MAY - - 2012
W9-BLH-850

Howard Hughes is the writer-researcher of the Filmgoers' Guides published by I.B.Tauris: *Stagecoach to Tombstone, Crime Wave* and *Once Upon a Time in the Italian West*. He is also the author of *Aim for the Heart: The Films of Clint Eastwood* and *Cinema Italiano: The Complete Guide from Classics to Cult* (both I.B.Tauris), as well as *Spaghetti Westerns* (Kamera Books) and *The American Indian Wars* (Pocket Essentials).

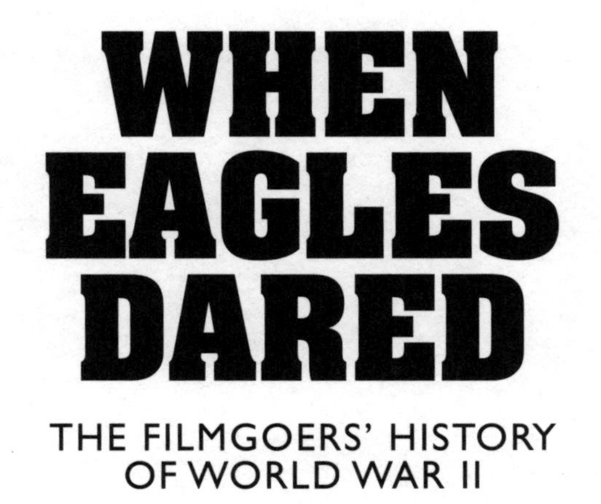

THE FILMGOERS' HISTORY
OF WORLD WAR II

HOWARD HUGHES

Published in 2012 by I.B.Tauris & Co Ltd
6 Salem Road, London W2 4BU
175 Fifth Avenue, New York NY 10010
www.ibtauris.com

Distributed in the United States and Canada Exclusively by Palgrave Macmillan
175 Fifth Avenue, New York NY 10010

ISBN: 978 1 84885 650 9

A full CIP record for this book is available from the British Library
A full CIP record is available from the Library of Congress

Library of Congress Catalog Card Number: available

Printed and bound in Great Britain by TJ International Ltd, Padstow, Cornwall

For Clara

CONTENTS

Preface

WAR AND REMEMBRANCE

World War II (1939–1945) was the most globally important historical event of the twentieth century. From Italian troops invading the Stone Age people of Abyssinia, to Adolf Hitler's mechanised Blitzkriegs and America's atomic bombing of Japan, it also charts the major developments of twentieth-century warfare. This was the first truly 'world war', with combat touching most continents. The principal theatres of war were Europe, Asia and the Mediterranean (including the North African coast, Greece and the Balkans) and the war on the Eastern Front in Russia – the campaign that ensured Hitler's grand designs were ruined. Germany's war with Russia was a massive conflict, where the fighting was on a larger, more ferocious scale, the distances were greater and the troop casualties higher than in any other area of the conflict.

When Eagles Dared is a salute to the men and women who participated in the war and the filmmakers who have immortalised their stories on screen. Each chapter discusses a theatre of war, an event, a campaign or battle, by explaining the historical background and then examines how filmmakers have depicted these events. Also in each chapter there is a 'focus film' which best represents the chapter's subject, though many further films are analysed within this format. To take one example, the chapter discussing the 'War Behind the Wire' focuses on *The Great Escape* (1963), the most famous and successful WWII prisoner of war film, but also discusses many other examples, from *The Wooden Horse* (1950) to *Escape to Victory* (1981). The selections are not restricted to American or British depictions of the war and throughout the book you will find films offering Italian, German, French, Japanese, Yugoslavian, Algerian and Russian perceptions of the conflict. Some films I discuss are famous, highly regarded and successful, while others are less so. All offer interesting perspectives on the conflict, as these storytellers brought history to life onscreen, however accurately. I imagine that almost all participants in WWII would agree that there has never been a movie made that has completely expressed the 'Hell on Earth' of combat.

There is no real way to fully convey the sensory experience of war – the smell of burning flesh, the acrid smoke, the screams, the noise, the blood, the fear.

WWII films have mirrored changing times and public tastes. During the war itself, films tended to be propagandist 'message' stories, designed to lift the nation's spirits. In Britain's case this included such films as *The Lion Has Wings, Went the Day Well?, The Way Ahead, We Dive at Dawn* and *In Which We Serve* and Hollywood produced *Back to Bataan, Casablanca, G.I. Joe, Mrs Miniver, Guadalcanal Diary, Objective, Burma!, Immortal Sergeant* and *They Were Expendable.* When the war ended, audiences demanded escapism, adventures which fed the imagination but gradually drifted further from the truth. In Britain audiences flocked to *The Colditz Story, The Dam Busters, Ice Cold in Alex, Dunkirk, Reach for the Sky* and *The Cockleshell Heroes*, while in America *Flying Leathernecks, From Here to Eternity, To Hell and Back* and *Stalag 17* were typical 1950s war fare. The beginning of the 1960s marked the emergence of the all-star international war epic, part of a trend that saw cinema reacting to the threat posed by television. This resulted in the release of widescreen spectacles such as *The Guns of Navarone, The Longest Day, The Great Escape* and *Where Eagles Dare*. There were war film comedies (*Kelly's Heroes*) and cynical, violent action movies (*The Dirty Dozen*). From the late 1970s onwards there has been a renewed attempt to bring authentically grimy realism to WWII films, from *Cross of Iron, The Big Red One* and *The Boat* (*Das Boot*) to *Saving Private Ryan, The Thin Red Line* and *Letters from Iwo Jima.* Since the turn of the twenty-first century, as the war fades ever further from memory, filmmakers have made films both in the ultra-cynical style of *The Dirty Dozen* – as

Douglas Bader (Kenneth More) returns from a sortie in Lewis Gilbert's popular screen biography of the WWII RAF hero, *Reach for the Sky* (1956). Note the Hurricane's bullet-riddled fuselage. Courtesy Kevin Wilkinson Collection.

in Quentin Tarantino's *Inglourious Basterds* – or else explored docu-realism, with such films as *Downfall*, a meticulous recreation of the fall of Berlin.

WWII films fall into four broad subgenres. The first is travelogue war movies, which follow a character or group of characters through the historical events of the war. These films include *To Hell and Back*, *The Victors*, *The Big Red One* and *Saving Private Ryan*, and also biopics such as *Patton*, *MacArthur* and *The Desert Fox*. The second is re-enactments of historical events, usually deploying star names in the principal roles. Key examples of this category include *The Longest Day*, *Battle of Britain*, *Stalingrad*, *Sink the Bismarck!*, *A Bridge Too Far*, *The Battle on the River Neretva*, *Tora! Tora! Tora!* and *Battle of the Bulge*. These films provide accurate depictions of historical events – often at great expense – with realistic drama, good stories and largely convincing performances. The third category is adventure movies, usually depicting a special mission, with scant regard for historical accuracy but plenty of action. Here the war is an excuse for larger-than-life heroism and explosive special effects. Good examples of this type include *The Guns of Navarone*, *The Dirty Dozen*, *Where Eagles Dare*, *The Heroes of Telemark*, Quentin Tarantino's *Inglourious Basterds*, *Von Ryan's Express*, *Objective, Burma!*, *The Dirty Heroes*, *Eagles Over London*, *The Eagle Has Landed*, *The Secret Invasion*, *Kelly's Heroes* and Enzo G. Castellari's *The Inglorious Bastards*. *The Great Escape* falls into this category also. Though it is loosely based on fact, it takes many liberties with history. War films of this type predominantly present a comic-book history of World War II. Having 'Eagles' or 'Heroes' in the title seems to help too. The fourth category is dramas that use the war as a backdrop to the story, such as *Ice Cold in Alex*, *The Boat*, *The Star* and *The Bridge on the River Kwai*.

On-set publicity shot depicting men on a mission and their target: the Navarone guns. The commandos (left to right) are Captain Keith Mallory (Gregory Peck), Corporal Miller (David Niven), Colonel Andrea Stavros (Anthony Quinn) and Private Spiros Pappadimos (James Darren), in J. Lee Thompson's *The Guns of Navarone* (1961). Courtesy Kevin Wilkinson Collection.

World War II was the first war to be photographed extensively by film crews (as opposed to still photographers) and film was used as a propaganda tool throughout its duration. Several Hollywood directors worked as documentary filmmakers during the war: for example, John Ford led a documentary crew for the US Navy in the Pacific War and George Stevens' unit covered the European theatre. Many actors served their country's armed forces during the conflict. Dirk Bogarde was a captain with Lieutenant General Frederick Browning in Normandy and Arnhem – he went on to play Browning in *A Bridge Too Far.* Henry Fonda enlisted in the US Navy and served on Admiral Nimitz's flagship *USS Essex* and later portrayed Nimitz for *In Harm's Way* and *Midway.* James Stewart served in the US Air Force and by 1945 had risen to the rank of colonel. Before he became a film star, Richard Todd was a lieutenant in the British 6th Airborne Division during the attack on the Orne River Bridge on D-Day and later played his paratroop commander Major Howard in *The Longest Day.* Hollywood star David Niven became a lieutenant with the commandos and was granted leave (termed 'special duty') to appear in two wartime propaganda films: *The First of the Few* (1942) and *The Way Ahead* (1944). While these 'reel heroes' were becoming real heroes, other actors remained in Hollywood. John Wayne became a star in Ford's *Stagecoach* (1939) and went on to appear in many patriotic war movies to keep wartime spirits up, but didn't see combat himself. The first Hollywood actor to be killed on active service was 1930s star Phillips Holmes, who was in the Canadian Air Force and died in 1942. Leslie Howard, the director-producer-star of *First of the Few*, which depicted the invention of the Spitfire, was shot down in 1943 by German planes on his way back to London from Lisbon. The Germans reputedly thought they had killed Winston Churchill.

When Eagles Dared is also about the millions of people – from many nations – who fought and died during World War II. For me this was a recent war. I grew up in the Cheshire village of Churton. In the 1970s I remember elderly uncles (it was always uncles) recounting their experiences of the war, or showing me faded photographs of their younger selves in uniform, posing with an array of smiling comrades-in-arms in front of army vehicles. During the war, members of my family enlisted in the Farndon Platoon, 'B' Company, 5th Cheshire Battalion of the Home Guard. Formerly the Local Defence Volunteers, this countrywide home defence against German invasion was the inspiration for the TV show *Dad's Army*. My grandfather William Hughes, who was a lieutenant in the Home Guard, was put in charge of 'stores and uniforms' and the company's headquarters was his house, 'Holly Bush' in Farndon. My other grandfather Philip Steel served in Malpas Auxiliary Fire Brigade and other relatives and family friends served in Burma, North Africa, landed on D-Day and fought through Italy and France. In Farndon churchyard stands a cenotaph, inscribed with 23 names: 18 men who died in the Great War (1914–18), five in World War II (1939–45). The names aren't famous, but this war memorial stands as a symbol of the village's loss, 'In perpetual memory of those men who died for their country'. These wars touched every family and every village cenotaph tells its own story – its little piece of history – of forgotten heroes, remembered once a year.

'When you go home, tell them of us and say:

"For your tomorrow, we give our today"'.

War memorial in St Chad's church, Farndon, Cheshire. The cenotaph erected in Farndon churchyard in 1922 to commemorate the 18 local men who died in the Great War. Five more names were added after World War II. Photograph: C. Hughes.

ACKNOWLEDGEMENTS

I'd like to thank Philippa Brewster, my editor at I.B.Tauris, for all her help, ideas and encouragement during the writing and research of this book. I'd also like to thank Paul Davighi, Stuart Weir, Cecile Rault and Thomas Abbs at I.B.Tauris, and Rohini Krishnan at Newgen, for their hard work on this project.

For providing most of the images reproduced in *When Eagles Dared* I thank dedicated archivist Kevin Wilkinson, who has an amazing array of rare film stills and posters in his collection. Thanks too to Andy Hanratty – it's always a pleasure working with him on the restoration of the images and assembling the montages. He's done a great job here: thanks for your help and the giant cups of tea. Unless otherwise noted the remainder of the images are from my own collection. Thanks also to Chris Bromley, who always designs such splendid jackets for my books.

Vital to the research of this book was Gareth Jones, who not only pointed me in the right direction towards many obscure and not-so-obscure WWII movies that weren't on my radar, but who also loaned me several key war films from his collection, helped with proofing material and shared his knowledge of WWII. Vital too was Chris Skinner, who also loaned me research material, and for his excellent advice and suggestions, particularly on Chapter 2: The War in the Skies.

Thanks also to my sister Belinda, Tom Betts, Lee Pfeiffer and Dave Worrall at *Cinema Retro*, Sir Christopher Frayling, Ann Jackson, Peter Jones, Steve and Sarah Holland, Paul Duncan, Andrew Collins, Alex Cox, Kim Newman, Frankie Holmes, Mike and Rhian Coppack, William Connolly, Mark and Louise Payne, Mary Alexander, Dave Lewis, Alex and Isabel Coe, Nicki and John Cosgrove, David Weaver, Mike and Tracey Oak, Paul Moss, Glyn Reece, Simon Hawkins, Sonya-Jayne Stewart and the staff of Chester library.

Thanks as always to mum (who suggested the title for this book and also proofread the manuscript) and dad, and of course to Clara and the zebra.

Introduction

BEFORE THE BLITZKRIEG

Adolf Hitler's rise to power took him from the rank of corporal during World War I (1914–18) to Germany's dictator, its Führer, by 1934. The right-wing Nazi Party's emergence coincided with Germany's economic depression in the 1930s. Hitler joined the Nazi Party – the National Socialist German Worker's Party (Nationalsozialistische Deutsche Arbeiterpartei or NSDAP) – after serving in the Great War. Voters became intoxicated by the party's ideals for a new, greater Germany – the Third Reich (empire) – and the party won seats in parliament, the Reichstag. The First Reich was the Holy Roman Empire, the second was the German Empire of 1871–1918. The Third Reich rose out of the Weimar Republic (as Germany was known after World War I) in 1933 and lasted until 1945.

Many Germans gravitated towards Nazism to counter a perceived threat from communism, while there were those factions in German society who blamed the Jews (*Juden* in German) for the country's defeat and compromised position in Europe after World War I. Hitler became Reich Chancellor (prime minister) in 1933 and then, following the death of Germany's President Von Hindenburg on 2 August 1934, he became all-powerful Führer ('leader'). Germany was by now a police state and the Nazi Party ruthlessly persecuted its political opponents and social victims – especially the Jewish population. Pre-war anti-Semitic purges reached a crescendo on 9–10 November 1938, the notorious Kristallnacht (Night of Broken Glass), when 7,000 Jewish homes and businesses were destroyed across Nazi Germany and between 25,000 and 30,000 Jews were transported to concentration camps. By 1941, Hitler and his collaborators concocted the 'Final Solution' to remove all Jews from Europe.

The rise of National Socialism in Germany has been depicted on film in *The Hitler Gang* (1944 – with Robert Watson as Hitler), *The German Story* (1956 – *You and Other Comrades*), *Mein Kampf* (1960), *The Life of Adolf Hitler* (1961), *Hitler* (1962 – with Richard Baseheart as Hitler), *The Black Fox* (1961 – narrated by Marlene Dietrich), *The Double-headed Eagle*, its sequel *Swastika* (both 1973), and Fred Zinnemann's *Julia* (1977), starring Jane Fonda, Vanessa Redgrave and Jason Robards. Edgar Reitz's West German TV series *Heimat* (1984) depicted life in the 'Homeland' between 1919 and 1980 and Volker Schlöndorff's unsettling Best Foreign Film Oscar winner *The Tin Drum* (1979), adapted from the novel by Günter Grass, was set against the Nazis' rise to power.

The November 1918 Armistice – which ended the 'War to End All Wars' – and the 1919 Treaty of Versailles resulted in Germany losing territory. Germany was also prohibited from building an army of any strength. When he became Führer, Hitler promptly ignored the Treaty of Versailles' restrictions. He cut unemployment by carrying out huge construction projects, infrastructure improvements (including extensive road building) and in 1935 a programme of rearmament. The chassis for the first two marks of the famed German Panzer tanks, for example, were disguised as agricultural tractors to bypass the treaty's restrictions.

The reorganised German armed forces, the Wehrmacht, included the mechanised Panzergrenadiers, which would be key to the German strategy at the outset of war in Europe, when they deployed ground troops, bombardments and air assaults in swift-striking Blitzkrieg attacks. Hitler became security conscious as his national and global profile grew. This is exemplified by his increasingly bomb- and bullet-proof chauffer-driven Mercedes cars which he travelled in for public appearances. The black-uniformed *Schutzstaffeln* (SS protection squads) originated as Hitler's personal bodyguards. The SS incorporated its military wing, the elite Waffen-SS and the Gestapo (the *Geheime Staatspolizei*, or State Secret Police). The SS became known for their fanatical Nazism and brutality, and their 'Death's Head' units ran the concentration camps, which were established soon after the Nazis rise to power in 1933. These were political prison camps in Germany – Dachau (near Munich) and Sachsenhausen and Buchenwald (northeast of Frankfurt) – where opponents of the Nazi party were tortured and starved. Every German soldier's belt buckle bore the inscription 'Gott Mit Uns', reminding them always that God was on their side in Hitler's anti-Semitic, anti-communistic war.

The most famous symbols of Nazism were the swastika emblem (the hooked cross, originally an Indian symbol which was hijacked by Hitler) and the Heil Hitler salute, the so-called 'Hitler greeting' of the Nazi Party, with the right arm extended. This was thought to have originated in ancient Rome – the 'Hail Caesar' that is seen so often onscreen in sword and sandal epics. The Italian Nationalists, in particular Gabriele D'Annunzio, allied the salutation to their extreme politics. Italian dictator Benito Mussolini later decreed that it should be used instead of a handshake and the German Nazi party made the salute compulsory in 1926. It will always be associated with Hitler's massive Nuremberg rallies in 1934, which were captured in the powerful propaganda film, Leni Riefenstahl's *Triumph of the Will* (1935).

Hitler annexed neighbouring land to allow Germany Lebensraum – 'Living Room' or 'Living Space' (literally room to live). He had seen how since World War I Germany had trailed other European powers, principally Britain and France, who owned and exploited territories abroad. Hitler's obvious intentions for German expansion were countered by a policy of 'Appeasement' by France and Britain, as they tried to avoid war. German troops occupied the Rhineland adjacent to France in March 1936 and took Austria in March 1938, in the so-called Anschluss. The occupation of Austria by Nazi troops features prominently in Robert Wise's musical *The Sound of Music* (1965). Hitler and Neville Chamberlain, the conservative prime minister of Britain, held a summit in Munich in September 1938 to discuss Czechoslovakia. Germany wanted to occupy Sudetenland – German-speaking territory in Czechoslovakia – after which there would be no more territorial demands in Europe. Chamberlain returned from Munich waving a worthless piece of paper promising 'Peace in our time'.

Hitler, a vegetarian and a non-smoker, was 50 years old when war was declared. On meeting the Führer in Munich, Chamberlain described Hitler's appearance – severely parted black hair and a trademark Charlie Chaplin moustache – as 'undistinguished': 'You would never notice him in a crowd'. Regardless of Chamberlain's opinion, Hitler is one of the most recognisable figures of the twentieth century and in history. It was Hitler's ambition, political views and charisma that defined the Nazis. His plans for Europe were outlined in his 1924 manifesto *Mein Kampf* ('My Struggle'). Hitler was the public face of Nazism and he was the one featured in Allied cartoons and newsreels as 'the enemy'. In North America, mock Western-style 'Wanted' posters were printed for the Führer 'Alias Adolf Schicklegruber, Adolf Hittler or Adolf Hidler', which read: 'For Murder ... For Kidnapping ... For Theft And For Arson, This Reckless Criminal Is Wanted – Dead Or Alive'.

Hitler has been portrayed many times in cinema and on TV, from the consummate, chilling impersonation by Bruno Ganz in *Downfall* (2004), to spoofs such as *That Nazty Nuisance* (1943) with Robert 'Bobby' Watson, who impersonated Hitler in several films, including *The Story of Mankind* (1957). Other actors to have played the Führer include David Bamber (*Valkyrie*), Anthony Hopkins (*The Bunker*), Alec Guinness (*Hitler: The Last Ten Days*), Rolf Stiefel (*Battle of Britain*), Billy Frick (*Is Paris Burning?*), Peter Miles (*The Eagle Has Landed*), Günther Bader (*Schtonk!*), Steven Berkoff (*War and Remembrance*), Günther Meisner (*The Winds of War*), Richard Basehart (*Hitler*) and Martin Wuttke (*Inglourious Basterds*). The self-styled 'Little Corporal' was mercilessly caricatured by Charlie Chaplin in *The Great Dictator* (1940), by Peter Sellers' barely-suppressed Nazi saluting *Dr Strangelove* (1964) and by British TV comedians such as Freddie Starr and Spike Milligan, though was the Führer ever a suitable subject for comedy? Chaplin later said that if he'd known about the Holocaust he'd never have made *The Great Dictator*, in which he played the dual roles of a Jewish ghetto barber and dictator Adenoid Hynkel of Tomania.

On 1 September 1939, the German battleship *Schleswig-Holstein* fired on the Polish fort on the Westerplatte peninsula, near Danzig (now Gdansk) in Poland. These were the first shots of the conflict and without declaring war Hitler's forces invaded Poland. Germany had signed a non-aggression pact with Russia in August 1939 and Joseph Stalin's Red Army invaded Poland from the east on 17 September. Warsaw fell on 27 September and the entire country had capitulated by 5 October. The stage was set – the 'War To End All Wars' was about to have a sequel.

Chapter I

THE FALL OF FRANCE (1940)

On 1 September 1939 Germany invaded Poland. Britain declared war on Germany on 3 September and there followed eight months of 'Phoney War'. The Germans called it the Sitzkrieg ('Sitting War') and in France it was Drôle de Guerre ('Funny War'). This was a strange stalemate, as Europe held its breath and waited for something to happen. The false security of this period appeared in many films, such as *In Which We Serve* (1942) and in Spike Milligan's autobiographical *Adolf Hitler: My Part in His Downfall* (1972), while Stephen Poliakoff's period espionage thriller *Glorious 39* (2009) – which featured Ramola Garai, Julie Christie, David Tennant, Bill Nighy, Jenny Agutter, Eddie Redmayne and Christopher Lee – was set in the uncertain summer preceding the declaration of war.

The British propaganda film *The Lion Has Wings* was released during the Phoney War in November 1939. It was produced by Alexander Korda and co-directed by Adrian Brunel, Brian Desmond Hurst and Michael Powell. Made in two weeks on a tiny budget, it combines newsreels, stock footage and dramatic re-enactments. The film begins by contrasting Britain's tranquillity with the political turmoil in Germany. 'This is Britain, where we believe in freedom', intones the patriotic voiceover by E.V.H. Emmett (from Gaumont British News). Pastoral scenes of the countryside, children at school and at play, holidays, sports and pastimes are intercut with goose-stepping parade footage from *Triumph of the Will*. 'What is your idea of a holiday?' asks the narrator. 'This?' (a shot of a fairground carousel) 'or this?' (Hitler delivering a speech). Britain's military power on land, sea and air is celebrated and factories churn out bombers, weapons and munitions. Newspaper headlines recount Hitler's territorial demands and gains in Europe (including 'Frightfulness In Occupied Poland'). We see a recreation of Wellington bombers attacking German ships in the Kiel Canal and a Luftwaffe bombing raid on south-eastern England (created from various footage, as Britain had not yet been bombed). The first wave of bombers is repulsed by

British fighters, the second wave is broken up by anti-aircraft fire ('Stand by boys to welcome the Nasties', notes an ack-ack gunner) and the third wave curtail their attack on London when they spot the area is protected by barrage balloons (blimps tethered by steel wires), which force the bombers to fly at an altitude too high for accurate bombing. This raid is compared to the Spanish Armada, via stock footage of Flora Robson as Elizabeth I in *Fire over England* (1937). *Lion Has Wings* also features a scene between a husband and wife, an RAF officer (Ralph Richardson) and a nurse (Merle Oberon), both of whom are doing their bit for the not-yet-at-war effort. Oberon delivers a speech extolling the virtues of land and freedom, and a Britain that believes in truth, beauty, fair play and kindness. The film is a naive view of what lay in store – the British Army was hopelessly outclassed in terms of tactics and armour, and it was going to take more than a few balloons to discourage the Luftwaffe. But the film served its purpose as encouraging, reassuring propaganda.

As the Phoney War simmered, the German navy sneaked into the Atlantic in preparation for hostilities. In the Allies' shipping lanes the Germans deployed magnetic mines, U-boat submarines and surface raiders, which sank commerce tonnage wherever they found it. The most famous was the 'pocket battleship' the *Admiral Graf Spee*. Pocket battleships were so-called because of their small size in comparison with true battleships, though they were heavily armed and armoured – the *Graf Spee* had 11-inch guns and 4-inch thick armour. Their size was necessitated by the Treaty of Versailles, which banned Germany constructing warships larger than 10,000 tonnes. The *Graf Spee* and her sister ship the *Deutschland* were loose in the Atlantic in August 1939, before the outbreak of hostilities. Under the command of Captain Hans Langsdorff, the *Graf Spee* struck in the South Atlantic and the Indian Ocean. From late-October to early-December she sank the following merchant ships: the *Clement* (30 September), the *Newton Beach* (captured 5 October, sunk 7 October), the *Ashlea* (7 October), the *Huntsman* (captured on 10 October, sunk on 17 October), the *Trevanion* (sunk 22 October), the *Africa Shell* (15 November), the Blue Star Line's *Doric Star* (2 December), the *Tairoa* (3 December) and the *Streonshalh* (7 December). The *Graf Spee* met her match on 17 December near Montevideo harbour in neutral Uruguay, following an encounter with British naval Force G (based on the Falkland Islands) in the mouth of the River Plate.

The Battle of the River Plate (1956) accurately retold the *Graf Spee*'s last month at sea. The film begins on Wednesday 15 November 1939, with the sinking of the *M.S. Africa Shell* in the Mozambique Strait of the Indian Ocean. Her captain, Patrick Dove (Bernard Lee) is taken prisoner and he's soon joined by other merchant captains and crew members captured by the German ship. *Graf Spee* refuels from the supply ship the *Altmark* and sets off around the Cape of Good Hope into the South Atlantic, sinking more merchant ships and eventually heading for South America. There she is attacked by Force G under Commodore Harwood: the cruisers *HMS Ajax*, *HMS Exeter* and the New Zealand *HMNZS Achilles*. Though outclassed, the trio of cruisers inflict heavy damage on the *Graf Spee*, which heads into port in Montevideo, while the *Exeter* heads for the Falklands for repairs. As running repairs are carried out on the *Graf Spee* and the British prisoners are released in neutral Uruguay, a diplomatic storm brews as to the German ship's rights in a neutral harbour. The newly repaired *HMS Cumberland* arrives from the Falklands. British intelligence, misinformation and whispered rumours on the streets of Montevideo inflate the British force lying in wait for the *Graf Spee* to be as many as 13 vessels. On the evening of Sunday 17 December, Langsdorff sails the *Graf Spee* out of the harbour, abandons ship and scuttles her in the Rio de la Plata.

The Battle of the River Plate was known as *The Pursuit of the Graf Spee* for US release. It was the penultimate collaboration between writer-director-producers Emeric Pressburger and Michael Powell, and was based on Patrick Dove's 1940 book *I Was Graf Spee's Prisoner* (Dove also acted as a technical advisor on the imprisonment scenes) and on Powell's 1956 book *Graf Spee*. The film was a factually accurate re-enactment of the events, using several actual naval ships, which are an improvement on the models and miniatures usually deployed in movie sea battles. Here the *Achilles* was played by the Indian Navy's *INS Delhi*, the *Exeter* was *HMS Jamaica*, *Ajax* was portrayed by *HMS Sheffield*, *HMS Cumberland* played herself and the US heavy cruiser *Salem* made a memorable *Admiral Graf Spee*. Peter Finch played Langsdorff, Anthony Quayle was Commodore Harwood aboard his flagship the *Ajax* and John Gregson was Captain Bell on the *Exeter*. Lionel Murton played American Mike Fowler, a fast-talking NBC news reporter, who provides a running commentary on developments in Montevideo harbour (filmed in Montevideo and Malta). In a cast of future stars, Patrick Macnee (later Steed in TV's *The Avengers*) had an early role as Lieutenant Commander Medley, Jack Watson played Swanson, the Cornish lookout who first spots the *Graf Spee*, John Le Mesurier (later of TV's *Dad's Army*) was the *Exeter*'s padre and Barry Foster played a rating (a non-commissioned sailor). Christopher Lee had a brief role as Manolo, a moustachioed bar owner in Montevideo. Michael Goodliffe played Naval Attaché McCall and Anthony Newley appeared as a captured merchant seaman.

The film loses momentum when the story arrives in Montevideo, becoming bogged down in diplomacy, but the naval scenes of Force G and the *Graf Spee* on the move are splendidly shot in colourful VistaVision and more than compensate for the film's talky lulls. The biggest failing is the stagy use of studio-bound interiors recreated at Pinewood for the warships' bridges: these are completely unconvincing, being both windless and motionless. The film also allows Langsdorff dignity in defeat and the climax concentrates on the victorious British ships sailing into the sunset. In reality Langsdorff committed suicide on 18 December in Buenos Aires.

The catastrophic fall of France amazed the world in May and June 1940 and still confounds historians today. The Phoney War ended when Hitler's Wehrmacht ('armed forces') turned its attention to Western Europe. First they invaded Norway on 9 April 1940, in operations that combined seaborne transporters and airborne landings. To the south, Denmark too was overrun on 9 April. Since the invasion of Poland, Hitler had amassed his army along the eastern borders of the Netherlands, Belgium, Luxembourg and France. By May, the Germans were prepared for an invasion, but the eight-month gap since Poland's demise had allowed the Allies to mobilise their forces. Eight Dutch divisions protected Holland; 18 divisions deployed in Belgium (with four in reserve); and 22 divisions protected France's northern border (with a further 22 in reserve). The British dispatched the British Expeditionary Force (BEF) under General Lord John Gort to the Western Front. Nine divisions joined the French line, with two in reserve in the Netherlands. Prime Minister Chamberlain was convinced that 'Hitler has missed the bus', but although the Allies outnumbered the German troops – the Allies numbered over 2.8 million troops and 3,600 tanks; the Germans 2.3 million troops and 2,700 tanks – Hitler's generals deployed their resources more effectively.

Crucially the Germans had the advantage in the air – 3,200 planes to the Allies 1,700 – and knew that their Luftwaffe air force could be best used in conjunction with their ground forces. This Blitzkrieg, or 'Lighting War', was a sustained spearhead push that would punch a hole through enemy defences. The fast-moving ground columns, a combination of armour and mechanised infantry (the *Panzergrenadiers*), were supported by air cover from the bombers – the two-engined fighter bomber the Messerschmitt Bf 110C and most significantly the Junkers Ju-87, the deadly Stukas. The Stukas were airborne artillery, swooping on their targets and obliterating them, their Junkers Jumo engines emitting a piercing scream as the planes dived. They bombed their opponents into submission while the well-drilled Panzer Corps – motorised infantry and tanks – provided a hammer blow on the ground. Behind enemy lines, paratroop and glider shock-troops secured vital objectives. The Allies, still labouring under the preconceptions and tactics of the last war, weren't prepared for Hitler's lightning bolts.

Hitler struck on 10 May, the day Chamberlain stepped down as prime minister of Britain and was replaced by Winston Churchill (the Conservative head of the Admiralty). The Allies had expected the Germans to avoid the Maginot Line – the French defences which ran from Luxembourg to Switzerland – and were prepared for an attack through Belgium. This would have been a replay of the Schlieffen Plan, the German tactics used in World War I. True to form, the German forces did attack in the north into Holland and Belgium on 10 May. *Operation Amsterdam* (1959) was set during the weekend the Germans invaded Holland. British intelligence's Major Dillon (Tony Britton) and two diamond experts, Walter Keyser (Alexander Knox) and Jan Smit (Peter Finch), infiltrate the city to extract the country's valuable supply of industrial diamonds before the Germans can loot them. Eva Bartok played their Dutch compatriot Anna and the film is more espionage-thriller than war movie, though the deserted Amsterdam streets, with their carnivalesque Pierement organ players, are rather eerie.

The German invasion of Holland and Belgium was a diversion – Hitler's strategist General Erich Von Manstein had formulated a new plan: Operation Sichelschnitt (Operation Sickle Cut). German airborne troops took the fortress at Eben Emael, which defended the Albert Canal and allowed German troops to attack Belgium. On 14 May, Rotterdam was levelled by German bombers in the so-called Horror Raid, which resulted in Holland's surrender on 15 May. Meanwhile Hitler's Panzers of Army Group A worked their way through the Ardennes forest, catching the Allies completely by surprise. The dense Ardennes in the Allies centre had been deemed impassable to armoured vehicles, but General Heinz Guderian found a way through, meeting only light resistance, and drove on to the River Meuse. The river was crossed at Sedan and Monthermé in the south and at Dinant in the north. The Germans achieved a breakthrough at Sedan and once the line was breached there was no stopping Guderian. French and British counterattacks failed and a German column reached the Channel coast at Noyelles on 20 May. The BEF and French forces fighting in Belgium now found themselves outflanked and surrounded. Boulogne was taken on 25 May and Calais the next day. On 28 May Belgium surrendered, leaving the remaining Allied forces hemmed in on the coast and low on supplies, with a further pocket of French forces surrounded inland around Lille.

In an attempt to salvage something from this shambles, the Allies evacuated the BEF, French and Belgian forces stranded on the Dunkirk coast back to England in Operation Dynamo. Vice-Admiral Bertram Ramsay oversaw the operation from the Dynamo Room, which was cut into Dover's white cliffs. The operation was a logistical nightmare, as the Royal Navy couldn't cope with such a large-scale expedition. The Admiralty provided 42 destroyers and other large transporters and assembled an armada of boats of all types – the Mosquito Navy – from boatyards and private owners along the Thames and the south coast. Anything deemed suitable was commandeered: fishing boats, cabin cruisers, motor boats, tugs, fire ships, pleasure boats, paddle steamers, barges, launches and yachts. They sailed from Sheerness, Ramsgate, Dover, Folkestone, Newhaven and Margate, and Southend and Deal were also used as return points. On the French coast, the evacuation began on 26 May from the beaches of Malo-les-Bains, Bray-Dunes, La Panne and St. Pol-sur-Mer, and the port of Dunkirk. The Luftwaffe strafed and dive-bombed the beaches, as the helpless soldiers waded out into the sea (to be picked up by the smaller boats and ferried to larger destroyers) or queued on makeshift jetties and piers. The Allies' saving grace was that the sand muffled the bomb explosions, minimising the radius of shell burst. The rescue ships had to avoid enemy E-boats (surface water motor launches), submarines, mines and artillery barrages. The beaches became littered with abandoned and burned-out vehicles and bodies, as grim Dynamo went on. All the BEF's equipment was left behind, including some 75,000 vehicles and 11,000 machine guns. On 2 June, the Germans bombed a hospital ship and by 4 June, when Dynamo was called off, 338,000 Allied soldiers had been rescued. On 5 June, the French rearguard finally capitulated, collapsing the beachhead defences.

Ealing Studios, a British company best-known for comedies, produced the finest version of these events. *Dunkirk* (1958) told the evacuation's story through three protagonists – cynical journalist Charles Foreman (Bernard Lee) and cowardly civilian John Holden (Richard Attenborough), both of whom are in England, and British 'Tommy' Corporal Tubby Binns (John Mills) with the stranded BEF. British soldiers were called 'Tommies' after 'Tommy Atkins', the name used as the example on specimens of official enlistment forms. These three protagonists' separate stories intertwine on the beach at Dunkirk during Operation Dynamo.

Stranded in France with the British Expeditionary Force, British 'Tommy', Corporal Tubby Binns (John Mills, right), contemplates his next move in Leslie Norman's *Dunkirk* (1958). Courtesy Kevin Wilkinson Collection.

In 1940, during the 'Phoney War', journalist Foreman tries to force straight answers from British Army spokesmen who are economical with the truth, while Hitler's divisions mass on the border. When the fury of the Blitzkrieg is unleashed, the Belgian, French and British forces are overwhelmed. Binns and his Wiltshire regiment are ordered to pull back from their defence of the River Dyle, destroying bridges as they go. An aerial attack kills Lieutenant Lumpkin (Kenneth Cope) and Binns takes command of the remaining four men, who are separated from their unit in the confusion of the war zone. They witness a Royal Artillery battery obliterated by a dive-bombing Stuka attack: 'That's murder, that's sheer bloody murder', notes a British Tommy. It is decided that the situation is hopeless and the BEF is ordered to pull back to Dunkirk for evacuation. In an effort to assemble a flotilla, the Royal Navy requisition 'anything that can float'. Foreman and Holden have their riverboats purloined and sail to Ramsgate, via Sheerness, where they volunteer to take their boats across the Channel. Meanwhile Binns and his men scrounge for food as the Germans close in. They manage to break through German lines and hitch a lift in a British lorry heading for Dunkirk. On the outskirts of the town they scuttle the lorry to prevent it falling into enemy hands (emptying the sump and running the engine until it seizes up) and join the thousands of soldiers waiting for rescue on the beaches. The troops are at the mercy of the Luftwaffe, who strafe the beaches and bomb the relief ships offshore. Foreman's boat is sunk and Holden's engine packs up, so they try to repair it on the beach. During an air attack, Foreman is killed. Holden, his boat fixed, ferries Binns and his comrades back to Blighty.

Produced by Michael Balcon and directed by Leslie Norman (UK film critic Barry Norman's father), *Dunkirk* was based on *The Big Pick Up*, a 1955 novel by Adam Hall (as 'Elleston Trevor') and the play *Dunkirk* by Lt-Col Ewan Butler and Major J.S. Bradford. The screenplay was written by David Devine and W.P. Lipscomb. Malcolm Arnold provided the rousing, patriotic score. Norman shot interiors at Ealing Studios and used authentic locations for the English scenes, including Fingringhole, Colchester and Sheerness Dockyards in Kent. The flotilla sails down the Thames past Westminster and Big Ben, and the cliffs of Dover also appear as a backdrop. The long flat beach backed by dunes on Camber Sands in East Sussex was 'Dunkirk'.

Dunkirk's parallel stories keep the plot moving. Mills is his usual stalwart self in a genre he excelled at. He made many war movies, including three in 1958: *Dunkirk, Ice Cold in Alex* and *I Was Monty's Double.* Bernard Lee (later M in the James Bond films) is good as the cynical journalist who stands on Dunkirk beach and witnesses the fiasco firsthand. He notes that the BEF are using 'last-war weapons, last-war methods'. But it's Attenborough who most impresses, with his portrayal of Holden, the garage owner and proprietor of a small engineering firm which makes belt buckles for the army. Holden thinks he's 'doing his bit', but others take him for a cowardly shirker with a 'soft job'. He initially claims that he's far too busy to pilot his boat to Sheerness, let alone to Dunkirk, and frets for his wife Grace (Patricia Plunkett) and their newborn baby. In a moving scene, he attempts to fit a cumbersome gasmask on the baby. Holden realises that he's not doing enough for the war effort. The navy requisition his vessel, the *Heron*, and his young employee Frankie (Sean Barrett) volunteers to go to France, convincing Holden to sail with the flotilla. It is Holden, not Foreman, who survives and returns a hero.

Dunkirk is convincing in its recreation of the period – the film's technical advisors were Ewan Butler and Lt-Cdr John Pidler. Historical figures General Lord Gort and Vice-Admiral Ramsay both appear (played by Cyril Raymond and Nicholas Hannen). Newsreel footage is used in the film's introduction, outlining the present political unrest in Europe. British Tommies in France watch cartoons mocking Hitler – 'Run Adolf, Run Adolf, Run Run Run', sung to 'Run Rabbit'. In England Bud Flanagan and Chesney Allen (appearing as themselves) entertain theatre audiences with 'Hang Out the Washing on the Siegfried Line' and Holden turns off a wireless broadcasting Lord Haw-Haw's pro-Hitler 'twaddle'. But soon the 'Phoney War' – the war of words and propaganda – gives way to the real conflict. Black-and-white war films have always been more realistic than their colour counterparts, mainly due to their resemblance to newsreels and propaganda films of the time. Monochrome cinematography also facilitated the use of actual war footage in battle scenes, cheaply adding an air of authenticity to the action. In *Dunkirk*, stock-footage Stukas dive-bomb an artillery emplacement in a wood and archive film of Hitler's 'lightning war' steamrollers though Belgium and France. When an Allied transporter is Stuka-bombed, the footage of men scrambling for safety and the sinking ship is recreated in a studio and the scenes of returning troops disembarking after the evacuation are a mixture of stock and recreated footage. Scenes of chaos in France bring home the grim logic of war. German planes don't bomb fleeing refugee columns, but machine-gun them: the Germans want the roads intact for their advancing tanks. In the actual battle, the French removed road signs to confuse the German advance, a tactic that would be unthinkable today, when even private cars have satellite navigation.

When Binns and his men reach the beach, *Dunkirk*'s depiction of the evacuation is its finest achievement, with expansive wide shots of Camber Sands crowded with troops. They resemble archive photographs and *Retreat from Dunkirk*, the painting by Charles Cundall, with palls of black smoke, circling German aircraft, shell bursts, boats and evacuees. The film's embarkation scenes are a combination of special effects (using backdrops, scale models, reproduction boat sets and a water tank) and recreations on Camber. A Tabac near the beach is converted into a makeshift field hospital, where medical officer Lionel Jeffries and his men draw lots to see who will remain to tend the wounded. An RAF pilot sheltering on the beach is harangued by Allied troops who complain about the lack of air cover, with the Stukas striking at will. In reality the RAF was largely powerless against the German air superiority, even though Churchill diverted precious aircraft earmarked to defend mainland Britain in the coming months. Binns and his men think they're on their way home when they board a transporter, but it is hit and the survivors struggle, spluttering and shivering, back to shore. German planes drop fliers urging the Allies to surrender and a padre leads the waiting troops in the Lord's Prayer during a service which is dispersed by a Stuka strike. It is during this attack that Foreman is mown down. The troops play football, gamble, clean their weapons or huddle in the sand, but all wait and hope for liberation. The finale depicts not defeat and retreat, but triumphs: the British and their 'miracle' rescue of the BEF, Holden's contribution to the war effort and Binns, whose men would have perished without his leadership and Holden's valour.

Apart from Leslie Norman's film, few outings have depicted this dark hour. Henri Verneuil's *Weekend at Dunkirk* (1964 – *Week-end à Zuydcoote*) had French soldier Jean-Paul Belmondo caught up in the evacuation. Verneuil's staging of the devastated beaches is convincing and was backed by an effective Maurice Jarre score. The film opens with a holiday poster advertising the sunny seaside resort with the tagline 'Ses Dunes, Sa Plage, Son Air' ('Its Dunes, Its Beach, Its Air') which fades into a shot of the beach overcrowded with retreating French troops. Dunkirk was also recreated in the romantic drama *Atonement* (2007), which featured a continuous five-minute shot along the beach and shattered seafront (filmed at Redcar, near Middlesbrough), as witnessed by British soldier Robbie Turner (James McAvoy). This sequence depicts a beached yacht, a carousel and Ferris wheel, and soldiers shooting their horses, disabling vehicles and singing the hymn 'Dear Lord and Father of Mankind' in a bandstand. In *Reach for the Sky* (1956), Douglas Bader (Kenneth More) flies an RAF sortie over the evacuation and during *In Which We Serve* (1942) *HMS Torrin* takes part in the evacuation. Sailor Shorty Blake (Mills again) hands out hot cocoa and biscuits to wounded British soldiers, while the BEF officers on the bridge with the ship's skipper, Kinross (Noël Coward), fare rather better. As Kinross notes of their tipple: 'It's just ordinary Bovril rather heavily laced with sherry'.

Mrs Miniver (1942), directed in Hollywood by William Wyler at MGM, highlighted the wartime plight of 'a quiet corner of England' for American audiences. As the trailer states, it was based on 'Jan Struther's Book-of-the-Month Club Hit!' The story begins in the summer of 1939 'when the sun shone down on a happy, careless people, who worked and played, reared their children and tended their gardens'. Greer Garson took the role of housewife Kay Miniver after Norma Shearer had turned it down. The war gradually encroaches on average middle-class family life in the fictional country village of Belham. Kay's architect husband Clem (Walter Pidgeon) joins the Mosquito Navy and sails to Ramsgate for Dunkirk. Kay herself is confronted by a downed Luftwaffe pilot brandishing a Luger, whom she finds under a bush in her garden. The Minivers' son Vin (Richard Ney, later Garson's husband) joins the RAF and fights in the Battle of Britain and Carol (Teresa Wright), his wife of two weeks, is killed during the battle by a stray bullet. Life goes on in Belham, as they endure air raids and the Minivers' house, Starlings, is hit by a bomb: 'Oh, it's not as bad as it looks – we just didn't have time to clear it all up', cheery Kay tells a shocked visitor. Dame May Whitty played Carol's mother, snooty Lady Beldon, and Henry Wilcoxon was the vicar, who in the film's climax delivers a rousing speech from the pulpit of a bombed out, roofless church. World War II films are predominantly a male-dominated genre and it was rare examples, such as *Mrs Miniver*, that headline a female star. Women were usually relegated to playing 'love interest' nurses, secretaries or radio operators. WWII films with prominent female characters tended to be set on the Home Front, such as *Mrs Miniver* or *Tender Comrade* (1943 – starring Ginger Rogers), or else behind the front lines, in hospitals (for example *Cry 'Havoc'*) or prison camps (*A Town Like Alice*). Garson won a Best Actress Oscar for *Mrs Miniver*, Wyler Best Director and the movie Best Picture. Despite many tragedies, the Belham locals occupy themselves with churchgoing, hymn-singing and their Flower Festival, in this melodrama which is still surprisingly powerful today. Churchill thought the film's plucky, positive message was worth more to the war effort than troops and armaments. A sequel, H.C. Potter's *The Miniver Story* (1950), again with Garson and Pidgeon, saw the family reunited in post-war England.

By far the most inventive deployment of the Dunkirk evacuation was Enzo G. Castellari's *Eagles Over London* (1969). The film begins with Captain Paul Stevens (Frederick Stafford) leading a BEF rearguard action against advancing German armour (the German tanks are 1950s vintage American US M47s and M48s). The British are ordered to withdraw and join a column retreating towards Dunkirk, which is strafed by a German fighter. Stevens' men destroy a bridge and proceed to the Dunkirk beachhead. Some money was obviously spent on *Eagles* by producer Edmondo Amati, as the Dunkirk evacuation scenes and the return to Dover port are impressive. The beaches are littered with personnel and equipment and three German planes swoop from the sky, machine-gunning and bombing the evacuees. This snapshot of history is shown being captured on film by a war cameraman on the beach. The troops wade out to the small boats, are transferred to transporters and sail for Dover. The bustling port is recreated, as Stevens is reunited with his lover RAF lieutenant Meg Jones ('Evelyn Stewart'/ Ida Galli) and French fliers enlist in the RAF. In an ingenious twist, during the retreat in France, German SS commandos led by Major Krueger (Luigi Pistilli) murder a squad of British soldiers, don British uniforms and travel to Dover in the rescue boats. The remainder of *Eagles Over London* has Kruger's men let loose in London. Their mission is to blow up aerial radar installations and the control room operations centre during the Battle of Britain.

'Hank Milestone'/Umberto Lenzi's *From Hell to Victory* (1979), another Amati production, was released in some territories as *From Dunkirk to Victory*. Spanning the entire war, it begins in August 1939 with four friends, an American, a German, a Frenchman and a Brit (played not wholly convincingly by George Peppard, Horst Buchholz, George Hamilton and Jean-Pierre Cassel) boating on the Seine. Soon the war arrives – we know this via a series of exclamatory titles: 'Poland Defeated!' 'France Invaded!' – and tears their friendship apart. Buchholz becomes a tank commander, Peppard an OSS agent, and Hamilton and Cassel are trapped at Dunkirk and shipped back to Dover. Their evacuation is depicted by chunks of footage from *Eagles Over London*.

With the departure of the BEF in June 1940, the second phase of the German invasion of France, codenamed Operation Red, began on 5 June. Paris fell on 14 June and the German army methodically mopped up French resistance in the south. Almost one third of the French army was employed defending the Maginot Line, which was never attacked. France signed an Armistice with Germany on 22 June in the same Parisian railway car that the Allies had accepted the German surrender in 1918. On 20 June Mussolini's Italian forces struck in the South of France and the French signed an armistice with Italy on 24 June. France was then split into zones. Occupied France – that is France under German control – was the northern and western territory, which encompassed France's Atlantic coastline (to guard against Allied amphibious invasion). Newly-formed Vichy France was the south-eastern part of the country, including its Mediterranean coast. From the town of Vichy, French prime minister Marshal Henri Pétain governed the collaborationist unoccupied zone (the 'zone libre') and also France's overseas colonies, including Tunisia, Algeria and French Morocco in North Africa. Charles De Gaulle was declared the head of France's 'government in exile' in London and formed the Free French, the French Resistance movement.

In May and June 1940 the Allies were tactically outclassed and the new model German army, defined by steel and speed, seemed to have risen mythically from another age. But despite the rapier Blitzkrieg, some German infantry units still used bicycles and the slow supply columns and artillery trains used horses and oxen to cart their kit. Sometimes Blitzkriegs were too quick for their own good, but the campaign in France was a resounding success. The Germans may have been well-drilled and efficient, but the Allies certainly proved they could improvise. If the Allies took anything from the debacle it was the indomitable 'Dunkirk Spirit' which drove the British war effort, as Britain stood defiantly against all-conquering Hitler across the Channel.

Chapter 2

THE WAR IN THE SKIES (1940–45)

With the evacuation of Dunkirk and the fall of France, Hitler expected Britain to surrender, but Churchill stood firm: 'The Battle of France is over. I expect that the Battle of Britain is about to begin'. In the summer of 1940, Hitler planned an amphibious invasion of Britain, designated Operation Seelöwe or 'Sealion'. Rather than attacking Britain through the rougher North Sea, the Germans decided on routes across the English Channel. From the peninsula at Cherbourg three divisions (Army Group B) would land in Lyme Bay at Lyme Regis and move north to Bristol. From Le Havre four divisions (Army Group A) would take the Isle of Wight and Brighton. Six divisions of Army Group A would leave Boulogne, Calais, Dunkirk and Ostend and attack the southeast coast, at Bexhill, Folkestone, Dover and Ramsgate. Objectives included the outflanking and surrounding of London, and a frontline (stretching from Southampton to Gravesend) which would move north to capture Gloucester, Oxford, St Albans and Maldon. For the German plan to succeed, it was vital that they gain air superiority to protect their invasion fleet – it would have more chance against the Royal Navy if they could deploy the Luftwaffe to its full potential.

In May 1940, Anthony Eden, Britain's Secretary of State for War, announced the formation of the Local Defence Volunteers (LDV), later renamed the Home Guard. It consisted of men aged between 17 and 65 who would defend Britain's home soil in the event of a German invasion. Their importance to Britain's safety considerably increased after Dunkirk. The big-screen spin-off from the UK TV series *Dad's Army* (1971) tells how the (fictitious) Walmington-on-Sea Home Guard was assembled. They are commanded by pompous Captain Mainwaring (Arthur Lowe), a bank manager in 'Civvy Street', whose military experience is that he served in France in 1919 (a year after World War I ended). His squad – who were familiar from the TV series – included urbane Sergeant Wilson (John Le Mesurier), miserable undertaker Frazer (John Laurie), black-marketeering spiv Walker (James Beck), whingeing 'Stupid Boy' Pike (Ian Lavender), deaf-as-a-post Godfrey (Arnold Ridley) and butcher Lance-Corporal Jones (Clive Dunn). Jones is a fine creation. A veteran of the Sudan (where he fought under Kitchener against the 'fuzzy wuzzies'), the Boer War and World War I, he gave the series some memorable catchphrases, such as 'Cold steel – they don't like it up 'em' and his famous 'Don't panic!' Other regular characters reprised in the movie include grumpy ARP Warden Hodges (Bill Pertwee), the Reverend Timothy Farthing (Frank Williams) and the verger (Edward Sinclair).

The brisk, episodic plot sent the bungling platoon on army manoeuvres, where they manage to flatten their own tents with a traction engine and send Major General Fullard (Bernard Archard) and his horse drifting downriver on a section of pontoon bridge. They later become heroes when they save the vicar and other villagers from three Luftwaffe crewmen who have bailed out and taken the locals hostage in the village hall. The Home Guard foil the invaders by disguising themselves as a church choir, emerging from the crypt singing 'All things Bright and Beautiful' dressed in cassocks and surpluses. The film was shot at Shepperton Studios and on location (Walmington-on-Sea's street was Chalfont St Giles in Buckinghamshire) and the film version retained the series' famous theme tune, 'Who Do You Think You're Kidding, Mr Hitler?' sung by Bud Flanagan.

The film is at its best when depicting the Home Guard's inadequate equipment. In that respect *Dad's Army* was historically accurate. The Home Guard were often poorly armed and the LDV designation was cruelly reinterpreted as 'Look, Duck and Vanish'. In the film, their first 'uniforms' arrive (simply arm bands reading 'LDV') and they receive ammunition, but no rifles. They muster their own weaponry – a formidable selection of assegai spears, shotguns, sabres, pitchforks and broom handles with knives taped to the end – and plan to defend the promenade from the Novelty Rock Emporium. Their home-made defences include two-dozen petrol bombs in lemonade bottles, a rocket-firing anti-aircraft device made from drainpipes, a one-man, bullet-proof tank (an upside down cast-iron bath on wheels), a gas-powered 'armoured car' (Jones' butchers van) and an 'anti-vehicle device' which emits an oil slick on the road.

Powell and Pressburger's *The Life and Death of Colonel Blimp* (1943) begins and ends with a Home Guard exercise – a mock defence of London against invasion – during which old soldier Clive Wynne-Candy V.C. (Roger Livesey), a retired general and Boer War and World War I veteran, realises that he is out of touch with modern 'total war'. Told 'the war starts at midnight', Blimp is captured when an enterprising young officer (James McKechnie) surprises him in a Turkish bath, by not playing by the rules and starting the exercise early – as the Germans would do. Featuring a wonderful performance by Livesey, *Colonel Blimp* is most interesting in its depiction of Candy's relationships with three women – Edith Hunter (whom he loses to German officer Theo Kretschmar-Schuldorff [Anton Walbrook]), Barbara Wynne (whom he marries) and Angela 'Johnny' Cannon (his young driver during World War II). All three are played by Deborah Kerr. Future *Dad's Army* regular John Laurie played Blimp's batman and butler Murdoch, who joins the Home Guard.

Operation Sealion was provisionally set for 15 September 1940. The Royal Air Force (RAF) were Britain's first line of defence – their motto was 'Per Ardva Ad Astra': 'Through Adversity to the Stars'. RAF Fighter Command, led by Air Chief Marshall Sir Hugh 'Stuffy' Dowding, consisted of 591 aircraft (though more were being rushed out on production lines). They were divided into four groups: Fighter Command Group 10 defended south-west England; Number 11 protected the southeast; Number 12 the east and Midlands; and Number 13 the north. The German aerial attacks began on 10 July 1940 in an attempt to disrupt shipping by bombing ports, docks and vessels at sea. With 13 Divisions massed on the Channel coast, on 17 July German troops began rehearsing embarkation and invasion drill under their commander-in-chief, Field Marshal Walter Von Brauchitsch. During this first phase of the invasion plan, Portsmouth was bombed on 11 July and on 8 August a convoy was attacked at Weymouth, as part of the ongoing campaign to weaken Britain's Channel defences. To counter Germany's aerial threat, Britain deployed anti-aircraft batteries, powerful search lights, barrage balloons ('shiners' as the RAF pilots called them) and the Observation Corps of spotters. The BBC stopped transmitting television programmes for the duration of the war, so the signal couldn't be used to guide in German bombers. Britain also deployed the newly invented radar system (the RDF, or Radio Direction Finding), which meant that the RAF didn't have to patrol the skies, but could 'scramble' (take off) when the early warning system alerted them to the presence of approaching enemy aircraft, which were then tracked on maps in the operations room.

Britain's principal air defences were fighter squadrons of Supermarine Spitfires and Hawker Hurricanes (both powered by Rolls-Royce Merlin engines) and a small number of two-seater Defiants. Against them was the formidable German Air Force, under its commander-in-chief, Reichsmarschall Hermann Göring, which was divided into Luft Flotten (air fleets). Luftlotte 2 launched from the Low Countries and north-east France, Luftlotte 3 was based in north-west France and Luftlotte 5 was stationed in Norway and Denmark. They consisted of Ju-87 Stuka (an abbreviation of Stukageschwader) dive-bombers (used so effectively as ground troop support in the Blitzkrieg), Messerschmitt Bf-109 fighters (with their brightly coloured yellow or red nose cones), twin-engined Messerschmitt Bf-110 fighter-bombers; Junkers Ju-88 bombers, Dornier Do-17 bombers (the long thin 'Flying Pencils') and Heinkel He-111 twin-engined bombers.

The German air assault on Britain began on 11 August 1940, with the bombers protected by fighter escorts. Designated Adler Tag ('Eagle Day'), the operation initially stalled due to low cloud and eventually got underway on 13 August. This was the first day of what became known as the Battle of Britain. By 18 August the bombing campaign wasn't going the Luftwaffe's way and Göring's assurances to Hitler of impending German air supremacy were unfounded. The RAF and the ground defences fought tenaciously and the Luftwaffe suffered great losses. On 20 August, Churchill made his famous speech which proclaimed: 'Never in the field of human conflict was so much owed by so many to so few'. The RAF bombed Berlin on 24 and 25 August. From 24 August until 6 September, the Luftwaffe changed tactics, concentrating its attacks on the airfields of

Fighter Command Group 11 in the southeast. On September 6, in response to the bombing of Berlin, Hitler ordered attacks on London to begin in earnest. The sustained bombing of Britain's capital, which lasted until May 1941, became known as the Blitz. This allowed depleted Fighter Command to reorganise and recuperate, and proved to be Hitler's biggest blunder of the battle.

The RAF's staunch defence pushed Hitler's Sealion plan back to 27 September. The Germans needed ten day's notice to mobilise the invasion, so the Luftwaffe had to gain air superiority by 17 September. Sunday 15 September 1940 was the decisive day in the engagement and was known thereafter as 'Battle of Britain Day', a swirling battle for control of the skies over London. At 11.35 am the first wave of German bombers and fighters arrived over the British coast at Dungeness on the Straits of Dover, and by noon the first planes had reached London. Battle was joined and between 11.30 and 12.30, the swirling dogfights stretched between London and the coast. Meeting sustained resistance from the RAF, the Germans dropped their bombs and returned swiftly to their bases. The encounter tailed off and another German attack began at 2 pm but was repulsed by the tenacious Spitfires and Hurricanes, who peeled off, swooped and attacked. The Spitfires attacked the fighter escorts while the Hurricanes harassed the bombers. Two unexploded bombs fell in the grounds of Buckingham Palace and a Dornier crashed into the front of Victoria Station. Its crew, hit for six, parachuted into the Oval cricket ground. The last attack of the day came at 5 pm, but the RAF triumphed. The RAF's victory on 15 September, the most famous aerial battle of the war, put Sealion on hold permanently. The aerial fighting over Britain continued, with 27 September planned by the Germans as the day they would finally wipe out the RAF, but it ended in failure. By 31 October, when the Germans conceded defeat, the RAF had lost 1,023 planes and the Luftwaffe 1,887. Just as Lord Nelson's victory over the French and Spanish fleets off Spain's Cape Trafalgar in 1805 curtailed Napoleon's invasion of Britain, so the Battle of Britain foiled Hitler's invasion plans.

Battle of Britain (1969) was an ambitious US-financed, British and European-shot recreation of the Luftwaffe's prolonged air strikes against Britain, with an all-star cast. Directed by Guy Hamilton (of *Goldfinger* fame), it was based on the 1961 book *The Narrow Margin* by Derek Wood and Derek Dempster. James Kennaway and Wilfred Greatorex fabricated a screenplay around the actual events and an early working title was *The Thin Blue Line*. The film begins in France in May 1940, with the Dunkirk retreat, and follows several RAF squadrons as their airfields in France are overrun and they return to England to defend London and the southeast of England. It also provides the German viewpoint, with scenes depicting Luftwaffe commanders and their strategies, and the preparations for Operation Sealion in the French Channel ports. Columns of trucks transport assault barges, harbours are crammed with ships and German troops mass on the coast, lifejackets at the ready.

Events are recreated as they happened and for audiences with no interest in the battle, the pace is slow. For historians however, *Battle of Britain* is a treat. It was produced by Harry Saltzman with finance provided by United Artists in New York. Initially budgeted at $3.5 million, the film was beset with problems – particularly bad weather during the dreadful wet English summer of 1968 – and the eventual cost shot up to $13 million. The troubled making of the film is told in Leonard Mosley's excellent first-hand account, *Battle of Britain*, published by Pan to tie-in with the film's release in 1969.

In addition to a costly star cast, Saltzman gathered an impressive roster of actual World War II aircraft. The Messerschmitt Bf 109s are repainted German-designed Hispano Buchon planes from the Spanish airforce. They are powered by Rolls-Royce Merlin engines, which sound quite different to their authentic Daimler-Benz originals ('Bf' means the plant in which they were made – Bayerische Flugzeugwerke). The technical manager was engineer Willy Messerschmitt. During the war, camouflage paint was applied to the top half of the plane and the upper side of the wings (so they blended with the landscape below when spotted from above) and they were painted pale grey or blue on their undersides (to merge with the clouds and sky when observed from the ground). The RAF planes are authentic Spitfires and Hawker Hurricanes. Twenty-eight Messerschmitts, Fifty Heinkel He-111s and a three-engined Junkers Ju-52 appeared for the Luftwaffe. They were flown with consummate expertise by Spanish pilots and four lively Texans from the Confederate Air Force. So many authentic aircraft were reconditioned, repaired and leased for the film that it was the 35th largest air force in the world at the time and was dubbed 'Saltzman's Private Air Force'.

Much of *Battle of Britain* was shot in Spain, with filming commencing in March 1968. The French Lafayette Escadrille air bases used by the Luftwaffe were filmed at the El Copero and Tablada air bases, near Seville. The Dunkirk evacuation scenes were filmed on Huelva beach, west of Seville, using Spanish extras, matte special effect shots and an artificial sandbank. A Luftwaffe HQ was a farmstead near the Guadalquivir River. On the northern Spanish coast east of Santander and near the French border, San Sebastian's harbour and beach became a French Channel port swarming with German troops preparing for the invasion. San Sebastian itself was redressed as Berlin for a night time air raid scene. The railway station at Irurzun, 60 miles from the Pamplona mainline, was used for the arrival of Marshal Göring in Pas De Calais, with a Spanish dining coach redressed for the period. By April the main unit returned to England to film on authentic British bases: RAF Duxford (Cambridgeshire), RAF Hawkinge (Kent) and North Weald Aerodrome (Essex). RAF Bentley Priory, Middlesex, the HQ of Fighter Command, appeared as itself. The main unit shot at Duxford, while the air unit was based at RAF Debden airfield. The attack on 'B Station', Duxford by the Luftwaffe was the film's biggest, most expensive special effects sequence, which called for several large explosions and a disused aircraft hanger to be destroyed – the smoking, burning devastation was captured in aerial shots. For the scenes of the bombing of London, the film company bought and burned down an old tea warehouse in London's Docklands. The scenes depicting ruined streets and fire crews tackling blazes were filmed in Dragon Road, Camberwell, London. These derelict streets were slated for demolition in the Greater London Council's slum clearance. Londoners shelter from the rain of bombs in the Aldwych underground tube station, which became a vast air raid shelter. Interiors were filmed in Pinewood Studios, Iver Heath, Buckinghamshire. Towards the end of August,

Spitfires, Messerschmitts and a B-25 relocated temporarily to Montpellier in the south of France, to get some flying shots bathed in sunshine. Awful weather, including sleet, ensured exterior shooting dragged on in England – at a daily cost of £55,000 – until the filming finally wrapped in September 1968.

Battle of Britain features an impressive roster of British talent, a mixture of established thespians, war movie stalwarts and 1960s new faces. The film began shooting in March, but Saltzman only announced his cast on 2 May 1968. Laurence Olivier played Air Chief Marshal Hugh Dowding (a role originally to have been played by Alec Guinness), Ralph Richardson was Sir David Kelly (British Minister to Switzerland), Patrick Wymark was Air Vice Marshall Trafford Leigh-Mallory, Michael Redgrave played Air Vice Marshal Evill and Kenneth More appeared as Group Captain Baker. Trevor Howard and Robert Flemyng

Battle of Britain (1969). Above: Field Marshal Milch (Dietrich Frauboes) arrives in his Mercedes to inspect rows of Heinkel bombers (filmed at Tablada air base, near Seville, Spain). Below: Eagles over London, as the bomb-laden Heinkels prepare to drop their payload on the capital. Images courtesy Kevin Wilkinson Collection.

played Air Vice Marshal Keith Park and Wing Commander Willoughby, who direct the action from the RAF's Operations Room. Rex Harrison was originally going to play Park, but had to drop out when weather delays pushed the filming dates back. Michael Caine, Edward Fox, Barry Foster and Ian McShane played the RAF's finest pilots. Most notable was Robert Shaw as ace squadron leader 'Skipper'. The idle boredom of waiting for the next 'scramble' is well illustrated – a Polish pilot reads *1000 Words in English* – and the cast model authentic RAF leather flying jackets, white polo necks and blue uniforms. The problem with this all-star-casting during the aerial combat scenes was noted by *Time*'s reviewer: 'Once they are airborne and covered with goggles and oxygen masks, it is impossible to distinguish between any of the actors'. Amongst the German contingent, Curd Jürgens played Baron Von Richter, Karl Otto Alberty played Jeschonnek, a Luftwaffe strategist, and Dietrich Frauboes played Field Marshal Milch, who arrives by Junkers and Mercedes to inspect the rows of Heinkels during Maurice Binder's colourful title sequence. Hein Riess (better known as a music hall singer in Hamburg) was a moonfaced caricature of Göring, who arrives in the Pas-de-Calais in September 1940 to oversee the invasion and who loses his jovial demeanour when his beloved Luftwaffe is dismantled. Having berated his commanders, he leaves on a train to report the bad news to the Führer.

Subplots on terra firma – including the troubled relationship between Squadron Leader Colin Harvey (Christopher Plummer) and his wife, WAAF Section Officer Maggie Harvey (Susannah York) – don't detract from the action. The pilots and WAAFs socialise in the 'Jackdaw Inn', Denton, near Canterbury, and the LDV drill outside the pub before popping in for a pint. Only York's 1960s-style blonde bob conspicuously lacks the film's visual authenticity. The moment when Maggie, having just met a facially disfigured RAF assistant controller, learns that Colin has been badly burned in a crash, is the most moving scene in the film. The controller she meets, Squadron Leader Tom Evans, was played by Bill Foxley, himself a WWII RAF pilot whose hands and face were severely burned in a plane crash. Due to the pioneering, untried plastic surgery that rebuilt his face and hands, he was a member of the so-called Guinea Pig Club. Air Chief Marshal Dowding visited the Pinewood set and was reduced to tears when he viewed rushes of the movie. In a separate incident, RAF hero Douglas Bader and other RAF veterans refused to meet with Luftwaffe pilots. Twenty-eight years later, the RAF were not yet ready to 'forgive and forget' – they didn't want the widows and children of RAF pilots killed in action to see them 'carousing with their murderers'. Even by 1968 it seems that for those who took part in the conflict, it was too soon to make peace with their 'enemies'. War heroes like Bader felt that a film of the Battle of Britain might demean their victory, at a time when Germany's role in the war was being re-evaluated. He certainly didn't want to be seen as their 'friends' and would reiterate to anyone listening 'We won!'

Bader needn't have worried. *Battle of Britain* is historical storytelling of the highest order, with great attention to detail – even down to the array of vintage cars and trucks on display. The film was shot in Panavision and Technicolor by Freddie Young. Key moments from the battle, including Eagle Day and Hitler's London blunder, are restaged on a grand scale. The Eagle Day attacks on RAF airfields is a spectacular sequence, with the German bombs raining fire down on the aerodromes, as the pilots scramble to take off. No expense was spared – there's even one of Hitler's rousing speeches restaged in showbiz Nazi style. The aerial sequences are the greatest World War II dogfights in cinema. Cameras were fitted to Messerschmitts, Spitfires and Heinkels, but most of the aerial filming was carried out by a customised twin-engined B-25 Mitchell Bomber, specially adapted as a camera plane, which was piloted by John R. Hawkes. The onboard cameramen in this 'flying studio' were Skeets Kelly and Johnny Jordon. The film's assistant director Derek Cracknell dubbed the Mitchell 'The Psychedelic Monster' due to the multicoloured paint job on its fuselage. Spitfires and Hurricanes swoop in picturesquely executed arabesques, filmed against magnificent cloud formations, as they attack the German Heinkels and their fighter escorts – unleashing hails of machine-gun bullets and spitting death at the push of a button. Stricken aircraft tailspin towards earth, a trail of smoke charting their last desperate flight, until they disintegrate on impact in showering explosions. Many of the aerial duels, heavenly and ethereal in their beauty, were filmed above the clouds, or else over the patchwork quilt of farmland or the rolling Channel.

The special effects work is above average, with row upon row of German aircraft in attacking formation. In addition to the shots of real planes, many scale models and matte shots were used, particularly when the burning planes explode in mid-air, or crash into the Channel. The Stuka attack on a coastal radar station has real Spitfires pitted against model Stukas. During the battle over London, a German He-111 bomber crashes into a railway station, while another makes it back to the German invasion fleet's harbour, trailing smoke. RAF Sergeant Pilot Andy (Ian McShane) returns from helping the emergency services to discover the church hall 'rest centre' where his wife and sons were sheltering is now a burning ruin. In a lighter moment, pilot officer Archie (Edward Fox) parachutes to safety and flattens a gardener's glass and timber flower cloche. A little boy appears and offers him a cigarette: 'Thanks awfully old chap!' coos Archie. The Canadians, Poles and Czechs who flew with the RAF are mentioned in the film and a downed Polish pilot who parachutes into English farmland is mistaken by a pikel-wielding yokel for a German. There are other moments of cinematic beauty, as in the depiction of the Blitz attacks on the London docklands, glowing red on the horizon – a burnished, burning Waterloo Sunset.

The score, by Ron Goodwin, is one of his finest. Goodwin excelled in the war genre, with memorable contributions for *Operation Crossbow*, *633 Squadron* and *Where Eagles Dare*. His rousing themes include an echo of 'Deutchland Über Alles' for the Luftwaffe. The film was originally to have been scored by Sir William Walton and conducted by Malcolm Arnold, but Saltzman rejected this music. Only Walton's darting 'Battle in the Air' can be heard in the finished film, during the RAF's defeat of the Luftwaffe on 15 September. This scene is played with Walton's score alone (no overlaid plane engines or sound effects) and is a fitting climax to the film. Walton's score has now been restored and there is a version of the film on DVD with his music in place of Goodwin's. *Battle of Britain* was released by United Artists in the UK in September 1969 rated U and in the USA in October. It was less-than-successful, losing UA $10 million.

But reviewers who complained about the film's lack of pace and plot missed the point. With the array of vintage aircraft, the cast is almost incidental and in the era of CGI action films, *Battle of Britain*'s authenticity soars high as a great film-making achievement.

The Battle of Britain also features in Enzo Castellari's *Eagles Over London* (1969 – *Battle Squadron* and *Battle Command*), produced by Edmondo Amati. Its original title, *La battaglia d'Inghilterra*, translates as 'The Battle of England' – presumably to cash in on Hamilton's film. German SS commandos under fanatical Major Krueger (Luigi Pistilli) disguise themselves as British Tommies and are evacuated back to England from Dunkirk. Their sabotage mission is to destroy a powerful radar station in Portsmouth and to overwhelm the control centre for Allied aerial operations, in preparation for Hitler's invasion, here codenamed 'Marine Lion' (a mistranslation of Seelöwe). Captain Paul Stevens (Frederick Stafford) organises Operation Valiant to track down the German agents in London.

Castellari partly filmed on location in London, including Tower Bridge and Westminster. Hitler orders his Luftwaffe to attack, but it is repulsed by the RAF. In retaliation for the Allied bombing of Berlin, the Germans turn their attention to London and 15 September 1940 is designated 'Day of the Eagle', an all-out attack on the capital (hence the film's title). Stevens is involved in a tug-of-love struggle for RAF Lieutenant Meg Jones (Evelyn Stewart) with Air Marshal George Taylor (Van Johnson). Stevens is befriended by Lieutenant Martin Donovan (Francisco Rabal), one of the German commandos, who rooms with him in London. Krueger's men successfully blow up the radar tower at Portsmouth and infiltrate the RAF's operations control room at RAF Bentley Priory, but in a shoot-out Stevens and his men scupper their plans, while the RAF are victorious in the skies. Air Marshal Taylor is shot down and killed during the Battle of Britain, leaving Stevens and Meg together for the fade-out in a railway station where they listen to Churchill's famous 'Never in the field of human conflict' speech broadcast over a tannoy.

Just as Sergio Leone's western *The Good, the Bad and the Ugly* (1966) recreated the American Civil War, Italian-style, Castellari's *Eagles Over London* restages Dunkirk and the Battle of Britain on a grand scale. Like *Battle of Britain* location scenes involving hundreds of extras were shot largely in Spain. Francesco De Masi provided the rousing score and Alejandro Ulloa's impressive widescreen cinematography is lost in cropped prints, especially the scenes when Castellari deploys groovy 1960s split-screen effects. Alberto De Martino was slated to direct the film, but Castellari convinced the producer Amati to hire him by screening split-screen footage which used a mixture of recreations and tinted archive footage. Castellari and Tito Carpi wrote the convoluted story in one week in a Madrid hotel. It was one of the most expensive Italian films ever made up to that time and was a massive success domestically, though it was never released theatrically in the USA.

Castellari's film is a comic-book depiction of 1940s Britain, which mixes thriller elements with wartime action. The Home Front subterfuge leads one British soldier to moan, 'This ain't a war, it's a crossword puzzle'. Teresa Gimpera

Vengeance Weapons: V-1 'Doodlebug' (foreground) and V-2 rocket (background) at the Royal Air Force Museum at Cosford, Shropshire, in England. Photograph: H. Hughes.

played a German spy who works as a barmaid in a London pub. Eduardo Fajardo was the German general overseeing Operation Marine Lion and Renzo Palmer played Stevens' cockney sidekick, Sergeant Donald Mulligan. The film features numerous scenes depicting aerial combat over the Channel and London, while the bombing of London by the Luftwaffe is depicted via archive footage combined with staged shots of burning buildings. The model and effects work for the dogfights at Cinecittà Studios was by Spanish special effects master Emilio Ruiz Del Rio (of *Conan the Barbarian*, *Dune* and *Pan's Labyrinth*). Numerous historical details are wrong, including the odd selection of planes that are deployed as the RAF and the Luftwaffe (with Hurricanes repainted with German livery). When the German commandos attack the Portsmouth radar installation they pack their knapsacks with dynamite and become human bombs. Murdered Allied soldiers are discovered across London with their identities stolen. A love scene between Stevens and Meg is filmed in a darkened room sporadically illuminated with flashes, as the Germans bomb London. A scene when Stevens' men corner a German commando on a London rooftop plays like a wild-west gunfight, and the numerous fistfights recall ex-stuntman Castellari's penchant for action. When a German commando is captured, what else can he do but commit suicide in time-honoured war movie cliché fashion, by taking a Cyanide capsule?

The London Blitz began in September 1940, but the night raids over the city continued during November and December 1940. 'Science fiction' visions of the future such as *Things to Come* (1936) and *Q Planes* (1937 – *Clouds Over Europe*) had predicted the bombing of Britain before war had broken out. *Midnight Menace* (1937) even featured bomb-laden pilotless planes years before the V-1 'Doodlebugs' were launched by Germany against British cities. Key German targets included Birmingham, Plymouth, Liverpool, Manchester, Glasgow, Cardiff, Southampton, Sheffield and Bristol. Five hundred bombers attacked Coventry on 14 and 15 November 1940, destroying a third of the city's houses and killing 600 people. 'Coventrize' came to mean the levelling of a city in one raid and by the end of the Blitz in 1941, 40,000 British civilians had been killed. The figures could have been much higher however. Prior to Germany's aerial attacks on Britain, millions of civilians, including many children, were relocated from cities and industrial targets, to rural communities.

The nine-minute documentary *London Can Take It* (1940) was propaganda for US audiences. It depicted one day in the life of London during the Blitz. Its US release title, *Britain Can Take It*, was somewhat inappropriate, as Britain could take it, but it could do with America's help. *In Which We Serve* depicted the bombing of Plymouth. *Confirm or Deny* (1941) looked at the dark days of the Blitz and Operation Sealion, via a tale of espionage, while John Boorman's semi-autobiographical *Hope and Glory* (1987) depicted life during the Blitz. The UK TV drama series *Danger UXB* (1979) followed bomb disposal engineer teams diffusing unexploded bombs in England, during the Blitz and thereafter. The interestingly offbeat *It Happened Here* (1963) was a mockumentary of 'what ifs', had Hitler invaded and Britain succumbed to fascism. On the Home Front, audience morale was kept up by comedy thrillers such as *Cottage to Let* (1941 – starring Leslie Banks) and by George Formby vehicles such as *Let George Do It* (1940), wherein ukulele-playing cheeky chappy George slaps Hitler during a rally. Alfred Hitchcock's *Foreign Correspondent* (1940 – starring Joel McCrea) was pro-British propaganda for American audiences disguised as a spy thriller, exhorting them to join the war. According to *The Lion, the Witch and the Wardrobe* (2005), the Pevensie children, four evacuees, discover the country of Narnia in an item of furniture.

George More O'Ferrall's *Angels One Five* (1953) was a monochrome British production shot on location at RAF Kenley, south of London. The fictional story begins in June 1940 and continues into the Battle of Britain. RAF pilots used their own slang jargon – 'bandits' were enemy aircraft, 'pancake' meant they were to land immediately and 'angels' was the height at which they flew in thousands of feet. Scottish Pilot Officer T.B. Baird, nicknamed 'Septic' (John Gregson) joins the RAF 'Pimpernel' squadron stationed at RAF Neethley (part of Fighter Command Group 11) commanded by Group Commander 'Tiger' Small (Jack Hawkins). Baird announces his arrival at the airfield by 'pranging' his Hurricane when he crashes into a house. The film depicts life at the aerodrome through various protagonists: the WAAFs (members of the Women's Auxiliary Air Force) and other staff of the Operations Room bunker (with its charts, radar and glass war map), flying ace Flight Lieutenant 'Batchy' Salter (Humphrey Lestocq), Squadron Leader Bill Ponsford (Andrew Osborn) and Betty Carfax (Veronica Hurst), Baird's love interest. Michael Denison was particularly good as Peter Moon, formerly commander of the Operations Room who takes over as squadron leader when Ponsford is killed. Denison's wife Dulcie Gray played nurse, Nadine Clinton, the 'lady with the lamp' – a guiding light for pilots landing on the airfield by night.

Much of *Angels One Five*'s aerial action occurs offscreen, with events mapped out on the Operation Room's war boards, or else seen as distant vapour trails and

WAAFs in the Operations Room at RAF Neethley await news of an impeding Luftwaffe attack in George More O'Ferrall's *Angels One Five* (1953). Courtesy Kevin Wilkinson Collection.

swirling clouds. When the Battle of Britain intensifies, 25 Ju-88 bombers attack the aerodrome, with horrific results. In the film's most memorable scenes, the airfield is devastated and the Operations Room suffers a direct hit, causing the hefty reinforced ceiling to collapse, a dusty tangle of concrete and twisted metal. The German planes are unconvincing special effect animation and matte shots, and the Spitfires are newsreel footage, but the film does have real Hurricanes, courtesy of the Portuguese Air Force. The stop-start life of the pilots is well depicted, their quiet moments interrupted by the scramble to 'action stations'. Planes return from sorties, shot up, low on juice, to patch up and refuel before returning to the fray. The film's ending is particularly powerful: as Betty prepares for her first night out with 'Septic' in Maidstone, it becomes apparent that he won't be making their date. No matter how depressing or downbeat the subject matter, most British RAF films deploy a chirpy score, in this case composed by John Wooldridge. For its simplicity and convincing performances, this remains one of the finest films to feature the Few, and aptly depicts that 'waiting was the worst part of war'.

The melodramatic *Dangerous Moonlight* (1941 – *Suicide Squadron*), another film that depicted the Few, is best remembered now for Richard Addinsell's melodramatic piano composition 'Warsaw Concerto'. Britain's air war also features in *Pearl Harbor* (2001). Hotshot US pilot Rafe McCawley (Ben Affleck) is transferred to the RAF in 1941 before the US has entered the war and dogfights with the Luftwaffe, where he's shot down over the English Channel and presumed lost. *From*

Hell to Victory (1979) frugally staged the Battle of Britain by reusing footage from *Eagles Over London*. Leslie Howard's *The First of the Few* (1942 – *Spitfire*) recounted the career of R.J. Mitchell, the aeronautical engineer who designed the Supermarine Spitfire, the fastest and best fighter of the war. The film begins on 'Zero Day, 15 September 1940' as RAF pilot Geoffrey Crisp (David Niven) tells his fellow fliers the story of how the Spitfire was developed. This includes interesting archive footage of the Schneider Cup seaplane races in the 1920s, which were won by the Supermarine S-6. A chance pre-war meeting between Messerschmitt (Erik Freund) and Mitchell in Germany at the Richthofen Club convinces Mitchell to develop the Supermarine as a fighter plane ('a spitfire bird'), with Rolls-Royce Merlin engines and Crisp – his race-winning pilot from Schneider Cup days – as his test pilot. Mitchell died from cancer in 1937 and never lived to see his creation's success at war. Rosamund John played long-suffering Diana Mitchell and producer-director Leslie Howard played Mitchell himself. *First of the Few* turned out to be the last of the lot for Howard: he was shot down and killed by German fighters on his way back from Lisbon in 1943.

Lewis Gilbert's *Reach for the Sky* (1956), a Rank Organisation release, was the screen biography of Douglas Bader and was based on the book by Paul Brickhill. Bader lost both legs below the knee in a biplane accident in 1931 but through Herculean determination, courage and perseverance, he became an RAF pilot, serving with distinction in the Battle of Britain and rising to the rank of Wing Commander. His prescient tactics, involving five squadrons of fighters (the so-called Duxford Wing) helped to win the battle. Kenneth More's moving, affably real portrayal of the war hero was instrumental in making the film a box office hit in Britain. It was filmed at RAF Kenley, Surrey and at Pinewood

Kenneth More as Douglas Bader, the RAF ace, in a publicity portrait for Lewis Gilbert's *Reach for the Sky* (1956). Courtesy Kevin Wilkinson Collection.

Studios. Much of the film details Bader's poignant relationship with his wife Thelma (Muriel Pavlow) and the tribulations of his rehabilitation. He was fitted with two artificial limbs (which earned him the nickname 'Tinlegs' Bader) and painstakingly learned to walk. This results in some rather odd dialogue – a flier colleague rouses Bader from his sleep to fly a sortie over the Dunkirk evacuation with, 'Come on Douglas, get your legs on'.

The film's clichéd depiction of pipe-smoking chaps and their prim, well-mannered love interests has dated badly, but the true-life drama of the story wins through. Originally 136 minutes, it was abridged for US release to 123 minutes. The battle footage is a combination of re-enactments (featuring real Hawker Hurricanes), model work and excellent aerial newsreel footage. Bader was later shot down over Occupied France, losing one of his artificial legs in the process, and the Germans allowed him to have a replacement flown in. They soon wished they hadn't, as Bader mounted three escape attempts from various prison camps. Eventually incarcerated in Colditz Castle, he was liberated by American forces in the spring of 1945. On 15 September 1945 – the five-year anniversary of the Battle of Britain – Bader led 12 survivors from the battle at the head of an immense fly-past over London.

As the war progressed, the Allies engaged in a sustained campaign of Strategic Bombing of targets in Europe, as a way of depleting German resources and morale, and in retaliation for the Blitz. The US Army Air Force (USAAF) carried out daylight bombing raids in their Boeing B-17 and B-24 Liberator bombers, while RAF Bomber Command carried out night-time raids (after daylight attacks became too costly) in Avro Lancasters and Wellingtons. In February 1942, Air Marshal Sir Arthur Harris (known as 'Butch' by his men) ordered the bombing of German cities, a tactic that helped shorten the war, but was criticised on moral grounds in some quarters and earned him the nickname 'Bomber Harris'. The first 'thousand bomber' raid was on Cologne in May 1942, but the most controversial raids were the night raid on Hamburg in July 1943 (where the planes also confused the German radar by dropping strips of tinfoil, called 'Window') and the infamous attack on Dresden. On the night of 13–14 February 1944, this raid killed thousands of civilians when the bombs and incendiaries created a huge inferno, a firestorm of such ferocity that it sucked the oxygen out of the air and suffocated victims in their shelters.

Twelve O'Clock High (1949) starred Gregory Peck as Brigadier General Frank Savage, the commander of daylight saturation bombing raids from Archbury airfield into Europe in 1942–43. Savage replaces Colonel Keith Davenport (Gary Merrill) who has begun to care too much for his men's welfare and cracks under the strain. Savage's rod of iron is intended to whip the 918th Bomb Group into shape – 'Consider yourselves already dead' he tells his pilots – but he too begins to push himself and his men to the limit, resulting in Savage's mental and physical collapse. All the air raid footage, of the American bombers coming under attack by German fighters during their operations over Germany, is archive filmed by the USAAF and the Luftwaffe. The scene where a B-17 crash lands and skids on its belly was staged especially for the film, with pilot Paul Mantz earning $4,500 for the risky stunt. Peck took the lead role after it had been turned down by John

Wayne and his towering performance is one of Peck's finest. He was nominated for a Best Actor Academy Award, but the cast is uniformly good. Millard Mitchell played General Pritchard and Hugh Marlowe was shirker, Lieutenant Colonel Ben Gately. Dean Jagger, as WWI veteran Major Stovall, won a Best Supporting Actor Oscar. Henry King's popular film was based on Sy Bartlett and Beirne Lay Jr's 1948 novel of the same title and deployed 12 real B-17 Flying Fortresses for the airfield scenes, which were shot at Ozark Airfield, Alabama and RAF Barford St John Air Base, England.

In Powell and Pressburger's *One of Our Aircraft Is Missing* (1941), a bomber crew bail out over Holland after a raid on Stuttgart and the locals help the RAF men make their way back to Blighty. The film never quite matches the eeriness of its opening scene, as crewless Wellington bomber 'B for Bertie' returns across the North Sea and crashes into a pylon. Erich Von Stroheim Jr and Boris Sagal's *The Thousand Plane Raid* (1969), starring Christopher George, Ben Murphy and Bo Hopkins, was based on the bombing of Cologne in 1942. *Memphis Belle* (1990), starring Matthew Modine, Eric Stoltz, Billy Zane and Harry Connick Jr, re-enacted the famous 25th daylight bombing mission over Germany by the title B-17, which was named after pilot Robert Morgan's girlfriend.

David Niven played an RAF pilot in Powell and Pressburger's best film, *A Matter of Life and Death* (1946), which was intended to encourage post-war transatlantic amity. Whilst returning from a one-thousand-plane bombing raid over Europe, Squadron Leader Peter D. Carter (Niven), a poet, bails out from his stricken Lancaster over a fog-shrouded Channel. Before he jumps, Peter has a long conversation with American radio operator June (Kim Hunter). Peter wakes up on a beach, meets June and they fall in love. But it appears that there has been a mistake in Heaven and Peter should have died. This leads to a Heavenly court case: Department of Records versus Squadron Leader Peter Carter. On Earth, Dr Frank Reeves , the physician who attempts to cure Peter of brain damage, headaches and hallucinations, is killed in a motorbike accident and becomes Peter's defence council in Heaven, where his key piece of evidence is one of June's tears on a pink rose. Roger Livesey played Dr Reeves, Richard Attenborough can be seen briefly as a deceased RAF pilot and Marius Goring played Heavenly messenger Conductor 71, who must convince Peter to return to Heaven. Raymond Massey was Abraham Farlan, the prosecuting council, who is eventually defeated as the power of love triumphs over all. The film's celebrated scenes of an immense escalator leading up to Heaven inspired the film's retitling in the USA, *Stairway to Heaven.* Filmed in monochrome (for the Heaven scenes) and Technicolor (for Earth) by Jack Cardiff, the film is a fantasy, a love story, a courtroom trial and a medical drama, but only briefly a war film.

Anthony Asquith's *The Way to the Stars* (1945 – *Johnny in the Clouds* in the USA) is the most reflective, nostalgic film to depict the wartime RAF and also the most moving. It was written by Terence Rattigan and producer Anatole De Grunwald. Set at 'Halfpenny Field', an airstrip in Yorkshire (filmed at RAF Catterick, North Yorkshire) it begins with RAF crews flying Blenheim bombers in daylight raids on barge concentrations in Calais in 1940, during the build-up to Sealion. Michael Redgrave played pilot David Archdale. He marries hotelier

'Toddy' (Rosamund John) and they have a son. David is killed when his burning plane crashes into a hill during a mission in France. His roommate, fellow pilot and close friend Peter Penrose (John Mills) tells Toddy the news and she asks him to read a poem written for her by David, which includes the lines: 'Do not despair for Johnny Head-in-the-air, he sleeps as sound as Johnny underground'. These words were actually penned by the poet John Pudney and are used to great effect throughout the film. In 1942, Peter is still flying missions but David's death has made him reluctant to become romantically involved with Iris Winterton (Renee Asherton), a resident of the Golden Lion hotel in the nearby village of Shepley. The film's excellent first half is disrupted by the arrival of the USAAF, who take over the base in 1942 to fly B-17 raids into Europe. Married US pilot Johnny Hollis (Douglass Montgomery) befriends Toddy, a platonic relationship between two lonely people. The film follows the airbase's story through to 1944, when Johnny has the opportunity to return to the USA as an instructor. But he stays on and is killed when he attempts to land his B-17 with one engine out, the rudder shot up and a bomb hanging from the hold. Loud, cocky B-17 pilot Joe Friselli (Bonar Colleano Jr) romances Iris, which eventually prompts Peter (now a Lancaster 'Pathfinder' pilot) to throw caution to the wind and propose to her.

The story is told through the personnel of the RAF base and the locals: planes take off, some return and the survivors mourn those who have perished. There are no scenes of combat or bombing but this film says more about war than its action-packed cousins. *The Way to the Stars* was a big success in the UK, surprisingly so given its downbeat, melancholic air, which nevertheless struck a chord with audiences. It is a film permeated with sadness and loss, of making the most of today when tomorrow is so uncertain. It's beautifully written and masterfully acted, particularly by Redgrave, Mills and John. The airfield scenes deploy authentic Blenheims, Hurricanes and B-17 Flying Fortresses. The nearby market town of 'Shepley' was filmed on two locations: the church and stone cross at Bedale, North Yorkshire and the Golden Lion Hotel in Northallerton. A panning shot of the main thoroughfare cleverly links these two locations with a cut concealed by a hay cart. Bill Rowbotham played gunner 'Nobby' Clarke in the film – as 'Bill Owen' he became famous as Compo in the long-running Yorkshire-set UK TV sitcom *Last of the Summer Wine*. Joyce Carey played Iris' meddlesome aunt, Trevor Howard was Squadron Leader Carter, Basil Radford played genial airfield controller 'Tiny' Williams and Stanley Holloway was Golden Lion resident Mr Palmer. David Tomlinson and Anthony Dawson played bomber crewmen and Jean Simmons appeared in an early role as the singer with a big band who performs 'Let Him Go, Let Him Tarry'. *Way to the Stars* begins with the camera roaming through the airbase, now derelict and abandoned after the war's end, which opens the story in haunting style – the ghosts from the past are still present at Halfpenny Field, which is now grazing for sheep.

Many of these aero-dramas blended love stories on the ground with combat in the air, with varying degrees of success, as cool US flyboys and 'chocks away' RAF pilots romanced blushing English Roses. Philip Leacock directed two such features: *Appointment in London* (1952 – *Raiders in the Sky* in the USA) and *The War Lover* (1962). In the first film, Dirk Bogarde, the pre-eminent post-war British film star, played Lancaster pilot Wing Commander Tim Mason. He is approaching his ninetieth successful bombing mission, but his nerves are beginning to fray. There is plenty of Lancaster footage (using three actual 'Lancs' at the airfield at RAF Upwood, Cambridgeshire), which is interrupted by the love story element of the film. Mason vies for the affections of intelligence officer Eve Canyon (Dinah Sheridan), a widow since Dunkirk, with US liaison officer Major Mac Baker (William Sylvester). The supporting cast includes Ian Hunter, Richard Wattis and Bryan Forbes, the latter as a pilot who loses his lucky harmonica and jinxes a bombing mission from which he doesn't return. The last half-hour of the film is a detailed, exciting recreation (using archive footage) of a large-scale night-time mission over Germany to destroy a newly built town which is to be used to assemble secret weapons. The planes approach the target, avoiding tracers, anti-aircraft fire and searchlights, and are led in by the Lancaster 'Pathfinder' squadrons, who marked the planes' bombing corridor with sky markers – the heroic Pathfinders were the subject of the 13-part 1972 UK TV drama, *The Pathfinders*. The bombing operation is a success and Mason miraculously completes his final mission.

In *The War Lover* (1962), two US B-17 crew members – manic Captain Buzz Rickson (Steve McQueen) and suave Lieutenant Bo Bolland (Robert Wagner) – fight over Daphne Caldwell (Shirley Anne Field). The fliers are on a 25-mission tour of duty carrying out bombing raids on 'Nazi Europe' in 1943. Buzz has a near-psychopathic obsession with the war and gets a literal 'buzz' from bombing missions and danger. The rule-breaking hotshot role is tailor-made for McQueen, though his acting is hammy by his own cool standards. The film plods while on the ground and the plot's rickety structure is barely nailed together with clichés, but the sequences featuring the B-17 Flying Fortresses are impressively done. The film was made on location in England (including Cambridge University), with interiors at Shepperton Studios, using actual Flying Fortresses. The US 8th Air Force's HQ was at High Wycombe: the film was made at RAF Bovington (Hertfordshire) and RAF Manston (Kent). The bombers fire up their engines and trundle in convoy to taxi into position, then open their throttles and roar into the sky. The B-17s have artwork painted on their fuselages. Buzz and Bo crew 'The Body', and other bombers are named 'Alabama Whammer', 'Angel Tread', 'House of Usher', 'Expendable VI', 'Hellcat Annie' and 'Chug Pug'.

The aerial scenes were arranged by Captain John Crewdson. There's an exciting moment when a Flying Fortress returns to base with no undercarriage and manages a 'belly landing', without wheels. Michael Crawford, in his film debut, played gunner Junior Sailen and Burk Kwouk (later Kato in the *Pink Panther* comedies) played another flier. The B-17s were heavily armed with machine guns and flew daylight bombing raids without fighter escort. They sometimes sacrificed accuracy by dropping their bombs through 'undercast' – cloud and fog which obscured the bombers' views of their precision targets. In the film Buzz sweeps his Fortress down below the cloud to knock out submarine pens. The Body's final mission, as part of a thousand-plane raid, is to attack a synthetic oil refinery in Leipzig. They run the gauntlet of fighters and flak to deliver their payload, but the bomb bay doors jam and one live bomb remains onboard. The Body is badly shot up, losing altitude, and over the Channel the crew bail out – except for Buzz who in attempting to land on the English coast crashes into the White Cliffs of Dover.

Throughout its history, Hollywood has never allowed facts to get in the way of a good story. As a response to Hollywood's rewriting and reinvention of WWII history, the spoof *Churchill: The Hollywood Years* (2004) was according to its tagline: 'Based on an Actual War'. It was directed by Peter Richardson, who had worked on the UK TV series *The Comic Strip Presents* (1988–2000). In this reimagining of history, Winston Churchill (Christian Slater) is a gung-ho, cigar-chomping US Marine. He romances and saves the life of Princess Elizabeth (Neve Campbell) – the future queen of England and the daughter of King George VI (Harry Enfield) – in the early part of the war, but dies in 1940 during the Battle of Britain (his gravestone epitaph is 'Give Me the Tools'). The politician and statesman we know as Churchill was actually 'after-dinner speaker and character actor' Roy Bubbles. The film assembled the cream of UK comedy talent – including Jon Culshaw, Vic Reeves and Bob Mortimer, Leslie Phillips, Steve Pemberton, Phil Cornwell, Sally Phillips, Mackenzie Crook, James Dreyfus and Rik Mayall – and frittered them away to little effect. Only Miranda Richardson's Eva Braun and Anthony Sher's Adolf Timothy Philip Hitler (who attempts to shanghai Elizabeth into marriage) gel in this disappointing film. It's a great idea but even with end titles and flub clips, it's thinly stretched to 84 minutes.

The most famous Allied bombing raid of the war – and one of the great exploits of the RAF – was recounted in Michael Anderson's *The Dam Busters* (1954), a British war film classic and *Boy's Own* adventure, par excellence. The theme tune – Eric Coates' stirring 'The Dam Busters' – builds to an inspiring 'Land of Hope and Glory'-style crescendo which epitomises the RAF, patriotism and daring do. In the spring of 1942, Dr Barnes Wallis (Michael Redgrave) an aeronautical engineer at Vickers, proposes an idea to destroy dams to the east of the Ruhr, Germany's industrial heartland. He invents a five-ton 'bouncing bomb' which will skim the surface of a reservoir and blow up the dam structures, depriving Germany of a valuable industrial commodity, stalling power stations and flooding factories and tracts of land. Air Chief Marshal Sir Arthur 'Bomber' Harris (Basil Sydney) of Bomber Command supports the idea, as does the Prime Minister, so Barnes Wallis proceeds with his experiments to perfect the unique device. Wing Commander Guy Gibson (Richard Todd) is put in charge of assembling a crack new team of Lancaster bomber pilots, 617 Squadron, for the task. They train on lakes and reservoirs in England and Wales, surmounting problems as they encounter them. For example, the pilots must fly at night only 60 feet above the water, to deliver their bouncing payload. In mid-May, conditions are right and by a full moon 617 Squadron fly in waves at low level across the Atlantic to avoid radar, through Holland and into the Ruhr. Their mission is a success, but 56 men are missing after the operation – a heavy price to pay – and Wallis wonders if it's all been worth it.

The Dam Busters was based on the 1951 book of the same name by Paul Brickhill and *Enemy Coast Ahead* (Gibson's own recollections) and was adapted for the screen by R.C. Sherriff. It is the true story of Operation Chastise, the bombing missions against the hydroelectric dams at Eder, Sorbe and Moehne. The film benefits from Erwin Hillier's monochrome cinematography and Gilbert Taylor's special effects. The production was lucky enough to have several four-engined Avro Lancaster bombers at its deposal and these impressive machines look tremendous, silhouetted on the airstrip against cold dawn skies, or sweeping across the shimmering surface of the moonlit lakes. The airfield at RAF Hemswell, Lincolnshire played the mission's base at RAF Scampton, Lincolnshire. The practice runs and the raids were recreated over the Derwent Water Dam in the Lake District, Cumbria, and Howden Reservoir and Ladybower Reservoir in the Peak District, Derbyshire. Interiors were filmed at Associated British Studios in Elstree, Hertfordshire. For its time the film's special effects shots are impressive. The Lancasters locate their targets and plunge low, running the gauntlet of tracer flak across the reservoirs before releasing the bombs on cue. As they hit their mark, the detonators explode in great plumes of water and flame. This action is intercut with Wallis and the RAF staff waiting anxiously back in the control room. The bomb resembles an oversized bowling ball when hurtling across the water, but when seen up in close it has flat sides. The actual bombs resembled large oil drums, but couldn't be depicted in the film as they were still top secret. In addition to 'The Dam Busters' march, the rousing incidental music was composed by Leighton Lucas and played by the Associated British Studio Orchestra.

The Dam Busters draws a contrast between eccentric, tweedy, bespectacled boffin Barnes Wallis and Guy Gibson, the sleeves-rolled-up 'doer', who puts Wallis' flights of fancy to strategic purpose. Here bombing is an exact science: the bombs must be dropped at a speed of 240 miles an hour, 600 yards from the dam for them to bounce correctly and hit their mark. A visit to a London show inspires Gibson to use two spotlights fitted to the underside of the planes, which will shine on the water – when the two spots meet, the aircraft are at the right height. Gibson has a beer-slurping black Labrador named Nigger, whose name has now been re-dubbed Trigger or removed altogether from TV prints. When Nigger is killed by a hit-and-run driver on the eve of the mission, Gibson asks that he be buried on the verge near Gibson's office around midnight, just as their attack is underway. Redgrave and Todd are both outstanding, in a well-chosen cast. Ursula Jeans appeared as Mrs Wallis, Harold Goodwin played Gibson's batman and the RAF crews were played by Brewster Mason, Nigel Stock, Anthony Doonan, Brian Nissen, Peter Assinder, Richard Leech, Richard Thorp, David Morell, John Fraser, Bill Kerr, George Baker, Ronald Wilson, Denys Graham, Basil Appleby, Tim Turner and Ewen Solon. Robert Shaw appeared as a member of Gibson's crew and Patrick McGoohan made his film debut as a sergeant guarding the briefing room door. The music, the action, the drama and the performances ensured the film was a great success, especially in Britain. The US print, entitled *The Dambusters* was edited to 102 minutes to make the film more of an action picture, while the UK print is uncut at 120 minutes.

Walter E. Grauman's *633 Squadron* (1964) is second only to *The Dam Busters* in the daredevil air mission movie stakes. It was based on the 1956 novel of the same name by Frederick E. Smith. Prior to D-Day, 633 Squadron are assigned to destroy a German factory hidden at the end of the Svartfjord (Black Fjord) in Norway. The factory is manufacturing special fuel for new rockets Hitler is preparing to launch against Britain. The multinational squadron includes Englishmen, an Australian and a Sikh. American Cliff Robertson played their Canadian commander, Wing Commander Roy Grant (named Roy Grenville in the book). They train over the highlands of Scotland, flying their Mosquito fighter-bombers low, to bomb their target. The plan is for the Norwegian Resistance to attack the German flak positions on the fjord, while the squadron's salvo of 'Earthquake Bombs' will fracture a huge overhanging precipice above the factory, which will be destroyed in the resulting rockslide.

Released by the Mirisch Corporation via United Artists, *633 Squadron* is essentially 'The Fjord Busters'. James Clavell co-wrote the screenplay with Howard Koch. The top-flight British cast included Harry Andrews as Air Vice-Marshal Davis, Michael Goodliffe as Squadron Leader Adams and Donald Houston as Group Commander Barrett. Angus Lennie (from *The Great Escape*) played Grant's co-pilot 'spotter' Flying Officer 'Hoppy' Hopkinson. The RAF airstrip scenes were filmed at RAF Bovingdon, Hertfordshire (called Sutton Craddock in the book) and the Highlands of Scotland (including Glencoe and Lochgilphead on the west coast) were used both for the Scottish training scenes and the Norwegian scenes. Johnny Briggs (later of *Coronation Street*) had a small role as one of the pilots who is killed during the training. The ground scenes are mercifully short – depicting the pilots' comradeship when drinking in their local, the Black Swan pub (actually the Three Compasses in Aldenham, Hertfordshire) – and the pre-mission briefing scenes mercifully brief. A subplot featured WAAF Mary (Suzan Farmer) and pilot Bissell (Scot Finch) getting married, but he is facially disfigured and blinded when his fiery Mosquito crash lands soon afterwards. Another subplot followed naval Lieutenant Erik Bergman, a Norwegian resistance leader, who escapes to Britain to help plan the operation and returns to Norway, where he's captured and tortured by the Gestapo. Grant has to fly a mission of mercy to bomb the Gestapo HQ in Norway to kill Bergman, rather than allow him to divulge information about the mission. Bergman's sister Hilde, who is also exiled in England and becomes Grant's love interest, was played by Maria Perschy. Bergman was played by George Chakiris (from *West Side Story* [1961]), who with his chiselled Latino looks and pompadour made an unconvincing Norwegian freedom fighter.

An RAF squadron designated 633 didn't exist, but Smith's novel purports to be a true story – the recollections of the landlord of the Black Swan, who has assembled biographical folders and photographs detailing the mission. The film deployed several actual twin-engined, two-man De Havilland Mosquito fighter-bombers, the so-called Wooden Wonders. They were the fastest allied combat aircraft of the war and their wooden structure made them easy to repair. The scenes of the attack on the fjord are well photographed (in Panavision and DeLuxe colour), with the actual planes intercut with convincing model work, amid plumes of flak bursts. The mission succeeds but at a very high price, with almost all the Mosquitoes downed by German fighters and ack-ack fire. German Bf 109s (actually

Wooden Wonders: Twin-engined, two-man De Havilland Mosquito fighter-bombers taxi into position at RAF Bovington, Hertfordshire, in Walter E. Grauman's *633 Squadron* (1964). Courtesy Kevin Wilkinson Collection.

Messerschmitt Bf 108 'Taifuns' [Typhoons]) strafe the RAF airfield and a Mosquito crashes into a fuel truck. Returning Mosquitoes perform emergency 'belly' landings and Bergman parachutes into Norway from a two-engined B-25 Mitchell bomber. When he is captured in a shootout, the German armoured car in the scene is actually a disguised British six-wheeled Alvis Saracen armoured personnel carrier of 1952 vintage. *633 Squadron* was a great success, but is perhaps best remembered today for its theme music by Ron Goodwin, the rolling brass and incessant, darting melody now as famous as its cousin, the theme from *The Dam Busters*.

Boris Sagal's *Mosquito Squadron* (1969) reused *633 Squadron*'s plot and plenty of Grauman's footage – the German attack on an airfield and reels of aerial stock – plus V-1 rocket footage from *Operation Crossbow* (1965). *Mosquito Squadron* starred David McCallum as improbably-named Squadron Leader Quint Monroe, who leads a bouncing bomb raid on a fortified French château where a V-3 rocket is being developed, even though the area houses a 'human shield' of RAF prisoners of war. This attack was possibly inspired by Operation Jericho in February 1944. An audacious jailbreak, this bombing mission carried out by 19 Mosquitos attacked Amiens Prison, breaching the walls to free French detainees held by the Germans, though in this historical ascendant the target of the raid was the prison itself. Films such as *633 Squadron, The Dam Busters, The Way to the Stars* and *Battle of Britain* serve as a lasting reminder of the valour displayed by RAF and USAAF pilots and their immense contribution to winning the war. The few saved the many – and for that the many are in their debt.

Chapter 3

THE WAR AT SEA (1940–45)

At the beginning of World War II, Britain had the world's largest navy. Germany had no navy as such, so Britannia could at least rule the waves. Even in the war's darkest days, naval war films were useful morale boosters. These films often depicted the Battle of the Atlantic, where the Royal Navy fought to keep solitary Britain supplied with imports and raw materials, as the freighter convoys were hunted by 'wolf packs' of German submarines, the predatory U-boats.

In Which We Serve (1942), presented by British Lion and dedicated to the Royal Navy, is the epitome of patriotic British wartime cinema which blurred historical fact with flag-waving, feel-good fiction. The destroyer *HMS Torrin* is sunk off Crete by Junkers-88 dive-bombers on 23 May 1941. One group of survivors cling to a dinghy in the oil-slicked water. Between strafing attacks by the Luftwaffe, the sailors keep themselves entertained singing choruses of 'Run Rabbit' and 'Roll Out the Barrel', while flashbacks tell the *Torrin*'s story, from dockyard and commission, to watery Mediterranean grave. *In Which We Serve* is 'The Noël Coward Show', with the multitalented playwright working as the writer-producer-composer of 'A Noël Coward Production'. For this *tour de force*, Coward received a special Oscar for his 'outstanding production achievement'. He also co-directed (with David Lean) and starred as the *Torrin*'s captain, E.V. Kinross, who was based on Lord Louis Mountbatten. The *Torrin*'s story is that of Mountbatten's ship, *HMS Kelly*, which was sunk off Crete in May 1941.

The film's opening scenes of the *Torrin*'s construction resemble inspiring promotional ads for the British Steel Industry. The Germans are 'The Hun' and their Italian allies 'Macaronis'. During the many flashbacks, the crews' very different class backgrounds are depicted in family vignettes. Their class differences are epitomised by upper-class Kinross and 'Cor blimey, Guv'nor' Ordinary Seaman 'Shorty' Blake (John Mills). Kinross and Alix (Celia Johnson in her film debut) have a nice country cottage, a maid and two adorable little tykes, Bobby

Publicity photograph of Noël Coward as Captain E.V. Kinross, the skipper of destroyer *HMS Torrin*, in Coward's wartime *tour de force In Which We Serve* (1942). Courtesy Kevin Wilkinson Collection.

and Lavinia. A scene depicts this idealised family picnicking on sunny Dunstable Downs, as the Battle of Britain rages overhead. Coward spouts such lines as, 'It was a good honeymoon as honeymoons go' in his inimitable, clipped style and runs a 'happy and efficient ship' with paternal care. Other key protagonists include Chief Petty Officer Walter Hardy (Bernard Miles) and Richard Attenborough (in his film debut) plays a young seaman who panics and leaves his post without permission during a naval engagement off Norway in 1940, when the *Torrin* is torpedoed, but is towed to port and repaired. Shorty falls for Freda Lewis (Kay Walsh), they marry and she gives birth to a baby boy (played by Mills' daughter, Juliet). Walter Hardy is less lucky – his wife Kath (Joyce Carey) and her mother Mrs Lemmon (Dora Gregory) are killed in an air raid on Plymouth. The scenes featuring Shorty and Freda are the film's best; they are a couple to which 'an extra half an hour together' during his brief shore leave means the world to them. When the survivors are eventually rescued and taken to Alexandria, they are reassigned as replacements for other ships. The scene when Kinross bids goodbye to his men says much about the comradeship, respect and even love that exists between men at war. For all its old fashioned-ness and dated dialogue, it remains a moving, powerful British classic, and no mistake.

Based on the diaries of German captain Bernhard Rogge, Duilio Coletti's *Under Ten Flags* (1960) recreated the activities of the *Atlantis*, a German raider which wreaked havoc on Allied shipping during 1940–41. Van Heflin starred as wily Rogge, who survived the war and at the time of the film's release was a NATO commander in the Territorial Allied Naval Force. The *Atlantis* impersonated shipping of many countries – hence the film's title – from Japan to Britain, by disguising the crew in appropriate uniforms, to mimic harmless cargo ships. But the *Atlantis* is actually a Q-boat, armed to the teeth with concealed deck guns and torpedoes. At the Admiralty, Charles Laughton delivered a large slice of ham as Rogge's arch-nemesis, surly Admiral Russell, who tracks the mysterious 'phantom ship' from his operations room. The interesting cast included Brigitte Bardot-alike Mylene Demongeot (as passenger Zizi), John Ericson, Peter Carsten, Gian Maria Volonté and Folco Lulli. Gerard Herter played a U-boat commander. Nino Rota wrote the score and the naval action deployed archive footage and re-enactments with full-size ships. The *Atlantis* is eventually tricked into a rendezvous with cruiser *HMS Devonshire* and is sunk.

Compton Bennett's *Gift Horse* (1952 – *Glory at Sea* in the USA) told the fictional story of the US destroyer *Whittier*, one of 50 ships transferred to the Royal Navy in 1940 as part of the US–UK Lend–Lease pact. In Halifax, Nova Scotia she is renamed *HMS Ballantrae* and sees action in the Atlantic, escorting supply convoys and staving off U-boats and aerial attacks. Her captain, widower Lieutenant Commander Frazer (Trevor Howard) is initially hated by his crew for his strictness, and their mission is less than successful, with the battered ship, already too old for active service, hitting a submerged wreck off the Lizard and suffering from mechanical glitches. But Frazer and his crew redeem themselves when they ram and sink a U-boat. James Donald appeared as Frazer's Canadian second-in-command, with Richard Attenborough and Bernard Lee as crew members. Token US star Sonny Tufts played Irish-American Flanagan, who falls in love with local girl Gladys (Dora Bryan) in Exeter, and Sid James appeared as the landlord of the Golden Bull pub. Gladys is killed in a bombing raid on Exeter and Frazer loses his son, a sailor, in action, and receives the news on Christmas Day 1941.

Howard is especially good as the emotionally spent captain and the scenes of Atlantic Convoy escorts are convincingly done, with footage filmed at sea combined with special effects. Eventually the *Ballantrae* is chosen for a special mission, which is based on old US destroyer *Campbeltown*'s role in the raid on St Nazaire dock in March 1942. With a commando escort, the *Ballantrae* sails up an estuary disguised as a German vessel and rams the dock gates, putting them out of action. In reality, the Normandie Dock was to be used as a base for the German battleship *Tirpitz* to raid into the Atlantic, but the mission's success ensured she never did. The *Ballantrae*'s valiant crew pay heavily in the attack, and many, including Frazer, are captured. The 'gift horse' which many thought fit only for the knacker's yard proved her worth.

Charles Frend's *The Cruel Sea* (1952), produced at Ealing Studios by Leslie Norman, is the high watermark for post-war British naval films, a recreation of events during the Battle of the Atlantic. It is based on the acclaimed 1951 novel by Nicholas Monsarrat. Jack Hawkins appeared in his finest, most memorable role as Captain Ericson, a merchantman in peacetime who is appointed skipper of the Flower Class corvette, *HMS Compass Rose*, which is despatched to escort convoys in the North Sea and later hunts U-boats on routes to Gibraltar. Despite the addition of the submarine location device known as asdic (an acronym of the Allied Submarine Detection Investigation Committee which developed it), the *Compass Rose* is torpedoed by a U-boat with heavy loss of life and the ship is sunk. Ericson and First-lieutenant Lockhart (Donald Sinden) survive and are reunited on a new ship, the Castle Class frigate *HMS Saltash Castle*, which patrols the bitterly cold routes through the Barents Sea to Murmansk, northern Russia. In their entire five years of active service, Ericson and Lockhart sink only two U-boats, but save many freighters and their crews.

Hawkins' narration establishes the film's grim mood from the outset: 'The men are the heroes, the heroines are the ships, the only villain is the sea ... a cruel sea, that man has made more cruel'. *Compass Rose* was portrayed by *HMS Coreopsis* and *Saltash Castle* was *HMS Porchester Castle*. It is accurately noted that U-boats were few and far between prior to the fall of France, when the Channel ports were used to launch U-boat operations. Stanley Baker played authoritarian, bullying First-lieutenant Bennett, who is transferred when he develops an ulcer. The film concentrated on events at sea, with few diversions to dry land. Lockhart courts Second Officer Julie Hallam (Virginia McKenna), an ops room Wren (a member of the Women's Royal Navy Service: WRNS). Sub-lieutenant Morell (Denholm Elliott) discovers his showgirl wife Elaine (Moira Lister) is an adulteress. When Bob Tallow (Bruce Seton) visits his sister Gladys (Meg Jenkins), he finds that his street has been levelled by the Luftwaffe and she is dead. She was to have married the ship's Chief Engineer Jim Watts (Liam Redmond). Most of these crewmen, who we come to know during the course of the film, go down with the *Compass Rose*, or else survive but suffer mental breakdowns, as with sublieutenant Farraby (John Stratton). Even Ericson's nerves are left shredded by the loss of his first ship and he is haunted by crewmen's dying screams. His tenacious search for and sinking of U-53 leads Ericson to come face to face with his enemy for the first time, when they pick up German submariner survivors. *Cruel Sea* contains one of the most famous scenes in war movie cinema. During a U-boat attack on a Gibraltar-bound convoy, Ericson has the opportunity to save several Allied seamen, who are in the water: when they spot the *Compass Rose* approaching, they cheer. Lockhart surmises that there's a U-boat directly beneath the floundering men. Ericson elects to ignore the survivors and drop depth charges, killing them. 'Bloody murderer' shouts one of his crewmen. Tension in this scene is ratcheted up by the corvette's blipping sonar. *The Cruel Sea*'s taut story and well-acted drama is the most accurate depiction of the Battle of the Atlantic in cinema.

A late edition to the British post-war naval films was Lewis Gilbert's historical drama *Sink the Bismarck!* (1960), which was unique in that it featured a landlocked hero. The story opens with newsreel footage of the launching of the KGM *Bismarck* in Hamburg on 14 February 1939 by the Führer. On 18 May 1941 the *Bismarck* sets off into the Atlantic to prey on Allied convoys. *Bismarck* is the pride of the German Navy, the Kriegsmarine, with guns that outdistance any Royal Navy ship. It is commanded by Captain Ernst Lindemann (Carl Mohner) and accompanied by the heavy cruiser *Prinz Eugen*, commanded by Captain Brinkmann. The two ships are overseen by Admiral Günther Lütjens (Karel Stepanek) aboard the *Bismarck*. The ships leave their base in Gdynia and are photographed by an RAF reconnaissance plane anchored in a Norwegian fjord near Bergen on 21 May, so they head into the North Atlantic. In the War Rooms, 200 feet below the Admiralty in London, Royal Navy strategists plot their next move under their new commander, Director of Operations Captain Shepard (Kenneth More). It is vital for British morale that the *Bismarck* is sunk and Prime Minister Churchill offers them his best wishes. The British Home Fleet is stationed at the Naval base at Scapa Flow, a bleak, haunting place in the Orkney Islands off the north coast of Scotland, between the largest island (Mainland, or Pomona) and the isle of Hoy. On 22 May, a naval force under Admiral Tovey (Michael Hordern), Commander-in-chief Home Fleet, sets off to intercept the raiders: the battle cruiser *Hood* and the battleship the *Prince of Wales* are sent to join the cruisers *Suffolk* and *Norfolk* in the Denmark Strait, between Iceland and Greenland. Tovey's force also includes battleship *King George V* (Tovey's flagship), the battle cruiser *Repulse* and the aircraft carrier *Victorious*, which guard the many routes that the German ships may use to break into the Atlantic shipping lanes.

There follows a meticulous recreation of the 2,000-mile chase, which intercuts scenes set in the Admiralty War Room with events at sea. On the 23 May, when the *Suffolk* sights the *Bismarck* and *Prinz Eugen* in the Denmark Strait, Force H (*Renown*, *Sheffield* and aircraft carrier *Ark Royal*) leaves Gibraltar. On 24 May the *Hood* and the *Prince of Wales* attack the *Bismarck* in the Denmark Strait – the *Bismarck* sinks the *Hood*, the best ship in the Royal Navy, with a 380mm shell (the *Hood* is hit in one of her magazines and blows in half). Three of her 1,400-man crew survived. The *Prince of Wales* is damaged and withdraws, while the *Prinz Eugen* retreated to the port of Brest (arriving on 1 June). Lütjens plans to plough on with their mission, but Lindemann would prefer to carry out minor repairs to the *Bismarck*. An attack by torpedo bombing Swordfish biplanes launched from the *Victorious* forces the *Bismarck* to change course. In the process, the British lose contact with the German ship on 25 May. Lütjens heads back across the mid-Atlantic towards the safety of the French coast, where two other German warships, the *Gneisenau* and the *Scharnhorst*, are in Brest for refitting. On 26 May, an RAF Catalina flying boat spies the *Bismarck* making a dash for France, where it will have Luftwaffe and U-boat cover. An attack by Swordfish biplanes from the *Ark Royal* mistake the *Sheffield* for the *Bismarck* but fortunately do no damage. Another strike by the *Ark Royal*'s Swordfish manages to jam the *Bismarck*'s rudder with a direct torpedo hit. The *Bismarck* is reduced to a speed of ten knots and is sighted by the British. *HMS King George V* and *HMS Rodney* close in for the kill. On 27 May, they blast the crippled *Bismarck* with repeated salvos. Lütjens orders the magazines to be flooded, to prevent them exploding, but the cruiser *Dorsetshire* torpedoes the *Bismarck*, finishing her off. Only 110 of her 2,300 crew survive, as the pride of the German navy sinks to a watery grave.

A slick blend of edge-of-the-seat drama and accurate, documentary-like history-telling, *Sink the Bismarck!* was filmed in monochrome CinemaScope. It was written for the screen by Edmund H. North, who later worked on the biopic *Patton*. Many protagonists are based on actual participants in the sea battle, but the film points out that Captain Shepard 'is in no way intended to depict Captain R.A.B. Edwards (now Admiral Sir Ralph Edwards KCB, CBE) who was the actual Director of Operations at the time of the *Bismarck*

Sink the Bismarck! (1960). Above: Royal Navy strategist and director of operations, Captain Shepard (Kenneth More), and his assistant, Second Officer Anne Davis (Dana Wynter), emerge from the War Rooms below the Admiralty in London. Below: UK poster for Lewis Gilbert's historical drama, depicting More, Wynter and the Swordfish biplane attack on the *Bismarck*. Images courtesy Kevin Wilkinson Collection.

engagement'. This allowed the filmmakers poetic licence with their story, as the events in the War Room are often as dramatic as the sea war. Shepard is a hard taskmaster – 'as cold as a witch's heart' – who has lost his ship to Lütjens in a previous engagement and has lost his wife in the Blitz. Tom, his son, is an air gunner on the *Ark Royal* and during the search for the *Bismarck* he is lost at sea, presumed dead. Later Shepard receives a telephone call to inform him that his son is safe, in the film's most emotional moment. Shepard's assistant is Second Officer Anne Davis (Dana Wynter), a Wren who lost her fiancé at Dunkirk. She and Shepard are drawn closer together during their days in the War Room. Shepard's gradual defrosting and Anne's growing respect for him – which sees her turn down a promotion in America – are excellently played by More and Wynter.

To add to the film's sense of documentary realism, renowned US radio and TV journalist Edward R. Murrow appears as himself, delivering 'This is London, Ed Murrow reporting' radio announcements. Amid a talented cast, Laurence Naismith played the First Sea Lord and Geoffrey Keen was the Assistant Chief of the Naval Staff (ACNS). Graham Stark and Ian Hendry can be glimpsed in bit parts and Johnny Briggs had a small role as a sailor on-board the *Prince of Wales*. Mohner and Stepanek are good as the German officers masterminding the *Bismarck*'s actions.

The pursuit across the North Sea is played out on the War Room map board, which resembles a war game. This narrative technique also helps to explain the various vessels' chart positions during the engagement and the film has a thriller's pace, due no doubt to its editor, Peter Hunt, who later worked on the James Bond films. The action at sea is created using a combination of newsreel footage and re-enactments using scale models. During these fog-shrouded sea battles, the story concentrates on the ships' bridges, with the various commanders issuing orders, intercut with blasting naval artillery. The mechanised loading of the battleships' heavy artillery shells is shown in detail. The Swordfish torpedo attacks are realistic, through a mixture of special effects and newsreel footage. The destruction of the *Hood* is a massive, convincing explosion and the *Bismarck*'s torpedoed demise ends with the wreck, smoking and aflame, slowly submerging into the boiling sea.

An awful single, the pop song 'Sink the Bismark' sung by Johnny Horton (which misspelt the ship's name on the 45's sleeve) was released as a tie-in. It was used in the trailer, but fortunately not in the actual film: 'We've gotta sink the Bismarck to the bottom of the sea. We'll find the German battleship that's makin' such a fuss. We've gotta sink the Bismarck, the world depends on us'. *Sink the Bismarck!* was the last of the great British war films set on the high seas and is a worthy climax to this patriotic, singularly British subgenre.

The newly built German pocket battleship *Tirpitz* was launched in 1941, but she posed an empty threat. She was largely inactive around Norway, which simply diverted British ships to shadow her movements. It was the reported presence of *Tirpitz* in the Barents Sea that created panic among Convoy PQ17 in July 1942. The convoy, bound for Archangel in Russia, scattered and was subsequently picked off and decimated by U-boats and aircraft, losing 22 of its 33 vessels. But *Tirpitz* did little else and was incapacitated by a daring commando raid in September 1943.

Ralph Thomas' *Above Us the Waves* (1955) was based on the 1953 book of the same name by James D. Benson and Charles Esme Thornton Warren, and Warren's 1954 book *The Midget Raiders*. The film was released the same year as *The Cockleshell Heroes* and also detailed a commando sortie, but *Waves* was a sombre affair in comparison. Commander Fraser (John Mills) trains Royal Naval volunteers for a special mission – to destroy the *Tirpitz*, which is 60-miles inland in Trondhjems Fiord in Norway. The men initially experiment with human torpedoes (two-man mini-subs which the commandos straddle like horses) but in September 1943 they use four-man midget submarines – X-1, X-2 and X-3 – to carry out their mission. Donald Sinden, John Gregson, Leo Genn and Anthony

Newley were among the submariners dispatched by James Robertson Justice on the mission. Once in the fjord, the subs negotiate mines and German patrol boats, cut through submarine and anti-torpedo nets, and avoid depth charges, in underwater scenes photographed in inky monochrome. The subs observe and stalk their target, and the audience has a periscope's-eye-view of proceedings, as Mills and his men position themselves to blitz the *Tirpitz*. Having planted explosives, one sub is trapped under *Tirpitz*' keel as the tide recedes, so the crew abandon ship and are captured as the sub is crushed. Fraser's craft is forced to surface and the crew are apprehended, but X-2 is destroyed. Eight tonnes of explosives detonate on cue and cripple the battleship. In reality the *Tirpitz* was badly damaged by the commando operation and was eventually sunk by Lancasters in November 1944 having contributed little to the Battle of the Atlantic.

A similar mission unfolds in *Submarine X-1* (1968). James Caan starred as Canadian Royal Navy submariner, Commander Richard Bolton, who has recently failed to sink the German destroyer *Lindendorf*. He also lost his submarine, *HMS Gauntlet*, and 50 crewmen in the process. Bolton's new assignment is to train and lead another attack on the ship anchored in a Norwegian fjord, this time using three 'X-craft' – untried X-perimental four-man mini-subs – rigged with explosive Amatol. Caan gives a one-note performance in the lead and the variable low-budget special effects were by the Bowie Organisation, but there's a good score by Ron Goodwin.

Other stories from the sea war include *Convoy* (1940) which recounts German pocket battleships attacking convoys, and *Corvette K-225* (1943 – *The Nelson Touch*), starring Randolph Scott as the captain of a corvette acting as escort to Atlantic convoys from Canada. *Action in the North Atlantic* (1943) starred Raymond Massey and Humphrey Bogart as blockade runners. John Ford's *The Long Voyage Home* (1940), an adaptation of Eugene O'Neill's *The Long Voyage Home: Seven Plays of the Sea*, featured many Ford regulars – including Thomas Mitchell, Ward Bond, Mildred Natwick, John Qualen and John Wayne (as Swedish sailor Ole Olsen) – in a tale of the tramp steamer *Glencairn*, freighting explosives from the West Indies to the US. Other blockade-running films include *Neutral Port* (1940), *The Navy Comes Through* (1942) and Pat Jackson's *Western Approaches* (1944 – *The Raider*), which boasted colour photography by Jack Cardiff and a cast that consisted of the seamen who actually carried out the heroism depicted: decoying U-boats in the Atlantic.

Alternative viewpoints of the sea war were depicted in *Morituri* (1965) and *The Sea Chase* (1955). Bernhard Wicki's *Morituri*, or *Saboteur: Code Name Morituri* pitted Marlon Brando's cultured German saboteur Robert Crain against Yul Brynner's Captain Mueller. Crain attempts to capture and divert the German blockade runner *SS Ingo* which is carrying seven thousand tonnes of rubber from Tokyo to Bordeaux in 1942. This aimless espionage drama featured Janet Margolin as captured Jewess Esther, Hans Christian Blech as the ship's stoker and Trevor Howard as Colonel Stetter, who sends Crain on his mission.

John Farrow's *The Sea Chase* (1955) follows the true story of the German tramp steamer *Ergenstrasse* from Sydney, Australia, via Valparaiso in South America to its final interception and demise in the North Sea, as the freighter rammed its Royal Navy pursuer. The German ship is caught in Australia at the outbreak of the war and makes headlines across the world as it leads the navy on a wild goose chase, on its way to Germany. Platinum blonde Lana Turner was little more than elegant set dressing in the role of German spy Elsa Keller, who is being transported to Germany aboard the *Ergenstrasse*, while creative casting deployed Tab Hunter, Claude Akins, Lyle Bettger, John Doucette, John Qualen and James Arness as the *Ergenstrasse*'s crew. John Wayne, playing the freighter's German skipper, Karl Ehrlich, made no attempt at a German accent. Wayne was also miscast in this period as Mongol Genghis Khan in *The Conqueror* (1956) and as Townsend Harris, ambassador to Japan, in *The Barbarian and the Geisha* (1958).

US attitudes to the war were changing by the mid-1950s so that all-American Wayne could portray a German sea captain – aided by the fact that Ehrlich is a sympathetic, anti-Hitlerian. Wayne is far from convincing in the role. He's 'John Wayne: cowboy' in a different hat and this remains one of his most tedious appearances. If many of Wayne's films – *The Searchers* for instance, or *The Alamo* – gave the actor great speeches, credos and words of wisdom, *Sea Chase* provides one of his most risible sayings: 'A man has weakness or strength ... weakness you can hide, like red lead over a sprung rivet, but it'll give under strain. Strength you cannot defeat, ever'. Such Hollywood purple prose often oversimplified these men of the sea and their war. But at least their fortitude, determination and sheer bravery survived intact in the transition from history book to silver screen.

Chapter 4

THE PACIFIC WAR (1941–42)

Japan, like Germany, was aggressively building its empire throughout the 1930s, creating the Greater East Asian Co-Prosperity Sphere. In 1937 Japan invaded China to gain land and raw materials needed for this expansion. It was during this offensive that the Japanese army gained its reputation for atrocities – in the Rape of Nanking in December 1937, for example, 250,000 Chinese were killed in a six-week killing spree. Atrocities such as this were intended to scare China into surrendering, but only turned public opinion in the USA and Britain against Japan. The Sino-Japanese War, a costly drain on Japan's resources, lasted until Japan's ultimate surrender to the Allies in 1945. The Japanese capture of Shanghai is featured in Steven Spielberg's *Empire of the Sun* (1987), based on J.G. Ballard's autobiographical novel, and the war was also the backdrop to the story of missionary Gladys Aylward (Ingrid Bergman) in *Inn of the Sixth Happiness* (1958).

David Miller's *Flying Tigers* (1942) cast John Wayne as Captain Jim Gordon of the American Volunteer Group (AVG), a group of pilots who fought in China for Chiang Kai-Shek against the Japanese in the early days of the war. They were nicknamed 'Flying Tigers' due to their winged tiger insignia (which was designed by Walt Disney Studios) and the distinctive jagged teeth painted on the noses of their Curtiss P-40 Warhawk fighters. Gordon is called 'Pappy' by his men and romances British nurse Brooke Elliot (Anne Lee), whilst fending off competition from heel Woody Jason (John Carroll), a mercenary to the core, whose sole reason for flying is the $600 a month wage and $500 bounty per Japanese plane shot down. The film deploys rare Japanese archive footage (of aerial combat and anti-aircraft guns) and ends with Gordon and Jason embarking on a suicide mission to blow up a railway bridge which culminates in Jason flying a nitroglycerine-laden plane into a Japanese train. This one-way trip is carried out in one of the ugliest planes of all time, the short-lived, two-engined Capelis XC-12 'Safety

US poster advertising the US–Japanese co-production *Tora! Tora! Tora!* (1970), one of the finest cinematic re-enactments of World War II history. Courtesy Kevin Wilkinson Collection.

Aircraft Transport', which looks as though it has been assembled at random from at least three other planes, with two desktop office fans strapped to its wings as propellers.

In September 1940, Japanese forces invaded French Indochina and on 26 September the USA imposed trade embargoes on Japan. The following day Japan signed the Tripartite Pact with Italy and Germany, becoming one of the three principle members of the Axis. Although Japan's figurehead was Emperor Hirohito, the government was controlled by the Imperial Japanese Army. In July 1940, it installed Prince Konoye as Prime Minister and in October General Tojo replaced him. In April 1941 Japan and the USSR signed a non-aggression pact. When Germany implemented Operation Barbarossa and invaded Russia in June 1941, Japan knew that Russia would be otherwise occupied. After much diplomatic toing and froing, with Ambassador Nomura negotiating in Washington with Secretary of State Cordell Hull, Japan decided to make war on the US, but failed to inform anybody else of this crucial development.

On 26 November 1941, the Japanese First Air Fleet sailed from Kurile Islands, northeast of Japan, and headed across the Pacific Ocean towards the Hawaiian Islands. The fleet included six aircraft carriers, two battleships, two cruisers, and nine destroyers, plus submarines. Their target was Pearl Harbor on Oahu (one of the Hawaiian Islands), the main base of the US Pacific Fleet. The Japanese reasoned that a surprise attack on the base would incapacitate US power in the Pacific and leave the way open for Japan's further expansion. The Japanese fleet maintained radio silence and ships elsewhere masqueraded as carriers, to confuse US Intelligence. The First Air Fleet were a well-trained force. They had practiced their attack in the bay of Kagoshima, on the island of Honshu (which resembled Pearl Harbor), honing their skill at bombing targets at speed. The First Fleet carried three types of planes: Mitsubishi Zero fighters, Aichi 'Val' navy dive-bombers and Nakajima Kate torpedo-bombers. Although US Intelligence had intercepted Japanese communiqués and suspected that a Japanese attack was imminent, the garrison at Pearl Harbor and at the airfields on the island were woefully unprepared. Admiral Husband E. Kimmel and General Walter C. Short, the US commanders at Pearl Harbor, failed to properly prepare for an attack and security and drill was lax. The base closed down over the weekend, with soldiers and sailors enjoying the local bars and dance halls by night. Radar stations on the island were new technology to their operators and when a large radar blip revealed aircraft moving in from the north it was presumed to be US B-17 bombers which were expected to arrive.

At 6 am on the morning of Sunday 7 December, the Japanese First Air Fleet launched its planes, which flew south across Oahu towards Pearl Harbor. At just after 6.30, the US destroyer *Ward* torpedoed and sank a Japanese sub which was shadowing it into Pearl Harbor. The first wave of 180 Japanese aircraft arrived unopposed and unannounced at 7.49. Seven minutes later they began their attack on the harbour and airfields. The US fleet was anchored in the harbour, with the destroyers *USS Cassin* and *Downes* and the battleship *Pennsylvania* in dry dock. The prime target was 'Battleship Row', ships anchored by twos along Ford Island in the middle of the harbour. *Maryland*, *Oklahoma*, *Tennessee*, *West Virginia*, *Arizona*, *Vestal* and *Nevada* were sitting ducks for the torpedoes and dive-bombers. Fortunately the attackers' main prize, the US Pacific Fleet's three aircraft carriers – *Saratoga*, *Lexington* and *Enterprise* – were delivering aircraft to US bases on Midway and Wake Island. In addition to the harbour, the Japanese attacked Schofield Barracks and the US airfields of Hickam Field, Kaneohe, Ewa and Wheeler Field, wreaking havoc among the US aircraft which were parked neatly in rows so they could be easily patrolled against sabotage. At 8.40 a second wave of 175 aircraft attacked, including bombers, but by 8.50 the raid was over and the Japanese departed, leaving smoking, burning ruins in their wake on what became known in the US as the 'Day that Will Live in Infamy'.

Little actual Pearl Harbor footage exists – US navy personnel shot 200 feet of 16mm black-and-white film and 250 feet of 8mm Kodachrome during the attack – though many photographs were taken. When it came to recreating the battle for cinema, it was essential that the shocking ferocity of the surprise attack should be depicted. *Tora! Tora! Tora!* (1970) is a recreation of that fateful Sunday morning and tells both sides of the story impartially. The first half of the film examines the diplomatic preambles to war, with onscreen captions specifying time and place, and introductory captions for key protagonists. Ambassador Nomura (Shogo Shimada) negotiates with Cordell Hull (George Macready) in Washington DC to no avail. In the USA, Lieutenant-Colonel Bratton (E.G. Marshall) races against time to decode crucial information, which he passes on to Lieutenant-Commander Kramer (Wesley Addy) but their warnings are ignored. They work for US Intelligence, the code breakers codenamed MAGIC, which intercept Japanese diplomatic codes and ciphers. Admiral Kimmel (Martin Balsam) fails to be suitably vigilante and General Short (Jason Robards) ignores all omens of impending attack and prepares for his Sunday morning round of golf. Joseph Cotten played Secretary of War Henry Stimson and Keith Andes was chief-of-staff General George C. Marshall. Tatsuya Mihashi played Japan's master strategist Commander Genda. Sô Yamamura played naval commander Admiral Yamamoto (overseeing the operation from Japan's Inland Sea), Eijiro Tono was Admiral Nagumo (commander of the First Air Fleet), Koreya Senda was Prince Konoye, Kazuo Kitamura played foreign Minister Matsuoka and Takahiro Tamura was ace commander Fuchida, who leads the aerial raid on Pearl Harbor. The casting, especially the US side, is not of superstar names, but rather of character actors – performers initially mentioned in connection with the project included Lee Marvin, Rod Steiger and George C. Scott.

This is neither a 'Day of Infamy', nor a 'Day of Glory', but a well-balanced depiction of the events as they happened. The Japanese aren't depicted simply as warmongers and the USA are not wholly incompetent. Although the first section of the film is talky, cross-cutting between the two sides keeps the pace brisk, as we see the Japanese training for the attack and the USA's lack of an adequate communication network. The fact that we know what lies in store also builds the tension. Following the film's 'Intermission', the attack proper commences, with the Japanese planes taking to the air. To sailors' cheers, engines splutter and roar, wheel blocks are removed and plane after plane takes off from the carrier decks into the rising orange ribbon of dawn. They fly in formation across the lush landscape of Oahu and then launch their attack on the unsuspecting harbour, the planes swarming overhead like mosquitoes, before peeling off and sweeping in for low-level attacks, machine-gunning the US troops and torpedoing and bombing the ships and airfields. So impressive were these scenes, they were reused in many subsequent productions, including the three-part TV miniseries *Pearl* (1978), the six-episode series *From Here to Eternity* (1979), and as battle footage in *Midway* (1976) and *Australia* (2008).

As with all truly great war movies, *Tora! Tora! Tora!* was a group effort. The screenplay by Larry Forrester, Ryuzo Kikushima and Hideo Oguni was based on two books: *The Broken Seal* by Ladislas Farago (detailing the code breaking that preceded the attack) and *Tora! Tora! Tora!* by Gordon W. Prange. The US scenes were directed by Richard Fleischer. On the Japanese side, Toshio Masuda shot

On the deck of the full-scale replica of Japanese battleship *Nagato*, which was built for the making of *Tora! Tora! Tora!* (1970). Courtesy Kevin Wilkinson Collection.

the drama scenes and Kinji Fukasaku lensed the action. Akira Kurosawa was to have directed the Japanese sections but following disagreements with the producers he was fired from the project. Produced by Twentieth Century-Fox, it cost $25 million. Filming took place in 1969, with two separate units: one working in the USA and Hawaii, and one in Japan. The US scenes were filmed at Fox Studios (on Stages 5, 9 and 15), in Malibu Creek State Park (the miniature work of the naval attack), Washington DC and San Diego. The Japanese scenes were filmed in Kagoshima Bay (on Honshu, for the mock Japanese training exercise); Kyushu, Ashiya, Osaka and Tokyo, with Japanese interiors at Shochiku Studios and Toei-Kyoto Studios in Kyoto. Location footage was lensed in Honolulu and in the actual Pearl Harbor, on Oahu, Hawaii. In the harbour, the full-scale front half of the *Arizona* was built on barges at a cost of $1 million. The battle scenes were a mixture of scaled down miniatures and full-scale replicas, with many aircraft employed for the assault and tonnes of explosives detonated during these scenes. For the Japanese scenes a full-scale battleship, the *Nagato*, and two-thirds of the *Akagi* aircraft carrier were built of plywood on a beach at Ashiya airbase, adding to the film's impressive sense of scale. This is meticulous war filmmaking of the highest order.

The attack sequences are a *tour de force*, as smoke plumes drift across the landscape and the Japanese planes wheel and buzz overhead. US fighters attempt to take off, but are strafed on the runways and career into parked aircraft, bursting into flames. Beached, helpless PBY Catalina flying boats are ripped by shuddering explosions on the tarmac. Heroic machine-gunners on the ground return anti-aircraft fire, while naval gunners blast away at planes over the harbour. A damaged Japanese fighter deliberately crashes into an aircraft hanger and crippled US warships burn, their crews scuttling for cover and abandoning ship. The moment when the *Arizona* is hit directly in the forward magazine by a well-aimed bomb is spectacular, with the ship exploding in a fountain of flame. The flight of US Boeing B-17s that arrived on the island mid-battle found themselves in the midst of the carnage. In the film, one bomber hits the airfield runway and manages to land, despite only one wheel of its undercarriage working. No other war film has captured the horror of an air attack's intensity. *Tora! Tora! Tora!* is now regarded as one of the greatest World War II films. Like *The Longest Day* it is an impressive historical record and a worthy testament to its makers' consummate moviemaking skill.

During the attack on Pearl Harbor the US forces lost 188 aircraft (plus 159 damaged) and 18 warships were sunk or severely damaged, including seven battleships. Over 2,400 US servicemen lost their lives – half of them were on the *Arizona* when she was hit. The *Oklahoma* was also sunk. The Japanese First Air Fleet lost 29 planes and pilots (plus 74 damaged), five midget submarines and one fleet sub (sunk by the *Ward*), plus their crews. But it was a hollow Japanese victory – 80 per cent of the damaged US aircraft were repaired and all the ships damaged in the attack (except the gutted *Arizona*) had been salvaged and refloated by 1943. US newsreels of the time mention that the garrison at Pearl presumed that this air attack would be followed by an amphibious landing and prepared themselves for an invasion. As depicted in *Tora! Tora! Tora!*, at 1 pm Admiral Nagumo decides not to launch a follow-up air attack – a third wave – which infuriates some of his commanders, particularly Genda and Fuchida. Nagumo surmises they've done enough damage to the US Pacific Fleet and when he realises that they have attacked before the Japanese declaration of war has arrived in Washington, Admiral Yamamoto notes, 'I fear all we have done is to awaken a sleeping giant and fill him with a terrible resolve'.

Pearl Harbor (2001) was directed by Michael Bay and co-produced by Bay and blockbuster specialist Jerry Bruckheimer. Despite splendid widescreen photography by John Schwartzman in 3-strip Technicolor (used for *The Wizard of Oz* and *Gone With the Wind*) and a budget topping $135 million, *Pearl Harbor* is one of the most derided war films. It tells the story of two Tennessee farm boys Rafe McCawley (Ben Affleck) and Danny Walker (Josh Hartnett) and their experiences in the US air force in Britain and Hawaii. Rafe is transferred to the RAF's Eagle Squadron, but is shot down over the Channel and presumed dead. Rafe's lover, US nurse Evelyn Johnson (Kate Beckinsale), and Danny are transferred to the US base at Pearl Harbor, where they begin a love affair, but the arrival of Rafe, very much alive, ends their idyll. Evelyn also discovers she's carrying Danny's child. Then the Japanese launch a surprise attack on the island and Rafe and Danny take to the skies in their P-40s to dogfight with the swooping Zeroes.

Pearl Harbor is a bizarre concoction. A hybrid of *Grease, Top Gun, Titanic, Tora! Tora! Tora!*, the 'Carry On' films, buddy movies and *Dick Dastardly and Mutley*, it slips into pop music video slow-motion at every opportunity – hence its hefty 183-minute running time. The action scenes, staged on a vast scale, are so overproduced as to resemble video game graphics. In typical Hollywood fashion, the not-so-beautiful, kooky, interesting characters die and the beautiful ones live on, a sort of 'survival of the hottest'. Affleck and Hartnett's scenes during the attack are the film's most risible – Affleck's 'Get me into a damn plane' is topped by Hartnett frantically informing us, 'I think World War Two's just hit us'. A newsreel voiceover reports, 'The German Luftwaffe relentlessly bombards downtown London', while when it looks like he's going fail his eye test to become a pilot, Rafe pleads with Evelyn, 'Ma'am, please, don't take my wings'. The presence of Dan Aykroyd (an actor so adept at spoofery) as US Intelligence code breaker Thurman doesn't help the material's gravitas and Jon Voight's President Roosevelt sports the most unconvincing jutting cleft chin in movie history. Only Beckinsale, a rose between two idiots, survives unscathed. She looks the part and is convincing when the hospital fills up with burned, bleeding casualties. Cuba Gooding Jr puts in a good performance too, virtually a cameo, as US navy cook Dorie Miller, who commandeers an anti-aircraft gun and fights back at the Japanese bombers. Miller was the first African-American recipient of the Navy Cross and was played in *Tora! Tora! Tora!* by Elven Havard.

Pearl Harbor's score by Hans Zimmer dawdles on the soundtrack, while the end titles play over a Faith Hill ballad with the Yoda-like title 'There You'll Be'. More than the bad acting, sludgy music and daft dialogue, the real problem with the film is the destruction and sinking of the *Arizona* and the capsize roll of the *Oklahoma*. The scenes are staged as though they belong in *Titanic* or *The Poseidon Adventure*, with drowning men trapped below deck and others falling from the listing, stricken ships. Why would anyone want to depict such a shocking disaster in such detail? To dwell on the tragic loss of life is voyeuristic and ghoulish, and its presentation as entertainment distasteful and insensitive. Presented are real events which cost real lives. Historically, the film isn't wide of the mark and most of the events are true to life – from the US Navy's negligence to Yamamoto's famous 'sleeping giant' quote – and it deploys dozens of real Mitsubishi Zeroes, which swoop impressively across the Hawaiian landscape prior to the attack. As per Hawaiian law, a priest blessed the crew before filming began in Pearl Harbor. He should have prayed harder.

A Japanese interpretation of events can be seen in Shue Matsubayashi's *Storm Over the Pacific* (1961 – *A Storm from the Sea*), made at Toho Studios. It was released, cut and dubbed, as *I Bombed Pearl Harbor*. Due to time differences, Japan is a day ahead, so the attack takes place on 8 December. Footage from this film (the carriers steering across the Pacific and some aircraft shots) was used in *Tora! Tora! Tora!* and star Tatsuya Mihashi appeared in both films.

An interesting twist on the Pearl Harbor story was Don Taylor's science-fiction movie *The Final Countdown* (1980). While on manoeuvres, the *USS Nimitz* is enveloped by a violent Pacific storm which transports the aircraft carrier, jet fighters and all, through a swirling time portal from 1980 to 6 December 1941, with the Japanese attack imminent. Kirk Douglas played Captain Matthew Yelland, who must decide if he will change the course of history, and Martin Sheen was systems analyst Warren Lasky, a civilian observer. The film, impressively shot in Panavision, was lensed on the actual *Nimitz* and deployed the officers and crew of Carrier Air Wing 8. The dogfighting Japanese Zeroes were provided by the 'Confederate Airforce'. The *Nimitz*'s crew included Ron O'Neal as Commander Dan Thurman and James Farentino as Wing Commander Richard Owens, who is working on a book about the Pearl Harbor attack. Katharine Ross played Laurel Scott, the assistant of prospective presidential candidate Senator Samuel Chapman (Charles Durning), both from the 1940s, who the carrier picks up when their launch is strafed by the Japanese. The story, which has some good twists, builds a steady tension as Yelland decides to deploy his jets, including F-14 Tomcats, against the Japanese Zeroes at the very moment the time portal reappears. Interestingly, as the carrier leaves Pearl Harbor at the beginning of the film, it passes the *USS Arizona* Memorial in the harbour, which marks where the wreck and many of those killed still lie.

John Ford's propagandist *December 7th* (1942) won Ford the Best Documentary Oscar in 1944. The celebrated ABC TV miniseries *The Winds of War* (1983) traces the gathering clouds of the conflict and culminates in the attack on Pearl Harbor and America's entry into the war. Fred Zinnemann's *From Here to Eternity* (1953) is set on Hawaii in the lead-up to Pearl Harbor. The attack, which climaxes the film, mixed recreations at the real Schofield Barracks on Hawaii with archive footage. Zinnemann filmed on location on Hawaii and also used the wild west town at Columbia Studios (from Zinnemann's *High Noon*) redressed as a Hawaiian street. Based on James Jones' 1951 bestseller of the same name, the film starred Montgomery Clift as Private Robert E. Lee Prewitt, a bugler and

Japanese Zeroes zero in on their targets in Fred Zinnemann's *From Here to Eternity* (1953). Courtesy Kevin Wilkinson Collection.

former champion middleweight boxer, who refuses to fight for the company team. Captain Dana Holmes (Philip Ober) ensures his sergeants make Prewitt's life hell. Prewitt becomes enamoured with prostitute Lorene (Donna Reed). Frank Sinatra played Italian-American Private Angelo Maggio, who is victimised and eventually beaten to death by bullying, racist stockade sergeant 'Fatso' Judson (Ernest Borgnine), who hates 'wops'.

A singing hero dubbed 'The Voice' by his bobby-sox fans, Sinatra's vocal chords haemorrhaged in 1952 and he was dropped by MCA. Desperate to forge a career for himself as an actor, Sinatra pleaded with Columbia to cast him as Maggio and worked for a mere $8,000, but was rewarded with a Best Supporting Actor Oscar. Sinatra's Mafia connections have led to his casting being cited as the inspiration for the scene in *The Godfather* (1972), when studio boss Jack Woltz (John Marley) is convinced to cast singer Johnny Fontane (Al Martino) in a 'war movie', by discovering the severed head of Khartoum, his favourite racing horse, in bed with him. Even bigger than the attack on Pearl is *Eternity*'s 'Big Love Scene'. Burt Lancaster played First Sergeant Milton Warden, who has an affair with Holme's wife, Karen (Deborah Kerr). During a beach date (filmed at Holcona Cove, Oahu) the pair, clad in bathing suits, embrace and kiss amid the foaming, crashing waves, in what was for its time a raunchy depiction of unfettered passion. Lauded at the Oscars, the film won eight, including Best Picture and Best Director, and was a massive box office hit, taking $12 million.

On 8 December 1941, the USA and Britain declared war on Japan. Britain was actually quite relieved by the attack on Pearl Harbor, as it finally brought the stalling USA into the war. Wake Island was next on the list of Japan's targets. John Farrow's *Wake Island* (1942) depicted the island's heroic defence, though it was filmed on the shores of the Salton Sea in the Californian desert. Alistair Grierson's brutal *Kokoda – 39th Battalion* (2006) portrayed Australian troops fighting advancing Japanese in Papua New Guinea in 1942. An immediate US reprisal for Pearl Harbor was the Doolittle Raid on 18 April 1942, an aerial attack by 16 B-25 Mitchell medium bombers which attacked industrial targets in Tokyo, Nagoya and Kobe. The raid was orchestrated by Lieutenant-Colonel James H. Doolittle and was launched from the aircraft carrier *USS Hornet*. The raid was a success, striking at the heart of Japan, and the bombers ditched in occupied China. The Japanese put a bounty of $5,000 on the heads of the 80 US fliers who carried out the attack – three US aircrews were captured by the Japanese and three of their officers were summarily beheaded. The *Hornet* was later at the Battle of Midway, but due to its involvement in the Doolittle Raid, the Japanese singled out and hunted the carrier and sunk her on 26 October 1942 during the fight for Guadalcanal.

Mervyn Le Roy's *Thirty Seconds over Tokyo* (1944) remains the best telling of the Doolittle Raid. Based on Lieutenant Ted Lawson's 1943 book of the same name it starred Spencer Tracy (as Doolittle) and Van Johnson, Robert Walker, Stephen McNally and Robert Mitchum, and boasted Oscar-winning special effects. Lawson's book renames the aircraft carrier the *Shangri La* and the names of US crew members still missing in action were altered, in case they were captured by the Japanese and identified as Doolittle raiders. The operation is also depicted in *Pearl Harbor* (2001). Following their heroism during the attack on Pearl Harbor, fighter pilots Rafe and Danny are sent on the 'Top Secret' raid piloting B-25s bombers by Colonel Doolittle (Alec Baldwin). Having bombed their industrial targets (which explode in apocalyptic fountains of flame), the planes continue on to China, but are low on fuel and crash land. In reality there was no way the B-25s could return to the *Hornet*, as the runway deck was too short to allow a landing.

In Harm's Way (1965), which deployed a dazzlingly starry cast (including John Wayne, Henry Fonda and Kirk Douglas), begins on the eve of Pearl Harbor, but is mostly concerned with events later in the war during the assault on the Solomon Islands. Wayne starred as construction boss Wedge Donovan in *The Fighting Seabees* (1944) which told of the formation of the Construction Battalions (the CBs). Donovan's tradesmen travel to Island X214 to build a US airstrip. When the Japanese invade, Donovan realises that his men need proper military training. The combat scenes are well handled, though much of the dialogue sequences are studio-bound. Wedge clashes with naval officer Bob Yarrow (Dennis O'Keefe) over feisty reporter Connie Chesley (Susan Hayward). The US Navy decided to form the skilled construction workers into a fighting battalion. They undergo basic training, with Donovan as their lieutenant commander. Donovan refers to their Japanese adversaries as 'Tojo and his bug-eyed monkeys' and it is one of the few opportunities to see tough guy 'Duke' Wayne cutting some rug, as he dances at a party with a 'champion jitterbugger'. Deployed on construction projects on Island X371, the Seabees come under attack from the Japanese. Yarrow and Connie are left together for the fadeout when Donovan dies heroically. He saves the day by driving their caterpillar-tracked bulldozer (christened 'Natasha') rigged with explosives into an oil depot to 'scorch those nips'.

Remember Pearl Harbor (1942) was quick-to-cash-in propaganda set in the Philippines, with Don Barry crashing a plane loaded with explosives into a Japanese invasion ship. Steven Spielberg's irreverent comedy *1941* (1979) is set in the immediate post–Pearl Harbor panic, as a Japanese submarine surfaces off California. Its eclectic cast included John Belushi, Toshirô Mifune, Warren Oates, Dan Aykroyd, Ned Beatty, James Caan, Elisha Cook Jr, Christopher Lee, John Candy, Slim Pickens, Mickey Rourke, Robert Stack and Treat Williams. John Wayne and Charlton Heston turned down roles in the film, deeming it unpatriotic.

Following the Doolittle Raid, Japanese expansion in the Far East and the Pacific continued, with many islands falling, including the Philippine Islands, Guam, Wake Island, Ceylon and Madagascar. The Philippine island of Luzon was invaded from Taiwan on 8 December 1941, with the main attack taking place on the Lingayen Gulf on 22 December. General Douglas MacArthur was now the Supreme Allied Commander in the Pacific and Admiral Chester Nimitz was head of the naval forces. On 23 December MacArthur was forced to withdraw to the island's Bataan Peninsula and Manila fell on 2 January 1942. Biopic *MacArthur* (1977), starring Gregory Peck, begins with General MacArthur's escape by PT boat from Corregidor in the Philippines to Australia in March 1942. After a lengthy battle, the jungles of Bataan fell on 9 April and the heavily fortified island of Corregidor, the key to Manila Bay, was also taken. After prolonged artillery barrages, the Japanese invaded the island and it was overrun on 6 May.

Tay Garnett's *Bataan* (1943) starred Robert Taylor as Sergeant Bill Dane, the commander of a ragtag bunch of assorted US and Filipino troops fighting a rearguard action to hold a bridge across a deep ravine on Bataan. As the opening blurb states: 'To those immortal dead, who heroically stayed the wave of barbaric conquest, this picture is dedicated'. George Murphy, Desi Arnez, Lloyd Nolan and Thomas Mitchell were among the brave defenders of a redoubt which overlooks the bridge. The squad demolish the crossing, only for the Japanese to rebuild it by night, so they destroy it again with grenades and later more permanently by flying a biplane into it, kamikaze-style. *Bataan* is surprisingly violent and realistic for its time. The cook comments on the defenders' meagre supplies: 'There ain't no sugar for the coffee and there ain't no coffee … there's maggots in the meat and the meat is mule'. The opening attack on a column of refugees graphically illustrates a Japanese air raid and the final battle, as camouflaged Japanese infantry launch a frontal assault, is *The Wild Bunch* of its day, as the depleted defenders mow down the onrushing attackers with machine-guns and wrestle them in fixed-bayonet, hand-to-hand action. Only Dane survives and he waits in his foxhole which will become his grave – with a cross already inscribed 'Bill Dane, Sgt. 31st Inf. USA' – for the final Japanese onslaught.

Cry 'Havoc' (1943 – starring Margaret Sullavan and Joan Blondell) depicted nurses involved in the Bataan fighting. *The Eve of St. Mark* (1944), based on Maxwell Anderson's play of the same name, recreated the heroic defence of Corregidor and starred William Eythe and Anne Baxter. Edward Dmytryk's timely *Back to Bataan* (1945), starring John Wayne, begins on 30 January 1945, with US troops liberating the prison camp at Cabanatuan, where survivors from the 'Bataan Death March' were incarcerated by the Japanese. Seventy-eight thousand exhausted, disease-ridden US and Philippine troops were captured on the Bataan Peninsula and their Japanese captors forced them to walk 65 miles to Camp O'Donnell, the nearest prison camp, resulting in the deaths of 650 Americans and an estimated 5,000 to 10,000 Filipinos – stragglers were bayoneted or shot on the roadside by the Japanese. Several actual survivors from this march appeared in *Back to Bataan*.

Following the liberation of Cabanatuan, *Back to Bataan* flashes back to tell the story of Colonel Joe Madden (Wayne) who following the siege of the fortress island of Corregidor is instructed by MacArthur to organise the American-aided Filipino guerrilla resistance movement against the occupying Japanese on Luzon. Madden is helped by Filipino captain Andrés Bonifácio in galvanising the local population in a sustained campaign of raids around the village of Balintawak. When Japanese forces occupy the village, the school principal, Señor Buenaventura J. Bello (Vladimir Sokoloff) is lynched from an American flagpole as a warning to the populace. Wayne is tough and unshaven as Madden, who in one impressive scene is blasted out of a crater by Japanese artillery fire. Anthony Quinn is excellent as national hero Bonifácio. A subplot details Bonifácio's love affair with beautiful Filipino woman Delisay Delgado (Manila-born Fely Franquelli from *Cry 'Havoc'*), who is ostensibly the voice of propaganda radio station

Radio Manila – run by the Japanese to undermine moral – but is really a spy for the Allies. Beulah Bondi played schoolteacher Bertha Barnes, who joins the rebels as a nurse and Paul Fix was their vagabond cook, Bindle Jackson. *Back to Bataan* is one of Wayne's best WWII movies and is a fine depiction of guerrilla jungle action. Fortunately the absence of love interest for Wayne keeps the pace brisk. The climax of the film depicts the rebels' endeavours to undermine Japanese defences as US troops land amphibiously at Leyte Gulf on 20 October 1944. No matter that the Japanese tanks are US M3s and Shermans – the straightforward action and winning drama survives such anachronisms. Like many of Wayne's monochrome movies, it is also available in a computer-colourised version.

They Were Expendable (1945) teamed John Ford and John Wayne in a tale of the US Navy's valorous Motor Torpedo Boat Squadron – the plywood-hulled PT boats – and depicted the outbreak of the Pacific War, the fall of the Philippines, the surrender of Bataan and MacArthur's escape. Wayne played Lieutenant 'Rusty' Ryan alongside Robert Montgomery (an actual PT boat skipper) as Lieutenant 'Brick' Brickley. Before the war commences, the Navy are reluctant to deploy the untried PT boats and Rusty considers quitting: 'Can't build a navy reputation riding a plywood dream'. Later the PTs come into their own as patrol and messenger craft, as well as in combat. The boats' crewmen featured several of Ford's 'Stock Company' regulars, including Ward Bond and Jack Pennick. Wartime pin-up Donna Reed was excellent as Second Lieutenant Sandy Davyss, a US nurse on Corregidor and Rusty's love interest, who is presumed captured or killed at the end of the film. Ford filmed this black-and-white movie – his first war drama – around Key Biscayne, Florida. *Expendable* is notable for its swirling, explosive sea combat scenes, helmed by second unit director James C. Havens. Japanese fighter-bombers swoop out of the sky in running battles with the PT boats and the PTs launch torpedo attack runs under heavy fire on Japanese cruisers. This timeless film is typically effortless, classic Ford: by turns moving, romantic, humorous, musical, nostalgic, artful, actionful and poetic.

Expendable was written by Commander Frank W. 'Spig' Wead, a well-known WWI flier whose naval career was ruined when a fall down the stairs at home broke his neck and left him paralysed. During his convalescence at San Diego Naval Hospital, Wead turned to writing and eventually forged a successful career as a playwright and screenwriter. Ford eulogised Wead in *The Wings of Eagles* (1957), with John Wayne as Wead, who overcame adversity in the manner of Douglas Bader in *Reach for the Sky* to write realistic tales of naval aviation with 'a pen dipped in seawater, not dry martinis'. Wead's naval chums included John Dale Price (Ken Curtis), Jughead Carson (Dan Dailey) and Arizona Pincus (Tige Andrews). Wead saw service during WWII – the only 'flattop' he was initially allowed near was a desk – and developed a naval tactic deploying smaller 'jeep carriers', which could swiftly restock the main carriers as they suffered aircraft losses during combat, until a heart attack forced him to retire. *Wings of Eagles* is an odd mixture of drunken slapstick comedy – as when Wead lands a biplane in a swimming pool during the admiral's garden party – and moving drama, particularly in his relationship with his wife Min (Maureen O'Hara). The film includes Wead's part in the US Navy team winning the Schneider Cup Race and the WWII sequences utilise some excellent colour archive footage from the Pacific War. When Wead becomes a screenwriter, he works for director 'John Dodge'. As played by Ward Bond, Dodge is a pastiche of Ford himself, complete with sunglasses, slouch hat, pipe, cowboy boots and hollowed-out cane concealing a slug of whisky. Dodge's office is littered with Oscar statuettes, and bits of western history and film ephemera, including portraits of cowboy stars Harry Carey and Tom Mix.

In the North African-set *Commandos* (1968), US commando Sergeant Sullivan (Lee Van Cleef) suffers post-combat trauma and relives flashbacks of charging Japanese soldiers, having witnessed a massacre on Bataan. The fall of Bataan is also the backdrop to Giuseppe Vari's *A Place in Hell* (1969 – *Commando Attack*). Following a Japanese air raid on Manila, alcoholic Pulitzer Prize–winning journalist Major Mac Graves (Guy Madison) escapes to the island of Lubang, with bombshell nightclub hostess Betsy (Helen Chanel) and Marine Mario Petrello (Maurice Poli). They team up with a mixed bag of Marines, Royal Navy personnel and Filipino jungle fighters to blow up an experimental radar base at Surigao, without realising the station is non-operational. As Graves' party try to leave the island at Tulong, they are bushwhacked. In the average film's best scene, their Japanese ambushers emerge from rifle pits hidden under the sand, and only Graves and Petrello survive.

The Japanese were swept with an overconfidence which would prove fatal, but two decisive naval battles halted Japan's gains in the Pacific and saved the US from a swift defeat. The first was the Battle of the Coral Sea. In May 1942 a Japanese invasion force set off to take Port Moresby on New Guinea and Tulagi on the Solomon Islands. Their aim was to control the Coral Sea and threaten Australia, but their plan had been intercepted. From 3 May to 8 May both sides sustained key losses, once they located each other in the vastness of the Pacific. It was a 'naval' engagement fought solely with aircraft attacks – the two naval forces didn't sight one another. The Japanese forces were led by Vice Admiral Inouye, while US forces were under Vice Admiral Fletcher. The Japanese carriers *Shokaku* and *Zuikaku* were heavily damaged and the US lost the carrier *USS Lexington* on 8 May, and the *Yorktown* was badly shot up. The Japanese suffered considerable loss of aircraft and without air cover their invasion plans were scuppered.

The principal turning point in the Pacific War was the Battle of Midway Islands – so called because they were 'midway' between the US and Asia – to the west of Hawaii and Pearl Harbor. A rapidly repaired *Yorktown* was lost in this epic encounter that saw Japanese naval power in the Pacific destroyed, along with four aircraft carriers: *Akagi, Kaga* and *Sorya* (all of which were sunk) and *Hiryu* (which was badly damaged and scuttled on 5 June). The Japanese attack, codenamed Operation MI (Midway Island), was anticipated by the US forces – Commander Rochefort and his codebreakers intercepted Japanese radio traffic and identified Midway (codenamed 'AF') as the target. Admiral Yamamoto launched a diversionary attack on the Aleutian Islands off Alaska on 3 June, but the real prize were the airstrips at Midway. The Battle for Midway began on 4 June 1942, when Vice Admiral Nagumo launched a raid against the US airstrips and defences on the two Midway Islands: Sand Island and Eastern Island. As the Japanese invasion force headed for Midway, a Catalina PBY seaplane spotted Nagumo's forces and planes from the US Task Force's three aircraft carrier 'flat-tops' (*Yorktown*, *Enterprise* and *Hornet*), attacked.

Jack Smight's *Midway* (1976 – *The Battle of Midway*) is the definitive screen depiction of this engagement. The brainchild of producer Walter Mirisch, it was written by Donald S. Sanford. World War II buff Mirisch had originally planned to make a documentary, but instead assembled a star-studded cast for this epic retelling of the battle. Henry Fonda played Admiral Chester W. Nimitz, who oversees the encounter from Pearl Harbor. Robert Mitchum had a cameo as Admiral Halsey, who should have been in command of the American naval forces, but was hospitalised with a severe skin disorder. In his stead, he nominated Rear Admiral Spruance (Glenn Ford), a commander untried in carrier warfare who proved his mettle in the battle. Robert Webber was Rear Admiral Fletcher, the Task Force's overall commander aboard the *Yorktown*, and Cliff Robertson, Robert Wagner and James Coburn appeared as other US top brass. Hal Holbrook played naval intelligence codebreaker Commander Rochefort, while a host of recognisable actors appeared in supporting roles: Christopher George, Gregory Walcott, Erik Estrada, Monte Markham, Dabney Coleman, Steven Kanaly and a pre-stardom Tom Selleck. Toshirô Mifune played Admiral Yamamoto and James Shigeta was Vice Admiral Nagumo, among many familiar faces as the Japanese naval commanders.

If these actors were familiar to cinema audiences, so was much of the footage. Realising that restaging the Battle of Midway would have been costly, Mirisch spent $60,000 on archive footage, assembling the action sequences before he began shooting his film. *Midway* was made in Panavision and Technicolor and colour archive footage had to be adapted to fit the 2.35:1 ratio. The title sequence, depicting the Doolittle Raid, is sepia-tinted clips from *Thirty Seconds over Tokyo*. The Japanese aerial attack on Midway's defences and airfields is a mixture of recreated footage, documentary footage and the attack from *Tora! Tora! Tora!* Much footage was reused from the Japanese film *Storm Over the Pacific* (which Mirisch bought) – the Japanese carriers on the move, US aerial attacks on the Japanese fleet and the fleet passing fishing boats. Mirisch used reels of Official Naval Archive footage of aerial combat. There's also footage from John Ford's 18-minute *The Battle of Midway* documentary (which featured Fonda on the voiceover) and Louis De Rochemont's documentary *The Fighting Lady* (1944), which detailed combat off Guam. Smight shot new scenes on studio soundstages and on location at Terminal Island Naval Base in Northern California, on the flat-top *Lexington* (off Pensacola, Florida) and also filmed miniature carriers under attack on Lake Castic. This melding of disparate elements is successful for the most part and offers a great opportunity to see colour naval archive footage.

The acting by some of the starry cast was emphatically gung-ho, but Fonda and Ford are notable for their dignified portrayals. To add a bit of human interest to the story, Sanford added the fictitious character of Captain Matt Garth (Charlton Heston), who is posted to the *Yorktown*. Heston has some awful dialogue with his son Tom (Edward Albert), a US pilot, as when he tells his son to keep his mind on the job: 'You better shape up Tiger, or some hotshot Jap pilot's gonna flame your ass'. The film ends with Tom surviving his sortie against the Japanese navy, albeit badly burned, while his father perishes as he attempts to land on a carrier.

Matt's relationship with Tom is strained when Tom announces that he is to marry his Nisei (American-born Japanese) girlfriend Haruko Sakura (Christina Kokubo). Haruko and her parents have been branded subversives by the FBI and are interred in a US 'relocation camp', which was a fate that befell many Japanese-Americans during World War II. While many Nisei were repressed, other Japanese-Americans fought in the US army in the much-decorated 442nd Regimental Combat Team, which was depicted in Robert Pirosh's *Go for Broke!* (1951) and Lane Nishikawa's *Only the Brave* (2006).

'Were we better than the Japanese', asks Nimitz in the quayside finale, 'or just luckier?' At two vital points in the battle, luck was on the US force's side. When Japanese scout planes spot the US carriers, their radio transmitter fails, preventing them from warning Nagumo. When the US dive and torpedo bombers pounce, in an attack coordinated by chance, they swoop down and in five minutes wreak havoc on the surprised carriers. *Midway* is stitched together by John Williams' sweeping score (including the rousing 'The Midway March' and the hymnal 'The Men of the Yorktown') and the film was given added punch in theatres on its release with the addition of attention-grabbing Sensurround, a sonic assault of the ears and body which had been deployed successfully in *Earthquake* (1974 – also starring Heston). This 'startling new multi-dimension' effect created audible and sub-audible air effects in the specially equipped theatres, a cunning ploy during the battles to detract from the vast change in film stock during the switch from newly shot scenes to grainy archive footage. As trailers stated, Sensurround 'surrounds you with the sights, sounds and actual sensations of battle – so real you can almost feel it'. A six-minute featurette *They Were There!* interviewed three veterans of the battle about their memories and the authenticity of the film. For TV showings the two-hour theatrical cut of *Midway* was beefed up to a four-hour, two-part drama, with advertising breaks and 40 minutes of additional footage depicting the battle of Coral Sea (which is only mentioned briefly in the feature) and a subplot of divorcee Matt's relationship with his lover Ann (Susan Sullivan) in Honolulu. If you're going to assemble a two-hour film using aged Hollywood superstars, archive footage, bits of old US and Japanese war movies and ground-shaking sound effects this is certainly the way to do it. It's a harebrained concept that works entertainingly and informatively as a Hollywood history lesson.

With the Japanese's attack on Pearl Harbor, the world was now at war. The Battle of Midway was an important tactical victory for the USA and allowed them to address the war on the Western Front against Hitler, whilst continuing to pin back Japanese empire-building. A US propaganda poster of the time is captioned 'Jap ... You're Next! We'll Finish the Job!' It depicts a manic-looking Uncle Sam rolling up his sleeves and brandishing a spanner. Until the Battle of Midway, Japan had been on the attack, but after this US success, the remainder of the war in the Pacific theatre saw the US forces in the ascendancy.

Chapter 5

THE SUBMARINE WAR (1940–45)

Germany may have had a paltry surface navy and the Luftwaffe may have been defeated during the Battle of Britain, but the German U-boat fleet was their one area of superiority during the early years of the war. After the sinking of the *Bismarck* in May 1941, Admiral Karl Dönitz's submarine fleet of Unterseeboots (U-boats) hunted in 'wolf packs', often attacking US supply convoys bound for Britain. The U-boat war was one of attrition, which involved some of the most callous actions of the conflict. The methods by which U-boats operated, often striking without warning and, early in the war, against civilian targets, makes their use difficult to rationalise morally today. The first ship sunk by a U-boat was the *Athenia*, an unarmed British passenger ship, which was torpedoed in the North Atlantic by U-30 on the night of 3 September 1939.

The supply lanes across the Atlantic, through the North and Baltic Seas, the Mediterranean and the Arctic to Russia, were the hunting grounds of the 'grey wolves'. One of their most prestigious scalps was the aircraft carrier *HMS Ark Royal*, sunk by U-81 off Gibraltar in November 1941. The U-boats were the only threat that Winston Churchill admitted really frightened him during the war. Until the Allies began to protect cargo freighters adequately with escorts, they were easy targets for U-boats. By 1943 the Allies had organised U-boat defences – special task forces, improvements in decoding, radar and the use of surface aircraft – and the wolves became the hunted. Forty-thousand men were sent to sea in U-boats, but only 10,000 returned, a good indicator of how successful these measures were.

Despite their name, U-boats were essentially surface boats. They needed to surface to launch their torpedoes and their speed underwater was much slower: 7 knots to 17 on the surface. U-boat commanders were noted for their cunning and stealth. An infamous U-boat attack on the Royal Navy base at Scapa Flow in October 1939 sank the battleship *HMS Royal Oak*. The area had particular resonance for the German Navy as it was at Scapa Flow at the end of World War I that the defeated German fleet had been scuttled by their German crews. Günther Prien's U-47 sneaked into Scapa Flow, avoided the sunken ship anti-submarine barricade and torpedoed *Royal Oak*, killing 833 crewmen. These events were dramatised in Harald Reinl's *U47 – Kapitänleutnant Prien* (1958), a West German war movie, with Dieter Eppler as Prien.

Unusually for an Allied wartime propaganda piece, Powell and Pressburger's Canadian-set 49th *Parallel* (1941) depicted the German point of view. It was both a 'flag waver' (it was commissioned as propaganda by the Ministry of Information to persuade the US to join the war) and a 'fee waiver' (with its big-name cast refusing payment, to help the war effort). In the early days of the war, U-37 sinks Allied shipping in the Gulf of St Lawrence, and then proceeds to the Hudson Bay. A six-man German landing party scavenge supplies, but while they are ashore the U-boat is sunk by an air attack. At the Hudson Bay Company depot at Wolstenholme Post, the submariners encounter Nick the Eskimo (Ley On), merchant The Factor (Finlay Currie) and trapper Johnnie (a check-shirted Laurence Olivier, displaying histrionic style, a wry moustache and a hammy French accent). The fugitives steal a seaplane, but run out of gas and crash on their way to Winnipeg. The film follows their attempts to reach Japan (via Vancouver) and later the US-Canadian border (to reach the US). They are decimated and the only survivor, Leutnant (Lieutenant) Ernst Hirth (played by Eric Portman), attempts to cross the border by train to claim immunity in neutral America, but Andrew Brock (Raymond Massey), a Canadian deserter, ensures he is taken back across the border to Canada.

The spectacular Canadian scenery – mountains, lakes, rivers and spruce forests – provides a dramatic backdrop to the tension-filled story. The fugitives' Nazi 'badness' is writ large, as they routinely murder innocent people. They massacre Eskimos and the seaplane crew at Wolstenholme, carve a swastika on the trading post's wall with a bayonet and Hirth is so evil he only takes cold showers. Anton Walbrook and Glynis Johns had cameos as members of a peaceful German religious community, the Hutterites. Niall MacGinnis played U-boatmen Vogel, who decides to stay on with the Hutterites, but Hirth has him executed for treason. Leslie Howard played cultured Canadian novelist Philip Armstrong Scott, the author of 'Indian books' such as *Red Men of the Rockies*, who notes similarities between the 'savage tribal methods' of the Blackfoot Indians and Hitler's indoctrination of his people. The Germans burn Scott's Picasso and Matisse paintings and his copy of *The Magic Mountain* by Thomas Mann. When Scott corners a pistol-packing Nazi in a cave, he beats him up: 'That's for Thomas Mann! That's for Matisse! That's for Picasso!' Of their confrontation, Scott muses, 'One armed superman against one unarmed decadent democrat – I wonder how Dr Goebbels would explain that?' Emeric Pressburger won the Best Original Story Oscar in 1942 for this film, which was shortened by 20 minutes in the USA and retitled *The Invaders*. It is this abridged version that won the Oscar.

Archie Mayo's *Crash Dive* (1943) is a typical example of Hollywood wartime propaganda. It depicted the *USS Corsair*, a US navy submarine. PT boat commander Lieutenant Ward Stewart (Tyrone Power) is transferred to the *Corsair*, under Lieutenant Commander Dewey Connors (Dana Andrews), as it patrols the North Atlantic. Most of the film is devoted to the landlocked love triangle between Ward, Dewey and schoolteacher Jean (Anne Baxter). The script for one of the few wartime war films to be shot in Technicolor pays high praise and lip service to the US Navy, which results in the movie resembling a naval recruiting film. Twentieth Century-Fox was allowed to film key scenes in the US Submarine Base in New London, Connecticut. Power enlisted as a private in the Marines during the making of the film and was granted four months leave to finish it, before serving in the Pacific as a transporter pilot.

Crash Dive features some good action, as when the sub confronts what appears to be a Swedish freighter but it's actually a heavily armed German Q-boat (a disguised merchant vessel). In the well-staged finale, the *Corsair* trails a tanker through protective submarine nets and a minefield and infiltrates a harbour being used as a U-boat base. This scene features the best piece of dialogue of these submarine adventures, between two *Corsair* crewmen: 'I wonder what'd happen if we ever hit one of those mines?'; 'I don't know, but here's that five bucks I owe you'. A landing party blow up the shore installations and the *Corsair* torpedoes shipping in the harbour (with some excellent model work and process shots, explosions and oil fires). The scene where the submarine partially submerges and Dewey becomes a human periscope to guide the *Corsair* out of the burning harbour is not to be missed.

Celluloid submarine action in the Atlantic includes the midget submarine attack on the *Tirpitz* in *Above Us the Waves* (1955) and the duels in *The Cruel Sea* (1952). *U-571* (2000), starring Matthew McConaughey, Bill Paxton, Harvey Keitel and Jon Bon Jovi, inaccurately depicted US sailors capturing a vital Enigma Code deciphering machine from a U-boat, a feat actually achieved by the Royal Navy. *U-boat Prisoner* (1944), starring Bruce Bennett, told the true story of Archie Gibbs. His ship was sunk and when he was captured by a U-boat he claimed he was a German sailor: with the aid of other Allied prisoners, he eventually took over the vessel. Alfred Hitchcock's *Lifeboat* (1944) crammed its title craft with the survivors of a torpedoed passenger ship (which has been sunk by a U-boat) and the unpopular U-boat captain.

In Anthony Asquith's fictitious *We Dive at Dawn* (1943), during April 1942 the Royal Navy submarine P61 *HMS Sea Tiger* returns from an uneventful patrol and its crew take shore leave. They are soon recalled, as the *Sea Tiger* is sent on a mission to sink the new German battleship *Brandenburg* which is heading out of the Kiel Canal into the Baltic. When three captured Luftwaffe pilots tell the *Sea Tiger*'s captain that the *Brandenburg* is already in the Baltic, he decides to give chase. Upon locating the *Brandenburg*, the *Sea Tiger* fires six torpedoes and then dives, as the German escorts drop depth charges.

We Dive at Dawn is a very British production – a Gainsborough Picture filmed at Gaumont British Studios and distributed by General Film Distributors – which is introduced by an early version of the Rank Organisation's gong-man. John Mills played the *Sea Tiger*'s skipper, Lieutenant Freddie Taylor, and Eric Portman was L/S (Leading Seaman) Hobson, who operates the sub's Hydrophone (underwater listening device). Made with the cooperation of the Admiralty and His Majesty's

Submarines, the film presents convincing action and the cramped, tedious life on board the sub is also conveyed. Hobson passes the time making wooden models of battleships and submarines for his son. Having evaded the *Brandenburg*'s escorts, the *Sea Tiger* puts into a Danish island harbour to purloin fuel and supplies. Although German propaganda has announced that the *Sea Tiger* is at the bottom of the Baltic, the submariners are greeted as heroes on their return to Blighty when they learn that their torpedoes have sunk the *Brandenburg.*

In Alfred Werker's *Sealed Cargo* (1951) set in 1943, halibut fisherman Captain Bannion (Dana Andrews) and his crew of the trawler *Daniel Webster* sail out of Gloucester, Massachusetts. Amid the fog-bound Grand Banks, they encounter a square-rigged schooner the *Gaunt Woman*, which resembles a ghostly galleon, with all on board dead – save for Captain Skalder (Claude Rains), who alleges they have been attacked by U-boats. The ship is bound for Halifax with its cargo of West Indian rum, so Bannion claims salvage rights and tows the schooner to Newfoundland. In port, Bannion discovers that the *Gaunt Woman* has a concealed ironclad hold and its 'sealed cargo' is hundreds of German torpedoes. The *Gaunt Woman* is in fact a mother ship, resupplying U-boats. In the finale, Bannion manages to blow up the ship and also two U-boats which rendezvous off Newfoundland. *Sealed Cargo* is an action-packed, suspenseful thriller – with fine locations and (for its time) excellent special effects – which is riven with topical 'trust no one' 1950s paranoia.

The finest Hollywood submarine movie is Dick Powell's *The Enemy Below* (1957), based on D.A. Rayner's 1956 book of the same name. Robert Mitchum starred as Captain Murrell, of the Buckley Class Escort Destroyer *USS Haynes*, which leaves Trinidad to patrol the South Atlantic. Murrell is an ex-freighter skipper who has recently lost both his ship and his English wife in a U-boat torpedo attack. The *Haynes* stalks a U-boat commanded by Von Stolberg (Curd Jürgens), but the wily commanders are a match for one another: Von Stolberg attempts to out-manoeuvre his opponent but Murrell always second guesses him. Murrell orders that the U-boat be pounded hourly with depth charges, which drives Von Stolberg to torpedo the *Haynes*. Murrell then orders that fires are lit on the ship's deck, to make her appear more badly damaged than she is, and the duped U-boat surfaces. The *Haynes* disables the sub with her guns and then suicidally rams the U-boat, sinking both vessels. Colourfully filmed in CinemaScope and DeLuxe Color, *The Enemy Below* is convincing drama. The *Haynes*' scenes were filmed aboard the *USS Whitehurst*. The vivid blue water of the South Atlantic leaves a frothing white wake, while great white plumes erupt when the *Haynes* discharges her depth charges. The Oscar-winning special effects by Walter Rossi add to the film's effectiveness. The cast includes Theodore Bikel (as Heinie Schwaffer) and Arthur La Ral (as Hitlerite Kunz) on the U-boat and Al Hedison (of cult movie *The Fly*) as the *Haynes*' executive officer, Lieutenant Ware. Future star Doug McClure can be glimpsed among the *Haynes*' crew. The film unfolds in an interesting, chess-like tactical game of destroyer-versus-sub, radar-versus-sonar and depth charges-versus-torpedoes.

The most famous film in the sub subgenre is from the German point of view. Wolfgang Petersen's *The Boat* (1981 – *Das Boot*) followed the exploits of U-96 in the North Atlantic. There are four different versions of Petersen's work. *Das Boot* was made as a TV series of six 50-minute episodes, in German for German TV. This is perhaps the most familiar version to European audiences, as it was broadcast on television in the 1980s. It was also released as a German-language film (with subtitles for the UK/US market) at 150 minutes as *Das Boot* (which is pronounced 'Das Bot'). In the 1990s, director Petersen prepared a 200-minute 'Director's Cut', which was a compromise between the lengthy TV series and the 150-minute film version. This is available in German (with English subtitles) and in English (a new English language version was recorded as part of the restoration), with a digitally enhanced soundtrack of new sound effects. My preferred cut (and the one I discuss below) is the fourth version: an English language 123-minute print which bears the onscreen title *The Boat*. It was released on home video in the UK in 1991 by RCA Columbia. In contrast to other German-language war films, it has excellent English language dubbing (the English dialogue differs from the later 'Director's Cut'). Whereas the sedate, six-part TV version meticulously depicts the often-boring life of a U-boat crew – 90 per cent tedium and 10 percent combat – this 123-minute version distils the sub's mission and plays like a fast-moving action movie.

In the autumn of 1941, the tide of the U-boat war is turning. Better escorts are accompanying the Allied convoys and inflicting heavy losses, resulting in younger crews being deployed by the Germans. U-96 leaves the submarine pens in La Rochelle harbour to seek out and destroy Allied shipping. As they scour the Atlantic, they are ambushed by a destroyer with depth charges, but they escape with minimum damage. They receive reports of a convoy and on a moonlit night they attack, but a destroyer escort replies with depth charges, driving them deeper and deeper to evade their persistent hunter. Under extreme pressure, the bolts of the U-boat's hull ping, ricocheting like bullets, pipes burst and water showers in, as U-96 'plays dead' until it's safe to resurface. When they surface they witness a stricken, broken-backed tanker burning. They decide to head back to La Rochelle to repair damage and refuel, but learn that they have been rerouted to the Italian naval base at La Spezia. This means they must pass through the Straits of Gibraltar, which is controlled by the Royal Navy. While trying to negotiate British-controlled waters, U-96 is bombed by an Allied plane. The U-boat dives to the seabed to a depth far greater than their gauges and almost to the point of pressurised implosion. To conserve oxygen, some of the crew go into 'hibernation' wearing oxygen masks, while others make running repairs. U-96 is embedded in the sand: the crew blow water out of the vessel to lighten it and finally the submarine loosens itself and breaks the surface. The engines are fired, the pistons spring to life and U-96 speeds for home.

The Boat/Das Boot was based on the 1975 novel by Lothar-Günther Buchheim. Petersen and Dean Reisner adapted it into a screenplay. Filming the $15 million production took a year, on location in the North Sea, in France and at studios in Hamburg. U-96's interior was recreated, copying every detail from an actual U-boat. This made filming cramped but authentic and enabled the camera to follow the sailors rushing through the vessel's hull and diving through the bulkhead hatches like bullets whizzing down a rifle barrel. These interiors were lit by dim lamplight, or else bathed in red and blue hues. U-boats were masterpieces of frugal, space-conscious design, incorporating torpedo rooms fore and aft, plus crew's quarters, a galley, the sonar and radar rooms, the engine room and the all-important control room and the conning tower, with its periscope: the vessel's eye on the surface of the sea. No number '96' appears on the outside of the U-boat's conning tower, an authentic detail as identifying numbers were painted out for security in wartime. Various scale models were used in the film for the submarine's exterior, including one full-scale, three-section replica which also appears in *Raiders of the Lost Ark* (1981).

The Boat was shot in sequence and the crews' beards grew longer as their mission progressed, ageing the fresh-faced raw recruits. A well-chosen cast portrayed the pasty-faced, hungry-looking, lank-haired crew. Jurgen Prochnow played the seasoned, gaunt U-boat captain, who was based on Captain Heinrich Lehmann-Willenbrock, at 30 a veteran U-boat commander. Nicknamed 'Recke' (Valiant Warrior), he commanded U-5 and U-96 and sank 25 ships during his successful career (he died in 1986). German rock star Herbert Gronemeyer played Leutnant Werner, a war correspondent who was based on author Buchheim. Klaus Wenneman was the sub's Chief Engineer and Heinz Honig was sonar operator Hinrich, with other pallid submariners played by Hubertus Bengsch, Martin Semmelrogge, Bernd Tauber and Martin May. Erwin Leder was memorable as Johann 'The Ghost', with his cabin-fevered red-ringed eyes and shattered nerves, who becomes a raving whimpering wreck when the British destroyer depth charges the sub.

The film's opening scene depicts the U-96 looming from the deep, a predatory monster, sleek and shark-like in the gloom. This unforgettable, menacing image is accompanied by Klaus Doldinger's unforgettably menacing music, which rolls and pitches like the sea. An intimidating composition, it is one of the great war movie scores. Doldinger used a mixture of electronic effects, synthesizers and strings to create the soundtrack for the U-96's exploits. Other orchestrations of the main theme accompany U-96 as she crashes across the surface of the sea, or glides towards a beautiful sunset. The film's detailed sound design incorporates sonar blips, crashing waves, hollow metallic clangs and scrapes, slamming doors and the chattering pistons of the engine room.

There's something unsettlingly powerful about the sight of a submarine breaking the surface of a desolate sea – the racing conning tower slicing through the surging, bubbling waves, the nose cutting through the water. It is majestic, but also ominously chilling. This same unnerving emotion is evoked by the sight of a torpedoed ship succumbing to the deep, its burning prow finally vanishing below the surface, leaving only the cries of those floundering in the water. When U-96 surfaces after six hours of deep-sea hiding from a destroyer, the stricken, blazing tanker they have torpedoed is still sinking, bathed in a blood-red sky. The crew watch from the conning tower as the captain orders the tanker torpedoed, to finish her off. It is only then that they realise that there are still crewmen aboard the ship – they haven't evacuated – and their cries can be heard by the U-boatmen. The captain knows they can't take prisoners, so the U-boat withdraws and the drowning men are left to their fate, a scene which echoes Captain Ericson's depth-charge dilemma in *The Cruel Sea*.

The Boat is artfully composed and the cramped interior scenes jar with the expansive seascape exteriors. A tracking shot explores the primeval sub pens in La Rochelle, with its plumes of smoke and showers of welding sparks. The harbour scenes were filmed in the actual concrete bunker pens of La Rochelle, dressed to resemble the 1940s. The cinematography was by Jost Vacano, the editing by Hannes Nikel and attention to detail was paid by art director Götz Weider. A picturesque scene shows the U-boat rendezvousing with the *Weser*, a German ship impounded in the Spanish port of Vigo, which resupplies and refuels U-96 while the naval attaché on board informs the captain of enemy ships located in Gibraltar's Straits.

The film's climax is a catastrophic, downbeat coda, which emphasises both the futility of conflict and the ties that bind men and machines together in times of war. U-96 returns to La Rochelle, but as the crew are being hailed as conquering heroes, an Allied air raid shatters the harbour, scattering the assembled dignitaries, a brass band and U-96's crew. During the attack many of the U-boat's crew – who have survived the cruel sea and Allied patrols – are killed or wounded. Werner finds his mortally wounded captain slumped beside the quay. Before he dies, the captain watches as his beloved U-96 sinks slowly beneath the water of the docks.

The Boat/Das Boot was a great success as both a film and a TV series. In addition to its TV miniseries format, it was released internationally to cinemas by Columbia Pictures, who were persuaded by Mark Damon and his partner John M. Hyde of PSO (Producers Sales Organisation) to distribute a foreign language film for the first time. It took $100 million worldwide and was the most successful German film of all time. The TV version was much more detailed in its depiction of claustrophobic, damp life aboard U-96 and supplied background characterisations and personalities to the crew that some critics found lacking in the abridged film versions. Damon also secured a $150,000 dubbing budget, with seven of the German cast re-voicing themselves in the 123-minute English language version. Petersen was nominated for an Academy Award for Best Director, and the film also received nominations for Best Adapted Screenplay, Cinematography, Editing, Sound and Sound Effects Editing. The film also picked up nominations for Best Foreign Language Film at the BAFTAs and the Golden Globes. A powerful, vividly realistic depiction of ordinary men at war, the film looks even better now than it did on its initial release. It is one of the finest films of the 1980s and the greatest depiction of the U-boat war in the Atlantic – in that respect it sinks all opposition.

Submarines were also deployed in the Pacific War by the US Navy, though due to the obsolescence of their craft and their outmoded, temperamental torpedoes, it wasn't until 1944 that they began to make a difference in the conflict. When the Pacific submarine war ended in December 1944, US submariners had succeeded in decimating the Japanese merchant fleet and strangled Japan's supply of imports.

Set during 1942, *Torpedo Run* (1958) was based on stories by Richard Sale. It followed the US submarine *USS Grayfish* commanded by Barney Doyle (Glenn Ford) and his lieutenant Arch Sloan (Ernest Borgnine). They are on the trail of the Japanese aircraft carrier the *Shinaru*, the pride of the navy, which led the attack on Pearl Harbor. Doyle learns that his wife and daughter have been taken prisoner by the Japanese in Manila. When the *Grayfish* has the opportunity to sink the *Shinaru*, the Japanese ship uses the *Hoshida Maru*, a transporter carrying 1,400 Allied prisoners of war, as a protective screen. Doyle torpedoes the wrong ship, condemning his own wife and daughter to a watery grave and the remainder of the film sees Doyle continue his vendetta with the Japanese 'flattop'. He eventually manages to sink the *Shinaru* in fog and the *Grayfish*'s crew are rescued by US submarine the *Bluefin*, when they are depth-charged. Good underwater CinemaScope photography, model work and Oscar-nominated special effects make the action scenes successful. L.Q. Jones and Dean Jones appeared among the *Grayfish* crew, and both Ford and Borgnine are memorable.

Gordon Douglas' *Up Periscope* (1959) was made by Warner Bros as a vehicle for their TV star James Garner (then best-known for the *Maverick* teleseries). Garner starred as intelligence officer and commando Lieutenant Ken Braden, who is assigned to the *USS Barracuda* skippered by Commander Paul Stevens (Edmond O'Brien). In 1942, as US forces make preparations for the invasion of the Marshall Islands, the *Barracuda* drops Braden near a Japanese island radio transmitter station, to photograph a vital Japanese code. As the submarine waits for him on the bottom of a lagoon, its oxygen runs low. When the story stops meandering and cuts to the chase, *Up Periscope* is a half-decent combat flick. When a Japanese fighter strafes the surfaced submarine and Stevens orders them to dive below the sea, the craft's wounded executive officer is left on deck to drown. It was shot in WarnerScope and Technicolor, with the collaboration of the Submarine Force Pacific Fleet, and features early roles for Edd Byrnes and Warren Oates as *Barracuda* submariners. The film deployed monochrome underwater and torpedo attack footage from earlier submarine movies and in the finale heroic Braden blows up a fuel dump and escapes with the code.

Other Pacific-set submarine movies include *Hellcats of the Navy* (1957), the only onscreen teaming of Ronald Reagan and his wife Nancy (then billed as Nancy Davis), Blake Edwards' comedy *Operation Petticoat* (1959) starring Cary Grant and Tony Curtis, and *Operation Bikini* (1963) featuring teen stars Tab Hunter and Frankie Avalon. Robert Wise's vengeful *Run Silent, Run Deep* (1958) starred Clark Gable, Jack Warden, Brad Dexter, Don Rickles and Burt Lancaster. Its remake – *Submarine Seahawk* (1959) – starred John Bentley and Brett Halsey.

Operation Pacific (1951) depicted life on the *USS Thunderfish*, a US submarine in the Pacific skippered by Commander John 'Pop' Perry (Ward Bond) and his executive officer, Lieutenant Commander Duke Gifford (played by the 'Duke' himself, John Wayne). This tribute to the 'silent service' depicts the problems faced by US submariners, especially their battle with unreliable dud torpedoes, which sometimes fail to explode on impact, or detonate too soon. During an attack on a Japanese freighter, which turns out to be a heavily armed Q-boat, Commander Perry is lost when the submarine is forced to dive and he is left on deck. Matters are further complicated when Gifford's estranged wife, Honolulu-based nurse Mary Stewart (Patricia Neal), dates flier Bob Perry (Philip Carey),

Commander Perry's younger brother. Bob blames Gifford for his brother's death. In an in-joke, the *Thunderfish*'s crew watch Delmer Daves' *Destination Tokyo* (1943), a wartime submarine movie starring Cary Grant, John Garfield and Alan Hale, and complain about the unrealism of these 'Hollywood guys'. *Operation Pacific*'s action culminates in the foiling of 'Operation Victory', the Imperial Japanese Fleet's attempt to repulse the US invasion of the Philippines on 20 October 1944. The *Thunderfish*, now under the command of Gifford, spots the enemy fleet in the Luzon Straits and radios for US aircraft to attack. This huge naval engagement – the Battle of Leyte Gulf over 23–25 October 1944 – shattered Japanese naval power in the Pacific. Neal, with her distinctive smoky voice and strong character, is not the usual pushover romantic interest of Wayne's war films and is more than a match for Duke. They were reunited years later, again as naval officer and nurse, for *In Harm's Way* (1965).

Offbeat submarine movies include the horror film *Below* (2002), starring Olivia Williams, which featured strange goings-on aboard a US sub following the sinking of a German vessel. In the contemporary thriller *Bear Island* (1979), starring Donald Sutherland, Vanessa Redgrave, Richard Widmark and Christopher Lee, and based on a novel by Alistair MacLean, a haul of Nazi gold is concealed in the Norwegian Arctic (ghostly subterranean submarine pens were created at Pinewood Studios). Duilio Coletti's *Submarine Attack* (1954) featured an Italian submarine, Renato Baldini, Folco Lulli and a pre–Miss Moneypenny Lois Maxwell, while Charles Frend's *Torpedo Bay* (1964), starring James Mason, Lilli Palmer and Gabriele Ferzetti, depicted Italian–British naval operations.

Peter O'Toole starred in *Murphy's War* (1971), which relocated submarine warfare to Venezuela in the last days of the war, in April and May 1945. Irish crewman Murphy (O'Toole) survives the torpedoing of his merchant vessel *RN/MS Mount Kyle* on the Orinoco River. His fellow crewmen are machine-gunned to death in the water by a U-boat commanded by Leutnant Lauchs (Horst Janson). Murphy is rescued by French oil company rep Louis Brezan (Philippe Noiret) and nursed back to health at a Society of Friends mission run by Englishwoman Dr Hayden (Siân Phillips). He discovers that the ship's biplane pilot, Lieutenant Ellis (John Hallam), has also survived, as has the ship's biplane (a seaplane, the Grumman J2F-6 'Duck'). The U-boat crew raid the mission and Lauchs kills Ellis (who has witnessed the *Mount Kyle* atrocity) but can't locate Murphy, who vows to take revenge for his murdered comrades. Directed by Peter Yates (an assistant director on *The Guns of Navarone* and the director of *Bullit*), *Murphy's War* is a well-told, cleverly plotted, beautifully shot, offbeat war movie that benefits from a fine Irish portrayal by O'Toole: once Lawrence of Arabia, now he's Murphy of the Orinoco. Murphy's tetchy relationship with Dr Hayden and elements of the plot recall *The African Queen* and Phillips and Noiret offer excellent support. But it's the underrated German actor Janson (later Hammer Horror's *Captain Kronos: Vampire Hunter*) as the most despicable U-boat skipper in war cinema that you'll remember.

Murphy's War was adapted for the screen by Sterling Silliphant from Max Catto's 1969 novel of the same name. The action was filmed in Panavision on the Orinoco River in Venezuela and at Pinewood and Twickenham Studios, England.

The Venezuelan Navy submarine *Carite* played the U-boat and John Barry provided the score. Murphy wages a one-man war against Lauchs, by attacking the U-boat in the biplane and bombing it with improvised Molotov cocktails. The aerial scenes of Murphy learning to fly the Duck – where his acrobatic baptism of fire proceeds from white-knuckle terror to loop-the-loop stunts – were performed by Frank Tallman. When the U-boat destroys the plane, Murphy attempts to ram the Germans with Louis' battered, flat-bottomed barge-crane. A torpedo fired from the U-boat beaches and the U-boat becomes embedded on a sandbank. Murphy hoists the unexploded torpedo off the beach with the crane and suspends it over the stranded U-boat, like the sword of Damocles: the torpedo drops on Lauchs' craft and destroys it. *Murphy's War* is a twisting, always-interesting tale of revenge and loss, made more moving by the fact that the final confrontation takes place after the German surrender in Europe in May 1945. As Murphy says when he hears the war is over: 'Their war ... not mine!'

Chapter 6

THE WAR IN THE MED (1940–45)

In October 1940, Italian dictator Benito Mussolini sought to further advance Italy's Mediterranean expansion. Italian forces had already overrun Albania in 1939, but Mussolini wanted to occupy the remaining Balkan countries – Bulgaria, Greece and Yugoslavia. Italian forces massed on the border and attacked Greece in October 1940, but Mussolini's army was no match for the Greeks, who had British air support, and was pushed back into Albania over the winter of 1940–41. By March 1941, the Greek army under General Papagos had not only contained the Italian invasion, but had taken half of Albania. Thus Germany was drawn into the war in the Balkans when it became obvious Mussolini's forces were insufficient to attain victory.

Bulgaria had joined the Axis – via the Tripartite Pact that bound together Italy, Germany and Japan. Yugoslavia joined too, but then quickly withdrew. Operation Punishment was Hitler's plan to bring Yugoslavia to heel. A Blitzkrieg was launched on 6 April 1941 and Yugoslavia surrendered on 17 April. The same day Hitler invaded Yugoslavia, he also struck in Greece, overrunning the Greek and Allied forces. By the end of April the Allies had fallen back to the Peloponnesian islands at the foot of Greece, and many were successfully evacuated to the island of Crete. The invasion of Greece was the last time the Blitzkrieg tactic was deployed successfully to invade and crush an entire nation. The Germans then turned their attention to Crete, launching an airborne assault – 'Sprung Nach Kreta' – on 20 May 1941 which landed on the north coast at Máleme, Caneá, Rétimo and Heràklion. General Kurt Student's strategy – the bombing of airfields, plus lightning paratroop and glider landings – guaranteed surprise. Although the Allies put up strong resistance, 15,000 Allies were evacuated and the remainder, some 18,000 men, surrendered on 31 May.

For filmmakers, the War in the Mediterranean was an exotic sideshow to the main conflict, providing interesting, unusual locales. Lewis Milestone's *They*

Who Dare (1953) starred Dirk Bogarde as Lieutenant Graham, an officer in the Special Boat Service (SBS) in Cairo. As the British 8th Army prepare to attack in North Africa in September 1942, Graham's band of commandos and partisans carry out two simultaneous attacks on Luftwaffe airfields on occupied Rhodes. Italian troops scour the island for the perpetrators and of the ten commandos and partisans assigned to the mission, only Graham and Sergeant Corcoran (Denholm Elliott) make their rendezvous with a Greek submarine. Eric Pohlmann had fun as the jovial Greek sub skipper, Captain Papadapoulos, and Akim Tamiroff played Greek officer, Captain Kounis. The film's retina-burning Technicolor and spectacular location photography are wasted for the most part, as much of the action takes place at night or in caves, or both. The scenes of the demolition of the Italian aircraft on the airstrip are well staged – the film deployed authentic Italian SM79 bombers borrowed from the Lebanese airforce. Not so authentic are the Italian troops' vehicles, which are a hodgepodge of disguised Chevrolet trucks, Daimler Scout Cars and tracked Bren Gun Carriers.

Ill Met by Moonlight (1957), the last film from the writer-producer-director team of Michael Powell and Emeric Pressburger, was set in 1944 on Crete. British commandos, working with the 'hungry wolves' of the Greek resistance in the Cretan mountains, kidnap the island's German commander-in-chief, paratrooper Major General Kreipe (Marius Goring). The ambush on his Mercedes between the German HQ and his villa goes smoothly, but the Germans hunt the kidnappers in the mountains. The wily general leaves a trail of clues (buttons, badges, coins, his hat) and deliberately tries to slow the commandos' progress. Eventually arriving at Rodhakinon Beach, the kidnappers find it patrolled by Germans but resourceful young resistance fighter Niko (Demetri Andreas) distracts them. The fine ending has the squad unable to flash the signal letters 'SB' to the rescue ship waiting offshore to take them to Cairo, as none of them know Morse Code.

The film was based on a true story – a wartime diary kept by one of the British kidnappers, Captain W. Stanley Moss (played in the film by David Oxley). His partner in the abduction is Major Patrick Leigh Fermor – also known as his alter ego, partisan Philedem, a Cretan Scarlet Pimpernel – as played with tired panache by Dirk Bogarde. Cyril Cusack played Sandy, another British commando, Christopher Lee had a bit part as a German policeman shot by Fermor at a dentist's and David McCallum (in his film debut) can be glimpsed as a sailor. The flavourful score was by native Grecian Mikis Theodorakis (of *Zorba the Greek* fame). The film benefits from a tension-filled plot, good performances (particularly by Bogarde and Goring) and evocative monochrome photography, which results in an erudite, poetic war film. Filmgoers' wishing to visit Crete on the strength of the spectacular locations depicted in the film – the beaches and coves, hilltop villages and majestic valleys and mountains – beware. *Ill Met by Moonlight* was shot at Pinewood Studios and on location on the Côte D'Azur on the French Riviera, and in the Alpes-Maritimes on the French–Italian border. As with many British-made war films (*Sea of Sand*, *Ice Cold in Alex*) the film's eloquent title was replaced by something more straightforward for its abridged US release – in the case of *Ill Met by Moonlight*, it was *Night Ambush*.

Other films depicting occupied Greece and its islands, and partisan resistance, include the Greek-set *Barefoot Battalion* (1954) and *Mediterranean in Flames* (1970). *The Naked Brigade* (1965) restaged the Battle for Crete in 1941, with Ken Scott leading a group of female guerrillas against the invaders. *The Battle for Crete* (1970), an Italian-Spanish-Greek co-production, was released internationally as *Hell in the Aegean. Mediterraneo* (1991) stranded Italian soldiers on a beautiful Aegean island in 1941, to Best Foreign Film Oscar success. The *HMS Torrin* went down off Crete in 1941 in *In Which We Serve* (1942) and Paul Wendkos' *Hell Boats* (1970) sent James Franciscus on a special mission which was shot on location around Malta.

Malta Story (1953) depicted an island under the hammer of incessant Axis bombing during 1942. Malta was a vital link in the Allies' supply lines from Gibraltar to Alexandria, Egypt. Alec Guinness played a reconnaissance pilot who falls for a Maltese girl, Maria Gonzar (Muriel Pavlow), while Flora Robson played her mother, Melita. Anthony Steel, Jack Hawkins and picturesque location filming in Malta (including the Grand Harbour of Valletta) aided the production, as did the extensive archive footage of air attacks and sea battles. The Allied forces on Malta were highly unorthodox – 'We have to make up our words and music as we go along' – and airfields on the island were used to launch attacks on Axis convoys resupplying their forces in North Africa. For its valour in the face of deprivation and adversity, the entire island was awarded the George Cross by King George VI in 1942. The film also depicts Operation Pedestal in August 1942, when an Allied relief convoy (including the oil tanker *Ohio*) was heavily decimated en route to Valletta.

Robert Aldrich's *The Angry Hills* (1959), set during the German invasion of Greece, was notable for Stanley Baker's turn as Gestapo officer Conrad Heisler and Robert Mitchum as war correspondent Mike Morrison trapped in Athens. Baker and his co-star Gia Scala were reunited in the Med for *The Guns of Navarone* (1961), a massively influential revamp of the war movie genre, which created an all-new, all-star, all-action template that is still used today.

In November 1943, 2,000 British soldiers are stranded on Kheros, a tiny island west of Turkey in the Aegean Sea. To convince Turkey to join the Axis, Hitler plans to blitz Kheros in one week's time and massacre those trapped there. Six British destroyers are to evacuate the island, but they can't reach Kheros because the route is guarded by a pair of long-range, radar-controlled guns on the island of Navarone. A bombing raid by Lancasters fails to knock out the artillery battery, so Commander Jensen (James Robertson Justice, who also served at the film's narrator) of the Subversive Operation Executive (SOE) assembles 'the best team in the business' under the command of Major Ray 'Lucky' Franklin (Anthony Quayle) for a five-day mission to spike the guns. The commandos are Corporal Miller (David Niven), a professor of chemistry and an explosives expert; Private Brown (Stanley Baker), a mechanic and knifeman known during the Spanish Civil War as the 'Butcher of Barcelona'; 'born killer' Private Spiros Pappadimos (singer James Darren, then better known as surfer Moondoggie in the *Gidget* films); Greek resistance leader Colonel Andrea Stavros (Anthony Quinn), a Cretan bull; and his comrade, Captain Keith Mallory (Gregory Peck), a mountaineering 'Human Fly'.

The Heroes of Navarone: Captain Keith Mallory (Gregory Peck) and Greek resistance leader Colonel Andrea Stavros (Anthony Quinn) in a US lobby card for J. Lee Thompson's *The Guns of Navarone* (1961). Courtesy Kevin Wilkinson Collection.

Travelling in a decrepit old chugger and posing as fishermen, the team sail to Navarone, blowing up a nosy German patrol boat incognito. During a storm they are dashed on the rocks of Navarone and access the island by scaling the sheer South Cliff: 'Lucky' Franklin proves to be anything but and breaks his leg as he climbs. They haul him overland by stretcher and Mallory takes command. The Germans scour the island with spotter planes, radar and patrols. The commandos negotiate snowy Mount Kostos and rendezvous in the ruins of St Alexis with their partisan contacts – Spiros' sister Maria Pappadimos (Irene Papas) and mute Anna (Gia Scala). Anna hasn't uttered a word since her torture at the hands of the Germans, a whipping which has left her back severely scarred. The squad make their way towards the fortress and guns, but the Germans anticipate their every move. In the town of Mandrakos, the commandos are captured but manage to escape and disguise themselves as Germans for the final part of the mission. Franklin, his leg gangrenous, is left behind and captured. Having been injected with scopolamine 'truth drug' he tells the Germans to expect an amphibious landing on the island (a lie fed to him by Mallory), so the Germans marshal their forces on the coast. Accessing the deserted town beneath the guns, the commandos discover their betrayer. Miller's equipment has been sabotaged and Anna is responsible. She wasn't tortured by the SS – her back is unscarred – and she has become a double-agent: for this, Maria executes her. Miller must now improvise, as the British relief convoy approaches.

The Guns of Navarone was based on Alistair MacLean's 1957 novel of the same name. The book is a mixture of high adventure, espionage and war story, and the film version retains this formula. Literally cliff-hanging, it features shoot-outs, subterfuge, silenced pistols, telescopic rifle sights, riddles, derring-do and betrayal. In this cloak-and-dagger scenario, the dagger usually ends up in the back of a German guard. Several changes were made to the plot of MacLean's novel. In the book Mallory is a New Zealander and a member of the Long Range Desert Group (LRDG), and his team are Lieutenant Andy Stevens RNVR (Royal Naval Volunteer Reserves), American demolition expert Corporal 'Dusty' Miller (also LRDG), Scottish engineer Casey Brown, and Greek resistance fighter Andrea. In the film, Mallory is American and Miller is British. There are only 1,200 men trapped on Kheros and the town of Mandrakos is called Margaritha. The Navarone partisans who aid them are male – Panayis and Louki – and it is Panayis who betrays the commandos. Partisan Maria is introduced to the film as love interest for Andrea Stavros. In the book, Andrea's wife and children were killed by a landmine and his father and stepmother were murdered by Bulgarians. The film adds an unnecessary vendetta between Mallory and Andrea: Mallory had inadvertently allowed the Germans to murder Andrea's wife and three children, and Andrea swears to kill Mallory when the opportunity arises.

Guns of Navarone was directed by J. Lee Thompson on a $6 million budget and the classy combination of a top-notch cast, fine music, taut story and photogenic locations gelled to create great cinema. The story was adapted for the screen by blacklisted Hollywood writer Carl Foreman and was shot on location on the island of Rhodes (the largest of the Dodecanese Archipelago in the Aegean Sea) in CinemaScope and Eastmancolor by Oswald Morris. The ruins at St Alexis were filmed at the Acropolis of Lindos. Despite rumours to the contrary, Navarone and Kheros are fictitious – the map in the front of MacLean's novel shows the islands off the coast of Turkey. The map inserts that appear in the film were by Halas and Batchelor Cartoon Films Ltd. Interiors were filmed at Shepperton Studios and Associate British Studios, Elstree in London. Filming on Greek locations gave the film a picturesque backdrop, with the landscape – harbours, whitewashed architecture, olive groves, cliffs, dust and sun – adding to the drama. Dimitri Tiomkin supplied the jaunty, rousing theme tune which was performed with gusto by the Sinfonia of London.

For such a big-budget production, the ordnance on display as Navarone's German garrison is lax. Excluding the odd VW Kübelwagon, the German equipment is US-made. The armour is M24 Chaffee light tanks, the trucks are Dodges, and when Mallory and his men are trapped in a house in Mandrakos, a six-wheeled American M8 light armoured car pulls up outside. It was often the case in 1960s war films that little attention was paid to locating or replicating original WWII vehicles. It was much easier to simply use current ordnance and pass it off as WWII vintage. After the war many authentic vehicles were scrapped and German tanks were in especially short supply. Yugoslavia was a popular filming destination for filmmakers wishing to make WWII action films, not just for its landscape but also for its abundance of actual weapons, tanks, trucks, artillery and other kit left over from the war. Developing technology resulted in newer designs, which to historians were obviously wrong for the 1940s period. Thus NATO armoured cars and 1950s tanks of Korean War vintage cropped up again and again in international war movies.

The Guns of Navarone's stalwart British supporting cast featured future film director Bryan Forbes as Commander Jensen's sidekick Cohn, Allan Cuthbertson as diffident British officer Baker (named Briggs in the novel) and Richard Harris as Australian Lancaster pilot Barnsby (Torrance in the novel), who fails to blow up the guns. The Germans are sketchily drawn, though there are vague attempts to differentiate between the regular army and the SS, such as torturer Sessler (George Mixell). The heroes' costumes are anachronistically 1960s in their style, though they are the best-dressed bunch of commandos in war cinema. Disguised as local fishermen, this unshaven crew of 'pirates and cutthroats' – who perpetually puff on 'gaspers' (cigarettes) – are garbed in a selection of sweaters, greatcoats, boots, goatskin jerkins, woolly hats, berets and caps, and weighed down with kit, supplies, bandoleers, binoculars and guns. The stars' performances are excellent. Niven's wisecracks (and a booby-trapped dead rat) add the only levity to proceedings, as these hard men demonstrate the importance of being earnest.

Guns of Navarone presents some spectacular action scenes and the sea storm which wrecks the fishing boat and a dive-bombing Stuka attack in the ravines of the 'Devil's Playground' are convincingly staged. But it is the finale that is most memorable – and here all credibility dispels. Maria and Brown steal a motorboat and Andrea and Spiros create a diversion, shooting it out with the German garrison. Brown is knifed in the guts, Spiros is gunned down and Andrea is wounded. Mallory and Miller infiltrate the fortress, where Miller rigs the ammunition hoist with explosives. The huge calibre guns and their cave lair are a formidable piece of set design and their destruction is fittingly grandiose. In their protective goggles, white cowls and gauntlets, the German gun crews resemble technicians watching an A-bomb test. When the Germans open up, finding their range on the approaching destroyers, the descending hoist triggers a cataclysm. The guns tumble into the sea below, the rock promontory is ripped asunder and the blazing wreckage of the emplacement resembles a smoking volcano. Sharing a gasper on a destroyer, Miller tells Mallory that he didn't think they could do it. 'Tell you the truth', smiles Mallory, 'Neither did I'. Mallory and Andrea's vendetta is forgotten by the finale. As they part company – with Andrea to continue the fight on Navarone with Maria – Mallory asks Andrea what chance he has of survival: 'I'm not so easy to kill', smiles the Greek.

The film's Oscar nominations included Best Picture, Director, Adapted Screenplay and Best Score, but it only won Best Special Effects awards for Bill Warrington (visual) and Vivian C. Greenham (audible). It was the biggest hit of 1961 when released through Columbia Pictures and spawned many imitators (for example *Tobruk*, *Raid on Rommel* and *Legion of the Damned*) and one direct sequel, *Force 10 from Navarone* (1978), with several of the original characters, but none of the cast.

Andrew V McLaglen's *The Sea Wolves: The Last Charge of the Calcutta Light Horse* (1980) reunited Peck and Niven on another mission improbable. It told the true story of a ragtag bunch of retired ex-servicemen from Boer War outfit the Calcutta Light Horse, who plan to sink three German freighters – the *Ehrensfels, Drachenfels* and *Braunfels* – which are moored in the neutral Portuguese harbour of Marmagoa in Goa, in March 1943. The *Ehrensfels* is a radio ship which is tipping-off U-boats with information on Allied shipping in the Indian Ocean. Robert Hoffmann and Dan Van Husen appeared as the U-boat commander and his first officer, and the impressive British supporting cast includes many familiar faces amongst the aged commandos: Trevor Howard, Patrick Macnee, Donald Houston, Patrick Allen, Percy Herbert, Kenneth Griffith, Graham Stark, Allan Cuthbertson, Brook Williams and Jack Watson. Incumbent screen James Bond Roger Moore played an SOE agent who becomes romantically involved with British ex-pat Agnes Cromwell (Barbara Kellermann): she is revealed to be a German agent. Moore's performance closely resembles that of 007 and Matt Monro (from *From Russia with Love*) crooned the ballad 'The Precious Moments' over the film's end titles.

Set 'Somewhere in the Greek Islands 1944' George Pan Cosmatos' *Escape to Athena* (1979) attempted to rekindle a little of *The Guns of Navarone*'s spirit, with an interesting cast and Rhodes locations. Major Otto Hecht is excavating an archaeological dig using Allied prisoners of war (POWs) as labour and plans to transport the unearthed treasures to Switzerland. An Allied invasion of the German-occupied island is imminent and the Greek resistance led by Zeno (Telly Savalas) – who operates from a brothel run by his lover Eleana (Claudia Cardinale) – work with the prisoners to take over Stalag VII Z. Zeno really plans to raid a mountainside monastery, supposedly to rescue a fortune in treasured antiquities, but really to destroy a V-2 rocket trained on the Allied invasion fleet.

Presented by TV mogul Lew Grade, *Escape to Athena* is all-star hokum of the highest order which bears absolutely no relation whatsoever to World War II. Roger Moore played German Major Hecht with tongue in cheek. He delivers a parodic performance as the opportunistic 'art collector' (Nazi looter) and such lines as, 'Svitzerland ain't just cuckoo clocks, chocolates and vatches'. Telly (real name Aristotle) Savalas, a New Yorker of Greek extraction, was ideal as the Greek resistance leader, though his black turtle neck jumper and bling silver crosses and chains make him resemble a cabaret show mind reader. Other cast members include Sonny Bono (half of Sonny and Cher) as Italian chef Bruno Rotelli, Anthony Valentine as SS Major Volkmann, David Niven as archaeologist Professor Blake and Richard Roundtree as US POW Sergeant Nat Judson. Michael Sheard played comedy relief German Sergeant Mann. Elliott Gould and Stefanie Powers were two captured USO entertainers: Jewish stand-up comic Charlie Dane and vaudevillian Dottie Delmar. Gould's mugging and wisecracks wear a bit thin, but he delivers the classic line 'Are you still here?' to William Holden (in an unbilled cameo as a POW) – a nod to Holden's performance in *Stalag 17*. Beautiful Powers resembles 1940s pin-up girl Betty Grable and performs a burlesque striptease to distract the German garrison, which enables the prisoners to escape.

The real star of the film is Rhodes. As photographed by Gilbert Taylor in Panavision, the locations are tremendous. The accomplished aerial photography shows off the setting to its best advantage, as the camera glides around the island. The spectacular clifftop acropolis at Lindos can be seen in the opening sequence and Lindos and Rhodes town were used for the fictional setting of Karya. The POW camp and the archaeological dig were filmed south of Rhodes, at the spa and beach cove at Kalithea. *Athena* throws everything at the audience, from U-boats and motorcycle chases, to POW escapes, heists and burning oil depots. There's also James Bond espionage (silenced pistols are in evidence, in addition to crossbows, garrottes, slingshots and machine guns) and prescient technology. When Zeno and the POWs abseil into the monastery, a colossal shiny black V-2 is wheeled out, its crew dressed in back uniforms and wearing helmets with mirrored visors, like extras from a sci-fi movie. When Major Hecht teams up with the POWs, Moore transforms into 007, wrestling German frogmen, rescuing imperilled Dottie and driving a burning speedboat through a fiery oil slick. The stunt work, overseen by Vic Armstrong, is dynamic. Every German falls over after being shot once, while the heroes survive hails of bullets without injury. Lalo Schifrin provided the twanging, Hellenic-flavoured bouzouki score and the choreographer was Arlene Phillips, later of BBC TV's *Strictly Come Dancing.* The film ends with Savalas and Cardinale dancing together in the town square during a night of celebration for the island's liberation. There is something undeniably moving about this simple scene – two movie stars laughing and dancing – that says more about a lost age of filmmaking than about any sentiment associated with the war.

With its partisan heroes battling against all odds for their liberty, the Yugoslavian theatre has proved popular with war filmmakers. Yugoslavia's Communist freedom fighters led by Marshal Tito (real name Josip Broz) represented the only occupied country to win its own liberation through partisan action and resistance. Since its invasion by Axis forces in 1941, Yugoslavia had been embroiled in a guerrilla war, as Tito's well-organised partisan rebels harassed the occupying Italian and German forces, in addition to fighting the pro-Nazi 'Chetnik' partisan faction led by Draza Mihailovic. Tito and his army hid out in the mountains and struck with ferocity, while the Germans and their allies fought back with equal savagery, shooting and hanging suspected partisans and collaborators. With the surrender of Italy in 1943, Tito's forces commandeered the Italian army's equipment and thereafter were a force to be reckoned with, eventually linking up with Russian troops. Yugoslavia was finally liberated in October 1944.

With its distinctive landscape – white limestone rock outcrops, lush grass valleys, mountains, forests and waterfalls – Yugoslavia became a popular filming location for international cinema in the 1950s and 1960s. When it came to their own history, proud Yugoslavians had no qualms about depicting their national heroes on film or for international war movies to be shot on location there. The finest film of the Yugoslavian struggle was the $12 million Yugoslavian-Italian-US-German co-production *The Battle on the River Neretva* (1969), which depicts the Axis offensive against Yugoslav partisans from January to April 1943. The partisans have no planes or tanks – only firearms and artillery – and cart everything with them, including their families, livestock and wounded. They are riven with hunger and further decimated by constant Axis air attacks, blizzards, mud and a Typhus epidemic.

Neretva was directed by Veljko Bulajic, who had helmed *Hill of Death* (1962 – *Kozara*) detailing partisans defending the mountain village of Kozara (now in Bosnia and Herzegovina) from German assault. *Neretva* recreates Plan Weiss, the Axis offensive masterminded by General Lohring (Curd Jürgens) and carried out by his field commander Colonel Kranzer (Hardy Krüger). The partisans are trapped between Kranzer's Panzers and Axis forces: the Italians under General Morelli (Anthony Dawson), the Chetniks and the fascist Yugoslavians, the black-clad Ustachians. The partisans trek 300km to the River Neretva, breaking through the fortified Italian lines at Prozor. But when they finally reach the Neretva Bridge, demolition experts have been ordered to blow it up, as Chetniks lurk in wait on the opposite bank. With their backs to the river, the partisans make a stand against Kranzer's forces. During this tactical game, the Partisans rig a temporary bridge and cross the Neretva, only to face the massed Chetnik cavalry.

In its original 175-minute version, *Bitka Na Neretvi* was nominated for a Best Foreign Film Oscar, but the US print, *The Battle of Neretva*, was cut to 102 minutes. The finest English language version is *The Battle on the River Neretva*, the 127-minute print released on UK home video in the 1980s. The film follows the story of the People's Army, which is portrayed by international star names and Yugoslavian actors. Yul Brynner played demolitions expert Vlado, with Sheyla Rozin his fellow engineer. Zagreb-born Sylva Koscina played field medic Danitza and Ljubisa Samardjic played her brother, machine-gunner Novak. Lojze Rozman was Danitza's lover, infantry commander Ivan. Pavle Vuisic was ambulance driver Jordan, Fabijan Sovagovic was Mad Bosko and Oleg Vidov played Typhus victim Nikola. In the film's most moving scenes, nurse Nada (Milena Dravic) catches typhus. When Nikola sees her emaciated by disease – her skin pale, her eyes red-rimmed and her beautiful long blonde hair shorn – he tells her comfortingly: 'You're beautiful'. Franco Nero and 'Howard Ross'/Renato Rossini played Italian artillerymen Captain Michael Riva and Sergeant Mario, who renounce fascism and join Tito's partisans. For the Chetniks, Orson Welles cropped up in a cameo as a senator and Addurrahman Shala played sadistic, long-haired Colonel Demarcozi. Ukrainian actor-director Sergei Bondarchuk played Partisan artillery commander Martin (Martik in the original version). Bondarchuk directed the four-part *War and Peace* (1968) and the feature film *Waterloo* (1970 – which also featured a cameo by Welles), both of which were praised for their sweeping Napoleonic battles.

The lavish budget allowed Bulajic to stage some of the greatest combat scenes in war movie history, which are in evidence even in truncated English language prints. This is no conventional war, but a 'saloon brawl' war of attrition. German planes bomb towns and strafe Partisan columns stumbling through winding valleys, mountain passes and snowscapes. The destruction of the Neretva Bridge is an impressive special effect and the numerous battles deploy hundreds of extras, weapons, artillery and vehicles. The German Panzers are an international mix of armour, mainly Russian T-34s and US Shermans. Tomislav Pinter's Panavision cinematography captures the film's earthy tones and the costumes – especially the partisans' ragtag collection of makeshift 'uniforms' – are authentically weathered. For the final pitched battle, a squad of partisans (including Novak, Danitza and Jordan) hold a hill to the last defender against a Chetnik cavalry charge in a memorably spectacular sequence. When the Germans attack a partisan field hospital in a church, the patients sing patriotically to raise moral, illustrating the power of music and its ties with national pride and identity. The original three-hour version was scored by Vladimir Kraus-Rajteric, but his music was replaced in English language versions by Bernard Herrmann compositions: huge, rumbling orchestrations which thunder over the dramatic Yugoslavian landscape. With the partisan army safely across the Neretva, Vlado torches the makeshift wooden bridge, as the proud, victorious People's Army march on, to forge a new nation.

Though it is neither the biggest-budgeted nor the most historically accurate war movie, Roger Corman's *The Secret Invasion* (1964) is one of the most entertaining. In Cairo in 1943, as the Allies are about to invade Italy, disgraced British Major Richard Mace (Stewart Granger) assembles a group of convicted criminals for a special mission: to create a second front in the Balkans and distract Axis forces. They must spring Italian commander-in-chief General Quadri (Enzo Fiermonte) from the Nazi fortress prison in Dubrovnik, so that Quadri, a non-fascist, will convince the Italian forces in Yugoslavia to join the Allies. The five convicts are forger Simon Fell (Edd Byrnes), assassin John Durrell (Henry Silva), Italian mafioso Roberto Rocca (Raf Vallone), art thief and master-of-disguise Jean Saval (William Campbell) and IRA demolition expert Terrence Scanlon (Mickey Rooney). They arrive in Dubrovnik and tunnel into the fortress from a graveyard mausoleum, but are captured by the Germans – which at least gains them access to Quadri.

Made on a $600,000 budget from United Artists over a six-week schedule, *The Secret Invasion* predated the similarly plotted *The Dirty Dozen* by three years. Corman filmed in the picturesque port of Dubrovnik. The red-tiled roofs, whitewashed architecture, sunshine and azure harbour look tremendous in grainy Eastmancolor and Panavision, considerably enhancing the production values. *Secret Invasion*'s other assets are its fast-moving story and good performances by a well-chosen cast of pros. Actors of the calibre of Vallone, Granger and Silva can do this kind of action-adventure in their sleep, though Rooney's variable Irish accent is a hoot. Mia Massina played partisan Mila, who carries explosives to the commandos hidden in her baby's blanket. There's a harrowing scene when Durrell, in attempting to stifle her baby's cries to avoid alerting Germans patrolling the graveyard, accidentally suffocates the child. If the film has a flaw it is its lack of German and Italian troops, with the fortress seemingly patrolled by half a dozen guards. But for the finale – as the commandos (disguised as Germans) escape into the hills with Quadri – Corman pulled out the stops (and his chequebook) as hundreds of Germans swarm from the fortress. The commandos and partisans are whittled down: Fell is felled, Saval selflessly catches a grenade and is blown up, Mila is shot, Scanlon dies while knocking out a pillbox and wounded Mace gives the German bloodhounds the runaround, until he slumps, dead. Rocca and Durrell discover that Quadri is in fact a pro-Nazi impostor so Durrell, still dressed in a Nazi uniform, executes him before the assembled Italian forces, affording 'Quadri' a martyr's death and inciting the Italian troops to storm Dubrovnik. *The Secret Invasion* was a deserved hit, taking $3 million when released by United Artists.

The Yugoslavian-shot *Operation Cross Eagles* (1969) was actor Richard Conte's only foray into directing. In 1943, US commando Sergeant Macafee (Rory Calhoun) and his men successfully blow up a German fuel depot in Capodistria, Yugoslavia. They are recruited by US Army Intelligence Lieutenant Bradford (Conte), whose company of commandos has been massacred as they landed on the coast at Piran. Working with Yugoslavian partisans – including beautiful double-agent Anna Di Paola (Aili King) – Bradford's mission is to rescue British Captain Scovill (Phil Brown) from the military prison at Socerb, near the Italian-Yugoslav border. Scovill is a courier who has important information pertaining to the Allied invasion of the Balkans, codenamed Operation Cross Eagles. Their initial attempt to raid the crumbling prison (disguised as red-robed monks) fails, so Bradford and crew kidnap SS Colonel Streich (Rick West) in the village of Socerb. They agree to exchange the colonel for Scovill in an elaborate hostage exchange staged in tidal salt fields. By clever timing, the German troop dinghies are beached by the ebbing tide, while Bradford's bunch free Scovill and kidnap German Admiral Von Vogels (Relja Basic) from his HQ. It transpires that Von Vogels' kidnap was Bradford's objective all along – Operation Cross Eagles didn't exist, but the Chief of the German Adriatic fleet will be useful during the forthcoming invasion of Italy.

Cross Eagles' low-budget roughness may discourage fans of big-budget war epics, but the well-crafted story is convincingly enacted. Imaginative characters include the admiral's always-suspicious aide, Fulda (Rada Duricin), and a partisan who wears a waistcoat which sheathes his many knives. This is primitive filmmaking, but like Corman's *Secret Invasion*, the authentically low-key settings and Spartan cast work in the film's favour. The salt fields, used at the beginning and end of the film, are particularly memorable. The scene where Bradford's squad are ambushed on landing, firstly by a German patrol near a beached boat and then by a fighter plane in the vast shallow harbours, demonstrates great imagination and visual flair.

Guy Hamilton's *Guns of Navarone* sequel *Force 10 from Navarone* (1978) was scripted by Carl Foreman from the 1968 novel by Alistair MacLean. The novel takes Miller, Mallory and Andrea into Yugoslavia, but the film has only Mallory (Robert Shaw) and Miller (Edward Fox) sent to occupied Yugoslavia in 1943 to kill their betrayer from Navarone, laundry-boy Nicolai, who tipped the Germans off about their mission. The duo are dispatched with Lieutenant-Colonel Barnsby and his US Rangers, codenamed 'Force 10' (a storm as measured on the Beaufort Scale), who are to blow up a bridge on the River Neretva and save a partisan army trapped by the Germans in the Zenica Cage. This scenario is loosely based on the Battle of Neretva. Barnsby's Rangers are decimated and Barnsby, Miller, Mallory and escaped US prisoner Sergeant Weaver are captured by Chetnik rebels sympathetic to the Nazis. When the raiders eventually contact friendly partisans, Mallory finds Nicolai posing as partisan Captain Lescovar.

Force 10 wisely dropped some of the novel's protagonists – Petar, a blind Chetnik folk balladeer with a speech impediment and his sister Maria – and instead cashed in on current film franchises. Harrison Ford, fresh from *Star Wars* (1977), was cast as Barnsby, while Barbara Bach and giant Richard Kiel from *The Spy Who Loved Me* (1977) also appeared – as partisan double-agent

Maritza Petrovich and sadistic Captain Drazak of the Chetniks (inspired by Chetnik leader Draza). Ex-American Football star Carl Weathers, best-known as boxer Apollo Creed in the 'Rocky' films, played Weaver and Robert Shaw was a hot property following the phenomenal success of *Jaws* (1977). In *Guns of Navarone*, bucktoothed laundry boy Nicolai was played by ferret-like Tutte Lemkow, who in this sequel has metamorphosed into Italian heartthrob Franco Nero. Nero is effective in one of his few villainous roles and Nicolai/Lescovar is shot dead by Barnsby when he's exposed as the traitor. The film's most interesting character is Miller from Churchill's 'Department of Dirty Tricks', who carries a suitcase loaded with explosive gadgets. This is the only WWII movie to feature booby-trapped, exploding dog turds and in a memorable scene a German officer is decapitated by a taut wire across the road, as he's standing up in his speeding half-track.

Force 10 was filmed on location in Yugoslavia, Malta and Jersey in the Channel Islands. Some of the Chetniks have bandaged faces, due to scars caused by flamethrowers, adding an eerie menace to their presence. The forested valley, a concrete dam and the bridge make a memorable setting for the climax. The saboteurs decide the only way to destroy the bridge and prevent German forces annihilating the partisans is to burst the Neretva Dam further upstream. When the German army mount their offensive across the bridge (in American M3 half-tracks and Russian T-34 tanks) the dam blows, washing away the bridge, which is staged convincingly with excellent special effects and miniatures. Ron Goodwin's busy score almost reprises the theme from *Star Wars* for this bridge demolition scene. Only after the bridge has been destroyed do the mission's survivors – Mallory, Miller, Weaver and Barnsby – realise they are stranded on the wrong side of the river.

Martin Ritt's *5 Branded Women* (1960) depicted five women (Silvana Mangano, Vera Miles, Barbara Bel Geddes, Jeanne Moreau and Carla Gravina) who are ostracised for fraternising with the enemy and become shaven-headed partisans. Yugoslavia's guerrilla war featured in Ealing's *Undercover* (1943). Louis King's *Chetniks* (1942 – *Chetniks: The Fighting Guerrillas*) inadvertently supported the wrong side when it didn't bother to check that Chetniks were pro-Nazi. The Yugoslavian-made *Bomb at 10.10* (1966) had partisans and US POW camp escapee airman George Montgomery versus the Nazis. Leonardo Bercovici's *Square of Violence* (1963), starring Broderick Crawford, Bibi Andersson and Valentina Cortese, was the Ardeatine Caves massacre perpetrated by the Nazis in Rome transposed to a Yugoslavian setting. The Yugoslavian-made epic *The Fifth Offensive* (1973 – *Sutjeska*) starred Richard Burton (as Tito) and Irene Papas (from *Guns of Navarone*). In the German-made, anti-Nazi *The Last Bridge* (1953) Catherine Schell's Nazi nurse is captured by Tito's partisans. The German invasion of Yugoslavia and the country's fight for freedom also appears in the decade-spanning *Underground* (1995).

In Hajrudin Krvavac's *Battle Squadron* (1979 – *Battle of the Eagles*), Major Dragan (Bekim Fehmiu) is assigned by Tito to counter the threat of the Luftwaffe against their ground troops with the formation by volunteers of the First Partisan Airforce, in May 1942. Filmed on location in Yugoslavia, the film has good aerial and landscape photography, and some explosive action scenes of ground-to-air combat and dogfights. Ljubisa Samardjic (from *Battle of Neretva*) is memorable as daredevil ace pilot Zare, though the film is a rather rose-tinted, sentimental version of events. The heroic if under-equipped partisans are pitted against typically clichéd German bad guys. Their airforce, which consists of ancient biplanes and stolen Luftwaffe fighters, operate from improvised airfields that are just fields. They are forever short on fuel and ammunition and their bombs (which are dropped by hand from the planes) are made from sewer pipes and gunpowder. The original title was *Partisanska Eskadrila*, literally 'Partisan Escadrille'. Rather like Tito's partisan forces, these dubbed-in-English, shot-in-Yugoslavia adventures are often vastly underrated. Aided by their authentic period kit, authentic action and daredevil stunt work, and good stories, these films – and particularly *The Battle on the River Neretva* – hold their own with Hollywood war epics of the era.

Chapter 7

THE DESERT WAR (1940–43)

The origins of the confrontation in North Africa – the desert war that was decided by the first and second battles of El Alamein in 1942 – had its genesis in the thirties. Italian dictator Benito Mussolini harboured ambitions to create a new Roman Empire in East Africa. Italy's occupied territories included Ethiopia (then called Abyssinia), Eritrea and Italian Somaliland, but it ran into trouble when it invaded British Somaliland in August 1940. British General Wavell retaliated into Ethiopia and Eritrea in January 1941 and the Italians were finally defeated in the region in November. Italian naval power was negated when its fleet was attacked by British Swordfish biplane torpedo bombers in the Bay of Taranto on 11 November 1940 and defeated at the naval Battle of Matapan (March 1941). Italian empire-building activities in North Africa featured in a trio of documentaries: *The Great Challenge* (1936), *The Paths of the Heroes* (1937) and *Abyssinia* (1939). Italian troops from Libya invaded Egypt (which was British territory) in September 1940. Wavell's army, the so-called Western Desert Force (later renamed the 8th Army), counterattacked and drove the Italians out of Egypt and into Libya, taking Bardia, Tobruk and Derna along the Mediterranean coast. By February 1941 the Western Desert Force reached El Agheila where they were halted, partly by overstretched supply lines and partly because Churchill required Wavell to combat the German invasion of Greece. This British Libyan offensive had been highly successful, with low British casualties for 130,000 Italian prisoners taken.

To protect Axis interests in North Africa – and to bail Mussolini out – Hitler sent two Panzer divisions to Libya in February 1941 under the command of master tactician Erwin Rommel. Rommel was a decorated infantry commander in WWI and had authored a book, *The Infantry Attacks* (1937). He'd been successful during the invasion of France and took the helm of this German-Italian Panzerarmee, the 'Afrika Korps'. The Axis forces planned to move east through Egypt and take the valuable oil fields of the Middle East, while the Allies strove to

The Desert Fox: James Mason leads from the front as master tactician Erwin Rommel in Henry Hathaway's biopic *The Desert Fox: The Story of Rommel* (1951). Courtesy Kevin Wilkinson Collection.

retain control of the Suez Canal. Rommel mounted a Libyan offensive in March 1941 and by April had driven through the fortified Gazala Line and pushed the British into Egypt. Only the redoubt at the port of Tobruk remained in British hands, but following a 242-day siege the fortress city and its vital stock of supplies fell in early 1942. One of the problems with the desert war was logistics: the British base was in Alexandria, Egypt, while the Axis' was in Tripoli, Libya. Whenever one force made inroads, it overstretched its supply infrastructure and enabled the enemy to counterattack. The climate didn't help, with scorching days followed by freezing nights, and desert winds whipped up sandstorms which filtered grit into equipment, rendering it useless. Landmine fields were laid by both sides, making seemingly harmless dunes and sand flats treacherous. During this campaign, the British mounted three offensives into Libya, but the Afrika Korps repulsed them. For his wily tactics and management of resources Rommel earned the epithet 'The Desert Fox'. In January 1942, Rommel attacked again, his bravado outflanking manoeuvres outwitting the British commanders. This time Rommel's Afrika Korps chased the British forces deep into Egypt and part of the British army was besieged in Marsa Matrûh on the Egyptian coast. The main British force pulled back to the El Alamein line, 60 miles west of Alexandria, as it seemed they were about to lose the North African campaign and with it control of Egypt.

Many war films have been set in this to-and-fro Libyan and Egyptian campaign. James Mason played the title role in Henry Hathaway's biopic *The Desert Fox: The Story of Rommel* (1951), which was controversial in its day for its sympathetic depiction of the master strategist. It was based on Rommel's meticulously researched biography, written by Brigadier Desmond Young, who appears as himself in the film, as a POW captive in North Africa. Through the use of archive battle footage, it followed Rommel's career from North Africa to his role in the overhaul of the Atlantic Wall sea defences in France, his part in an assassination attempt on Hitler and his subsequent suicide in 1944.

Robert Wise's *The Desert Rats* (1953) had Mason reprise his role as Rommel in a brief cameo, but mainly detailed the siege of Tobruk in 1941. It was during the North African campaign that the British 8th Army earned the name 'The Desert Rats'. The film depicts the heroism of the 9th Australian Division under the command of Captain Tammy MacRoberts (Richard Burton) and their defence of the Tobruk perimeter. The monochrome combat scenes are particularly impressive, with the Afrika Korps looming out of the desert and the 'Rats' crawling from their defensive foxholes in the ground to open fire. These scenes, a combination of staged and stock footage, are very convincing. As the siege progresses, the Australians launch night-time hit-and-run raids on the German positions and on 9 July MacRoberts leads a commando attack on an ammunition dump. By air and artillery barrage, Rommel keeps up the relentless assault and MacRoberts' men are ordered to hold El Duda, a strategically important hill on the Allies left flank, until General Claude Auchinleck's relief column can arrive (depicted by archive footage of Mk IV Churchill tanks). *Desert Rats* is an excellent war movie and one of Burton's finest films. He's ideally cast as MacRoberts, the tough taskmaster who hopes one day to see his newborn son. About to set off on the commando raid, MacRoberts chats to Tommy Bartlet (Robert Newton), his aide who was also once his schoolteacher. 'If I don't …' MacRoberts begins, then stops himself and smiles: 'I'll see you tomorrow'. *Desert Rats* was shot on studio-bound 'exteriors' at Twentieth Century-Fox and on location in San Diego and Palm Springs, California. Charles Chauval's *The Rats of Tobruk* (1944) also depicted Australian involvement in North Africa.

Burton was again a British officer in Nicholas Ray's *Bitter Victory* (1957), a US-French co-production shot in Libya. Set during the desert campaign against Rommel, the film detailed a love triangle between cowardly Major David Brand (a horribly miscast Curd Jürgens, who attempts to pass his German accent off as South African), his wife Jane (Ruth Roman) and her lover Captain James Leith (Burton). Brand and Leith lead a commando raid on a German command post in Benghazi, to steal vital papers from a safe. The mission is successful, but on the return journey Brand eliminates his competition for Jane's affections by allowing Leith to be bitten by a scorpion, then abandons him in the desert and in the ambiguous ending, perhaps even strangles him during a sandstorm. On his return, Brand receives the DSO for bravery. Christopher Lee played commando Sergeant Barney, Nigel Green was safecracker Private Wilkins and Raymond Pellegrin played the commandos' Arab guide, Mokrane. Fred Matter played German officer Oberst Lutze, who manages to burn many of the captured documents before Brand can hand them over to Army Intelligence. Leith was a typical Burton role: intelligent, tough and Welsh. *Bitter Victory* was cut from it original 100-minute UK release to a pacier 82 minutes in the US.

Probably the most famous war film set in this theatre has few reference points to the historical conflict. J. Lee Thompson's *Ice Cold in Alex* (1958) told the story of a desert trek by British 'crate' Katy – an Austin K2 ambulance with a leaky pump – from besieged Tobruk to Alexandria through the Libyan and Egyptian wastelands of dunes, rocks, quicksand and the salt marsh of the Qattara Depression. The party consists of alcoholic Captain Anson (John Mills), his sergeant-major, Tom Pugh (Harry Andrews) and two nurses, Sister Diana Murdoch (Sylvia Syms) and Sister Denise Norton (Diane Clare). They pick up Captain Van Der Poel (Anthony Quayle), who claims to be South African but is later revealed to be Otto Lutz, an Axis spy. During his latrine visits he radios information to his comrades. The narrative, based on a true story by Christopher Landon, is set in 1942, when the Germans have broken through and the British are in retreat towards Alamein. The cross-country truck trek resembles *The Wages of Fear* (1952) and the story's tension is played for every last bead of sweat.

Ice Cold in Alex was shot on location in the Libyan desert, in Tripoli and at Elstree Studios, Borehamwood. The monochrome cinematography by Gilbert Taylor is stark and the cast deliver stalwart performances, which has established *Ice Cold* as a British classic. The ambulance is an actual Austin K2, though the German patrol half-tracks are US M3s marked with the Afrika Korps' swastika and palm tree insignia. In a memorable scene, the party toil to manoeuvre Katy up a steep, soft sand dune by winding the starting handle to drive the wheels in reverse. The scene when the ambulance gingerly crosses a minefield is the best such sequence in war movie cinema. 'There's something under my foot', says Van Der Poel nervously. Jittery-when-sober Anson carefully unearths the 'mine' which turns out to be a bean tin. When drunken Anson's rash actions cause the death of Denise, he vows his next drink will be in his favourite bar in Alexandria – an ice-cool Carlsberg lager in Bar Canopus. Despite Van Der Poel being their enemy, the group bond and though sheer grit, determination, sweat and ingenuity make it to Alexandria. In the final scene, Anson instructs the barman to 'Set 'em up Joe' and downs the precious liquid that was 'Worth waiting for'. This scene took six takes, with Mills swallowing a glass of lager in each one. The US print, cut from 125 minutes to 76, was retitled *Desert Attack*, though with its protagonists and their vehicle pitted against an inhospitable landscape it could easily have been called 'The Wages of Beer'.

Released as *Desert Patrol* in the US, Rank's *Sea of Sand* (1958) was shot on location in Libya, in the region known as Tripolitania. The film was dedicated to its subject, the British Long Range Desert Group (LRDG): scruffy-but-ruthless crack units who operated behind enemy lines during the North Africa campaign in heavily-armed 4x4 Jeeps and Chevrolet WA trucks. *Sea of Sand* features a raid by one such 'pirate' crew on the Omara supply depot in October 1942. The mission is led by unshaven Captain Cotton (Michael Craig) who clashes with smart Captain Williams (John Gregson), a specialist in minesweeping. Other members of the unit are sapper Corporal Matheson (Barry Foster), White, called 'Blanco'

(Percy Herbert), a farmer in civvy street, and drunken Brody (Richard Attenborough). At the depot, Cotton discovers the compound unexpectedly contains two divisions of brand new Panzers. Their mission is a costly success; the depleted unit is pursued by spotter planes and the Afrika Korps (driving American M3 half-tracks) and few make it back to base alive. Directed by Guy Green, *Sea of Sand* has worn well. Attenborough may be the star, but it's charismatic Craig's film, as the ex-architect who used to build things: 'Now I knock them down'. The monochrome photography adds realism and the LRDG drive authentic Chevrolet trucks. There are some effective combat scenes of running battles between the LRDG and German light armour, but nothing quite matches the incongruity of badly wounded Blanco, left behind in a machine gun nest to hold off the pursuing Afrika Korps, listening to a gardening programme on the wireless in the middle of the desert. When the Afrika Korps arrive, he puts up a fight against two half-tracks, blasting one, but is riddled with bullets as the radio plays Vera Lynn's 'What a Day We'll Have'. *Sea of Sand* was influential on antiheroic, cynical 1960s war movies and the LRDG were also the focus of the popular US TV series *The Rat Patrol* (1966–68).

By far the most popular North African-set war films are a series of generic 'desert' movies, where the mere presence of sand dunes tells us all we need to know about the theatre. Any historical perspective is subverted by camel-riding nomads, palm-treed oases, belly dancers and bazaars. Arthur Hiller's *Tobruk* (1967) is set in September 1942, as Rommel pushed on towards El Alamein. A disparate group of Allies are sent on a special mission behind enemy lines, across 800 miles of Sahara. They are pitted against what the introduction calls, 'Adolf Hitler's high-stepping Afrika Korps', which sounds like a dance troop. The Allies must blow up a concrete gun emplacement dominating Tobruk harbour and detonate Rommel's underground fuel dumps, which will stall his Afrika Korps' push east. The Special Identification Group (SIG, a squad of German-Jews fighting with the British) led by Captain Bergman (George Peppard, deploying a ropy German accent) disguise themselves as Afrika Korps. British Long Range Desert Group forces led by Colonel Harker (Nigel Green) pose as their prisoners of war. American Major Craig (Rock Hudson) is their guide through the minefield-infested desert. The film was written by Leo Gordon, who also plays one of the SIGs.

Tobruk was filmed in arid locations at Tucson (Arizona), Almeria (Spain) and California by Universal Pictures, with help from the 40th Armored Division of the Californian Army National Guard. It was a big box office success, despite losing its way in unnecessary subplots: when it is discovered there is a murderous traitor in their midst, the film begins to resemble a whodunit. In other diversions, the Allies encounter nomadic Tuareg tribesmen and two German agents. The cast includes Percy Herbert and Norman Rossington as two bickering soldiers (Irishman Dolen and cockney Alfie), and Jack Watson played tough Sergeant-Major Tyne. The film is well photographed, with impressive helicopter shots of the Allies' truck and half-track convoy sweeping through the desert. The SIG travel in half-tracks which are supposed to be German, but are actually American M3s, while the German and Italian tanks are American M47s.

Much ordnance did change hands during the desert war, but each side did have a few vehicles of their own and German SdKfz 251 half-tracks don't resemble US M3s. The action scenes, especially the pitched battle climax beneath the cliffs of Tobruk, are well handled, with flamethrowers and tanks put to good use. The special effects blend well with the action and the scene when Hudson and co commandeer a German tank and blast the fuel dump results in an impressive fireball inferno. Having achieved their mission, many of the Allies are captured but Bergman and Craig make it to their naval pick-up point at Sollum.

For Henry Hathaway's *Raid on Rommel* (1971) the makers also raided the Universal archives. Captain Foster (Richard Burton) from 8th Army intelligence and a group of 5th Commandos attack the harbour guns in German-held Tobruk. They also spot a stockpile of Panzers and deduce that Rommel's underground fuel supply must be nearby. Virtually half the film is footage lifted from *Tobruk* – all the scenes of Foster's column driving towards Tobruk, an attack by a shark-nosed Kittyhawk, the destruction of the fuel dump and the detonation of the guns – with Burton and the new cast skilfully edited into the action. *Raid on Rommel* was originally made for TV and has that bland, made-for-television look. Burton went through the motions as Foster, Wolfgang Preiss made a cameo appearance as philatelist Rommel and Karl Otto Alberty played Afrika Korps commander Schröder. To ensure the footage matched, Foster's team (posing as Afrika Korps) travel in US M3 half-tracks and the Germans drive US M47 tanks. Viewed back-to-back, *Tobruk* and *Raid on Rommel* make a highly entertaining double bill.

At the end of June 1942, the first Battle of El Alamein was initiated when Rommel attacked. By mid-July, his forces were contained, suffering considerable losses. General Claude Auchinleck led the British 8th Army in a counterattack, but all offensives failed. It was then that a key change was made to the British strategy. In August, General Bernard Law Montgomery was appointed commander of the 8th Army, against Churchill's wishes. Montgomery's forces numbered units from New Zealand, Australia, India, South Africa, Greece, France and Britain, and had been reinforced with troops and the recently-developed US Sherman tank. Both the Axis and British forces licked their wounds, regrouped and laid minefields in the Egyptian desert. At the end of August, the Germans attacked Alam Halfa, but the offensive was aborted on 2 September. Rommel was withdrawn from command in late September to recuperate from exhaustion and his successor was General Georg Stumme. On 23 October 1942, the second battle of El Alamein began with a British advance, which picked its way through the German minefields – the 'Devil's Garden'. On 24 October, Stumme suffered a heart attack when his car came under fire from Australian troops. Flown back into action, Rommel was in command of the Afrika Korps by 25 October. Late October was a stalemate until Montgomery instigated Operation Supercharge on 2 November, an all-out attack to break through the enemy defences. Low on fuel and ammo, and physically exhausted, the Afrika Korps began to retreat on 3 November and over the following months the British pursued the Afrika Korps all the way to Tunisia.

Giorgio Ferroni (as the pseudonymous 'Calvin Jackson Padget') directed *The Battle of El Alamein* (1968), a big-budget recreation of these events made with the cooperation of the Italian Ministry of Defence and the Italian Army General Staff. Mounted in some style by Zenith Cinematografica (Rome) and Les Films Corona (Paris), it was an ambitious attempt at telling the story of the engagement through the various combatants. Michael Rennie played an unsympathetic General Montgomery, the villain of the piece, and Robert Hossein played wily Rommel. Ferroni focuses on the Italian contribution to the campaign via two brothers. Strict, unpopular Lieutenant Giorgio Bori (Austrian 'Frederick Stafford', whose real name was Freidrich Strobel Von Stein) of the Folgore paratroopers and brave Sergeant-Major Fabio Bori (Enrico Maria Salerno) of the Bersaglieri infantry.

The screenplay, by Ernesto Gastaldi and Remigio Del Grosso, telescopes history to entertaining, sometimes confusing effect. The action begins in June 1942, with the Axis forces pushing towards the Nile, hoping to overrun Egypt and take the vital Suez Canal. 'Mussolini had given explicit orders', informs the opening blurb, 'The Italians must arrive first!' British troops ambush an Italian Bersaglieri column and Fabio's heroics save the day (this is the film's representation of the British halting Rommel's push across the desert). The narrative then jumps to the replacement of Auchinleck by Montgomery in August 1942. Montgomery complains that the British have been 'chased for 1,500 miles by a German fox', but now it is he who will do the chasing. Rommel's men are exhausted and their armour low on fuel, but he reckons that one decisive battle will open up the route to the Middle Eastern oil fields. The Axis forces set up fake fortifications, with wooden artillery and dummy troops, to confuse the British as to their strength, but the British discover the ruse. Rommel outwits the Brits however and when Montgomery orders an advance through the fortifications, they are now manned by Giorgio's paratroopers. The paratroopers' superior officer (Ettore Manni) is killed and Giorgio takes command and repels the attack. Suffering from an inflamed kidney and exhaustion, Rommel is withdrawn to recuperate and is replaced by General Stumme (Giuseppe Addobatti).

When Fabio and Giorgio reconnoitre a British minefield, Fabio is injured and Giorgio is captured by the British, where he's impressed by his humane treatment in defeat at the hands of Lieutenant Graham (George Hilton). Giorgio escapes and wanders through the desert (accompanied by stirring strings and Biblical choir on the soundtrack) and steals a jeep. He's so unpopular that when he returns to his unit in the purloined British vehicle his men consider 'accidentally' shooting him in mistake for an enemy. The British produce a bogus map of minefields, which they allow to fall into Italian hands. During an ambush, Italian paratroopers kill Lieutenant Graham, to Giorgio's regret. The Germans launch an attack through the 'safe' minefield passages clearly marked on the British map, are shelled by British artillery and decimated. During this action it is reported that Stumme has been killed and Rommel is brought back to head the Afrika Korps. The Axis forces are now outgunned. With the commencement of Operation Supercharge, Rommel orders a retreat to Tobruk. Giorgio's Italian paratroopers must act as the rearguard in the southern sector and hold for 24 hours – from midnight on 3 November – delaying Montgomery's advance. Woefully under-equipped, the paratroopers and the Italian Ariete tank unit stall the British long enough to allow Rommel's escape. Fabio, retreating with the remnants of his Bersaglieri unit, learns that the paratroopers are outflanked and rushes to warn his brother. In the final battle, Giorgio is killed and Fabio and the surviving paratroopers surrender to the British. Rommel notes: 'One day they'll say the real victory of Rommel was his retreat from El Alamein'.

In this Italian-French co-production the Germans and the British are the villains, and the Italians the heroes. The British are referred to throughout as 'the English' and 'Limeys' and this is probably the bitterest depiction of British forces' involvement in WWII. British Sergeant O'Hara (Luciano Catenacci) executes unarmed, surrendered Italian prisoners with a grenade. When Italian prisoners are loaded into a lorry, a cockney guard's voice pipes up, 'Alright you geezers, on your feet. You're taking a trip, you bloody wops'. Rennie does an excellent impersonation of Montgomery: his uniform and manner are very accurate, even down to Monty's two badges on his cap. His officers are ruddy-faced, moustachioed twits, with the sole exception of handsome Lieutenant Graham, played by suave Argentinean actor Hilton.

The Italians dislike both their German allies and their British foe. 'Those Krauts are a pain in the ass', notes Fabio and when Rommel hears of the annihilation of the Italian forces in the south, he surmises: 'Don't blame me – our corporal Hitler wished it'. The Italian army was often derided by the Allies as the most inefficient, under-equipped army of the war, with an implication of cowardice via such jokes as Italian tanks having four reverse gears and one forward. They did indeed surrender in droves when the opportunity arose, but this was more due to their sagging belief in fascism and low morale. As Rommel notes in this film, 'It's not my fault that Mussolini sent his people off to war without necessary means'. The Italian prisoners in *Battle of El Alamein* don't want to escape from a British compound when Giorgio suggests it – they are happy with the way they are being treated. The supporting cast is mostly Italian. Nello Pazzafini, Massimo Righi, Riccardo Pizzutti and Sal Borgese played Italian paratroopers, and Marco Guglielmi and Tom Felleghi were Rommel's staff. Gerard Herter played General Schwartz, a staunch Hitlerite, who ensures that Rommel is removed from command to recuperate and who is convinced the 'western plutocracies' (America) won't intervene to help the British in North Africa.

Where *Battle of El Alamein* really scores is in its scenes of desert combat, which are frantic swirls of dust and noise. The film's Military Consultant was Colonel Vittorio Giacchero and on the whole he appears to have done a fine job. The uniforms and arms for all combatants are convincing. The Italian Bersaglieri infantry are noteworthy for their helmets decorated with distinctive plumes of black feathers, which were surely the conflict's most ridiculous battledress. The production assembled a formidable array of military vehicles. Dotted throughout the film can be glimpsed Canadian three-tonne Chevrolet trucks, a German VW Kübel staff car, British 4x4 Jeeps and even an Italian Fiat 508 staff car. The Italian Ariete armoured command deploys authentic Fiat L6/40 Light Tanks, which were no match for the British armour – as an Italian paratrooper notes, it's 'Mosquitoes against elephants'. The remainder of the tanks are a mixed bag. British hardware is depicted by sandy-coloured Shermans and 1950s

American M47 Pattons (which were used for many years by the Italian army). The German armour is a mixture of US M47s and M48 Pattons and when British infantry attack the beleaguered Italian paratroopers in the finale, they deploy anachronistic US M113A2 armoured personnel carriers (which date from the early 1960s). The scenes of rolling armour and artillery barrages are well orchestrated by Ferroni and the film's ambition is to be commended. For the finale, Giorgio and his paratroops wait in ambush in their foxholes for the advancing British tanks. The paras use dynamite, Molotov cocktails and 'Human Mines' – the troops attach mines to the underside of enemy tanks from their foxholes, or suicidally rush the tanks carrying the devices. This noble defence is based on a true incident at Alamein. The battered, ragged Italian survivors surrendered to the British, having assisted Rommel's escape. After viewing this film – with its emphasis on Rommel's glorious withdrawal and the Italians' rearguard heroism – it's hard to believe that El Alamein was a British victory.

The box office success of such films as *Tobruk* established a much-copied formula. Most of the combat films set in the North African theatre depend on the plot device of blowing up or capturing a fuel dump, supply depot or oasis. Fuel and water were vital commodities for keeping the armoured columns on the move. Andre De Toth's *Play Dirty* (1968) was an ultra-cynical remake of *Sea of Sand*, with Colonel Masters (Nigel Green) sending Special Forces 'gangsters'

Captain Douglas (Michael Caine) in Axis disguise endures a dust storm (on location in Almeria, Spain) in Andre De Toth's gritty desert movie *Play Dirty* (1968). Courtesy Kevin Wilkinson Collection.

400 miles behind enemy lines through the Qattara Depression to destroy an Axis fuel depot near the coast. As posters noted: 'Forget the Medals, Throw away the Rulebook. If you want to survive ... Play Dirty'. This crack squad – including a demolitions expert, a weapons expert and two gay Arab guides – are ex-convicts, as is their leader Captain Leech (a sneering Nigel Davenport, who replaced original choice Richard Harris). Visually, this motley crew resemble the LRDG: Leech's trucks are Mercedes, but they are dressed to resemble the distinctive Chevvies. The German troops drive US M3 half-tracks with German livery. The screenplay was written by Lotte Colin and Melvin Bragg. Producer Harry Saltzman fired the original director René Clément and replaced him with De Toth. Almeria, the rock-littered desert and dunes of southern Spain, stood in for the North African desert. The palm trees at an oasis had been planted for *Lawrence of Arabia* (1962).

Leech's ruffians disguise themselves as Italians and are assigned petroleum expert Captain Douglas (Michael Caine) who clashes with scallywag Leech. 'You play dirty, Captain Leech', Douglas tells him, after Leech and his men watch the massacre of fellow British troops in an Afrika Korps ambush. The party encounter the usual desert hazards – sandstorms, Barasi nomads, booby traps and mines – but at almost two hours the film is overlong. One elaborate scene depicts the party winching their trucks up a steep incline, seemingly forever. As *Time* noted: '*Play Dirty* plods across the screen like a camel in a sandstorm'. Early in his career Caine had small roles in two World War II movies, Hammer's *The Steel Bayonet* (1957) and *A Foxhole in Cairo* (1960). In *Play Dirty*, when the squad steal a German ambulance to tend to one of their wounded and discover they have inadvertently kidnapped a nurse, the cons try to rape her: from *Ice Cold in Alex* to this. Eventually they discover the fuel dump is a dummy: the real depot is in a well-defended port. Montgomery meanwhile has achieved a breakthrough at El Alamein and is steaming along the coast. The British top brass now want the dump taken intact, but are unable to contact their commandos, who blow it up. When the British forces arrive at the port, Douglas and Leech, still disguised as Italians, surrender under a flag of truce but are mown down by a British soldier. 'Sorry sir, I didn't see the white flag'; 'Don't do it again', snaps his commanding officer.

Further North African-set action movies include *Sahara* (1943), *El Alamein* (1953), *Rommel's Treasure* (1958), *Desert Mice* (1959), *The Battle of the Damned* (1969), *Desert Battle* (1969 – *Battle in the Desert* and *Desert Assault*), *Desert Tigers* (1977) and *The Heroes* (1972 – *Kelly's Heroes* relocated to the desert, co-starring Terry-Thomas and Rods Taylor and Steiger). *Heroes Without Glory* (1971) had a group of US commandos led by a British officer up against an Afrika Korps driving post-war NATO vehicles and 'Panzers' that were US Shermans. The siege of Tobruk featured in the multi-Oscar winning drama *The English Patient* (1996), while action in North Africa was also staged as part of *The Young Lions* (1958). Sydney Lumet's *The Hill* (1965) depicted a British-run detention centre for their own soldiers, who are forced to climb a dirt hill in the compound under the sweltering Libyan sun. In Richard Lester's spoof *How I Won the War* (1967), British troops (including Michael Crawford, Roy Kinnear, Jack MacGowran, Lee

Montague, Jack Hedley and John Lennon) attempt to set up a cricket pitch in enemy-occupied territory.

Several war movies wallow in a world of espionage and spies in North Africa, the exotic locale providing added atmosphere to *The Man from Morocco* (1944) and *Hotel Sahara* (1951). *Five Graves to Cairo* (1943), Billy Wilder's imaginative remake of *Hotel Imperial* (1939), relocated the intrigue to the desert war zone. During the British retreat, fugitive soldier John Bramble (Franchot Tone) hides out in a hotel run by Farid (Akim Tamiroff) and Mouche (Anne Baxter), which becomes the headquarters for Rommel (Erich Von Stroheim). Bramble poses as a deceased hotel servant who was a German agent. Bramble finds himself entrusted with preparations for Rommel's attack east to Cairo, codenamed 'Five Graves', as it pivots on a map which indicates five points where Rommel has buried supplies and ammunition in the desert. *A Foxhole in Cairo* (1960) featured British intelligence officers tracking one of Rommel's German secret agents who is attempting to glean information about the British strategy. *Casablanca* profited from its timely release in November 1942. With its Moroccan setting, resistance leader in hiding and Nazi villains, *Casablanca* was among other things a cleverly-disguised piece of anti-Nazi propaganda which just happened to be a classic love story.

The Casablanca Conference (codenamed Symbol) took place between Roosevelt, De Gaulle and Churchill over 14–24 January 1943. The winter of 1942–43 was used as the setting for Umberto Lenzi's *Desert Commandos* (1967), with German commandos targeting Roosevelt, Churchill and Stalin ('The Big Three') in Casablanca. Stalin attended the conferences at Teheran in September 1943 and Yalta in February 1945, but wasn't in Casablanca in early 1943. *Desert Commandos* remixes the ingredients of the 'desert war movie' from the German viewpoint. Four German specialist commandos have their Christmases ruined when they are called to take part in a mission to attack the high-level conference at Casablanca to kill the trio of world leaders. Ken Clark played their commander Captain Fritz Schöeller, with Horst Frank, Carlo Hinterman, Howard Ross and Hardy Reichelt as his squad (posing as British desert commandos) and Jeanne Valerie as their Moroccan contact Faddja Hassan (a double-agent). When the commandos burst in on Churchill's speech, they discover the voice they can hear is a gramophone record. It's a trap set by the allies and US MPs mow down the would-be assassins.

Filmed on location in North Africa, *Desert Commandos* features a lively camel chase between the commandos and Tuareg nomads, and such clichés as a minefield scene (with located mines being marked out by cigarettes stuck in the ground) and an MP asking the Germans (now disguised as Americans) who was the winner of the 'Double-header between the Yankees and the Cardinals?' Such sport-orientated questions were actually employed by US intelligence to root out impostors and spies. *Desert Commandos* deploys French ordnance as US armour. The US tanks are distinctive French AMX-13s (which began production in 1952) and the US armoured cars are actually Panhard EBRs, a wheeled variation on the AMX-13.

Casablanca Express (1988), starring Jason (son of Sean) Connery and Francesco (son of Anthony) Quinn, must have used *Desert Commandos* as its research source, as it featured a plan for German paratroopers to kidnap Churchill from his train en route to a conference with Roosevelt and Stalin. *Teheran* (1947) was set around the Iranian summit between Stalin, Roosevelt and Churchill, and was also released by the tell-all title *The Plot to Kill Roosevelt. Kill Rommel* (1969) reversed the set-up, with the German commander in jeopardy from British commandos. This may have been inspired by the Keyes' Raid, a plan on the night of 13–14 November 1941 to kidnap Rommel, blow up his HQ and destroy a communications pylon near Cyrene. But Rommel wasn't in the 'Rommelhaus' in Beda Littoria and only two of the commandos survived the badly planned operation.

Following the German defeat at El Alamein, the next significant development in North Africa was the arrival of US forces. Operation Torch, the US landings in Morocco and Algeria on 8 November 1942, left the Afrika Korps caught in a pincer movement, as the Allies closed in on Tunisia from both east and west. There were three main landings in Morocco and Algeria. The Western Task Force of US troops led by General George S. Patton sailed from America and landed at Casablanca, Morocco. The Central Task Force of US troops led by General Fredendall sailed from the UK and landed at Oran in Algeria and the Eastern Task Force under General Ryder was Anglo-American and sailed from the UK to Algiers. The occupying French forces in North Africa surrendered on 10 November but German reinforcements arrived in Tunisia from Sicily to cover Rommel's retreat. The Allies pressed west but the Germans held their bridgehead. Rommel withdrew behind the defensive Mareth Line near Medenine and turned his attention to the Allied forces at his rear in Tunisia. Rommel's last victory in North Africa was the Battle of Kasserine Pass in February 1943 but the Allies managed to retake Kasserine when Patton came to the rescue. Rommel left North Africa for Berlin in March 1943 on sick leave and soon afterwards Montgomery broke the Mareth Line. The Axis forces were pushed back towards Tunis and finally surrendered on 11 May 1943.

British director Roy Boulting made two documentaries on the desert war: *Desert Victory* (1943 – detailing Montgomery's pursuit of Rommel following Alamein) and *Tunisian Victory* (1944 – co-directed by Frank Capra). Of the films set in the final phase of this campaign, Armando Crispino's *Commandos* (1968) is the most action packed. Prior to the Torch landings in October 1942, a group of Italian-American commandos posing as Italian soldiers parachute into the desert to secure an oasis and its vital water pumping station in a mission designated 'Operation Torch'. They take the oasis and imprison the Italian garrison, but German Panzer troops stationed nearby unmask the impostors, precipitating a bloody pitched battle from which there are few survivors. Lee Van Cleef and Jack Kelly played the mission's commanders: manic Sergeant Sullivan and neophyte Captain Valli. Mario Nascimbene's atmospheric oscillations on the soundtrack added atmosphere to this Italian-West German co-production. Sullivan's aide Dino was played by Romano Puppo (Van Cleef's stunt double) and the Afrika Korps officers were portrayed by Götz George and Joachim Fuchsberger. *Commandos* was shot in Sardinia with a mixed bag of modified French AMX-13s and US M47 tanks as the Panzers and their support vehicles. Western star Van Cleef trades his six-shooter for a bazooka, but he's not quite quick enough on the draw in the finale and dies a hero's death whilst facing a Panzer in the showdown.

Carol Reed's *The Way Ahead* (1944) followed a group of conscripts from all walks of life. In the wake of Dunkirk, they are transformed into soldiers of the Duke of Glendon's Light Infantry by Lieutenant Perry (David Niven) and taskmaster Sergeant Fletcher (future TV Doctor Who, William 'Billy' Hartnell). The platoon includes Stanley Holloway, Raymond Huntley, James Donald, Leslie Dwyer, Hugh Burden, Jimmy Hanley and John Laurie. On their way to Tunisia to take part in Operation Torch, the platoon's transport ship is torpedoed and they are evacuated by a destroyer (a well-staged sequence, which features Trevor Howard's film debut as a naval captain) to recuperate in Gibraltar. In March 1943 they are posted to French North Africa to face Rommel's counteroffensive. Niven recalled that *Way Ahead* was backed by the Army and screened as a training film for ten years at Sandhurst officer's college. The film was co-scripted by Peter Ustinov (who also has a cameo as the sullen French owner of Café Rispoli) and Eric Ambler. It was retitled *The Immortal Battalion* in the USA and shortened to 91 minutes. The film climaxes with the battle for a Tunisian village, as German bombers and mortars rain down a barrage. Our last sight of the heroic platoon – as they fix bayonets and vanish into a smokescreen – anticipates the 'You Have Been Watching' end title sequence of TV sitcom *Dad's Army*, in which Laurie starred as grumpy undertaker Frazer.

Samuel Fuller's *The Big Red One* (1980) followed a sergeant (Lee Marvin) and four of his men of the US 1st Infantry Division from landing in North Africa in November 1942, though Sicily and into Europe. Their episodic exploits were based on Fuller's own experiences of the war as a member of 'The Fighting 1st'. In North Africa, the 1st see action in the Kasserine Pass – they conceal themselves in foxholes and an Afrika Korps tank column rolls over the top of them. These desert scenes, like much of the film, were shot in Israel. The sergeant is wounded in action and treated in a German hospital in Tunis, until the US army liberate him (and Tunis), so he is reunited with his unit before they assault Sicily.

American actions in the Torch campaign featured in *Immortal Sergeant* (1943 – starring Henry Fonda and Thomas Mitchell), *Hell Squad* (1958), *G.I. Joe* (1945) and *Darby's Rangers* (1958). *The War Devils* (1969) opened in Tunisia 1943, as US paratroopers led by Guy Madison blow up M Battery, a gun emplacement. The subsequent US desert offensive, an atmospheric, dusty tank and infantry battle, is hampered by the fact that although the US tanks are authentic M4A2 Shermans, the Germans oppose them in ochre-painted Sherman variants, the M4A3.

Franklin J. Schaffner's *Patton* (1970 – *Patton: Lust for Glory*) was a biopic of the finest US commander of World War II, General George S. Patton Jr, as played by George C. Scott. He won a Best Actor Oscar for his accurate portrayal of 'Old Blood and Guts' but refused to accept his statuette, calling the awards a 'meat parade'. The film begins with Patton's arrival in Morocco, where he's honoured in Rabat with a parade following the Torch landings. After the US defeat in the Kasserine Pass, Patton is brought in by Eisenhower to replace incumbent 2nd Corps commander General Fredendall. Patton's arrival, in an M3 half-track silhouetted against a magnificent sky, is suitably heroic. He already has a reputation as an ace tank commander and counterattacks the Afrika Korps, bushwhacking them on a

Tunisian plain. This impressive desert ambush features sandy-coloured US M47 tanks redressed to resemble Panzer 'Tiger' tanks and US M48s as Patton's forces, while planes dogfight overhead. The rival commanders – Patton and Rommel (Karl Michael Vogler) – are master tacticians. Patton's bedside reading is *The Tank in Attack* by Erwin Rommel and when the battle is won, Patton gloats at the retreating Rommel: 'I read your book!'

The first hour of *Patton* depicts the general's exploits in North Africa. It opens with a patriotic speech from Patton (which actually dates from 4 June 1944) where he notes that 'America's never lost a war' and they are going to 'murder those lousy Hun bastards by the bushel'. This is followed by panoramic shots in DeLuxe Color and widescreen Dimension 150 of the 'Tunisian desert' (the sierras and dried-up riverbeds of Almeria, southern Spain), accompanied by Jerry Goldsmith's memorable title music: commencing with an echoing, ebbing trumpet post (using a delaying device called an echoplex), drum rolls and a church organ, it springs into life in a lively, patriotic march. Our introduction to the desert war is one of defeat. In a haunting scene, as Arabs loot and strip the corpses of US soldiers in desolate Kasserine Pass, General Omar N. Bradley (Karl Malden) surveys the carnage.

The Oscar-winning script, by Francis Ford Coppola and Edmund H. North, was based on Bradley's 1951 book *A Soldier's Soldier* and Ladislas Farago's *Patton, Order and Triumph*. The film accurately depicts its hero as a larger-than-life figure. When German fighter-bombers shell and strafe a whitewashed village where Patton's HQ is based, he stands defiantly amid the confusion and fires his pistol at the planes. Patton believes in reincarnation and writes poetry, but can't stand cowardice and won't take 'battle fatigue' as an excuse for soldiers to be hospitalised. Patton is also a military historian and learns from the past. He visits the ruins of the ancient city of Carthage (filmed at Volubilis, near Meknès, Morocco), which had been sacked by Rome 2,000 years ago. Patton turns his poorly disciplined, lax troops into 'fanatics' and drives them on to victory, making himself a war hero in the process. Critic Judith Crist deemed Scott's portrayal, 'One of the great performances of all time' and the film won Best Direction and Best Picture Oscars, among many other awards.

The North African campaign of 1941–43 provided the Axis forces with their first taste of defeat and diverted vital resources for both sides. Most importantly it gave the Allies a strong position in preparation for a sustained campaign against Europe, with the island of Sicily their next target. As *Patton* depicts, it was just a case of whose strategy they would use to take the island: Patton's or Montgomery's.

Chapter 8

WAR BEHIND THE WIRE (1940–45)

The Geneva Convention of 1929 was signed by all the major world powers except Japan and the Soviet Union. Most signature countries adhered to its rules on the treatment of prisoners, with the US and Britain providing the best conditions for their captured enemies. Germany usually treated their prisoners well, with the exception of those from Russia. As Göring remarked of Russian prisoners to the Italian Foreign Minister Count Galeazzo Ciano: 'After having eaten everything possible, including the soles of their boots, they have begun to eat each other, and what is more serious, have eaten a German sentry'. Of the five million Russian POWs taken by the Germans, only a sixth survived the war. On the Eastern Front, the SS didn't take prisoners and killed all defeated Russian soldiers, which had severe repercussions for Germany when Russia invaded German soil later in the war.

Hollywood POW films generally depict British or American prisoners of war held in Europe by German forces, and thrive on their own set of clichés. Rigid German commandants often inform their inmates 'For you ze vor is over', while unobservant guards plod the corridors and sweep the compound with searchlights, but always miss the agile prisoners. Even the most unhealthy-looking POWs suddenly become escapologists, gymnasts and acrobats, and the infirm rise, Lazarus-like, from their beds to escape. There were two principle methods of escape: 'over' and 'under' (over the wire or tunnelling under it). German POW camps in British war films tended to resemble Butlins holiday camps, or English public schools, providing reason enough to break out. Until the 1960s most British films depicted only the imprisoned English officer classes. Internationally co-financed POW movies tended to include a more interesting multinational cross-section, though in reality many camps did separate officers and enlisted men. Camps were designated 'Oflag' for officers and 'Stalag' for enlisted men. Compared to combat films, which require at the very least jeeps, tanks, artillery and explosions, POW films were cheap films to make. All that was required was a fence, some sheds, a few Nazi uniforms, some makeshift shovels or at most a vaulting horse. Audiences marvelled at the prisoners' ingenuity – an ability to create something out of nothing – which is all the more surprising as most POW films were based on fact.

The first British POW film was Basil Dearden's *The Captive Heart* (1946), which was filmed in a documentary-like realist style which later outings abandoned. Michael Redgrave played a Czech concentration camp escapee who has stolen the identity of a British soldier and writes to the dead man's wife to continue the subterfuge. Others in the cast include Jack Warner, Mervyn Johns, Jimmy Hanley, Gordon Jackson and Rachel Kempson.

British Lion's *The Wooden Horse* (1950) was based on Eric Williams' true story, *The Tunnel Escape*. It was directed by Jack Lee and filmed on location in a compound constructed in Lower Saxony in Germany, at Luneburg Heath near Soltau. Interiors were filmed in London Film Studios, Shepperton and location scenes were shot in Lübeck, Germany and Copenhagen, Denmark. The story is set in 1943 in the East Compound of Stalag Luft III, a camp for Allied officers run by the Luftwaffe. John Clinton (Anthony Steel) and Peter Howard (Leo Genn) concoct a plan to escape, by tunnelling out of the camp from beneath a wooden vaulting horse during gymnastic classes in the camp compound. Their plan succeeds and Clinton, Howard and Philip Rowe (David Tomlinson) tunnel out. Rowe heads for Danzig, while the other two make for the German port of Lübeck. Posing as French labourers, they gain passage to Copenhagen by ship and finally make it to Gothenburg in neutral Sweden, where they meet up with Rowe.

The cast included Bryan Forbes, Bill Travers, Peter Burton, Michael Goodliffe, Anthony Dawson and David Greene as POWs, Patrick Waddington played Group Captain Wardley, the Senior British Officer, and Peter Finch had a small role as an Australian officer in the prison hospital. Helge Erickssen played Sigmund and Lis Løwert his sister Kamma, who hide the escapees from the Nazis in Copenhagen. Franz Schaftheitlin was the Stalag's commandant and Hans Meyer played German guard 'Charlie', the nosy 'head ferret'. In POW slang, ferrets were special guards employed to watch for escape plans. The prisoners referred to themselves as 'kriegies' and in *The Wooden Horse* Scots engineer 'Wings' Cameron (Russell Waters) runs the 'Kriegie Construction Company', which builds the sturdy horse used for the escape.

In the film, the names of the three escapees are fictitious: Clinton is actually Captain Michael Codner (Royal Artillery), Rowe is RAF Flight Lieutenant Oliver Philpot and Howard is author Williams, also an RAF Flight Lieutenant. The final escape attempt in October 1943 is suspensefully done, the claustrophobia of the narrow crawl space illuminated by torchlight captured in the monochrome photography, as the escapees dig with trowels. The film's locale and props – wire fences, searchlights, guard dogs and towers – established the template for subsequent prisoner of war films. The excavated earth is hidden inside the horse in bags made from old trousers and then disposed of in the huts, either under the floor or up in the roof space. Scenes where guards and locals are bribed with a couple of 'gaspers' or an egg, look ridiculous today, but would have had added resonance to British audiences still enduring rationing. *The Wooden Horse* holds up as an excellent prison drama. It was a brave film to make in Germany only five years after the end of the war, which adds to its sense of realism today.

The popular 1953 book *The Colditz Story* by Patrick R. Reid was set in Colditz Castle, a foreboding medieval fortification in Saxony, which was supposedly Germany's most escape-proof prison. The castle had high, thick walls, turrets and towers, and was the stuff of gothic horror – it dropped to cliffs on three sides and had a dry moat, crossed by a bridge. The Third Reich's most troublesome prisoners were housed there – most were recaptured escapees from other camps. Reid spent almost two years as X: the chief British 'escape officer'. With four companions he escaped from Colditz in October 1942 and reached Switzerland. In 1955 Reid's book was made into a British Lion film of the same name, directed by Guy Hamilton and shot on location in shadowy monochrome in the actual Colditz Castle, Saxony. John Mills starred as Pat Reid, although all other character names in the film are fictitious. Under the command of Colonel Guy Richmond (Eric Portman), the international mix of French, Dutch, Polish and British prisoners decide to liaise and coordinate their escape, despite threats from the Kommandant (Frederick Valk) that anyone trying to abscond will be shot, as escape is 'Verboten'.

The Allies' 'escape committee' is a result of early escape attempts by the individual nationalities getting under each other's feet. In one scene a British tunnel is caused to collapse by a rival French one. Initial escape attempts fail, thanks to a Polish mole who betrays their plans to the Germans. According to the film there were 320 escape attempts until the prison's liberation in April 1945. Of these there were 56 'home runs' (successful escapes): five Polish, 15 Dutch, 14 British and 22 French. Throughout the film various ingenious methods are employed. Prisoners distribute earth excavated from tunnels via trousers with pockets which allow the soil to trickle down their legs and be dispersed on the ground. Jimmy Winslow (Bryan Forbes) is hidden in a sack of supplies and driven out of the camp in a truck. The Germans offer the prisoners special privileges if they will put their skills to work for the Third Reich. A French prisoner agrees, saying he would rather work for ten Germans than one Frenchman. The Germans ask his occupation: 'Undertaker'. During an athletic bout of gymnastic exercises, a French prisoner is launched over the wire by an accomplice and bolts for freedom, never to be seen again. In reality French cavalry lieutenant Pierre Mairesse-Lebrun did successfully escape from Colditz by this method – catapulted by an accomplice over the nine-feet high fence, he fled to neutral Switzerland. Richmond (wearing a false moustache) and Harry Tyler (Lionel Jeffries) impersonate a German officer and a sentry, in an attempt to allow a group of prisoners to escape in a tunnel from the canteen, but Richmond is rumbled and the escape foiled. This was also based on a true incident: Michael Sinclair, known as the 'Red Fox' by the Germans, attempted to escape from Colditz seven times by impersonating the garrison's sergeant major. He was shot during his final attempt, in September 1944, having made a break for it over the wire.

Colditz's monocle-wearing Kommandant is a walking cliché and the Germans are mostly portrayed as faceless 'goons' – POWs called all Germans 'goons' and enjoyed 'goon-baiting'. 'Goons' were moronic characters in the *Popeye* comics and the prisoners' slang usage of the word inspired Spike Milligan when he created the 1950s radio show *The Goons*. In *Colditz Story* Denis Shaw played goon Priem, the portly, wily head of the German security and German-born Anton Diffring played German officer Fischer. Although much of the film is light in tone, with the prisoners wisecracking and generally humiliating the Germans, it is not without moments of drama. Tall 'Mac' McGill (Christopher Rhodes) feels the 'Colditz Blues' when he is told he won't be able to take part in an escape attempt that he has conceived; his height and reputation will attract attention to the escape party. In a futile, depressed attempt to escape – a dash over the wire – he is shot by the guards.

McGill's plan is an excellent one – Reid, Tyler, Winslow and a German-speaking Dutchman disguise themselves as German officers and leave the castle to return to their billets in the village. It's an old ruse ('the idea's got a beard'), with a clever twist – they will exit through the officers' mess hall. The prisoners concoct an escape route under a stage, while in the theatre other inmates distract the officers and guards with a revue, 'Colditz Capers'. This includes a parody of the standard 'I Belong to Glasgow' (as 'I Belong to Colditz') and two officers, Robin Cartwright (Ian Carmichael) and bespectacled Richard Gordon (Richard Wattis) perform a skit as Flanagan and Allen. The quartet breaks out disguised as German officers, but Tyler and the Pole are soon caught. Later Richmond receives a postcard, which he reads aloud to the prisoners, from his two 'aunts', Gert and Daisy, informing him that they are enjoying the refreshing Swiss air: 'How we wish you could be with us'. Although it's stated in the film that Reid and Winslow are the first British home runs, it also mentions that the escapee who actually earned that accolade is Lieutenant-Colonel Airey Neave. It was Neave and Dutchman Toni Luteyn who carried out the theatrical escape described above, on 5 January 1942, and made it the 350 miles to the Swiss border.

In 1963, ingredients from these previous POW films were blended in the greatest escape movie of all. Originally entitled *The Last Escape*, John Sturges' *The Great Escape* is one of the most continually popular war films. Stalag Luft III was the Germans' attempt at a maximum security prison, where all the worst prisoners could be housed. Also the setting of *The Wooden* Horse, it was located in fir-treed woodland at Sagan near the German-Polish border, southeast of Berlin. In fact the wooden vaulting horse ruse was a diversionary measure during the tunnelling for the so-called 'The Great Escape', a breakout planned by some of the 10,000 allied airmen who were detained at the Führer's pleasure.

Like all great stories based on fact, the historical 'The Great Escape' of 76 prisoners from Sagan sounds outlandish and implausible. In Sagan's North Compound in April 1943, the escape committee put into practice a bold plan to dig three huge tunnels – deep enough to avoid the ferrets' sound detectors and illuminated by electric lights powered by the camp's electrical system – called Tom, Dick and Harry. They were so sophisticated that in Harry there were 'rest stop' way stations ('Piccadilly' and 'Leicester Square'), a workshop,

The Great Escape (1963). Above: Steve McQueen waits to film the tunnel escape scene. Below: Hilts and Bartlett (McQueen and Richard Attenborough) emerge in no man's land between the wire and the woods. Images courtesy Kevin Wilkinson Collection.

trolleys on rails to remove the excavated sand and ventilation bellows pumping fresh air into the shaft. In fact for such a feat of engineering, the only error the tunnel designers made was a grave and costly one – they dug beyond the perimeter fence, but were 10 feet short of the woods. On the night of 24 March 1944 escapees emerging from the hole found themselves in no man's land and though the plan was to free 220 men, just over a third got away and only three RAF men managed to reach England. The rest were rounded up in two weeks by the German manhunt that engulfed the area. Fifty of them were executed in cold blood – as they tried to escape, the Germans claimed – and 23 went back behind the wire.

The film *The Great Escape*, based on Paul Brickhill's 1951 memoir of the same name, was set in 1944 in Stalag Luft North; prisoners complain of being confined for four years. Brickhill, an Australian-born RAF Spitfire pilot, was held in Sagan during the venture and was unable to go on the escape because he was claustrophobic. The film opens with the disclaimer that this is a 'true story' and that although the characters are 'composites' of real men, and time and place has been 'compressed': 'Every detail of the escape is the way it really happened'. Luftwaffe Stalag Luft Nord (actually an 'Oflag') is designed by the Germans as an escape-proof prison for Allied air force officers, which confines all the 'rotten eggs in one basket'. During high-spirited 'Yankee Doodle' American Independence Day celebrations by POWs fuelled by moonshine, the Germans discover Tom. Thereafter, all efforts are concentrated on Harry. The POWs plan to free 250 men and the tunnel is 20 feet short of the woods, but in the main the film recreates the historical events.

The international nature of the film ensured a starry cast for the POWs. Steve McQueen played misfit US flier 'Cooler King' Virgil Hilts, who spends long portions of the film locked in a solitary confinement 'cooler' cell as punishment. There he passes the time, alone in his boredom, slumped against the cell wall, endlessly tossing a baseball against the opposite wall and catching it with a pitcher's glove. Charles Bronson played Polish Danny Valenski (a tunneller who suffers from claustrophobia) and actor-pop singer John Leyton (famous for the haunting hit 'Johnny Remember Me') played his English friend Willy Dickes.

Publicity photograph of Steve McQueen as Virgil Hilts, on a 1960s vintage 650 Triumph TT Special motorcycle during the filming of the famous chase scene from John Sturges's *The Great Escape* (1963). 'Achtung 100m Schweizer Grenze' translates as 'Attention 100m Swiss Frontier'. Courtesy Kevin Wilkinson Collection.

Danny and Willy are the 'Tunnel Kings'. James Coburn played Australian Sedgwick, the resourceful 'Manufacturer' and James Garner appeared as Bob Hendley, the 'Scrounger', who can acquire anything in the camp by bribery, blackmail and guile.

In the British contingent, Richard Attenborough played Squadron Leader Roger Bartlett, called 'Big X', who was based on Squadron Leader Roger Bushell, the actual planner of the escape. Gordon Jackson (from *The Captive Heart*) played Andy MacDonald, James Donald (incarcerated in *Bridge on the River Kwai*) was the Senior British Officer (SBO) Group Captain Ramsey and David McCallum (soon to be a Man from U.N.C.L.E.) was Eric Ashley-Pitt, in charge of 'Dispersal' of the excavated soil (he invents the trouser pocket method). Donald Pleasence played bird-watching forger Colin Blythe, who creates false documentation for the escapees and in the film's most moving scenes discovers he's going blind; he is allowed to go on the escape only when Hendley assures Bartlett that he will look after Blythe. Robert Desmond played Griffith, the tailor who makes disguises for the men and Nigel Stock was Dennis Cavendish, the tunnel's surveyor. Angus Lennie played ace tunnelling 'Mole' Archibald Ives, the pint-sized Scottish jockey nicknamed 'Piglet' who eventually goes 'wire crazy'. When tunnel Tom is discovered by the Germans, Ives attempts to scale the wire and is machine-gunned in a scene which recalls Mac's demise in *Colditz Story*.

This multinational cast was rather more multinational than the actual escapees. The American prisoners in Sagan had been moved to another camp by the time of the actual breakout. In the film both Hilts and Hendley escape, but their fellow American Goff (Jud Taylor) doesn't quite make it before the Germans discover the tunnel, when Cavendish trips over and alerts a guard. For the German contingent, Hannes Messemer played the camp Kommandant, Colonel Von Luger. Robert Graf was nervous 'Ferret' Werner, who is blackmailed by Hendley (and is petrified of being sent to the Russian Front), Ulrich Beiger played bespectacled Gestapo interrogator Preissen and Hans Reisser was leather-coated Gestapo agent Kuhn. Reisser had been a POW in America, Messemer had been held by the Russians and Donald Pleasence, who was in the RAF, spent time in a German POW camp.

Sturges had read Brickhill's book in 1951, but couldn't interest investors until he'd had a major hit with *The Magnificent Seven*. *The Great Escape* was financed by the Mirisch Company and released through United Artists. The script was adapted by James Clavell (who had been a prisoner of the Japanese) and William Riley Burnett, the author of many novels, including *The Asphalt Jungle* (1950), which featured a group of specialists breaking into a jeweller's. *The Great Escape* was shot on location in Germany in DeLuxe Color and Panavision by Daniel Fapp. The prison camp was constructed in pine woodland (which was later replanted) near Geiselgasteig Studios, Munich in Bavaria, with interiors filmed in the studios themselves. The historic town of Sagan, with its railway station, was renamed Neustadt ('Newtown') for the film and the train was an original 1944 locomotive on the Munich-Hamburg railroad.

The first 105 minutes of the 165-minute film recreated the escape's meticulous planning, while the remainder recounted how the 76 POWs fared once loose in Germany on their separate routes to freedom. When Danny begins to dig, he chalks a '17' beside the hole: it's his seventeenth escape attempt. Willy looks down the passage to freedom, festooned with lights, and marvels that it reminds him of 'Blackpool at the height of the season'. In addition to the sturdy construction of the three main tunnels – using scrounged timber which leave both huts and bunk beds rickety – the film also featured 'mole' tunnelling, where an escapee dug very quickly and pushed the earth behind them in a shallow tunnel, a method that was ideal for small-scale escapes.

The story of the escape is fairly true to history, but once the POWs are on the run, some licence is taken with their exploits. Ashley-Pitt is caught and shot at the Neustadt railway station. Bartlett and MacDonald, plus 50 other prisoners including Cavendish, are rounded up and interrogated by the Gestapo. MacDonald gives himself away as he's boarding a bus and a German officer wishes him 'Good luck' in English, to which MacDonald instinctively replies, 'Thank you'. Bartlett is cornered outside a 'Zigaretten' (tobacconists) following a chase though the streets of a German town (shot on location in Füssen, near Munich) by German SS officer Steinach (Karl Otto Alberty). The 50 prisoners are then trucked to a desolate spot and machine-gunned to death. Brickhill's book was dedicated 'To the Fifty' and the film ends with a similar dedication. The massacre's SS perpetrators were tried and executed after the war.

While the film's British contingent is wiped out, the international players fare rather better. Danny and Willy steal a boat and calmly row to freedom,

No Escape: Squadron Leader Roger Bartlett, codenamed 'Big X', is cornered by SS officer Steinach. Karl Otto Alberty (left) and Richard Attenborough (right) on location in Füssen near Munich during *The Great Escape* (1963). Courtesy Kevin Wilkinson Collection.

eventually reaching a port and boarding a Swedish ship. Sedgwick steals a bicycle and manages to reach France, where he contacts the Resistance, who safely escort him across the border into Spain. Hendley and Blythe steal a German training aircraft (a 1937 Bücker 181) but crash before they can reach the Swiss border. Blythe is shot and Hendley is returned to the camp. McQueen's penchant for speed provides the film with its most famous scenes; he took the role when Sturges introduced a motorbike chase into the script. McQueen's *Hell Is for Heroes* and *The War Lover* hadn't drawn the crowds and he was reticent about making another war movie. Hilts steals a German motorcycle and is pursued by German patrols along roads and across picturesquely verdant rolling Bavarian countryside near Füssen and the Alps. McQueen did most of his own stunt riding and can also be seen, in a German uniform and goggles, as his German purser. Almost attaining freedom, Hilts manages to leap the first border fence but as his pursuers close in, he's machine-gunned and crashes into the second fence, where his captors corner him. Tangled in barbed wire, he's bloody but defiant, in what is probably McQueen's iconic screen moment. The border fence jumps were performed by McQueen's biker friend Bud Ekins on a 1960s vintage Triumph. Hilts is returned to the camp at 'The End', where he's reacquainted with the cooler.

The other vital ingredient of *The Great Escape* is Elmer Bernstein's immortal theme music. The piece commences with great rolling chords, then syncopated brass backs a jaunty march. Bernstein had also composed the memorable music

A Glorious Saga of the RAF: UK poster promoting John Sturges's *The Great Escape* (1963) depicts Bartlett, Hilts and Hendley (Richard Attenborough, Steve McQueen and James Garner) on the run. Note US pilot Hilts' RAF uniform. Poster courtesy Kevin Wilkinson Collection.

to *The Magnificent Seven.* For scenes of tension – including the breakout – Bernstein deploys ominous tidal strings. The escapees' progress through beautiful rural landscapes is accompanied by pastoral themes and Hilts' chase is scored in fine dramatic style. To coincide with the film's release, John Leyton recorded a vocal version of *The Great Escape* theme (attributed to 'A. Stillman and E. Bernstein') through His Master's Voice records, which cheapened the tune with facile lyrics: 'Fickle, I may be fickle – but it's a dollar to a nickel. That when I'm kissin' the one I'm kissin', she is the one girl for me'.

McQueen, Garner and Bronson were the top-billed stars of the US promotional campaign. Bronson was ousted by Attenborough on UK posters, which advertised *The Great Escape* as 'A Glorious Saga of the RAF', with McQueen wearing an RAF uniform. Critical reception was mixed – 'A strictly mechanical adventure with make-believe men' wrote Bosley Crowther of the *New York Times*'; 'First class' opined *Variety* – but it was one of the biggest box office successes of the 1960s. It made McQueen a star and helped Coburn, Bronson, Pleasence and Garner's careers too. Thanks to its ensemble cast – which enact their little dramas that interweave into a great story – *The Great Escape* survives repeat viewings. This is just as well as it is a holiday season TV schedule favourite, especially in the UK. If the film isn't the whole truth, it's still great escapism.

Another action-filled POW adventure, Mark Robson's CinemaScope *Von Ryan's Express* (1965), was released by Twentieth Century-Fox. As the Allies invade Italy, an Italian prisoner of war camp becomes crammed with prisoners. The inmates are mostly British, but there are some Americans, and all are kept in appalling conditions. The camp commandant, Major Battaglia (Adolfo Celi) hoards the prisoners' Red Cross parcels to sell on the black market. The arrival of downed US pilot Colonel Joseph L. Ryan (Frank Sinatra) causes friction with Major Eric Fincham (Trevor Howard), when Fincham realises that Ryan is the ranking officer and thus takes command. Ryan surmises that with the war going well for the Allies in Italy, they should stop any escape attempts; Fincham sees this as compliance with the Axis and christens the American 'Von Ryan'. Ryan orders the prisoners to burn their clothes, forcing the Italians to issue them with fresh uniforms. With the liberation of Italy the Italian guards flee and the 400 prisoners escape. They are recaptured by the Germans and loaded on a train but take over the locomotive and steam for neutral Switzerland, with the Luftwaffe and a German military troop train in pursuit.

Von Ryan's Express is one of the great war movies of the 1960s, which offers an imaginative twist on the standard POW film. Routed from Rome, via Florence, to Innsbruck, Austria, the POWs divert the train to Milan and then through the Alpine Malajo Pass into Switzerland. It was filmed on location in Italy, on the Capranica-Viterbo railroad (also used for Enzo Castellari's *The Inglorious Bastards*), in Rome and Florence, and further north towards the Swiss border. The production thanked the executives and staff of the Italian State Railroad (Ferrovie Dello Stato) who allowed the production to use their rolling stock and lines. The supporting cast included several reliable 'Brits and Yanks' as POWs: John Leyton (from *The Great Escape*) played Orde and Brad Dexter played Sergeant Bostick. Edward Mulhare gave a great turn as Captain

Captain Oriani (Sergio Fantoni, with eye patch), Major Eric Fincham (Trevor Howard), Colonel Joseph L. Ryan (Frank Sinatra) and their watchful German captors in Mark Robson's POW movie *Von Ryan's Express* (1965), Sinatra's biggest box office hit of the 1960s. Courtesy Kevin Wilkinson Collection.

Constanzo, a British chaplain, who impersonates a Nazi officer with gusto to bluff the train's passage through Florence. Austrian-born William Berger played a delving Gestapo agent, Paul Muller and Mirko Ellis were Nazi officers, and Ivan Triesault had a brief role as vain Lieutenant-General Von Kleist. Italians Vito Scotti and stuntman Remo De Angelis were train driver Peppino and his fireman.

As per all international war films shot in Italy, the Italians are absolved of blame for fascism: the officers were 'following orders'. The sympathetic presence of Captain Oriani (Sergio Fantoni), on hand to help the POWs navigate the Italian rail system, ensures the audience realise this. The camp's commandant, played by Celi, is presented as a sadistic, corset-wearing fascist buffoon. When the prisoners are loaded onto the train, the Allied wounded are shot (offscreen) at Battaglia's orders, a direct result of Ryan sparing Battaglia's life earlier in the film. Wolfgang Preiss played Major Von Klemment, who is taken hostage by the prisoners on the hijacked train, and Raffaella Carra was his consort Gabriella.

Von Ryan machine-guns her in the back when she tries to escape, taking no chances following his soft-hearted treatment of Battaglia.

As the train hurtles towards the Swiss border via the mountainous Malajo Pass – through tunnels and over bridges – three rocket-firing 'Messerschmitts' attack. This excitement is pure Hollywood fiction. The planes are actually disguised US P-51 Mustangs, as the Germans never deployed rocket-armed planes. The Luftwaffe manage to obstruct the line, almost derailing Von Ryan's Express, but the prisoners resourcefully dismantle track from behind them, to repair the rails ahead. Ryan, Fincham, Bostick and others fight a heroic rearguard action, as a German troop train commanded by Colonel Gortz (John Van Dreelen) catches up. In the shock dénouement, the POW train starts to roll with the prisoners on board, but as Ryan sprints to catch the departing loco, Gortz machine-guns him down and he sprawls on the track. Fincham notes as the train departs: 'Remember Ryan, if only one man escapes, it's a victory'. *Von Ryan's Express* is one of Sinatra's finest performances and his biggest box office hit of the 1960s.

POW films weren't all motorbike stunt jumps and careering, hijacked trains. David Lean's *The Bridge on the River Kwai* (1957), which is discussed elsewhere in this book, is one of the great POW movies. It differs significantly from other POW films in that those captured don't try to engineer their escape, but instead engineer a bridge and help their Japanese captors construct a railway line. Their collaboration and collusion goes far beyond Von Ryan's. The narrative is now social commentary, though the sequel, *Return from the River Kwai* (1988), is a conventional 'escape' narrative, which featured POWs being transported by train. Other Far Eastern POW films, such as *A Town Like Alice* and *King Rat*, were similarly unconcerned with escape. *A Town Like Alice* (1956 – *The Rape of Malaya*) was set in a Japanese POW camp for women and starred Virginia McKenna and Peter Finch as lovers who meet in extraordinary circumstances. *The Camp on Blood Island* (1958) and *The Secret of Blood Island* (1964) were Far Eastern POW narratives, Hammer Horror-style: *Camp*'s tagline was 'Jap War Crimes Exposed!' *Three Came Home* (1950), set in Borneo, starred Claudette Colbert. *Southern Cross* (1982) depicted Australian POWs in a Japanese camp and *Merry Christmas, Mr Lawrence* (1982) was set in 1943 Java and starred Tom Conti and singer-actor David Bowie. *Paradise Road* (1997) confined its formidable cast – Glenn Close, Pauline Collins, Cate Blanchett, Frances McDormand and Jennifer Ehle – in a women's camp in Sumatra; Buzz Kulik's TV movie *Women of Valor* (1986) depicted women prisoners (including Susan Sarandon) held on Bataan. Ralph Thomas' *The Wind Cannot Read* (1958) detailed a love affair between RAF officer Dirk Bogarde and Japanese girl Yoko Tani.

POW films often spawned TV spin-offs. *A Town Like Alice* became the highly-rated *Tenko* (1981–84) and the follow-up TV movie *Tenko Reunion* (1985). *The Colditz Story* spawned *Colditz* (1972–74) and Billy Wilder's cynical black comedy *Stalag 17* (1953) became *Hogan's Heroes* (1965–71). In Wilder's film, William Holden gave an Oscar-winning performance as Sefton, the scamming hero who is suspected by his fellow inmates of being a 'stoolie', a German spy betraying his fellow prisoners. Set in a camp for American airmen 'somewhere on the Danube' in late 1944 where 'life was confining but never dull', *Stalag 17*'s irreverent style was a great success with the public. The opening narrator moans that most war films depict airmen or soldiers – never POWs – and the great cast includes Don Taylor, Robert Strauss, Harvey Lembeck, Gil Stratton Jr, Sig Rumann, Peter Graves, Neville Brand and Richard Erdman, with film director Otto Preminger as the camp Kommandant, Oberst Von Scherbach.

Lewis Gilbert's *Albert, RN* (1953 – *Break to Freedom*) was the true story of an escape engineered around a lifelike dummy, which stood in for escapees at roll call. Such mannequins were used during the war. The Swiss-made *The Last Chance* (1945) had US and British prisoners escaping in 1943 from Italy to Switzerland. The propagandist *The Cross of Lorraine* (1943) had Jean-Pierre Aumont and Gene Kelly up against Nazi Peter Lorre. Robert Bresson's *A Man Escaped* (1956) featured a French Resistance POW escaping from the Nazis. In *Fraulein* (1958), US POW-in-hiding Mel Ferrer is helped by German woman Dana Wynter in post-war Berlin. *Danger Within* (1958 – *Breakout*), written by Bryan Forbes and starring stalwarts Richard Todd, Michael Wilding, Bernard Lee, Richard Attenborough, Donald Houston and Dennis Price, used a subplot from *Colditz Story*, with prisoners suspecting a betrayer in their ranks. *No Time to Die* (1958 – *Tank Force*), starring Victor Mature, Leo Genn and Anthony Newley, featured Allies in an Afrika Korps' POW camp. The Japanese *Human Condition* trilogy (1959–61) began in *No Greater Love* (1959), with everyman hero Kaji the Idealist (Tatsuya Nakadai), a soldier and conscientious objector, trying to improve the lot of iron ore mine labourers in occupied Manchuria, and ends, in *A Soldier's Prayer* (1961), with Kaji himself in a Russian gulag.

The Password Is Courage (1962) featured Dirk Bogarde as resourceful Sergeant-Major Charles Coward in the tragicomic true story of his various scrapes and escapes whilst in captivity. It was based on John Castle's biography of Coward and was directed and scripted by Andrew L. Stone. Though it was set in France, Germany and Poland, the film was shot in England. The German railway marshalling yard where Coward and his cohorts sabotage trains (redirecting green paint to the Russian Front and canned food to concentration camps) was actually Gateway Service Station, at Scratchwood in Hertfordshire. In the film's most famous scene, George is wounded and is taken to a German hospital, where he is mistakenly awarded the Iron Cross. Maria Perschy played Irena, an optometrist who is Coward's Polish Resistance contact in Breslau. Alfred Lynch was Coward's partner-in-crime, Corporal Billy Pope, and Ferdy Mayne, Victor Beaumont and Richard Marner cropped up as German officers. It features a tunnel escape from Lamsdorf prison camp (Stalag VIIIB) and a well-staged train crash. Coward and Pope finally make it through German lines to the US army by posing as firemen driving their engine to an emergency call.

Michael Winner's offbeat *Hannibal Brooks* (1968) had Allied prisoners (including Oliver Reed) escape over the Alps to Innsbruck with Lucy, an elephant from the Munich zoo; it was scripted by Dick Clement and Ian La Frenais. Sydney Lumet's *The Hill* (1965) depicted a British military camp for British soldiers in North Africa – Sean Connery shed his 007 image as a resilient detainee and the supporting cast included Ossie Davis, Harry Andrews, Jack Watson,

Michael Redgrave, Roy Kinnear, Alfred Lynch and two tough Ians: Bannen and Hendry. *Don't Look Now, We're Being Shot At* (1966 – *La grande vandrouille*) was a send-up starring Louis de Funès and Bourvil, with Terry-Thomas and other downed Allied pilots evading the Nazis' clutches in Paris. *Paris Underground* (1945 – *Madame Pimpernel* in the UK) was a serious treatment of similar subject matter, starring Constance Bennett and Gracie Fields.

Very Important Person (1961 – *A Coming Out Party*) begins during a TV show called *Memory Album*. The guest, renowned boffin Sir Ernest Pease (James Robertson Justice), recalls events in 1942 when he was flying on a reconnaissance mission over Germany in a Wellington. He was shot down and ended up in a POW camp (filmed at Independent Artists Studios, Beaconsfield, London). Most of the film is a farcical 'Carry On'-style parody of POW movies such as *The Wooden Horse*, as brusque Pease – a scientist and very important person – engineers his escape from the camp disguised as a member of the Swiss Commission from Geneva, who inspect prison living conditions. The comic cast included Stanley Baxter (in the dual roles of compulsive tunneller 'Jock' Everett and the camp's German Kommandant), John Le Mesurier as the Chairman of the Escape Committee and Eric Sykes as the PE instructor. Leslie Phillips and Jeremy Lloyd played two randy RAF fliers, Flying Officer Jimmy Cooper and Flight Lieutenant 'Bonzo' Baines, for whom everything is 'tickety boo'. On *Memory Album*, Pease is reunited with his cohorts: Baines now designs ladies' 'foundation garments', Cooper is a missionary in India, Everett works as an undertaker ('still digging') and the Kommandant is the entertainment manager at a British holiday camp.

The German POWs' point of view was depicted in Roy Ward Baker's *The One That Got Away* (1957). It was based on the true story of Oberleutnant Franz Von Werra, a Luftwaffe fighter ace shot down on 5 September 1940 at Winchet Hill, Kent, east of Tunbridge Wells, during the Battle of Britain. Hardy Krüger played resourceful Werra in this Rank release filmed at Pinewood Studios and on location. Werra is incarcerated in Grizedale Hall in the Lake District, Cumbria, but escapes while taking exercise. An extensive manhunt involving the army and Coniston police through the bleak, windswept, rain drenched landscape eventually apprehends him. He's then taken to a POW camp at Swanwick, near Derby, but he tunnels out and poses as a Dutch pilot who has crash landed. This time he's apprehended at RAF Hucknall, attempting to steal a Hurricane. Werra and his fellow prisoners are transported to Canada in early 1941. While travelling by train to the camp, Werra jumps through a window and escapes. He poses as a torpedoed Dutch seaman and toils through the icy wastes, finally crossing the border into then-neutral USA. Via Mexico, Peru, Bolivia, Brazil and Spain, Werra reached Berlin on 18 April 1941. A larger-than-life figure, Werra had a pet lion cub named Simba and sent his interrogator at RAF Intelligence, Cockfosters in London (played in the film by Michael Goodliffe) a postcard from New York on his escape. Werra's first contact with an American national on crossing the snowbound US frontier was played by Canadian character actor Al Mulock. Werra was the only German POW to make it back to Germany after being captured in Britain, but he was later lost at sea while on patrol on 25 October 1941.

While Grizedale Hall in the Lakes is hardly Colditz, *The One That Got Away* does attempt to redress the balance and show German prisoners of war in a sympathetic light and their British captors as villains.

Lamont Johnson's *The McKenzie Break* (1970 – *Escape*) depicted German prisoners held in Scotland (though it was actually filmed on location in Ireland). Camp McKenzie, a 'desolate chicken farm', is ruled by anarchy as the insubordinate Germans run riot. Ineffectual camp commandant Major Perry (Ian Hendry) is powerless, but when Captain Jack Connor (Brian Keith) – a tough Irishman working for military intelligence – arrives, he brings the camp to heel. The senior German officer is U-boat Kapitan Willi Schleutter (Helmut Griem), who stops at nothing to irritate his captors. The prisoners are in radio and code contact with Germany and plan an escape, which involves 28 Kriegsmarines (submariners) tunnelling out. They succeed and travel by truck to a remote rendezvous with a U-boat on the Scottish coast, where Connor intervenes. Many of the submariners make their escape, but the sub is forced to dive when a British torpedo boat arrives and Schleutter is left stranded in a dinghy. Connor had assured his commanding office General Kerr (Jack Watson) that he would apprehend the prisoners and destroy the U-boat, but as he notes to Schleutter in the finale: 'Willi, looks like we're both in the shithouse'.

The story was based on Sidney Shelley's 1968 book of the same name and the Germans are stereotypical 'Bad Nazis', especially disruptive Schleutter. Ex-crime reporter Connor discovers that Schleutter has murdered the elderly senior German officer in order to take command of the prisoners and Schleutter has Luftwaffe Lieutenant Neuchl (Horst Janson) beaten and throttled (his death is made to appear that he hanged himself). During the rain-sodden night-time tunnel escape, Schleutter deliberately collapses the earth-laden attic of barrack hut 3, which kills several of his own men, buries many others in mud and creates a diversion to cover the escape. *McKenzie Break* has some gritty action, especially in the scenes showing the German prisoners rioting and Connor quelling the disruption with water jets from the local fire service. Riz Ortolani supplied a suspenseful score and Keith and Griem are fine, grudgingly respectful adversaries.

Perhaps the most ridiculous POW movie and one that continues to enjoy surprising cult popularity is John Huston's patriotic *Escape to Victory* (1981), which features the most talented POWs. In a variation on the prisoners-versus-guards American Football movie *The Mean Machine* (1974), Allied prisoners take on the German national team. For the Germans it is a propaganda exercise, but for the allies it's an opportunity to stage a daring escape. Michael Caine starred as Captain John Colby, an ex-West Ham and England international footballer, now a POW, who is recognised by Major Von Steiner (Max Von Sydow), another international football player. Steiner proposes that Colby captains a team to face the German national squad. The game takes place in the Colombes Stadium in Paris (actually filmed in the MKT Stadium in Budapest) in front of a French crowd and German top brass. The Allied players are supposed to escape at half time through the sewers with the aid of the Resistance, but they are trailing the Germans 4–1. Instead of escaping, they return to the pitch and draw 4-all. When

POW goalkeeper Hatch (Sylvester Stallone) saves a last minute penalty, a pitch invasion enables the crowd to disguise the prisoners, who escape in the melee.

Set sometime after the Dieppe Raid in August 1942 but before the liberation of France, *Escape to Victory* was shot in Hungary for $15 million. It was based on the true story of a group of prisoners who played the Germans and won, but were executed. In the film the prison camp has an Escape Committee overseen by SBO Colonel Waldron (Daniel Massey), who view Colby as a collaborator. Among the British officers were Tim Pigott-Smith and Julian Curry. Clive Merrison played a forger who moans that summer is his busiest time, as everyone wants to escape in the good weather. George Mikell played the eye-patched Kommandant, Gary Waldhorn was Muller, the German team coach, and Anton Diffring played the German match commentator. The fly in the ointment is drawling Stallone, the big American star of the film, who plays a Canadian prisoner (captured during the Dieppe Raid) and the team's goalkeeper. Too much time is devoted to his exploits, as he breaks out of the camp and organises the team's escape in Paris. Carole Paure played his love interest, Renee. It is in the football scenes where the film really scores. The prison team consists of famous professional footballers – including Pelé, Osvaldo Ardiles, Bobby Moore, Kazimierz Deyna, Hallvar Thorensen, Paul Van Himst, Mike Summerbee, Co Prins, Russell Osman, John Wark, Soren Listed and Kevin O'Calloghan – augmented with players from Ipswich Town, while the German squad are the Hungarian national team. Pelé also designed the 'soccer plays' featured in the film. With four minutes remaining, injured Pelé comes off the bench and scores the vital equaliser with an overhead, slow-motion bicycle kick.

The film was retitled *Victory* in the US, where association football is called soccer. It is this film more than any other that unites many English males' preoccupations with football, World War II and Michael Caine. Even today the England supporters' band plays the theme to *The Great Escape* and 'Self Preservation Society' from *The Italian Job* (Caine's 1969 heist film) at England's international football matches. *The Great Escape* was even rereleased on DVD in the UK to coincide with the World Cup in 2006, with a free Cross of St George flag and a set of patriotic temporary tattoos. *Escape to Victory* is a fantasy film melding two old rivalries – the England-versus-German enmity of football and war. As the POW team argue at half time whether to escape while they climb into the sewers, national pride and winning the game – a very 'British' attitude – becomes more important than freedom itself.

Chapter 9

THE WAR IN THE FAR EAST (1941–45)

The day after Japan's attack on Pearl Harbor on 7 December 1941, it embarked on further empire building. On 8 December Japan invaded the colony of Hong Kong from China, forcing the British and Indian garrison to surrender on Christmas Day. On 8 December, Japanese forces invaded Southern Thailand and Malaya. On 10 December, British naval Force Z was attacked by air and the battleship the *Prince of Wales* and the battle cruiser *Repulse* were sunk. The Japanese drove south, down Malaya's east coast, taking Kuala Lumpur on 11 January 1942. British and Empire forces withdrew to the island of Singapore at Malaya's southernmost tip, on 31 January 1942. On 15 January, Japanese forces in northern Malaya struck north and invaded Burma, to join up with the main invasion force, which launched from Thailand into Burma on 20 January 1942. The Japanese strove to sever the Burma Road, a vital supply link to China. Control of Burma would also strengthen their position in Malaya, which was yet to be conquered. During months of ferocious fighting, the well-drilled Japanese forces drove the occupying British, Burmese and Indian army northwards. Cut off, fortress Singapore fell on 15 February – the fortress' guns faced the sea, so the Japanese attacked from the mainland. Through Burma the British and their allies were aided by Chinese troops sent by Chiang Kai-shek, but the Japanese pushed on. The retreat through Burma was the longest fighting retreat in British military history. British forces eventually crossed the Chindwin River and relinquished Burma on 15 May 1942.

This valiant but fruitless Allied campaign has seldom been depicted in films and the accent on this theatre of war has tended to concentrate on the Japanese treatment of prisoners following their incarceration. The 1929 Geneva Convention outlined the humane treatment of prisoners of war, but the Soviet Union and Japan didn't sign the agreement and both countries forced their prisoners to work in terrible conditions. The international prisoners captured by the

Japanese in the Far East were deployed constructing a railway connecting Bangkok in Thailand to Rangoon in Burma. Fighting monsoon rains, appalling living conditions, tropical disease, mud and heat, and under the watchful eyes of their brutal Japanese and Korean guards, the prisoners constructed the link, which became known as the 'Death Railway'. To link the existing rail system, a 260-mile stretch of railway was constructed between Ban Pong in Thailand to Thanbyuzayat in Burma. 61,000 prisoners (about half of which were British) toiled from autumn 1942 to finish the work on schedule by November 1943. Many of the British soldiers had been captured at the fall of Singapore. Other nationalities included Dutch, Australians and 650 Americans, many of whom were sailors captured following the sinking of the cruiser *Houston* in the Battle of Sundra Strait near Java on 1 March 1942. The most renowned incident during the Death Railway's construction was the building of an 800-foot long railway bridge near the confluence of the Khwae Noi River (also called the River Kwai) and the Mae Klong River, from October 1942 to February 1943. The railway link, which was a vital supply line for the Japanese, was finally opened in October 1943, at a cost of thousands of prisoners' lives.

The bridge's construction is recreated in David Lean's *The Bridge on the River Kwai* (1957). It is a meditative wartime story depicting psychological warfare in a Japanese work camp in 1943. British soldiers captured in Singapore arrive at Camp 16 in the Siamese jungle (Thailand was then known as Siam) which is commanded by the ruthless Colonel Saito (Sessue Hayakawa). The prisoners work on a section of the Rangoon–Bangkok railway, including the bridge over the River Kwai, which must be completed by 12 May. Colonel Nicholson (Alec Guinness) refuses to allow his British officers to take part in the project, which brings him into conflict with unbending Saito, who punishes Nicholson by confining him to a cramped corrugated iron shed, 'The Oven'. The project falls behind, Saito's threats fall on deaf ears and he is forced to lose face and give in to Nicholson.

When Nicholson takes over the bridge operation he becomes obsessed with its construction, seeing it as a morale-boosting exercise for his men and a matter of national pride. Working with his advisory engineers Captain Reeves (Peter Williams) and Major Hughes (John Boxer), they resite the bridge further downstream to a bedrock foundation and progress on the bridge and the rail link intensifies. As Nicholson strives to complete the bridge on time, he puts his officers to work and turns out malingerers in the sick bay, which appals Dr Clipton (James Donald), who disagrees with Nicholson and the POWs helping the enemy. Meanwhile Commander Shears (William Holden), a US sailor from the *Houston* who was a captive in the camp, escapes to Ceylon. As he recuperates from his trek, he's contacted by Major Warden (Jack Hawkins) of Force 316, who convinces Shears to go back into the jungle as the expedition guide to a commando squad who plan to obliterate the bridge.

Released by Columbia Pictures and produced by Sam Spiegel, *Bridge on the River Kwai* is the first of several meticulous, epic productions by British director Lean. The screenplay adaptation was credited to Pierre Boulle from his 1954 novel *Le Pont de la Rivière Kwai* (*The Bridge Over the River Kwai*) – in reality the bridge crossed the Mae Klong River, not the Khwae Noi. The screenplay was written by

Adversaries then allies, Colonel Nicholson (Alec Guinness, left) and Colonel Saito (Sessue Hayakawa, right) call a truce and work together to construct *The Bridge on the River Kwai* (1957). Courtesy Kevin Wilkinson Collection.

Carl Foreman and Michael Wilson, but neither was credited, as they were on Hollywood's Communist blacklist. Andre Morell played Force 316 mastermind Colonel Green, Percy Herbert and Harold Goodwin played British POWs Grogan and Baker, and Ann Sears was a nurse, Shears' brief love interest in Ceylon. Early casting proposals included Cary Grant as Shears and Charles Laughton as Nicholson, with Howard Hawks as director, but Holden and Guinness turned out to be ideal choices. Holden's antihero is introduced digging graves. He bribes a guard with a lighter to be excused work and is placed on the sick list in hospital – he's one of the malingerers Nicholson detests. We discover that he's posing as a naval officer in a bid to ensure better treatment from his Japanese captors, but he's later made an honorary major for the commando mission. Guinness' role as Nicholson remains probably his best performance in a career littered with awards and fine portrayals.

With a budget of $3 million, Lean filmed from November 1956 to May 1957, mostly on the island of Ceylon (now called Sri Lanka) in the Indian Ocean, which provided the range of locations required for the film. The 425-foot long bridge took eight months to build with logs, using labourers and elephants, at a cost of £85,000. It was the largest film set built up to that time. The score by Malcolm Arnold memorably deployed Kenneth J. Alford's jaunty 'Colonel Bogey' march. The rowdy lyrics to this piece are entitled 'Hitler Has Only Got One Ball'. This tune is whistled proudly by the British POWs, without lyrics, and is augmented by Arnold's 'River Kwai March'. The cinematography, in CinemaScope and Technicolor by Jack Hildyard, make this the most poetically picturesque of all war films. Noteworthy are the film's scene transitions, with images dissolving into one another, or fading to black. When the commandos are ambushed by a Japanese patrol at a waterfall, thousands of bats wheeling overhead dapple the shadowy jungle scene. There are majestic sunsets, spectacular scenery and jungle splendour, but there's also a sense of the prickly heat and a soundtrack that foregrounds the jungle's ominous natural sounds, as Hildyard's camera prowls through the undergrowth in lengthy dolly shots. The appalling conditions of the sun-scorched, rag-clothed inmates in Camp 16 – the monsoons, mud and disease – contrast strongly with Shears' Shangri La convalescence at the Mount Lavinia Hospital in Ceylon, as he sips Martinis on the palmed beach with his pin-up blonde nurse.

At first glance, *River Kwai* appears to be a POW movie, but there is no Escape Committee here – there's no need for one, or for towers, fences or stockades. Escape is futile, as the hazardous jungle takes no prisoners. Building on its POW premise, *River Kwai* fuses several plot threads, which layer the narrative. Boulle asked: imagine if the POWs were helping their captors' war effort and one of the prisoners escapes and returns to destroy the fruits of their toil. The cross-cutting between these parallel stories keeps the pace brisk over the film's 155-minute running time.

Saito and Nicholson's antagonism is defined by psychological warfare and extreme cruelty. In Camp 16, Nicholson cites Article 27 of the Geneva Convention, which states that officers should have to work alongside their men only in a supervisory capacity. Saito doesn't care for the etiquette of war. In one scene he slaps Nicholson with a copy of the Geneva Convention, which contravenes the Convention. When Saito gives the POWs 'presents', they receive the Red Cross supply packages they should have already been issued. Saito threatens to compel the sick and infirm to work, the POWs food rations are cut when they don't work hard enough and starving Nicholson is forced to watch Saito eat supper. Saito threatens Nicholson and his officers with a machine gun and they endure an entire day standing in the hot sun of the camp's parade ground. This endurance test, a battle of wills between two equally stubborn men, is only resolved when Saito concedes. Later, with the project completed on schedule, Nicholson is proud that his men have made such an excellent job of the bridge and a plaque is erected reading: 'This Bridge was Designed and Constructed by Soldiers of the British Army. Feb-May 1943'. In reality the prisoners constructing the Mae Klong bridge attempted to sabotage it, using rotten timbers and wood-eating white ants. Nicholson's morale-building exercise has worked, as Saito's credo states: 'Be happy in your work'. On the eve of the railway's grand opening, Nicholson and Saito share a lyrical moment on the bridge at sunset. After 28 years in the army, Nicholson takes stock of his life, realising he's nearer the end than the beginning.

The introduction of the commando raid plot takes over the narrative and dominates the film's latter stages. When they parachute into the jungle, commando Chapman is killed, leaving Warden, Shears and Canadian Lieutenant

Joyce (Geoffrey Horne) to carry out the mission with help from Siamese village guerrilla Yai (M R B Chakrabandhu) and Siamese women bearers (Vilaiwan Seeboonreaung, Ngamta Suphaphongs, Javanart Punynchoti and Kinnikar Dowklee) who carry their kit. Despite Warden suffering an ankle injury, they arrive at the bridge on time. Yai, Shears and Joyce float their plastic explosive downriver on a raft, rig the bridge under cover of night and trail the detonation cable to a sandy beach downstream. Meanwhile, Nicholson tells his men, 'Here in the wilderness you have turned defeat into victory' and proudly leads the men – who are soon to be moved to another camp and another bridge – in the National Anthem.

The following day, the water level of the river has dropped dramatically: the explosives strapped to the bridge stanchions, once below the waterline, are now exposed and the detonation wire is snagged on a submerged branch and is visible. Nicholson investigates with Saito, as a Japanese army train carrying troops and VIPs approaches. Joyce, hidden on the beach with the detonator, knifes Saito but Japanese guards shoot him as Nicholson tries to stop him reaching the detonator. Shears splashes across the river under fire – bullets slam into him and he staggers to the other side, then slumps dead. Nicholson recognises Shears as an escapee from the camp, but Warden fires his mortar and the shell blast hits Nicholson. In a moment of clarity, shell-shocked Nicholson realises his blunder ('What have I done?') and collapses. His fall pushes the detonator plunger and demolishes the bridge, as the Japanese train crosses it. This spectacular explosion ruptures the bridge in a cascade of timber and flames, as the train swan dives into the Kwai. Experts from Ceylon's Imperial Chemical Industries acted as advisors for this sequence. As a final comment on the futility and folly of war, Dr Clipton surveys the bodies of Shears, Nicholson, Joyce and Saito, and the ruined bridge, and utters disbelievingly: 'Madness! Madness!'

The Bridge on the River Kwai was the box office hit of 1957 – *Film Review* in 1959 noted that it revived cinema going in Britain and 'achieved the rarity of bringing back the long queues outside every cinema at which it was shown'. At the 1957 Academy Awards, it won Best Picture and did well in all departments. Lean was named Best Director, Guinness Best Actor, with other statuettes going to Arnold's score, Peter Taylor's editing, Hildyard's cinematography and Boulle (who spoke no English) for Adapted Screenplay. It also won BAFTA's for Guinness, Boulle and Best British Film. During the film's restoration in 1996, Foreman and Wilson's names were finally added to the film's title sequence by the Writer's Guild of America. It remains one of the pre-eminent World War II movies, through its combination of great acting, locations, music and a timeless story.

A belated sequel, *Return from the River Kwai*, followed in 1988. In February 1945, US fighter-bombers destroy the bridges on the River Kwai. As the end of the war approaches, Lieutenant Tanaka (George Takei), the Japanese commandant of Kanburi work camp, is instructed to move his British and Australian prisoners, who have been toiling on the railway, to Japan by train. Meanwhile US pilot Lieutenant Crawford (Christopher Penn) is shot down in the jungle and joins commando Colonel Grayson (Denholm Elliott) and his Siamese guerrilla raiders, who

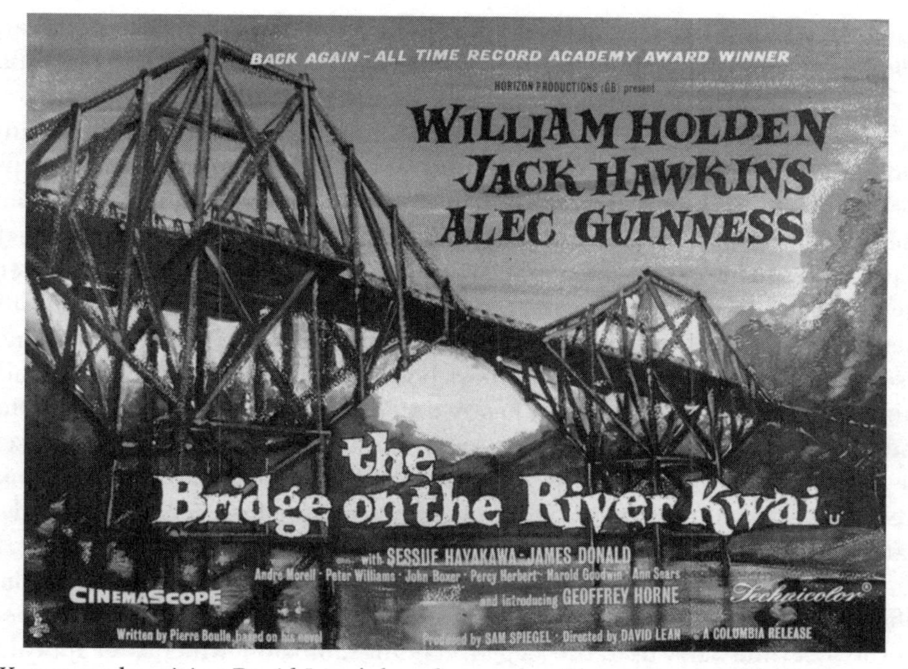

UK poster advertising David Lean's hugely popular, Oscar-winning *The Bridge on the River Kwai* (1957). Poster courtesy Kevin Wilkinson Collection.

plan to waylay the train and free the POWs. They fail and Crawford is detained on the train. Eventually reaching Saigon, the POWs board a cargo ship, the *Brazil Maru* and with a destroyer escort, set off for Japan. Crawford escapes and steals a Japanese plane, but ditches in the China Sea, where he's picked up by US submarine *USS Sealion*. The POWs manage to overpower their guards and take over the ship, but at the moment of their freedom the US sub torpedoes the cargo ship, despite Crawford's warnings. The ship is flying the Japanese flag, with no indication of POWs on board, and the sub picks up the survivors. The film was based on a true story as retold in Joan and Clay Blair's 1979 book of the same name. Only 809 of the 2,218 POWs travelling on two Japanese freighters on 12 September 1944 were saved.

Often derided as a cash-in on Lean's film, *Return from the River Kwai* has much to recommend it. The story is well told by action director Andrew V. McLaglen and has scenic locations in Malaysia, Thailand and Manila, including an authentic railroad and docks. Edward Fox gives an excellent performance as sympathetic British doctor, Major Benford. The supporting cast includes Nick Tate as Australian Commander Hunt, Timothy Bottoms as Aussie sailor Billy Miller (who in a brutal scene is beheaded by Tanaka) and Tatsuya Nakadai (from *The Human Condition* trilogy and Akira Kurosawa's samurai epics) as Tanaka's alcoholic superior, Major Harada.

In Robert Parish's *The Purple Plain* (1954), Gregory Peck played a pilot downed in the Burmese jungle. This theatre of war was also the setting for the UK BBC TV sitcom *It Ain't Half Hot Mum* (1974–81), which featured a concert party in the jungle. It was the second of writers Jimmy Perry and David Croft's trilogy of wartime sitcoms, between the Home Front *Dad's Army* (1968–77) and *'Allo 'Allo!* (1982–92), set in Occupied France. The TV series *Tenko* and films such as *A Town like Alice* (1956) were Far Eastern-set POW scenarios.

Best-selling author James Clavell had been imprisoned in a Japanese camp and his experiences were recounted in his first novel, *King Rat*, in 1962. Bryan Forbes directed the film version in 1965, with George Segal as King, the lying, cheating hustler, who feathers his own nest with profits made from others. Set in 1945 Singapore in notorious Changi jail for US, British and Australian prisoners, the film shows how King, a mere corporal, has created an empire for himself in the POW camp. He lives in luxury while his fellow rag-clothed, malnourished, disease-ridden inmates starve. He enjoys hot-towel shaves, has manicured nails, shined shoes, laundered clothes, neatly cropped hair and sells POWs watches and other personal effects to the Japanese, skimming off the profit for himself. He serves a meal of cooked dog and in one of his schemes, he and his cronies breed rats and sell their meat on to officers as 'mouse deer', which they understandably find a little 'stringy'.

King Rat is Forbes' best film, with its themes of humility, greed, love, class difference and survival. John Barry's haunting score adds to the downbeat mood. It's the first time Barry used the jagged, echoing cimbalom which later appeared as Harry Palmer's theme 'A Man Alone' in *The Ipcress File* (1965). The remainder of the Changi inmates are perched precariously on the edge of sanity. Tom Courtenay was beady-eyed, needling Lieutenant Robin Grey, who is constantly trying to nail corruption, thievery and dishonour in the British ranks. John Mills was Colonel Smedley-Taylor, who turns a blind eye to such activities. Cheating quartermaster Lieutenant Colonel Jones, who tampers with the weights used for dolling out the prisoners' food, was played by Gerald Sim (later the rector in the UK TV series *To the Manor Born*) and a pre – *Rising Damp* Leonard Rossiter was Major McCoy. Patrick O'Neal was Top Sergeant Max, who outranks King, but is his flunky. James Donald, from *Bridge on the River Kwai*, was again cast as the camp doctor. Denholm Elliott was Lieutenant Larkin, who survives the war only to be informed that his wife and daughter have been killed in a German air raid on Coventry in 1941. James Fox played Peter Marlowe, who is able to speak Malay and acts as King's interpreter. They become close friends – much of the film is their strange love story – and when Marlowe injures his arm and it becomes gangrenous, King pays for the necessary medical supplies to prevent it being amputated. When the camp is liberated following the Japanese surrender, and King is back to his subordinate corporal's rank, he no longer wants to know officer Marlowe. Something unspoken has changed between them and King leaves without saying goodbye. The film's poster stated, somewhat misleadingly: 'They made the toughest among them king', which isn't the point of the story at all. Changi is a place where human life does have a price – and if you can afford it, you'll live. Burnett Guffey's Oscar-nominated monochrome cinematography captured every bead of sweat and cloud of dust in the stifling, rotten camp, a place where King is king of a dung heap with an ever-growing graveyard.

Val Guest's *Yesterday's Enemy* (1959) recounted a British patrol in Burma who victimise and execute Japanese prisoners, including civilians. Filmed in black-and-white Megascope, *Enemy* starred Stanley Baker and an excellent cast: Guy Rolfe, Leo McKern, Gordon Jackson and Bryan Forbes. Leslie Norman's *The Long and the Short and the Tall* (1960 – *Jungle Fighters* in the USA) takes its title from the rousing standard 'Bless 'Em All'. Based on the play of the same name by Wallis Hall, it is set in 1942 (as British troops fight the Japanese) but bears the hallmarks of 1960s British 'Kitchen Sink' drama. A squad commanded by Sergeant 'Mitch' Mitchem (Richard Todd) is on patrol to test sonic warfare equipment which plays tape recordings of troop movements to confuse the Japanese. The bickering unit consists of pugnacious Corporal 'Johnno' Johnstone (Richard Harris), irritable Scot Lance-Corporal 'Jock' MacLeish (Ronald Fraser), mule-skinning Welshman Private 'Taff' Evans (John Rees), diplomatic Englishman Private 'Smudger' Smith (John Meillon), cowardly Geordie radio operator Private 'Sammy' Whitaker (David McCallum) and niggling cockney Private 'Bammo' Bamforth (Laurence Harvey).

The patrol captures a Japanese soldier (Kenji Takaki) whom they christen 'Tojo'. As the fractious group argue, they humiliate their prisoner. Surprisingly it is indolent, disruptive Bamforth who tries to protect the prisoner. Tojo is accused of looting British cigarettes and is roughed up, but Bamforth reveals that he gave their prisoner the smokes. While they are holed up in a tin mine, Whitaker machine-guns their prisoner in cold blood, alerting the enemy to their position. Bamforth and Mitchem fight a futile rearguard action, but the patrol is ambushed in the jungle. All are wiped out, save for Johnstone and Whitaker, and the latter begins to suffer the same humiliation at the hands of his captors that the British had meted out on Tojo. The powerhouse ensemble cast – especially Harris, Harvey and Todd – is excellent. Peter O'Toole had starred as Bamforth in the stage version. With its casual racism (Japanese are the 'Yellow Peril' and 'Nippos'), bad language (it was originally an X certificate in the UK) and testosterone-fuelled macho rivalry, the film's taut drama is spoiled by its obvious use of interior 'jungle' sets at Elstree Studios, though the sharp monochrome photography almost compensates for this. Had it been made on location it would have packed an even greater punch, but it still delivers its share of visceral psychological drama as the squabbling, disreputable squaddies pick at each other like a festering wound and seal their own fate with their petty, thoughtless actions.

John Sturges' *Never So Few* (1959 – working title *Sacred and Profane*) was based on the 1957 book *Never So Few* by Tom T. Chamales and shot on location in Burma, Thailand and Ceylon in Metrocolor and CinemaScope. In the Kachin Hills of north Burma in 1942, 1,000 Kachin warriors, who are outnumbered by the Japanese 40–1, become a formidable raiding force under Allied OSS officers – captains Tom C. Reynolds (Frank Sinatra) and Britisher Danny DeMortimer (Richard Johnson). Dean Jones played radio operator Sergeant Jim Norby, Steve McQueen was army driver William Lewis 'Bill' Ringa, Philip Ahn was Kachin leader Nautaung and George Takei (later Sulu in the *Star Trek* TV series) had a bit part as a hospitalised raider. Peter Lawford appeared as army doctor Captain Grey Travis and Charles Bronson played Sergeant John Danforth, a Navajo code talker. This may sound like a fanciful gimmick, but the US Army did employ 400 Navajos during World War II, from the Guadalcanal campaign in 1942 onwards, to relay messages. The Navajo language was difficult to learn and almost never written down, so it fooled the Japanese, who had no hope of cracking the code. The entire battle for Iwo Jima in 1945 was directed by Navajo code talkers. Adam Beach played Navajo code talker Ben Yahzee in John Woo's *Windtalkers* (2002 – also starring Nicolas Cage and Christian Slater), which is set during the battle for Saipan in the Pacific War.

In *Never So Few*, Reynolds' force repulses Japanese ambushes and embarks on a mission to destroy a Japanese airstrip, fuel dump and barracks. Over 300 Kachin fighters trek through the jungle and their mission is a success, but they encounter a US military convoy of 34 GIs who have been massacred by Chinese bandits operating across the border – these renegades have no allegiance to Generalissimo Chiang Kai-shek's government in Chungking and steal US army kit to sell to the Japanese. Reynolds and his force attack the bandit warlord's stronghold and take the bandits prisoner. When DeMortimer is killed, Reynolds orders their Chinese prisoners be executed in cold blood, an atrocity that the film glosses over. This massacre causes an international incident, for which Reynolds is arrested on his return to India. His commander General Sloan (Brian Donlevy) defends Reynolds' actions when he shows the general the dead men's personal effects and dog tags, and Chiang Kai-shek exonerates him. The film's combat scenes are well staged, with McQueen on fine form. In the early scenes Sinatra sports an ill-advised Abe Lincoln goatee and a bush hat, and unfortunately the Kachin fighters' exciting Burmese exploits form only part of the two-hour narrative. The plot becomes bogged down in India with Reynolds romancing Carla Vesari, played by Italian Gina Lollobrigida, whose general mangling of the English language slows the pace to a crawl.

The Allies offensive to take back Burma from the Japanese began in October 1942. The US commander was Lieutenant General 'Vinegar Joe' Stilwell, while General Slim coordinated the British and Commonwealth forces. Between February and March 1943 a daring raid by two groups of unorthodox Brigadier Orne Wingate's 'Chindits' – British, Ghurkha and Burmese guerrilla troops who were resupplied by air – was successful, causing disruption to Japanese supply lines. A second large Chindit operation was mounted from February to August 1944, though Wingate himself was killed in an air crash on 25 March. Barry Foster played Wingate in the three-part TV biopic *Orde Wingate* (1976). Heavy fighting from 1943 to 1945 saw the Japanese pushed back, as the Allied forces won victories at Imphal, Kohima, Madalay (secured in March 1945), Meiktila (taken in early August 1945) and finally Rangoon (May 1945). Burma was finally secured by the Allies in August 1945.

Merrill's Marauders (1962), Samuel Fuller's rough-edged adaptation of Charlton Ogburn's book *The Marauders*, depicted US raids by the 5307th Composite Provisional Unit, known as 'Merrill's Marauders', the US equivalent of the Chindits. Jeff Chandler starred as Brigadier General Frank Dow Merrill, who led his men on a special mission from India into Burma. They carry out three tough assaults: on the main Japanese supply base at Walawbum; the railhead at Shaduzup; and their famous victory to take the airfield at Myitkyina in north Burma in 1944. This shot-in-the-Philippines production – filmed in Technicolor and CinemaScope by William Clothier – is Fuller's best World War II film. The cast featured Peter Brown, Claude Akins, Will Hutchins and John Hoyt. Chandler and Ty Hardin (as Second Lieutenant Stockton) were excellent in this moving, arduous, actionful chronicle of a seemingly impossible mission behind enemy lines. Of the 3,000 men who arrived in Burma, only 100 remained fit for action by the campaign's close. Before *Merrill's Marauders* was released, Chandler died of blood poisoning following back surgery, aged only 42, though his trademark grey hair made him appear much older.

Raoul Walsh's *Objective, Burma!* (1945) was one of the most exciting – and certainly the most controversial – war film set in the Far East. As the Allies set about taking back Burma from the Japanese, Colonel Carter (Warner Anderson) at his HQ in Dibrugah, India, implements the 'Red Robin Operation' which sends a squad of US 503rd Parachute Infantry under Captain Charlie Nelson (Errol Flynn) into the green hell to obliterate a Japanese radar base 'somewhere near Point W on Operations Map B'. The party, who travel in two DC-3 Dakotas, consists of 36 paratroopers, two Ghurkha guides with local knowledge, a Chinese officer and Mark Williams (Henry Hull), an aged American News Service journalist. They succeed in obliterating the radar base, but are attacked at an abandoned airstrip as they await rescue. Two hundred miles from safety, Nelson leads his men out of Burma on foot, as Japanese forces mobilise and hunt the raiders.

Objective, Burma! is the template for every 'well-planned special mission that careers off the rails' war movie. It is also the epitome of macho, men-only combat cinema: there isn't a single woman onscreen for the film's 142-minute duration. The taut screenplay by Ranald MacDougall and Lester Cole ensured the pacy story retained its momentum and the tremendous cast featured James Brown as Sergeant Treacy, George Tobias as moaning corporal Gabby Gordon, John Alvin as Hogan, Anthony Caruso as Miggleori and Richard Erdman as 'Nebraska' Hooper, with Mark Stevens as Dakota pilot Lieutenant Barker. The paratroopers split into two groups: one led by Nelson, the other led by Lieutenant Sidney Jacobs (William Prince). The latter group is ambushed and massacred by the Japanese – in a moving scene, their tortured remains are found by Nelson's squad in a native bamboo village.

James Wong Howe's crisp monochrome cinematography captured the jungle landscape in vivid detail, while Franz Waxman's Oscar-nominated score also helped to create and sustain the mission's tension. Much of the action was filmed in the Los Angeles Arboretum and Botanic Gardens, with location shots on the Santa Anita ranch near Pasadena. The jungle is alive with animal noises on the soundtrack which adds to the film's oppressive atmosphere. The action is augmented with actual Burma campaign footage (particularly the aerial shots of the jungle and Dakotas dropping supplies to the paratroopers on the ground). Eventually the battered, starving remnants of Nelson's force – having lost their radio and hacked through disease-infested jungle, rivers and swamps – make it to a hilltop, dig in and await their fate. They repulse a night-time attack by the Japanese and are saved when Colonel Carter launches the airborne invasion of Burma, which is depicted with authentic paratroop drops and glider landing footage. The human cost of the radar's destruction is visualised by Nelson's handful of identity 'dog tags'. The film ends impressively with Nelson and his men, now recuperated, being picked up: an aircraft swoops down and catches their tow rope, hoisting their glider into the air.

The trailer trumpeted, 'The Most Heroic Adventure ever Hurled from the Screen!' The casting of Flynn, a swashbuckling womaniser and the screen's most dashing Robin Hood and General Custer, was seen by some as somewhat disingenuous, as Flynn had sat out the war in Hollywood, rather than enlist. This wasn't his fault, as he was classified '4F' (unfit for service) – due to a dodgy heart, tuberculosis and bouts of malaria – which wasn't widely known at the time. The film opens with a quote from Stilwell and creates the impression that the US alone liberated Burma. In the UK the film met severe criticism for its depiction of the campaign and was withdrawn, banned effectively, until 1953. When it was finally released, *Objective, Burma!* ensured a prologue and epilogue stressed the contribution of the British, Chinese and Indian forces (though it still omitted the Australian contribution to the campaign). This entertaining, moving, never sentimental adventure film remains one of Flynn's finest outings and one of the great wartime combat movies. But in terms of UK and US WWII cinema, the Far Eastern campaign was something of a forgotten war. There have been many more films depicting the glorious campaigns in North Africa, Europe and the Pacific than the slog through the fetid, muggy jungles of Burma.

Chapter 10

THE EASTERN FRONT (1941–45)

Adolf Hitler's foolhardy decision to invade Russia was his most disastrous of the war. The appalling conditions on the Eastern Front during the campaign are legendary in the history of warfare, through a combination of the subzero winter temperatures and the ferocity of the fighting. On 30 November 1939, Russia invaded Finland, with whom they had previously maintained a non-aggression pact. The Finns surprised everyone with their well-organised, obstinate defence of their country against massive odds. Nevertheless, they were defeated in this Winter War and on 12 March 1940 agreed to cede 16,000 square miles of their country to Russia in the Russo-Finnish Treaty.

Following the invasion of Europe and a failure to gain air supremacy during the Battle of Britain in 1940, Hitler put the amphibious invasion of Britain on hold and shifted his attention to the wide open spaces of Mother Russia, with its bountiful resources, raw materials, manpower and industry. Germany signed a non-aggression pact with Russia in August 1939, which facilitated the German invasion of Poland. But beneath the subterfuge, Hitler planned to attack Russia and oust his arch-enemy, the Communist dictator Joseph Stalin. Stalin, whose name means 'Man of Steel', had taken control of Russia in a series of purges in the 1930s and his rise to power – destroying political opponents and radical politics – was not unlike Hitler's own. Operation Barbarossa, the German invasion of Russia, was planned for 5 May 1941, but Hitler was diverted by the war in the Balkans, which sapped vital troops from the Russian invasion force and delayed the operation's start date. This last factor was to prove most costly in the coming months.

'Barbarossa' was the nickname of Frederick I, Holy Roman emperor from 1152–1190. The German invasion force was some three million men, organised into three vast army groups and augmented with half a million allies: Rumanians, Slovaks, Hungarians, Vichy French and Italians, plus the Finns, who

Cold War: US poster advertising Sam Peckinpah's brutal war film, *Cross of Iron* (1977), which was set on the Russian Front. Poster courtesy Kevin Wilkinson Collection.

wanted to regain their Russian-occupied land. Facing them were an equal number of Russians, who were poorly organised and equipped. Barbarossa rolled into action on 22 June 1941. Army Group North, led by General Wilhem Von Leeb, headed for Leningrad; Army Group Centre under Fedor Von Bock went for Moscow; and in the South Gerd Von Rundstedt drove into the Ukraine and the Crimea.

The Blitzkrieg lightning strikes worked again, with the German pincer movements outflanking, surrounding and isolating entire Russian army groups. The Germans deployed two gigantic, long-range, railway-mounted siege guns, the Schwerer Gustav and the Dora, which had 31-and-a-half-inch calibre barrels. But the pockets of Russian resistance fought hard and protected their soil more determinedly than Hitler had anticipated. In the Eastern Front's most famous encirclement, Leningrad was besieged from September 1941 for 882 days (often rounded up to 900 days) by Army Group North. The plan was for the Germans to starve the defenders, but the population survived on supplies which were ferried across Lake Ladoga. In the winter the lake froze and a road was chiselled through the ice. The city was finally liberated by the Soviet army on 24 January 1944, amid reports of cannibalism and extreme suffering.

Italian director Sergio Leone had long planned to make a film of the siege, but died in 1989 before he could begin filming. The project, known variously as *The Siege*, *The 900 Days* and *Leningrad*, was to have been a co-production involving Russian and Italian finance and was based around Dmitri Shostakovich's 'Leningrad Symphony'. Writer-director Aleksandr Buravsky made the unrelated project *Leningrad* (2009 – released internationally as *Attack on Leningrad*), a UK-Russian co-production which was shot on location in St Petersburg. English press photographer and journalist Kate Davis (Mira Sorvino) is separated from her lover – fellow journalist, American Philip Parker (Gabriel Byrne) – and trapped in the besieged city. Based on a true story, *Leningrad* is visually impressive in its depiction of snowbound Leningrad and early action scenes – in particular a rain-drenched, muddy pitched battle – bode well, but the film becomes convoluted and somewhat sluggish. Mostly the story recounts Kate's relationship with the malnourished Russian population, including Nina Tsvetkova (Olga Sutulova), a member of the Russian militia. The English journalist poses as a Spanish communist (the Russian secret police are attempting to locate Kate) and following a trek across frozen Lake Ladoga, she is reunited with Philip on the eastern shore. But she has become emotionally involved with the people of Leningrad and when Nina and the supply trucks head back towards the city, Kate goes with them to an uncertain fate. Both Nina and Kate died in 1943 during the siege.

As the Germans advanced, Stalin stalled them with his cannon fodder army. This allowed Stalin some breathing space, as he ordered the dismantling of Russia's industrial equipment and moved it east, safely beyond the Ural Mountains. The Germans drove on towards Moscow, but their elastic supply lines were becoming overly stretched and the autumn saw a turn in the weather: rain washed away roads and turned them into quagmires. The delay in Barbarossa's start date proved costly, as the German objectives – Leningrad, Moscow and the Volga – had been reached, but not taken. The Germans launched Operation Taifun (Typhoon), their attack on Moscow, on 2 October 1941. But they weren't equipped for a winter war and certainly not for one where the temperature dropped to 40 below freezing. As the Germans dug deeper into the Russian vastness, they were digging their own graves. On 5 December, 25 miles from Moscow, the advance ground to a halt. On 6 December 1941, the Russians counterattacked and broke the German encirclement, saving their capital city. When winter set in, the Germans prepared for the long haul and waited for the spring thaw. But the Russians attacked relentlessly, exploiting their superior winter kit and familiarity with the conditions. Stalin's Siberian Reserves – crack troops expert in winter warfare – were key to this victory. So disappointed was Hitler with what he saw as the failure to take Moscow that he personally took charge of the army. As Mussolini (Rod Steiger) says in *The Last Days of Mussolini* (1974), Russia has three great generals: 'General Snow, General Mud and General Distance – no one's ever beaten them'.

Hitler had learned nothing from history. His defeat by the weather was a retread of Napoleon's ill-fated invasion of Russia in 1812, during the Napoleonic Wars. Though he took the capital, Napoleon found it abandoned and had no choice but to retreat. The long trudge home, over the winter of 1812–13, resulted in catastrophic losses for Napoleon's army. To repulse Hitler's invasion the Russians deployed two great technological innovations and one great tactician. The T-34 tank, the best tank of the war, with its heavy armour, hard-hitting firepower (a 76.2 mm gun, plus two 7.62 mm machine guns) and speed (34 mph). In 1943, the Russian's deployed the whooshing tubular missile batteries, the Katyusha (nicknamed 'Stalin's Organs'), which fired 16 missiles in ten seconds. Their other great advantage was the Russian's commander, Marshal Georgi Zhukov, who in addition to leading the successful defence of Moscow, went on to many great victories, including the final attack on Berlin in 1945. A lesser Russian innovation and an inhumane weapon were the Russians' dog bombs – literally dogs with explosives strapped to their backs who were trained to forage for food under German tanks.

While two of the German army groups struggled to their objectives, Army Group South launched a fresh offensive in the summer of 1942 – a push into the oil fields of the Caucasus, the mountain region of south-eastern Europe. This was part of Hitler's wider 1942 strategy, a giant pincer movement which was also to capture the oil fields of the Middle East, through North Africa. The operation was codenamed Fall Blau (Case Blue). Army Group South divided into two: Army Group A headed for the Caucasus oil fields, while Group B headed for the River Volga and Stalingrad, where factories churned out a quarter of Russia's armour and weapons. Stalingrad was a heavily fortified city, with an important industrial sector and a power station, which were the Germans' chief objectives. The offensive began on 28 June 1942 and by 9 August Group A had reached the Maikop oilfields. By 23 August, the advanced guard of Group B – the XIV Panzer Corps – reached Stalingrad. The city was defended by the Soviet 62nd and 64th Armies, commanded by Generals Chuikov and Shumilov. German General Paulus and the VI Army supported XIV Panzer Corps, and the Russians fell back to within the city limits on 2 September 1942. This marked the beginning of the Battle of Stalingrad, as the suburbs were engulfed in fighting. The opposing forces were roughly equal, with one million troops deployed on each side. The Luftwaffe had attacked the city but the defenders dug in the bombed-out rubble. The Germans' Panzers were useless at street fighting, which they christened Rattenkrieg ('Rat War'). On 15 October, after hard-fought battles, the Germans captured the Tractor factory (where the Russians had assembled their production line T-34s) and on 23 October the Barrikady (Barricade) and Krasny Oktyabr (Red October) factories, and fought for the city's grain elevators, great multi-story grain store houses which resembled blocks of flats. By the end of October, Paulus controlled most of Stalingrad.

On 19 November, the Russians counterattacked the ill-equipped, understrength German auxiliaries in the north. The following day, a similar counterattack was launched in the south. A Russian pincer movement enveloped the city and on 23 November the pincers met, trapping Paulus and the entire VI Army and part of the Panzer Army – some 330,000 men – in Stalingrad. The Luftwaffe failed to drop adequate supplies on Stalingrad and Paulus fed his able soldiers, but not his starving wounded. The Germans' ammunition dwindled and frostbite gnawed away at the beleaguered defenders. 12 December saw the start of Operation Winter Storm, an attempt to relieve Stalingrad from the southwest by Army Group Don led by General Von Manstein, the architect of the Blitzkriegs in Europe. But the Russians halted this offensive 25 miles from Stalingrad and on Christmas Eve 1942 the Russians pushed Manstein back. Trapped in the southernmost of two defensive pockets, Paulus was promoted to field marshal on 30 January 1943. On 31 January the new field marshal surrendered the city and on 2 February, the northern defensive pocket capitulated. Ten-thousand Germans died in the city's defence and many were evacuated by air. Ninety-one thousand were taken prisoner and marched to Siberia. On their release ten years later, only 7,000 had survived. History has viewed Stalingrad as one of the greatest tactical victories (for the Russians) and greatest tactical failures (for Paulus' encirclement and destruction). It was a major turning point, not only in the war on the Eastern front, but also in the war as a whole.

Josef Vilsmaier's *Stalingrad* (1992) remains the greatest depiction of the battle. It follows a group of German soldiers from their idyllic leave in the sunny Italian seaside town of Porto Cervo in August 1942, to their involvement in the Stalingrad encirclement and their subsequent attempts to break out of the city. The principal characters are Leutnant (Lieutenant) Hans Von Witzland (played by Thomas Kretschmann), Unteroffizier (literally sub-officer) 'Rollo' Rohleder (Jochen Nickel), Obergefreiter (Senior Lance-Corporal) Fritz 'Fritzi' Reiser (Dominique Horwitz) and soldiers GeGe (pronounced 'Jay Jay') Müller (Sebastian Rudolph) and Otto (Sylvester Groth), plus their commanders, Hauptmann (Captain) Musk (Karel Hermanek) and Hauptmann Haller (Dieter Okras).

Travelling from Italy by train, the Germans pass through the sweeping Russian Steppes, where farm workers till the land and disembark at a rain-drenched marshalling yard. The new arrivals are thrust into the front line offensive to take the factory district of Stalingrad, in ferocious street fighting which proves costly. One of the Germans is badly injured, losing his leg in a booby-trapped sewer, and his cohorts take him to a vast field hospital and demand at gunpoint treatment for him. For their actions, Von Witzland and his men are punished: they are sent to the frozen wastes around the city to work as mine-sweepers. When the Russians counterattack during Christmas 1942 and the Germans' weak Rumanian auxiliaries give way on the flank, the German prisoners are reinstated in the army to aid an attempted breakout from the city. Despite being undernourished and under-equipped, they ambush and defeat a Russian tank offensive at Marinovka. But Paulus' forces are doomed to defeat and Vilsmaier unflinchingly depicts his heroes' demise.

Stalingrad is an accurate recreation of the infamous battle. It was shot on location in Italy, Finland and the Czech Republic, and Norbert J. Schneider's looming score, performed by the Münchner Philharmoniker, rumbles and crashes like a vast rolling war machine. The dismal, clattering railway marshalling yard is filled with columns of disembarking troops and beaten, mistreated

Russian POWs. The ordnance on display includes field artillery, anti-aircraft guns and authentic SdKfz 251/1 half-tracks. The Russians deploy real T-34 tanks, which the dug-in German defenders hold off with an anti-tank gun. During the battle for the industrial sector of Stalingrad, German troops scramble over dust-caked rubble through streets reduces to piles of bricks, to take the factories. In this close fighting men shoot their friends by mistake, hand-to-hand combat becomes necessary and the city's sewers – harbouring rats and Russians – are cleared with flamethrowers. Vilsmaier's strong visual imagery is the film's major asset. Tanks loom out of the snow, entire multi-storey buildings are reduced to rubble in an instant and a transporter plane attempts to take off amid the panic of the rout.

These epic scenes contrast with the story's drama and moments of individual cruelty, human suffering and matter-of-fact brutality. The field hospitals are charnel houses of screaming, blood-drenched wounded, hideously disfigured or missing limbs. When all seems lost, Reiser decides to desert. Having shot himself in the hand, he arrives at an airfield for the last plane out of Stalingrad in January 1943. A fellow soldier feigns shell shock. Neither escapes, as the Russians shell the airport and the plane departs. Soldiers exposed as cowardly traitors – their self-inflicted gunshot wounds given away by tell-tale powder burns on their skin – are rolled off their stretchers and shot. Dead bodies are burned on funeral pyres or left to rot as hideous waxworks in the frozen landscape. After repulsing the Russian tanks at Marinovka, the German soldiers have no horses to tow their wheeled anti-tank gun, so manhandle it through a blizzard back to their HQ (in reality many of the German draft animals were eaten by starving troops). The retreating Germans suffer frostbite, which disintegrates and burns their extremities, while others, unable to cope with the suffering, commit suicide.

Lieutenant Witzland is the film's moral compass. The Russian Front is his first action, while some of his men – such as Rohleder – are hardened veterans. In Russia, Witzland almost immediately clashes with his superior officers. He opposes the treatment of Russian POWs and is judged a 'Russian lover'. A mass prayer meeting in the field delineates Hitler's fanatical 'holy war' between the German troops (with 'Gott Mitt Uns' – God With Us – forged on their belt buckles) and the 'scourge of Bolshevism'. Witzland and his platoon are 'tested': they are forced to act as a firing squad to execute several Russian saboteurs, including a young boy. The Luftwaffe airdrop supplies with 'Greetings from the Führer', which comprise chocolate bars and Iron Crosses. Their commander, Captain Haller, accuses Witzland and his men of looting. Gege is shot by Haller, who is then wounded by Rohleder and killed by Otto. The soldiers search the cellar of Haller's billet and discover stockpiles of food and supplies, while his men have been starving.

There were terrible atrocities perpetrated by both sides on the Eastern Front, with many Russian civilian casualties. In *Stalingrad*, we see German troops burning villages and herding Russian peasants. In Haller's cellar, when Witzland's men find Irina (Dana Vávrová), a Russian captive who has been assaulted, Witzland protects her from his men. The misty, blizzard-swept snowscapes, broken only by clusters of shivering trees, have none of the picturesque romance that is often found in snowbound war cinema. It is a desolate wasteland, an ice desert where refugees starve and wounded soldiers who have fallen by the wayside beg to be shot by their comrades. It is in this nowhere land that the heroes meet their destiny. Irina leads Reiser and Witzland towards her own lines, but she is mistaken for a German and shot. Witzland can go no further and dies slumped in Reiser's arms. In blizzard conditions, their corpses gradually vanish into the landscape, enveloped by the drifting snow.

Stalingrad's trailers announced 'From the producers of *Das Boot*' – Günther Rohrbach and Mark Damon were among the producers of both films – and cut the action to music by Gustav Mahler, with the tagline: 'In the winter of 1942, it was too cold for tears'. Two 132-minute prints exist – one in the original German language (with English subtitles) and one with an English dubbing track, which offers some variable German accents, unsynchronised lip movement and copious profanity. In its original German language, *Stalingrad* is a masterpiece of World War II cinema, while the English dub is just about saved by its powerful

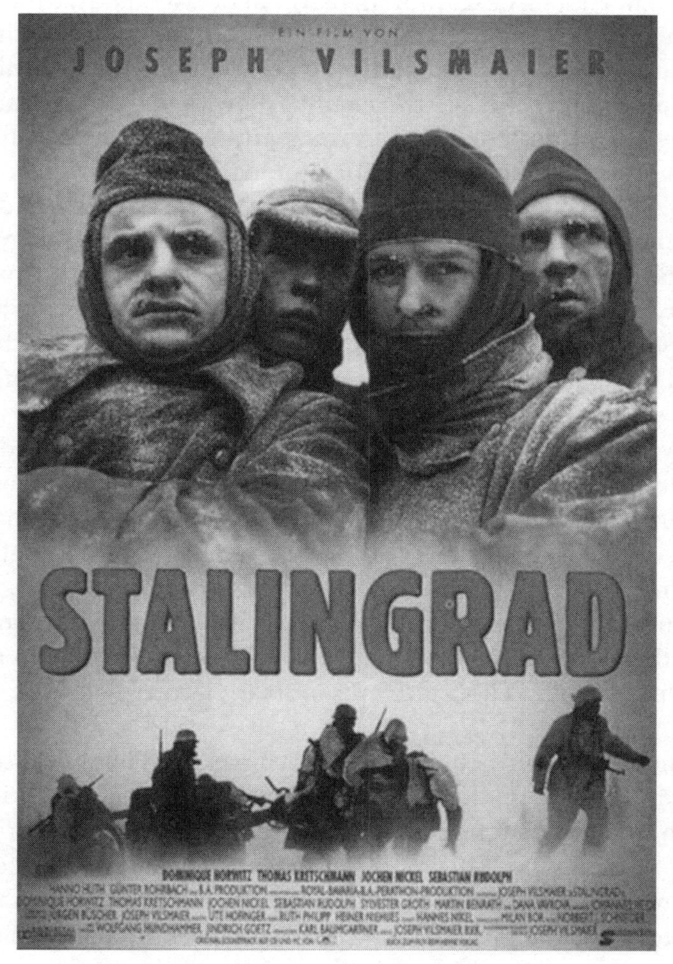

German poster advertising Josef Vilsmaier's *Stalingrad* (1992), starring, left to right, Dominique Horwitz, Sebastian Rudolph, Thomas Kretschmann and Jochen Nickel.

visuals, convincing performances and strong story. It was praised at the time for its unheroic, human depiction of the war on the Eastern Front and remains an unsettling viewing experience.

Two Russian productions re-enacted the engagement: Friedrich Ermler's *The Great Turning Point* (1946 – *The Turning Point*) and Vladimir Petrov's *The Battle of Stalingrad* (1950). Frank Wisbar's *Battle Inferno* (1959 – *Stalingrad*) – starring Peter Carsten, Horst Frank, Wolfgang Preiss and Joachim Hansen – presented the German view of the battle. Jean-Jacques Annaud's *Enemy at the Gates* (2001) used the rubble of Stalingrad as a backdrop to a battle of wits between two ace snipers: Russian Vasily Zaitsav (Jude Law) and German Major König (Ed Harris).

As the Germans fought in Poland and Russia, specialist killing squads shadowed the army, slaughtering the civilian population in its wake. These Einsatzgruppen squads shot or burned their victims, or gassed them in specially adapted trucks. This genocide was depicted in Elem Klimov's *Come and See* (1985 – *Idi i smotri*), a Russian production presented by Mosfilm. In Byelorussia in 1943, teenage Russian Fliora (Alexei Kravchenko) wanders a muddy, wintry landscape which gradually becomes more hellish as his full realisation of the Germans' activities blurs into focus. Fliora joins the partisans and is left behind in camp when they move off to engage the enemy. He witnesses a German parachute drop, is temporarily deafened by a German artillery barrage and finds himself trapped in a peasant village which is surrounded by Einsatzgruppen.

Klimov's film, the last he directed, conveys the randomness and savagery of the war on the Russian civilian population. The atmosphere is edgy, menacing, as it would be in a horror film. Fleeting moments of beauty – a burnished sunset or a showery rainbow – are hollow images amid such savagery. Fliora returns home with young partisan Glasha (Olga Mironova), to hide out with his mother and sister. The village is sinisterly deserted and buzzing flies proliferate. Fliora and Glasha eat a meal, which they find still warm in his mother's oven, and as they leave we see a grisly pile of slaughtered villagers' corpses piled against the house. *Come and See* is filled with troubling imagery and strange moments, such as a perpetually patrolling German plane, which at one point disperses propaganda leaflets ('Kill the Bolshevik kikes; smash a brick in their ugly mugs'), or the unsettling stork stalking the deserted partisans' camp. Fliora joins a group of starving peasants sheltering on an island in a swamp and later goes in search of food for them. He finds a cow, but when the animal is killed in the crossfire of a night-time firefight, Fliora attempts to steal a farmer's hay cart, to transport his booty.

Come and See builds to a sickening climax, as Fliora realises that he's behind enemy lines. From the chilly morning fog, the spectral SS killing squads emerge. On a speeding motorbike and sidecar, the sidecar carries a corpse which is 'holding' a sign: 'This morning I insulted a German soldier'. During a chaotic round-up in the village of Perekhody, the SS herd the peasants into the church, which they then grenade and torch with the villagers inside. The end titles inform us that 626 villages were dealt with in this way. Fliora escapes this atrocity, but is traumatised by witnessing extermination and rape, and visibly ages by the film's conclusion. He rejoins the partisan army, who have since taken revenge on the perpetrators of the Perekhody massacre. Klimov's film is emotionally heavy going, but a more powerful and disturbing film of events on the Eastern Front is yet to be made. The film's disconcerting, uncomfortably claustrophobic atmosphere is some achievement, as most of the action takes place outdoors.

In Russia, the conflict on the Eastern Front was known as the Great Patriotic War. With the tide turned at Stalingrad, the Russians pressed home their advantage – Stalin's war machine went into overdrive and his army didn't suffer another significant defeat until the war's end. On 5 June 1943, the German's mounted a counteroffensive, called Operation Citadel, an attempt to isolate Russian forces around Kursk. The German pincer movement pushed from Kharkov in the south and from Orel in the north, but the Russian defences held firm. In the southern sector, the II SS Panzer Corps faced the Russians' Fifth Guards Tank Army on 12 July. This massive tank battle –the largest of the war – stopped the German advance and by the end of July the offensive had been pushed back to where it began. Thereafter the German forces on the Eastern Front were on the defensive, as the invaders were driven back to their own borders and beyond, in a series of immense land battles. The land the Germans had fought on was where they were now buried.

The internationally acclaimed, multi-award winning Russian films – Mikhail Kalatozov's *The Cranes are Flying* (1957) and Grigori Chukrai's *Ballad of a Soldier* (1959) – both used the broad canvas of the Eastern Front as a backdrop to their tales of humanity and love. Three-hundred-thousands Italians were deployed on the Eastern Front, but they suffered terrible casualties and only 10,000 returned home. Giuseppe De Santis' epic *Italiano Brava Gente* (1965 – *Attack and Retreat*) depicted the Italians who fought on the Russian Front and recreated Mussolini's involvement in Operation Barbarossa; it starred Arthur Kennedy, Peter Falk, Tatyana Samoilova, Rafaelle Pisu and Andrea Checchi. Douglas Sirk's downbeat *A Time to Love and a Time to Die* (1958) was set on the Russian-German Front in 1944. During his three week's leave, German soldier Ernst Graeber (John Gavin) returns to a Berlin all but levelled by Allied bombers. There he falls in love and marries Elizabeth Kruze (Lilo Pulver). He returns to the front and learns that Elizabeth is expecting a baby, but as he reads her letter he's killed by a partisan whose life he has spared. Larissa Shepitko's *The Ascent* (1976) depicted Russian partisans fighting the invaders in 1943. Andrei Tarkovsky's *Ivan's Childhood* (1962 – *My Name is Ivan* and *The Youngest Spy*), a Golden Lion winner at the Venice Film Festival, had little Ivan (Kolya Burlaev) escape from a German prison camp and becoming a spy for the Red Army. *Liberation* (1969) an East German-Italian-Polish-Russian-Yugoslavian co-production, depicted the war on the Eastern Front from 1943–45 and was cut down to a two-hour English dubbed version, *The Great Battle* (1971). In its original form it comprised four films: *The Flaming Bulge, The Breakthrough, The Direction of the Main Blow* and *The Battle for Berlin.*

Sam Peckinpah's *Cross of Iron* (1977) is told from the Germans' point of view, at the very moment of their defeat on the Eastern Front. It is an unusual international

Corporal Rolf Steiner (James Coburn, left) and Krüger (Klaus Löwitsch, background) in Sam Peckinpah's uncompromising depiction of combat on the Eastern Front, *Cross of Iron* (1977). Courtesy Kevin Wilkinson Collection.

concoction: a British–West German co-production shot in Yugoslavia with interiors at Jadran Film, Zagreb, which deployed a British–German–Yugoslavian cast and an American star playing a German platoon leader. In early 1943 on the Taman Peninsula of the Black Sea, German troops are besieged by the Russians. German Corporal Rolf Steiner (James Coburn) returns from a reconnaissance mission and informs his superior, Colonel Brandt (James Mason), that the Russians are planning an offensive. Idiosyncratic, unconventional Steiner clashes with new arrival Captain Stransky (Maximillian Schell), an aristocratic Prussian who has requested a transfer to the Russian Front: 'I want to win the Iron Cross'. Steiner is promoted to senior sergeant, but soon afterwards the Russians launch an onslaught, with armoured support, which is somehow repulsed by the ragged German defenders. Steiner suffers shell-shock concussion and convalesces in a hospital far from the front, where he begins a relationship with Eva (Senta Berger), a nurse. Back in action, Steiner is asked to be one of the witnesses for Stransky's commendation for the Iron Cross – for leading the counterattack which repulsed the Russians – which was actually led by Lieutenant Meyer (Igor Galo) who was killed in the action. Steiner refuses. The German divisional commander orders Brandt's troops to pull back, but Stransky orchestrates a breakdown in radio communications. When the Russian offensive strikes, Steiner's platoon is trapped behind enemy lines. When the Germans evacuate the peninsula, Steiner and his men make it to their own lines. As the depleted platoon emerge from the no man's land – with some of the men posing as Russian POWs – Stransky's conniving aide Lieutenant Triebig (Roger Fritz) opens fire on them – only Steiner, Krüger (Klaus Löwitsch) and Anselm (Dieter Schidor) survive. Steiner machine-guns Triebig and goes looking for Stransky, as the Russians attack.

Cross of Iron is a typically blood-drenched venture from 'Bloody Sam'. Nonconformist, psychologically disturbed Steiner fights a war he doesn't believe in, while his loyal men teeter on the brink of madness. It was based on Willi Heinrich's novel *The Willing Flesh*. The score, by Ernest Gold, blends violin 'love themes' with patriotic marches. The titles, depicting archive footage of Eastern Front combat footage, refugees and prisoners, is accompanied by a children's choir. This juxtaposition of moods is echoed in Peckinpah's trademark style. The combat scenes, staged in open country, woodland and a wrecked factory – are filled with slow-motion bloodletting, as action filmed at normal speed is intercut with bodies pirouetting or flying through the air in slo-mo. The combat is swathed in smoke and explosions, as troops charge forward and are impaled on barbed wire, or are blown to pieces by grenades. The Germans' trenchwork bunkers are under almost permanent artillery barrage and the distant thud of mortars punctuates many dialogue scenes. The $4 million budget quickly ran out and Peckinpah ended up spending $90,000 of his own money to complete the film. His producer could only muster three T-34 tanks for the Russian offensive, but by deft editing and by filming them from every angle, they appear more numerous.

Brian Ackland-Snow and Ted Haworth's production design is authentically decrepit, with the embattled defenders' lice-infected rags contrasting with new arrival Stransky's spotless uniform. John Coquillon's steely cinematography is impressive and Coburn, with his white, haggard face and German army cap, resembles a Sven Hassel paperback cover brought to life. James Mason was Steiner's superior and David Warner played Mason's adjutant, Captain Kiesel, who eulogises Steiner as, 'A myth, but men like him are our last hope'. Slavko Štimac played a young harmonica-playing Russian boy soldier captured by Steiner's men. Stransky orders him to be executed – German policy on the Russian Front – but Steiner shelters him in the platoon's bunker. When Steiner allows the boy to return to his own lines, the lad is mistaken for a German and is shot by his own comrades.

Peckinpah was at pains to stress the futility of war and the fakery of 'glory'. Cowardly Stransky can't bear to return home without winning the Iron Cross, an award Steiner deems 'just a piece of worthless metal'. He hates such 'Iron Cross scavengers' and as the Russians attack through a burning railway marshalling yard, Steiner tells him: 'I will show you where the Iron Crosses grow'. In this final battle, as Brandt leads a counterattack, Steiner laughs maniacally at Stransky struggling to reload his rifle. The end titles feature images of civilian hardship during wartime, including Vietnam and other contemporary conflicts, pounding home Peckinpah's anti-war message. Though badly received in the US, the film was a hit in Germany and Austria. Its reputation has since improved and it now rated as one of the best combat films of the 1970s. A lesser sequel, *Breakthrough* (also released as *Sergeant Steiner*), starring Richard Burton and Robert Mitchum, was released in 1979.

Like *Come and See*, director/co-scriptwriter Nikolai Lebedev's *The Star* (2002 – *Zvezda*) was from the Mosfilm stable. By the summer of 1944, the Red Army had pushed the Germans westward, to begin the liberation of Poland from Nazi tyranny. *Star* told the story of a squad of Russian army scouts who infiltrate behind enemy lines on a fact-finding reconnaissance mission, with instructions not to engage the enemy, nor take prisoners. The group consists of Lieutenant Travkin (Igor Petrenko), Sergeant Kostya Mamochkin (Alexei Panin), Sergeant Anikanov (Alexei Kravchenko, from *Come and See*) and four men. Each member of the squad possesses specialist knowledge – one is an expert marksman, one a local who knows the terrain, another a German-speaking translator. Kitted out in camouflage gear, they successfully cross the German lines and learn from captured soldiers (who they later kill) that the Germans are concentrating their forces for a counteroffensive which will mobilise in a matter of days. These forces appear to be gathering at a station – this is subsequently destroyed by a Russian airstrike – but the depot is a decoy. The tanks and armour are being assembled in an industrial quarry by night. Travkin's scouts are decimated by an immense Wehrmacht manhunt, Operation Trap, which is launched to track down the 'Green Ghosts'.

The Star was based on a true story by Emmanuil Kazalevich and the real scouts were posthumously decorated for their bravery in 1964. The project obviously meant a lot to director Lebedev and his passion for the subject is conveyed during this moving, eloquent film. Flares light up the night sky, plunge to earth and fizzle out in the river that marks the Russian front line, in imagery which represents the young men's lives lost in the war. The photographs which Travkin hands over as his personal effects before he embarks on the mission are actually pictures of Lebedev's own family, who were killed in the conflict. Fans of militaria will be pleased to see much armour on display, from Russian T-34 tanks to German SdKfz 251 half-tracks and the SdKfz 2 tracked motorcycles. The German Tigers look authentic, but are built over T-34 chassis.

Artfully photographed by Yuri Nevsky on location in Russia, *The Star* succeeds in depicting both the natural beauty of the vast landscape – woods, rivers, rolling open grassland – and the smoking, shattered ruins left in the war's wake. A German barrage levels a village and throughout the action the squad encounter such grisly sights as hanging corpses and executed, naked prisoners (with their hands bound and backs scarred) drifting downriver. *Star* bears certain similarities to *Cross of Iron*, told from the Russian perspective and with an added romantic subplot. The mission is the film's primary focus, but Lebedev also depicts the relationship between Travkin and radio operator Katya (Yekaterina Vulichenko), which recalls the British film *A Matter of Life and Death*. Katya falls in love with Travkin – her first sight of the young lieutenant is as an idealised hero riding his horse to HQ. As Travkin keeps in touch with his command via radio, it is to Katya he speaks. Travkin's call sign is 'Star', the command post's 'Earth'. The two plot threads meet in the film's actionful, dreadful climax, when the remnants of Travkin's squad are trapped, outnumbered, in a barn. Travkin desperately tries to radio the vital information to his superiors, warning them of the counteroffensive of 40,000 men and 2,000 tanks, as his men are wiped out. He manages to send the message in time, before a German flamethrower immolates the barn, burning the occupants. Katya, no longer able to hear an answer from 'Star', refuses to leave her radio post.

The Russian army continued its advance into Poland and by August 1944 it had reached Warsaw, where the Red Army met severe German resistance. The Polish 'Home Army' rose up against the German occupiers in the Warsaw Uprising, but by October 1944 the rebellion had been crushed and the city destroyed – with still no sign of the Russians. Some sources speculate that Stalin paused his army and allowed the rebellion to be suppressed before he entered the shattered city – Poland became a Communist nation under Stalin's rule following its liberation. Increasingly oppressive conditions and Nazi brutality in the Warsaw ghetto during the German occupation featured in Roman Polanski's Oscar-winning *The Pianist* (2002), starring Adrien Brody and Thomas Kretschmann. Andrzej Wajda's *Katyn* (2007) detailed the massacre of 22,000 Polish POWs by the Russians in 1940 and Jon Avnet's TV movie *Uprising* (2001) depicted the events of the Warsaw Ghetto Uprising in 1943 and starred David Schwimmer, Jon Voight, Donald Sutherland, Leelee Sobieski, Hank Azaria and Sadie Frost.

Kanal (1956 – *They Loved Life*), the second part of Andrzej Wajda's war trilogy (following *A Generation*) saw most of the cast spending most of the film wading through effluence in Warsaw's sewer (kanal) system. It begins in late September 1944, on the fifty-sixth day of the Warsaw Uprising, as the Russian Red Army neared the city. A company of the Polish Home Army (as the resistance movement was called) are ordered to withdraw from the defensive perimeter and head for the centre of town, where chaos reigns. As the Tiger tanks close in and German troops herd civilians into cellars and set the houses on fire, the freedom fighters climb down into the bowels of the city in an attempt to escape the smoking ruins. Once descended into this otherworldly nightmare – 'a land of dreams and shadows' – the film doesn't let up in its depiction of squalor, as the last heroes of the resistance become sewer rats. Throughout these subterranean brick sewer tunnels, wreathed in misty vapours, horrors include disease, delirium, the moans of the dying, gas attacks, dead ends, rushing water and booby-trapped exits hung with barbed wire and stick grenades. The film also offers a rare chance to see Goliath tracked mines, a German remote-controlled killing machine resembling a scale model of a tank.

As the narrator intones at *Kanal*'s outset: 'Watch them as they live their last hours'. Liaison officer Halinka (Teresa Berezowska) shoots herself when she discovers her lover, drunken Lieutenant Mądry (Emil Karewicz), is married. Mądry himself emerges from a manhole into a courtyard filled with filthy Polish prisoners, German guards, a firing squad wall and a heap of corpses. The company's leader, Lieutenant Zadra, eventually makes it out of the sewer into the levelled city but after insanely shooting his own batman, Sergeant-major Kula (Tadeusz Gwiadowski), he climbs back into the manhole. A musician, Michael, goes mad and dazedly wanders the tunnels playing an ocarina. The most riveting segments follow wounded Sub-Lieutenant Jacek Korab (Tadeusz Janczar) and his lover, Daisy Stokrotka (Teresa Izewska), a 'sewer guide' for the underground. Izewska delivers the film's best performance, an exceptionally modern portrayal of a cynical anti-heroine, who in the film's best scene refuses to read graffiti spelling out

'I love Jacek' to her dying lover, saying 'I love Johnny' instead. Daisy asks, 'Do you want my life story now?'; 'Is it long story?' asks Jacek. 'Longer than this sewer', she answers. They toil on through unspeakable filth, only to find that the light at the end of the tunnel, the sewer's outlet into the river, is barred. This nihilistic movie remained unreleased in the USA until 1961.

By 1945, the Russian landscape had swallowed Hitler's legions in its vastness. Stalin's army had faced and defeated the bulk of the Wehrmacht and without Hitler's arrogant invasion of Russia, Nazism would never have been crushed. With Warsaw taken on 17 January 1945, the Red Army pushed on towards western Poland and into Germany. By the beginning of February, the Russians had pushed towards the River Oder and were less than 50 miles from the gates of Berlin. They were determined to reach the prized capital before the Allies.

Chapter 11

THE BATTLE FOR ITALY (1943–45)

Once North Africa had fallen in May 1943, it was inevitable that the Allies would turn their attention to the invasion of Fortress Europe. The Germans expected the Allies to land in Sardinia, thanks to deception by the British 'Double Cross' organisation involving an elaborate red herring. The corpse of Allied Major William Martin was washed ashore in Southern Spain with fake plans for the Allied invasion of Sardinia. This ruse – codenamed Operation Mincemeat – was depicted in the film *The Man Who Never Was* (1956). But the Allies invaded the island of Sicily in Operation Husky, on 10 July 1943. Meeting relatively little opposition, they soon secured the island, though the German forces managed an orderly withdrawal to the mainland. The landings in Sicily were the largest amphibious assaults of the war. General Patton's US 7th Army landed in the Gulf of Gela, while Montgomery's British 8th Army attacked the Gulf of Noto, south of Syracuse. Patton arrived first at Messina in the north-eastern tip of Sicily on 17 August 1943.

It was during this campaign that the infamous incident occurred when Patton slapped a shell-shocked soldier suffering from 'battle fatigue'. This unheroic gesture was recreated in *Patton* (1970), when the general (George C. Scott) slaps a quivering hospitalised soldier (Tom Considine) and brands him a 'yellow bastard', not fit to share a ward with brave men injured in battle. *Patton* also accurately recreates some key moments from this poorly orchestrated campaign. Following his exploits in Tunisia, Patton lobbies General Alexander to deploy his plan to attack Sicily. Patton wants to attack Palermo, with Montgomery landing at Syracuse – Patton knows his history and the Athenians conquered the island this way. Montgomery (Michael Bates) has his own ideas and convinces Eisenhower to use his method, with Patton landing in Gela. Patton is to protect Montgomery's left flank, but he pushes north towards Palermo and on to Messina, arriving ahead of his 'rival'. When Montgomery, his Scot's Pipers and the 8th

Army liberate Messina, they discover the city square packed with US tanks and Patton is waiting for them. The film's depiction of the Sicilian fighting (filmed in Spain) demonstrates Patton's disregard both for orders and human life. He pushes on to Palermo (the most conquered city in history), swinging west when he should be aiding Montgomery. He also leaves US General Omar Bradley hacking his way through the mountains against stiff Axis resistance. When Patton discovers a peasant's mule wagon blocking his column's advance, he simply shoots the mules, which are summarily thrown off a bridge. Patton may be 'Old Blood and Guts', but as a soldier notes, 'Our blood, his guts'. Following the slapping incident, for which Patton had to apologise formally to all concerned, he was relieved of his command and took no further part in the Italian campaign, prompting his comment: 'I wish I'd kissed that son of a bitch'.

In Samuel Fuller's brutal, often surreal, *The Big Red One* (1980), the US 1st Infantry rifle squad led by a nameless sergeant (played by Pacific War veteran Lee Marvin) land in Sicily in July 1943. After the North African campaign, the four surviving members of his 12-man squad are named 'The Sergeant's Four

The Conquering Hero Comes: General George Patton (George C. Scott) arrives in Palermo, Sicily, in Franklin J. Schaffner's Oscar-winning *Patton* (1970). Patton's travelling in a Dodge truck, known by servicemen as 'Beeps', or 'Big Jeeps'. Courtesy Kevin Wilkinson Collection.

Horsemen': they are marksman Griff (Mark Hamill from *Star Wars*), Italian-American Vinci (Bobby Di Cicco), Johnson (Kelly Ward from *Grease*) and Zab (Robert Carradine). Cigar-chomping Zab, a would-be writer and the film's narrator, is partly based on Fuller himself, while the name Griff appeared in many of Fuller's films in tribute to a GI of that name whose injuries following an encounter with a landmine left him without arms or legs. In Sicily the Four Horsemen look upon the steady stream of replacements who arrive to reinforce their squad as 'Dead men who temporarily had the use of their arms and legs' and avoid getting to know them too well. One such replacement activates a tripwire mine, designed to castrate its victim. The sergeant tends the wounded soldier and picks up a bloody lump of flesh lying nearby: 'It's just one of your balls, Smitty', he says matter-of-factly, 'You can live without it, that's why they gave you two'. In the Sicilian episodes of the film (filmed in dusty Israel), the squad clear a village of snipers, hide in a cave to pick off a German troop convoy and take a self-propelled gun emplacement. A young Sicilian boy carries his mother's body off for burial on a cart and as thanks for liberating them, local Sicilian women colourfully decorate the sergeant's helmet with flowers. Fuller's anti-war message is articulated by a GI: 'Survival is the only glory of war'.

Using Sicily as a springboard the Allies mounted a three-pronged assault on Italy's mainland. On 3 September 1943 Operation Baytown saw the 8th Army crossing the narrow Straits of Messina and landing on the 'toe' of Italy's boot. On 9 September, the 1st Airborne Division of the 8th Army landed at Taranto (Operation Slapstick), on Italy's 'heel' to link up with their allies in the west. Also on 9 September, the US 5th Army under General Mark Clark undertook Operation Avalanche, an ambitious amphibious landing in the Gulf of Salerno. This disastrous landing proved costly, as troops of Field Marshal Albert Kesselring's Panzer Divisions offered a resolute defence. The '21 days of horror and carnage', as the battle for the Salerno beachhead would be described, almost stalled the Allies plan until the arrival of the 8th Army, driving north, forced Kesselring to withdraw to the Gustav Line (also called the Cassino Line), a defence stretching from the east to the west coast, south of Rome. When the Allies landed in September, Italy surrendered and Mussolini was rescued by German paratroops, to set up the Italian Socialist Republic in the north. The German army disarmed Italian troops, who became their prisoners and many were transported to Germany as slave labour.

The most famous film detailing the Salerno landings is Lewis Milestone's *A Walk in the Sun* (1945), which was rereleased as *Salerno Beachhead*. Filmed on Twentieth Century-Fox's Ranch in Malibu Creek State Park, *Walk in the Sun* follows an American platoon's mission – from dawn until noon – to take a German-occupied farmhouse six miles inland. During the Salerno landings their lieutenant has his face blown off, their platoon sergeant is killed and soon afterwards their next in command, another sergeant, cracks and collapses weeping. They make their way inland though woods, avoiding strafing German fighter planes, and ambush a German half-track (a US M3). Eventually they attack the farmhouse and blow a bridge, though they suffer heavy casualties. Dana Andrews, Richard Conte, John Ireland and Lloyd Bridges are convincing among the GIs.

Most of the battle for Salerno takes place offscreen – the GIs hear barrages, see smoke and aircraft overhead, and pass burning Panzers – and the human depiction of the confusion of war is very effective. These are frightened, real men waging a frightening, real war. As the title song says: 'It was just a little walk in the warm Italian sun', which turned out to be anything but.

The Gustav Line – with its bunkers, barbed wire, defences and mines – gave the German X Army a strong position and the invasion of Italy was a stalemate. The Allies took Naples on 2 October 1943, but further advances were hindered by swollen rivers, flooded valleys and bad weather. The US Army advanced up the western Mediterranean coast, with the British in the eastern Adriatic sector. The strongest point in the line was at Cassino, which protected routes north to Rome via panoramic views of the approaches. Despite sustained aerial bombardment the following March, particularly on the heights of Monte Cassino which was dominated by a Benedictine monastery, its German paratrooper defenders dug in. It wasn't until 18 May 1945 that Polish troops finally took Monte Cassino and opened up the route north. In Andrew V. McLaglen's *Dirty Dozen* clone *The Devil's Brigade* (1968), William Holden moulded convicts (augmented with Canadian regulars) into the First Special Service Force (an actual unit) to take Monte La Difensa during the Cassino campaign.

RKO's *The Bold and the Brave* (1956) directed by Lewis R. Foster, was set during the Italian stalemate spring of 1944 (though it was filmed in the Simi Valley, California), when the Allies couldn't break the Gustav Line. Three US comrades provide differing perspectives on the war. Pious sergeant 'Preacher' (Don Taylor) becomes involved with an Italian woman Fiamma (Nicole Maurey), whom he later discovers to his disgust is a prostitute. Cowardly Dave Fairchild (Wendell Corey) eventually musters some guts during a recon patrol and takes on and destroys a German tank (actually a Korean War American M47 from the 1950s) and Mickey Rooney (who was Oscar Nominated for Best Supporting Actor) played motormouth gambler Willy Dooley. He wins over $30,000 at craps, facilitating his dreams of opening his own fancy restaurant back in the US, but dies riddled with bullets, surrounded by his winnings.

Though it begins in Tunisia, where green US recruits receive their baptism of fire at the Battle of Kasserine Pass, William A. Wellman's *G.I. Joe* (1945 – *War Correspondent*, *The Story of G.I. Joe* or *Ernie Pyle's Story of G.I. Joe*), is primarily set in the slog through Italy towards Rome, specifically the muddy, rain-sodden stalemate siege at the monastery atop Monte Cassino. It was based on the 1943 book *Here Is Your War* by popular Scripps-Howard war correspondent Ernie Pyle (played in the film by Burgess Meredith). The film is antiheroic, heavy on drama and light on action, with a good sense of period realism. 'You know, when the war's over, I'm gonna buy me a map to find out where I've been', moans a soldier. Dug in their foxholes and bunkers, the soldiers become muddier, shaggier and more ragged as the siege progresses. Wellman cast many actual combat veterans from Africa, Sicily and Italy as the soldiers. The film features a towering, Oscar-nominated performance from Robert Mitchum, as the unshaven, heavy-lidded, laconic Lieutenant (later Captain) Bill Walker. Wally Cassell was womanising Private Dondaro. Private Murphy (Jack Reilly) marries army nurse 'Red' (played by Wellman's wife, Dorothy) and Freddie Steele played Sergeant Warnicki, who is perpetually in search of a gramophone to play a recording from home of his child's voice. When he eventually hears it, he loses his sanity and is carted off to hospital. *G.I. Joe* was shot on location in California (including Lone Pine) and at Selznick International Studios, Culver City. Robert Aldrich worked as the assistant director and its influence can be seen in Aldrich's *Attack* (1956) and Sam Fuller's *The Big Red One*. Pyle, who won the Pulitzer Prize for journalism in 1944, died in a Japanese ambush on Iejima while covering the Pacific War on 18 April 1945.

The early part of writer-director-producer Carl Foreman's cynical *The Victors* (1963) depicts the Italian campaign, as a squad of GIs (including George Peppard, George Hamilton, Jim Mitchum and Peter Fonda) led by Sergeant Craig (Eli Wallach) negotiate war torn villages and romance local women. Vince Edwards falls for an Italian woman (Rosanna Schiaffino) who has a young child, while other GIs visit prostitutes and get drunk at a winery they are supposed to be guarding; fortunately their captain mistakes their drunkenness for battle fatigue. The film ambitiously attempts to intercut frivolous wartime newsreel footage and newspaper headlines – for example the marriage of Shirley Temple and John Agar, or Mrs Truman attempting to smash a bottle against the front of a newly launched air ambulance – with the 'real war', where US troops loot bombed-out buildings, street kids empty drunken GIs pockets and racist soldiers tour bars 'coon hunting' (finding and beating up black soldiers). But Foreman's lengthy, ahead-of-its-time exercise is episodic and structureless, and only occasionally realises its potential.

During the Gustav Line impasse, the Allies decided on a new strategy – a land attack on the Gustav and an amphibious assault landing on the west coast, behind the defences, in January 1944. Codenamed Operation Shingle, the amphibious assault saw a British-Canadian-US force cross the Tyrrhenian Sea and land at Anzio, to the south-west of Rome. It was intended as a diversion to allow the breakthrough of the Gustav Line and open the route to Rome up Highway 6. The US 6th Corps was commanded by Major-General John Lucas. With most of the Allies' amphibious craft being assembled for operations in the Normandy landings, under-equipped and overly cautious Lucas landed and consolidated his position. This allowed the German XIV Army to react and attack in force, which developed into a three-month siege with the Allies boxed-in. The Allies' position became so precarious that the commanders envisaged another Dunkirk. In addition to heavy armour, the Germans deployed secret weapons including midget submarines, radio controlled glider bombs and 'Anzio Annie', a huge railway-mounted gun, which enabled the Germans to level Anzio harbour from a distance. Lucas' blunder led Churchill to observe: 'I had hoped we would be hurling a wildcat ashore, but all we got was a stranded whale'.

The failure of the Allies to push home their advantage and take Rome was well-illustrated in *Anzio* (1968 – *The Battle for Anzio* in the UK). Originally titled *Lo Sbarco di Anzio* ('The Anzio Landing'), it was a US–Italian co-production between Columbia Pictures and Dino De Laurentiis based on the 1961 book *Anzio* by war correspondent Wynford Vaughn-Thomas. The film is scathingly critical of the Allied officers and their tactical decisions, via the character of non-combatant Official US War Correspondent Dick Ennis (Robert Mitchum). Co-directed by Edward Dmytryk and Duilio Coletti, *Anzio* was filmed on location in Italy and follows a group of US Rangers from their embarkation in Naples to the Anzio landings and beyond. Though many of the names have been changed, the main protagonists are easily identifiable. Arthur Kennedy played cautious Major-General Jack Lesly (a thinly-disguised Lucas) and Robert Ryan was his superior General Carson (General Clark). Commandeering a jeep, Ennis drives unopposed into Rome – the German garrison is but a few SS and Military Police. Having secured a beachhead behind the Cassino Line, Lucas digs in, much to the disgust of British generals Marsh (Anthony Steel) and Starkey (Patrick Magee). Kesselring (Wolfgang Preiss) can't believe his good fortune and with General Eberhard Von Mackensen (Tonio Selwart) and the XIV Army sets about repulsing the invaders. When Lesly finally sends forward a sortie of the 1st and 3rd Ranger Battalions, they are ambushed and massacred by well-concealed defenders en route to Cisterna, a town on the edge of the Pontine Marches. Ennis and seven survivors are trapped behind enemy lines in the Alban Hills and witness Kesselring's master plan – massive construction sites deploying forced labour toil through the night to build a new defence of concrete pillboxes and gun emplacements, the Caesar Line, to defend Rome. The Rangers are whittled down and the remnants finally make it back to Anzio. Ennis informs Lesly of the defences, but Lesly has already been replaced by Major-General Luke Howard (Arthur Franz) – historically, Lucas was replaced by General Truscott on 23 February 1944.

Anzio's cynicism is surprising even today. Ennis, fresh from the Cassino front, mentions by name the recent fiascos at Salerno and an aborted crossing of the River Rapido. Mitchum, who'd just visited US troops in Vietnam, thought the script 'violently anti-American' and demanded changes. During the battle at Cisterna, non-combatant Ennis pretends to be dead and Ranger Wally Richardson (Mark Damon), having risked his neck to check the reporter's well-being, snaps, 'We can't play dead Ennis – we got guns'. Von Mackensen and Kesselring joke about the bottled-up beachhead: 'Anzio is now the cheapest prisoner of war camp in Europe – 50,000 men who feed themselves'. The film's most interesting character is Peter Falk's pathfinder Corporal Jack Rabinoff, assigned to guide the Rangers to Cisterna. In Naples he pimps prostitutes from the back of his Dodge ambulance and when asked by Ennis why he fights, he replies that 'it's got nothing to do with democracy'. When Ennis and Rabinoff discover Rome undefended, Falk quips: 'This is an open city' (an apparent in-joke reference to Roberto Rossellini's *Rome, Open City* [1945]). Throughout the film Ennis asks big moral questions of himself and is eventually forced to take up arms to shoot a German sniper (Wolfgang Hillinger) who has decimated the Rangers. Back at Anzio, Ennis pessimistically surmises to Lesly that men kill each other 'because they like it'.

The sunny Italian countryside was picturesquely photographed in Technicolor and widescreen Panavision by Giuseppe Rotunno. These locations, to the west of Rome (including Anzio Cape) and Rome itself, add authenticity to the story. Scenes of the Allied troops marching through the streets of Naples – the Scots pipers and infantry stiffly well-drilled, the 'Yank' GIs slovenly hip – and their embarkation in Naples harbour are convincing for their epic sweep, with innumerable columns of extras, railroad rolling stock, tanks, 4x4 jeeps and ordnance. Riz Ortolani provided suitably ominous musical cues for the embarkation and invasion scenes. Unfortunately there is also an awful title song 'This World Is Yours', belted out Las Vegas–style by Jack Jones ('Where have you gone, you bright-eyed gentle dreamer?') The film's impressive trailer warned: 'Off Shore the Invasion Fleet – On Shore Who Knows What?' The Anzio invasion is restaged with landing craft and ships, as colour WWII archive footage of a naval barrage shells a model of Anzio town. This was familiar territory for Mitchum, who'd played Brigadier General Norman Cota for the D-Day landings on Omaha Beach in *The Longest Day* (1962).

Anzio's big action set piece is the ambush at Cisterna (26 January, 1944), a 'royal foul-up', staged in a yellowy-grassed valley. As the Rangers emerge from a

All Roads Lead to Rome: US poster advertising *Anzio* (1968), Dino De Laurentiis' Italian-shot production of Operation Shingle, starring Robert Mitchum and Peter Falk. Poster courtesy Kevin Wilkinson Collection.

deep drainage ditch, the Fossa Di Pantano, the 3rd Panzer Grenadiers open fire from machine-gun positions concealed in haystacks. Little wonder the German tanks are heavily camouflaged with foliage – they are Korean War vintage US M47 Pattons masquerading as Panzers. These same vehicles, minus their camouflage, are also deployed as the US armour in the film. Dmytryk noticed that the US troops' rifles were waggling about in the action scenes and discovered they were rubber. He confronted producer De Laurentiis who conceded, 'What can I do? The dealer with the good guns cheated me. You'll just have to use them'. At Cisterna, the Ranger operation's leader, Captain Pete Burns (Venantino Venantini), is shot dead and his men scatter. In reality only 6 of the 767 Rangers involved in this sortie escaped death, wounding or capture. In the film the Ranger survivors are Richardson (Damon), radio operator Andy (Thomas Hunter), randy Private Movie (Reni Santoni), Italian Cellini (Giancarlo Giannini), Doyle (Joseph Walsh) and their platoon sergeant Abe Stimmler (Earl Holliman). They are a B-movie all-star-cast: Damon (who fractured his neck during filming) had worked for Roger Corman, Hunter was a spaghetti western star, Holliman a supporting player in 1950s Hollywood and Giannini was just beginning his journey to international acclaim, but all acquit themselves well. Wayde Preston played their regimental commander, Colonel Hendricks, Dante Maggio had a cameo as a Neapolitan street vendor flogging nylons, and stuntman Tiberio Mitri cropped up as a Scottish-accented Military Policeman in Naples.

Once behind enemy lines in the Alban Hills, *Anzio* becomes a familiar tale of a disparate group of soldiers in peril. As Reni Santoni put it: 'There was no script … it turned into seven dwarves lost in the woods'. The survivors, plus Ennis and Rabinoff, are trapped in a ruined farmhouse by a flame-throwing Panzer and negotiate a minefield by hurling large flat stones to detonate the mines, creating stepping stones to safety. They witness a huge Nazi construction site working by night (filmed at Tor Caldara Nature Reserve on Anzio Cape) and shelter in a farmhouse with an Italian mother and her daughters, before they attempt a breakthrough to the beachhead and are picked off by four proficient German snipers. Only Ennis, Stimmler and Movie survive. Falk's bloody death – a splattered shot to the chest – is missing from afternoon TV prints of the film. *Anzio* ends on an upbeat note, with General Carson having his day of triumph in Rome. These liberation scenes were shot on the streets of Rome, with the Colosseum, the Castel and Ponte (bridge) Sant'Angelo, and the Arch of Constantine visible. The final image is of the crowds and troops celebrating in a packed Piazza San Pietro (St Peter's Square), as befits a US–Italian co-production. Advertising for the film stated: '*Anzio* – Where All Roads Lead to Rome'. When the Allies managed to move out of the Anzio beachhead, they linked up with troops that had broken through the Gustav Line on 26 May, enabling the push to Rome. Clark's insistence on taking the city allowed the German X and XIV armies to withdraw to fight another day, rather than the resounding victory it should have been.

Jesse Hibbs' *To Hell and Back* (1955) depicts the Italian campaign – from Sicily to the liberation of Rome – through the exploits of the most decorated GI of WWII, Audie L. Murphy. It was based on Murphy's 1949 autobiography of the same name. Refused entry to the Marines, the Navy and the paratroopers, Texan Murphy enlisted in the US 3rd Infantry Division and underwent training in North Africa. He fought in Sicily and Salerno and was at the forefront of the push north, crossing the River Volturno in October 1943. He was involved in action on the Cassino Line (accurately depicted as a muddy, rain-sodden slog through the mountains). After a brief romance for Murphy in Naples, the 3rd land at Anzio and in a lengthy battle attempt to secure an OP (observation post) in a two-storey house. Following the breakout, the 3rd embark on further amphibious landings as part of the US 7th Army in Operation Anvil into the south of France, and fight through France into Germany, where at Colmar Murphy was badly wounded in the hip and hospitalised. His injuries prevented him attending West Point and in the post-war period he took acting lessons and became a movie star, mostly in B-westerns.

Throughout the campaign, Murphy distinguished himself in battle, demonstrating initiative and valour under fire. 'Little Texas' rose from private, via corporal and sergeant, to second lieutenant, galvanising his comrades with his gung-ho, 'up and at 'em' vigour. His many decorations, 28 in all, include three Purple Hearts and a Congressional Medal of Honor. In the film's most famous scenes, Murphy single-handedly clears out German machine gun nests and later stands atop a burning Sherman tank wielding a machine gun and routs advancing German infantry. Location scenes were filmed in the USA. The Volturno crossing was on the Yakima River, in the north-western state of Washington. Open country combat in Sicily, Italy and France was shot in the Oak Creek Game Reservation 'Wildlife Area' in Naches, Washington. When Murphy visits Naples on leave, the location resembles a redressed wild west Mexican pueblo set, and the parade ground at Fort Lewis appeared for the decoration ceremony epilogue. This Universal-International version of World War II is convincing: the well-staged, exciting scenes of combat, aided by Technicolor and CinemaScope, were re-enactments of actual events mixed with archive footage. The US armour is authentic Sherman tanks, but the German 'Tigers' are US M47s with German insignia. Murphy's only other war movie was the fictitious *Battle at Bloody Beach* (1961 – *Battle on the Beach* in the UK), in which he supplied Filipino guerrillas during the Pacific War.

The battle for Sicily and Italy also featured in William A. Wellman's *Darby's Rangers* (1958 – *The Young Invaders* in the UK) with then-TV star James Garner as Major (later Lieutenant-Colonel) William Orlando Darby. With his aide, Sergeant Saul Rosen (Jack Warden), Darby moulds a formidable force. They train in Scotland at the British commando training school near Dundee and are thrown into action during Operation Torch in North Africa in November 1942 and in Sicily, spearheading the attack at Gela. Later they fight their way up Italy's 'boot' and are involved in the Anzio landings. The film frugally recreates the Battle of Cisterna on studio soundstage 'exteriors' fogged in dry-ice. The German armour is again disguised US tanks. Almost all the exterior action scenes are shot on unconvincing studio 'exteriors', which hamper their effectiveness and the mediocre monochrome photography makes the film resemble a TV show. Perhaps this was intentional: as Stephen H. Scheuer's *Movies on TV* guide notes, 'The supporting cast includes the entire Warner Bros TV talent roster at that time'. Only the scene in a rubble-strewn town, when the Rangers are ambushed by a sniper in a bell tower, passes muster. The Rangers include Stuart Whitman, Torin Thatcher and Edward Byrnes, and the story, based on Major James Altieri's book *Darby's Rangers*, frequently diverges to concentrate on the Rangers' courting of local women, be they Scottish, English or Italian – there's too much romance and not enough Rangering.

When Rome was liberated by General Clark on 4 June 1944, the war in Italy was far from over. The propaganda value of taking the first 'Axis capital' was useful on the eve of D-Day, but Kesselring retreated first to the Albert Line and then to the Gothic Line, another fortified defence 100 miles north of Rome. In this crawl up Italy by the Allies, which would last the duration of the war, there were many attempts at breaking the resolute Germans. John Huston made one of the most highly acclaimed documentaries of the war, *The Battle of San Pietro* (1944), during this hard-fought campaign. Several war films recreated special ops and partisan activities throughout Italy, including *Achtung! Banditi!* (1951), *Then There Were Three* (1961), *Warriors 5* (1962) and *The Quick and the Dead* (1963). In 'Frank Kramer'/ Gianfranco Parolini's actionful *Five for Hell* (1969) five US commandos carry out a mission behind the Gustav Line to steal 'Plan K' (the Führer's plan to reinforce Kesselring's troops and encircle 50,000 US troops) from a safe in the HQ of the German High Command in Villa Verdi. Phil Karlson's *Hornets' Nest* (1970) cast Rock Hudson as Captain Turner, who leads a group of US paratroopers into Italy on a special mission. His squad are massacred on landing and he is injured and nursed back to health by a doctor (Sylva Koscina). Turner recruits a band of Italian street urchins (whose parents have been executed by the Germans) to blow up a dam. Ennio Morricone provided the score. Trailers christened these raiders 'Captain Turner's Baby Brigade' and Sergio Fantoni played their opposition, German officer Von Hecht.

Von Ryan's Express (1965) was an excitingly staged, Italian-shot Allied prison break. Other films set in the Italian theatre include *Force of Arms* (1951 – an update of Hemmingway's WW1-set *A Farewell to Arms*), *Eight Iron Men* (1952), and AIP's *Paratroop Command* and *Tank Commandos* (both 1959). *General Della Rovere* (1959) starred Vittorio De Sica, who is forced by the Germans to impersonate a partisan leader. *The Four Days of Naples* (1962) recounted in semi-documentary style a revolt by the population of Naples in 1943. Mike Nichols' *Catch-22* (1970), a sprawling adaptation of Joseph Heller's war satire, was set on an island off Italy in 1944. The cast included Alan Arkin, Martin Balsam, Richard Benjamin, Martin Sheen, Jon Voight, Bob Newhart, Anthony Perkins, Art Garfunkle and Orson Welles.

Tonino Ricci's wintry *Salt in the Wound* (1969 – *War Fever*, *The Liberators* and *The Dirty Two*) starred Klaus Kinski and Ray Saunders as condemned GIs, who redeem themselves in their selfless defence of the hilltop town of San Michele against German attack. Their uniforms make these thieving killers heroes and liberators. The incredible final battle for San Michele (filmed in the town of Montecarlo, Lucca) deploys US M47s as German armour. One of the great 'forgotten' war movies, *Salt in the Wound* is as cynical in its message as *Anzio*. As Kinski notes of men at war: 'We're all killers'.

Ari Taub's *The Fallen* (2004) was set in the autumn of 1944 in northern Italy, as the Allies and their partisan compatriots attempted to break through the German-Italian defences on the Gothic Line. The main plot follows a squad of US supply company staff pressed into combat to deliver ammo and a radio to frontline troops. For a film on which the DVD cover claims is '*Saving Private Ryan* but even better', *The Fallen* is a disappointment. Evidently made on a low budget (a reported $600,000) and shot on location in Italy and Germany, this US–Italian–German co-production features acting and action which recalls TV drama-documentaries, or weekend re-enactment societies. Small groups of GIs encounter small groups of refugees and are aided by small groups of partisans in their fight against small groups of Germans. In the film's only interesting scene, partisans harangue Italian soldiers loyal to Mussolini and the Nazis from cover in the woods. The film has its moments, mostly of unintentional comedy, and with the exception of the German performers, the acting is poor. Ruben Pla's eye-popping turn as psychotic GI Corporal Packard is not to be missed. The film ends suddenly, implying the filmmakers ran out of film and it may be the worst World War II movie ever made. There is a sequel also set in Italy and directed by Taub, entitled *Last Letters from Monte Rosa* (2009).

As the liberators fought their way through Italy, the Germans exacted terrible revenge on their one-time allies. In the immediate post-war period, Roberto Rossellini directed two films – *Rome, Open City* (1945) and *Paisà* (1946) – which depicted the German occupation and the country's liberation. Set in the winter of 1943–44, *Open City* detailed with documentary-like realism the hunt for Giorgio Manfredi (Marcell Pagliero), a resistance leader in Rome. Another member of the resistance, Francesco (Francesco Grandjacquet), is due to marry widow Pina (Anna Magnani), but on their wedding day the Gestapo and Italian fascists raid their apartment block. In one of the most famous scenes in cinema, pregnant Pina is mown down in the street as she pursues the truck taking Francesco away. Later SS Major Bergmann (Harry Feist) captures Manfredi (who dies under torture rather than betray his friends) and orders the execution of priest Don Pietro Pellegrini (Aldo Fabrizi), who has aided the resistance. Rossellini had made three fascist propaganda films during the war: *The White Navy* (1941 – detailing hospital ships), *A Pilot Returns* (1942 – depicting the air force) and *Man of the Cross* (1943 – set on the Eastern Front).

Paisà is perhaps Rossellini's greatest film, in which the grit of neorealism is combined with newsreel combat footage to moving, powerful effect. The six-episode film is set during the Allied campaign to liberate Italy: it begins in Sicily in 1943 and concludes in the Po Delta in the winter of 1944. In episode one, Carmela (Carmela Sazio), an indolent young Sicilian woman, acts as a guide to a GI patrol on a night-time sortie. When GI Joe (Robert Van Loon) befriends her, he attempts to show her a photo of his sister, but when he strikes a light, a German sniper picks him off. Later the GI patrol think Carmela is responsible for Joe's death. In Naples, orphaned street urchin Pasquale (Alfonso Pasca) steals the boots off drunken black American military policeman Joe (all Americans in

Italy seemed to be named 'Joe') played by Dots Johnson. Later the MP meets Pasquale again and when he sees Pasquale's squalid living conditions and those of other Neapolitan civilians, he realises why the orphan needs to steal boots. In Rome following the Anzio landings, Sherman tank crewman Fred (Gar Moore) hitches up with a prostitute. He drunkenly remembers that six months ago, on his first arrival in Rome, he met a wonderful Roman girl called Francesca. He is too drunk to realise that the woman he is with is Francesca, who has been compelled to become a 'working girl' to avoid starvation. She arranges to meet Fred again tomorrow, but he fails to keep their appointment, thinking she is just 'some whore' and not the lover he has been seeking.

Paisà continues with the German retreat north through Tuscany, as the fighting envelopes Florence. British nurse Harriet (Harriet White) and Massimo (Enzo Tarascio) attempt to cross the River Arno: she to contact her lover Guido Lombardi who is now heroic partisan leader Lupo (Wolf), he to see his wife and child whose house is caught up in the fighting. They cross the river through the Uffizi passageway, as the only bridge standing is the heavily guarded Ponte Vecchio. Traversing rooftops and rubble, and avoiding fascist snipers and patrols, they make contact with partisans in the German occupied zone and Harriet learns from a dying fighter that Lupo has been killed. At the Gothic Line, three US chaplains – Captain Bill Martin (William Tubbs), Captain Feldman (Elmer Feldman) and Captain Jones (Newell Jones) – seek shelter in a Franciscan monastery in the Apennines. The chaplains give the monks Hershey bars and their supplies of tinned food, including tinned eggs: 'Those Americans, they think of everything', the monks marvel. But when the monks discover that two of the chaplains are not of the 'true faith' – but are Jewish and Protestant – they begin a fast. In the final episode, anti-fascist partisans and American OSS operatives work together against the Germans in the Po Delta, south of Venice. They negotiate the reed-strewn shallows of the delta in canoes. This episode is the most actionful and climaxes with a shootout between the partisans and German gunboats on the delta. The episode begins with a partisan's corpse drifting down the delta supported by a lifebelt, with a placard 'Partigiano'. Later the Germans massacre the defenceless inhabitants of Casel Madelena, who have collaborated with the partisans, leaving only a screaming child and lifeless corpses in their wake. Partisans are hanged, or else barbarously executed by being tied up and pushed off the gunboats into the delta. Cornered partisans shoot themselves rather than fall into enemy hands and OSS agent Dale (Dale Edmonds) is mown down when he accuses the Germans of being murderers. *Paisà* depicts a realism that makes Hollywood and British war films of the time look ridiculous in comparison.

Vittorio De Sica's *Two Women* (1960) followed the wartime experiences of widowed mother Cesira (Sophia Loren, in an Oscar-winning performance) and her daughter Rosetta (Eleanora Brown), who become refugees from Rome when the Allied bombing intensifies. When Mussolini is jailed and the Americans invade in 1943, Cesira and Rosetta set off home, but Moroccan auxiliaries fighting for the Allies assault both women. George Pan Cosmatos' *Massacre in Rome* (1973) recounted the true story of the Ardeatine Caves massacre, a Nazi atrocity on 24 March 1944. Following the ambush of an SS patrol by partisans,

10 Italians were executed for every one of the 33 Germans killed. Lieutenant Colonel Hubert Kappler (Richard Burton) of the Gestapo is given the task of overseeing the executions. Marcello Mastroianni played Father Pietro Antonelli, who opposes the Gestapo and the film closes with a roll call of those executed, including Antonelli. In *The Assisi Underground* (1985) Italian Jews are protected from German Anti-Semitism in 1943. Italian fascists had refused to carry out Hitler's extermination programme, but with the Italian surrender and German occupation, the situation changed, as depicted in Vittorio De Sica's *The Garden of the Finzi-Continis* (1971 – a Best Foreign Film Oscar winner) and Paolo and Vittorio Taviani's *The Night of the Shooting Stars* (1981).

In the 1960s, with the war fading further from memory, the Italian occupation and liberation were deployed in several lighter Hollywood-backed films. Charlton Heston and Harry Guardino played two GIs sending information from occupied Rome in *The Pigeon That Took Rome* (1962). Anthony Quinn, Anna Magnani, Virna Lisi and Hardy Krüger starred in the comedy *The Secret of Santa Victoria* (1969): the secret is a million bottles of wine concealed from the occupying German forces. Blake Edwards' *What Did You Do in the War, Daddy?* (1966) starred James Coburn, Dick Shawn, Aldo Ray, Harry Morgan, Carroll O'Connor, Giovanna Ralli and Sergio Fantoni (the resident Italian in such Italian-shot Hollywood movies). A Sicilian village only agrees to surrender to the US Army if they are first allowed to stage a wine festival and football game. In *The Secret War of Harry Frigg* master escapologist Harry Frigg (Paul Newman) is sent to northern Italy to spring five Allied generals from house arrest in a villa guarded by the Italian army. Newman gives an oddly dopey, twitchy performance as Frigg, who plans an escape route but tarries too long to romance the villa's beautiful contessa, Francesca (Sylva Koscina). When the Italians surrender to the Germans in autumn 1943, Frigg and company are taken to an altogether more escape-proof POW camp for interrogation. These films – wherein the Italians are usually 'Mamma mia!' stereotypes, the Germans are mostly buffoons and the 'Yanks' are hip and funny – sit oddly beside *Rome, Open City* and *Two Women*.

Following the liberation of Rome, the war in Italy dragged on for almost another year, with the German forces in Italy finally capitulating on 29 April 1945. Mussolini had been captured on 27 April by communist partisans. George C. Scott played the dictator in the seven-hour TV biopic *Mussolini: The Untold Story* (1985) and Jack Oakie spoofed Mussolini in *The Great Dictator* (1940), as Benzino Napaloni, the Dictator of Bacteria. Carlo Lizzani's *The Last Days of Mussolini* (1974 – *The Last Four Days*) starred Rod Steiger as Il Duce, a hunted man who flees Milan as the noose tightens around his ankles. The Americans, communist partisans and the National Liberation Committee all seek the dictator – the Americans to interrogate him, the partisans to try him – but as Mussolini heads for Switzerland disguised as a German soldier, he is captured by red-scarved Italian communists of the Garibaldi Brigade in Dongo, on Lake Como. They hand Mussolini and his mistress Claretta Petacci (Lisa Gastoni) over to Colonel Valerio (Franco Nero) of the Liberation Committee, who shoots them both, 'Rendering justice to the Italian people'.

Shot on beautiful Lake Como, Lombardy locations, Lizzani's film is an underrated gem. Like *Massacre in Rome,* the dissonant score was by Ennio Morricone. Steiger, dubbed into Italian and subtitled in English, bears a startling resemblance to the dictator and his usual histrionics are reined in by the sombreness of the subject matter. A strong supporting cast included Henry Fonda as Cardinal Schuster and Andrea Aureli (wearing an eye-patch and a long leather coat) as Mussolini's tough henchman Barracu. After his capture, Mussolini distances himself from Hitler and fascism, leading one partisan to ask: 'Was anything ever your fault?' The film is punctuated by flashbacks to better days – the glory that was Mussolini's fascist Rome – and ends on a freeze-frame of Mussolini's machine-gunned corpse. Lizzani doesn't depict his final public humiliation, when his corpse was hung by its heels in Milan. Lizzani and Steiger aside, following the fall of Rome in 1944 filmmakers showed little interest in the Italian theatre, as more interesting subject matter had presented itself in the Allies' next major offensive: the invasion of France.

Chapter 12

SPECIAL OPS IN EUROPE (1940–44)

Britain's initial forays into Occupied Europe were a series of disruptive commando raids. They began as low-key strikes on Boulogne and Guernsey, but quickly escalated into larger undertakings. Operations in Norway included the Lofoten Islands raid in March 1941 (against fish factories and shipping), the Spitzbergen Raid in August 1941 (which burned stockpiles of coal) and December 1941 raids on Vaagsö and Maalöy Islands (which destroyed fish oil factories, shipping and the German garrison). In France, the raid on Bruneval (February 1942), which destroyed a radio installation north of Le Havre, was carried out by paratroopers led by Major John Frost, later of Battle of Arnhem fame. Operation Chariot, the raid on St Nazaire (March 1942), used the US destroyer *Campbeltown* as a battering ram to destroy a dock, while the famed 'Cockleshell Heroes' sank German shipping moored in Bordeaux in December 1942.

The largest of these raids on France's Iron Coast was Operation Jubilee, a horror show now known as the Dieppe Disaster. Described as 'a reconnaissance in force' by Churchill, it was an ill-organised attempt to ascertain how well defended the port of Dieppe was against amphibious attack. Six thousand Canadian troops and commandos landed on 19 August 1942, but the operation was a total failure against the German shore batteries. Almost 4,500 men were lost in the action, plus all their equipment (including 28 tanks). Following Dieppe, the British Army developed the Churchill AVRE (Assault Vehicle Royal Engineers), a customised tank which was used to clear beach defence obstacles. The Dieppe fiasco is referenced in *D-Day the Sixth of June* (1956), when US Lieutenant-Colonel Timmer (Edmond O'Brien) tags along with the Canadians on Operation Jubilee as an observer (though the actual raid occurs offscreen) and in *Triple Cross* (1966).

Paul Wendkos' lively *Attack on the Iron Coast* (1968) was a fictionalised rehash of these early raids. The film begins with Canadian commando Major

Jaime Wilson (Lloyd Bridges) watching footage of his disastrous commando raid, La Plage, which strongly resembles Dieppe. He is the mastermind behind an equally suicidal new raid, codenamed Operation Mad Dog. The plan is to sail an explosives-laden destroyer into the dock gates at Le Clairé, which is obviously based on the St Nazaire attack. The dry dock can be used to refit German raiders such as the *Ostwind*, which has recently suffered heavy damage. Envisioned as a combined operation between the RAF, the navy and the army, the RAF are unable to offer any air cover and the best the navy can contribute is a rusty old minesweeper and four motor launches. Despite this lack of resources, the mission is a success, but the commandos and navy pay a high price in casualties.

Andrew Keir played naval captain Franklin, who clashes with Wilson over Mad Dog – he lost his son in the La Plage assault and is critical of Wilson's capabilities and the operation's viability. Sue Lloyd was underused as Wilson's wife Sue. Mark Eden played the navy's Lieutenant Commander Donald Kimberly, who is blinded during Wilson's rigorous assault rehearsals. Maurice Denham was Rear Admiral Sir Frederick Grafton and Ernest Clark played Air Vice Marshall Woodbridge, while Le Clairé's German garrison commander, Oberst Von Horst, was played by Walter Gotell. The film was shot at MGM's British Studio at Borehamwood (including the French château exterior from *Dirty Dozen*) and Operation Mad Dog is discussed at Gaddesden Place, Hemel Hempstead, Hertfordshire. The commando training scenes and the Le Clairé raid were staged in London's Docklands, with Tower Bridge in the background. The minesweeper and its entourage are depicted by rather obvious model work by the Bowie Organisation and a scene where Lancasters carry out a bombing raid was from *The Dam Busters.* Posters imaginatively stated: 'They turned a dead ship into a live bomb and sailed it down the throat of the enemy'.

Terence Young's *The Red Beret* (1953 – *Paratrooper* in the USA), a UK-shot Alan Ladd vehicle, recreated two early paratroop raids against the Germans. Ladd starred as Los Angeles-born, Canadian national Steven 'Canada' MacKendrick, who joins the British 1st Airborne Division and earns his wings at a parachute training school in post-Dunkirk England. Canada participates in two airborne missions and the film recreates the Bruneval Raid on a radar installation on the French coast (here called Operation Pegasus) and a raid to take an airstrip on the North African coast east of Algiers (loosely based on the Oudna operations in Tunisia in December 1942). These convincing action spots and the numerous parachute drops (from real Dakotas) are the film's best scenes – despite the Germans driving British Humber armoured cars and the African airstrip and its environs being portrayed by the landscape at Trawsfynydd, in Gwynedd, North Wales.

The parachute training scenes in *Red Beret* were shot at RAF Abingdon Parachute School, Oxfordshire, with interiors at Shepperton Studios, London. Stanley Baker (who is dubbed by someone else even in the English language version) played the school's bullying sergeant, Breton, who is killed in a training drop when his 'chute fails to open. The multinational paratroopers included Donald Houston (as Welshman 'Taffy' Evans), Harry Andrews (as the Scottish Regimental Sergeant Major [RSM]) and Anton Diffring (as a Pole). Leo Genn played their commander Major Snow (loosely based on John Frost). Ladd portrayed a mysterious 'man with a past' (here an ex-pilot who caused the death of his best friend), who plays it mean and moody during his romance with parachute packer Penny Gardner (Susan Stephen) and in the unlikely finale fires a path through a minefield with a bazooka to save his unit from the Afrika Korps. Ladd's turn as a Red Beret didn't go down very well with the British press, who thought a British actor such as Richard Todd should have received the role.

Compton Bennett's *Gift Horse* (1952) was mostly concerned with the North Atlantic exploits of *HMS Ballantrae* – a clapped-out old US destroyer donated to the Royal Navy in 1940. In early 1942 it is chosen for an operation to destroy a dry dock in France. The *Ballantrae* has her bows loaded with high explosives and rams the dock gates. These events were based on the US destroyer *Campbeltown*, which was commissioned for Operation Chariot in 1942 to demolish the huge dock at St Nazaire, at the mouth of the River Loire on the French coast. The 'Normandie Dock' was to be used by the new German battleship *Tirpitz* as a base to attack Atlantic convoys. Leaving from Falmouth, the explosive-loaded *Campbeltown* was accompanied by commandos in 16 motor launches and a motor torpedo boat. On the night of 27–28 March the *Campbeltown* sailed up the Loire, surviving intense German fire, and hit the dock gates, while the 600 commandos razed facilities in the dock area, including submarine pens used by U-boats. The cost of the raid was heavy – only two of the motor launches made it back to England and a quarter of the raiders were killed. On 28 March the explosives rigged to a timer in the *Campbeltown*'s bows detonated and the dock was put out of action.

The Cockleshell Heroes (1955), directed by and starring José Ferrer, recounted another factual raid in Occupied France. In March 1942, unconventional Royal Marine Commando Major Stringer (Ferrer), strict World War I veteran Captain Thomson (Trevor Howard) and Sergeant Craig (Victor Maddern) whip a group of marines into shape. From an initial contingent of 43 volunteers, Stringer selects eight to undertake their dangerous mission – Operation Cockleshell – to blow up German blockade runners harboured in Bordeaux. In December, the commandos are dispatched from a British submarine and travel up the estuary of the River Gironde in two-man canoes ('cockles') to attach limpet mines to enemy ships. The leader of the actual raid, Major Herbert G. Hasler, and Bill Sparks (one of the surviving commandos) acted as the film's technical advisors. They were members of the Royal Marine Boom Patrol, who became the S.B.S. (Special Boat Service). The film was co-scripted by Bryan Forbes and Richard Maibaum, from Sparks' book *The Last of the Cockleshell Heroes* and *Cockleshell Heroes* by C.E. Lucas Phillips. In the actual raid there were 12 commandos in six canoes (named *Conger, Catfish, Crayfish, Coalfish, Cuttlefish* and *Cachalot*), but in the film there are ten commandos and no *Cachalot*. The canoes are launched from a sub on the night of 7 December on the edge of a minefield. The *Coalfish* vanishes during the night, *Conger* capsizes in the tidal estuary and the *Cuttlefish* is also lost. Only two canoes manage to navigate the river to their targets, avoiding German patrols boats, guards and searchlights. As depicted in the film, all the commandos who were captured were shot as spies, despite the fact that they were in uniform (official paperwork stated they had been found drowned in Bordeaux harbour). Seven ships were sunk or damaged, including a Sperrbrecher (minesweeper) but only Hasler and Sparks lived to tell their tale.

Cockleshell Heroes is what might be termed *Buoy's Own* adventure. It is historically inaccurate and there are some ill-judged comedy moments during the training scenes, but the format of meticulous preparation followed by the mission's execution was widely adopted by later war films. The film was shot in CinemaScope on location in Eastney Barracks, Southsea, Hampshire (as the commandos base in Portsmouth), the actual naval dockyard in Portsmouth, and off the coast of Portugal (as the French estuary). Ferrer and Howard played officers at opposite ends of the discipline spectrum (lax maverick versus by-the-rules stickler). The marines included Anthony Newley, David Lodge, Percy Herbert, John Fabian and John Van Eyssen. Lodge played a marine who finds that his wife (Beatrice Campbell) has been unfaithful, so he goes AWOL to sort out the interloper. Dora Bryan played Newley's lover, Myrtle, Christopher Lee has a bit part as a British submarine commander and Walter Fitzgerald was the Gestapo agent who interrogates those commandos taken prisoner. In a notable scene, a Wren (played by Yana) – who resembles an idealised image of women-in-uniform, as presented by wartime recruitment posters – sings the moving 'The London I Love' in a forces pub. *Cockleshell Heroes* was a great success in the UK when released through Columbia.

One of the most famous early raids into Europe was the attack on the Vemork 'Norsk Hydro' plant near the town of Rjukan in Telemark, Norway on the Scandinavian Peninsula. The plant was producing D^2O (heavy water) which is essential for atomic bomb research. In November 1942, Operation Freshman was an attempt by 34 British commandos to combine with Norwegian partisans to destroy the hydro plant. The commandos' gliders crashed and all were killed, or captured and executed. Operation Gunnerside was more successful, with the Norwegian resistance partially destroying the plant on 27 February 1943. On 16 November 1943 an American bombing raid destroyed the power station and the remaining water was loaded onto a train. When the cargo was transferred to the Hydro Ferry, the Norwegian resistance sank the vessel, destroying the remaining heavy water.

This true story was the basis for Titus Wibe Muller's *The Battle for Heavy Water* (1947 – *Operation Swallow*) a French–Norwegian co-production which recreated the events using many of the actual Norwegian saboteurs. It also inspired Anthony Mann's *The Heroes of Telemark* (1965). Kirk Douglas starred as Rolf Pedersen, a doctor of physics at the University of Oslo, who is recruited by Norwegian Resistance fighter Knut Straud (Richard Harris) to destroy the German Norsk Hydro factory in an inaccessible gorge near Rjukan. They flee to England in a hijacked freighter to plan the raid and parachute back into the mountains of Telemark. When a 50-strong British commando force is wiped out when their gliders hit a mountain, seven Norwegian partisans disguised in British uniforms, led by Rolf and Knut, blow up the water production facility. The Germans soon have replacement water tanks from Berlin and the plant is back to full production. An Allied bombing raid does little damage to the factory, but does kill 67 civilians in nearby Rjukan. Rolf and Knut learn that the remaining stock of heavy water is being exported on a train guarded by 1,000 crack troops. They decide to sink the Hydro Ferry on Lake Tinnsjø – train, passengers and all – but with the explosives set to detonate in the bow hold, Rolf is horrified to see Knut's wife and baby boarding the ferry.

The Heroes of Telemark's interiors were filmed at Pinewood Studios and exteriors were filmed in Norway: in Oslo (the university and harbour docks), in Rjukan, Vemork and on Lake Tinnsjø. Mount Gausta can be seen looming over Rjukan. Filmed in Technicolor and Panavision most of the action takes place in magnificent snowscapes, or else near the water factory, on bridges, roads and railway lines. The expansive landscapes are augmented by a sweeping, romantic musical theme from Malcolm Arnold. The opening sequence depicts the resourceful partisans nudging a German armoured car off a mountain road with a well-timed boulder and Mann stages many suspenseful action scenes. Knut and Rolf are pursued by German ski-troops across snowfields and many sequences – for example the parachute drop scenes and the commandos' snowbound radio hut – anticipate *Where Eagles Dare* (1968). One of the Norwegian fighters was played by Brook Williams, who was also a commando in *Eagles*. Roy Dottrice played Jensen, a traitorous Norwegian, Anton Diffring appeared as German Major Frick and Jennifer Hilary played Knut's wife, Sigrid. During the operation, Rolf encounters his ex-wife, Anna (Swedish actress Ulla Jacobsson) and her uncle (Michael Redgrave), who are resistance fighters. Rolf and Anna rekindle their love, but the scenes between these lovebirds in chunky knitwear are the film's weakest. Mann is unsentimental in his storytelling – Norwegian civilians are executed in reprisals for partisan attacks and one of Rolf and Anna's romantic moments, when they spot a rabbit in the snow, is curtailed when the rabbit steps on a mine. The film is also one of few to depict a 'Quisling', a term meaning a traitor who collaborates with the occupying forces. The original 'Quisling' (V. Quisling) was a renegade Norwegian officer. The film follows the true story closely, but condenses the time frame. For the Hydro ferry's demise, recreated on a grand scale, the train slides off the stricken vessel and the ferry tips upright, its stern sinking beneath the waters of icy Tinnsjø.

Other films featuring the commandos and the Norwegian underground include *The Commandos Strike at Dawn*, *They Raid by Night* and *The Day Will Dawn* (all 1942), *Edge of Darkness* (1943 – with Errol Flynn as a Norwegian fisherman), *Suicide Mission* (1956) and Norwegian-made films such as *Little Ida* (1981) and *The Last Lieutenant* (1993). *Max Manus* (2008) is the biopic of much-decorated Norwegian resistance fighter Maximo Manus. Aksen Hennie starred as Manus and the story is based in part on Manus' memoirs, as adapted for the screen by Thomas Nordseth-Tiller. Manus begins in the resistance movement distributing anti-Nazi propaganda newspapers. In January 1941 he is captured by the German police, but escapes by leaping through a window into the street. He is severely injured but survives the fall and escapes from his hospital bed. Manus arrives at Forest Lodge Army Training Camp, Scotland, where he is schooled in sabotage by the British army and becomes part of the 1st Norwegian Independent Army. He carries out Operation Mardonius in Oslo harbour in April 1943. This is an excellently staged commando raid on the moonlit harbour, as Manus and his cohorts place limpets on three ships: *Ortelsburg*, *Von Knipprode* and *Tuguela*. The film depicts Manus' stint fighting on the Salla Front in Finland (March 1940) against the Russians and his sinking of the German troop transporter *Donau* outside Drøbak in January 1945. This operation, with Manus and his men disguised as electricians to plant limpet mines rigged to timers, is recreated in detail. The ship's demise is a memorably haunting moment, as the stricken hulk is discovered, floundering at sunrise, hours after it has left Oslo harbour.

Max Manus was co-directed by Joachim Rønning and Espen Sandberg and photographed in widescreen by Geir Hartly Andreassen on location in Oslo, Scotland and at Norsk Filmstudio. Trond Bjerknes provided the epic score. Hennie is excellent as Manus, a sentimental man at heart, who admits that he cried when he watched *Gone With the Wind*. He is haunted by flashbacks of his time fighting for the Finns in the Winter War of 1940. Nicolai Cleve Broch portrays Manus' close friend and co-saboteur Gregers Gram, who is scythed down in a café ambush engineered by the Gestapo in November 1944. Stig Hoffmeyer played Norway's King Haakon VII, and Christian Rubeck and Mads Eldøen played Norwegian resistance fighters Kolbein Lauring and Eduard Tallaksen. Agnes Kittelsen was Ida 'Tikken' Lindebraekke, Manus' alluring Stockholm contact in neutral Sweden. In reality Tikken divorced her husband, a British diplomat, in 1947, to marry Manus. Manus himself died in September 1996, aged 81. Ken Duken played Siegfried Fehmer, the disingenuous head of the Gestapo in Oslo, and Viktoria Winge was Solveig Johnsrud, a Norwegian secretary he romances, despite his fervent anti-Norwegian stance and his persistent hunting of the resistance. If the film has a fault it is the over-glamorisation of some scenes, particularly those of romance, when a realistic, documentary-like approach would have better served the story. Manus himself acknowledges: 'They torture and kill my friends to get their hands on me' and the film is altogether more convincing in the scenes of torture, sabotage and violent action. With the war over, Manus has lost his closest comrades and has no one to raise a toast with. In a moving scene, he stands alone in an empty room and imagines his friends are there with him. The international DVD bills the film as *Man of War*, though the onscreen title is *Max Manus*, a name perhaps unfamiliar to non-Norwegian audiences.

Clandestine activity by the French Resistance movement – freedom fighters who were a thorn in the side of the occupying German forces – has featured extensively in cinema and TV. The resistance was given the comedy treatment in the UK TV sitcom *'Allo 'Allo!* A café run by flustered café proprietor René Artois (Gordon Kaye) is the hub of resistance activities in a small, occupied French town. René spends most of his time avoiding the attentions of the German officers who frequent his café, especially the Gestapo's Herr Flick (Richard Gibson), while juggling the women in his life, including his wife Edith (Carmen Silvera) and sexy waitress Yvette Carte-Blanche (Vicki Michelle). The local French policeman (Arthur Bostrom) is actually a British agent, Officer Crabtree, and one of the series' running gags was his mispronunciations of basic French phrases ('Good moaning'). Kirsten Cooke played Michelle, the leader of the French Resistance cell, who would begin to impart key details of the resistance's plans with her catchphrase: 'Listen very carefully: I shall say this only once'. The series was a spoof of the UK TV series *Secret Army* (1977–79), which depicted the Belgian Resistance movement.

Other depictions of the French Resistance include Jean-Pierre Melville's haunting thriller *Army of Shadows* (1969) starring Lino Ventura, Simone Signoret and Jean-Pierre Cassel, and the UK TV series *Wish Me Luck* (1987–1990). *Odette* (1950) starred Anna Neagle as the Special Operations Executive (SOE) agent Odette Churchill (later Odette Hallowes) who worked with the French Resistance and was awarded the George Cross for her bravery. Odette also acted as one of the technical advisers on the best-known film about British involvement with the French Resistance, Lewis Gilbert's *Carve Her Name with Pride* (1958). Virginia McKenna played Violette Szabo in this true story of her exploits working for the SOE. In London, Violette marries Ettienne Szabo (Alain Saury), a French officer and the early part of the film depicts their *Mills & Boon* romance. Following his death at El Alamein, Violette is recruited by the SOE for special operations in France. Her first mission – reorganising a shattered resistance cell in Rouen, which manages to blow up a railway viaduct – is a success. But when she returns to Le Havre, in the aftermath of D-Day, June 1944, she is ambushed, captured and tortured, but refuses to divulge her encoding method, which was Ettienne's love poem 'The Life that I Have'. She is sent to the Ravensbrück concentration camp with two other captured agents, Denise Bloch (Nicole Stephane) and Lillian Rolfe (Anne Leon), and is executed by the SS in 1945. In 1947 Violette was posthumously awarded the George Cross, which was collected by her daughter, Tania (Pauline Challoner). Paul Scofield played SOE agent Captain Tony Fraser, Bill Owen was Violette's instructor at the commando training school, Maurice Ronet played resistance fighter Jacques and Michael Caine can be glimpsed holding out a tin and shouting 'For God sake, we want water!' on a prison train bound for Ravensbrück.

Jean-Paul Salome's *Les Femmes De l'Ombre* (2008 – 'Women in the Shadows') was anglicised to the self-explanatory *Female Agents* for international DVD release. In the lead-up to D-Day, five French women are convinced by the SOE to embark on a mission to rescue a captured British geologist (Conrad Cecil) who was taking soil samples of the Normandy beaches. The women are resistance fighter Louise Desfontaines (Sophie Marceau), Susy (Marie Gillain), Jeanne (Julie Depardieu), Gäelle (Deborah François) and Maria (Maya Sansa). They infiltrate the hospital and free the geologist, putting him safety on a plane back to Britain, but then discover that they must also travel to Paris to assassinate SS Colonel Karl Heindrich (Moritz Bleibtreu), Susy's one-time fiancé. Though it strives for the lyrical intensity of the best in French cinema, *Female Agents* is an odd mixture of old-fashioned heroics, fashion magazine glamour, romance and brutality. This last aspect features in the film's sadistic SS interrogation scenes, when Gäelle, Louise (who discovers halfway through the mission she is three-months pregnant) and her brother Pierre (Julien Boisselier) are ruthlessly grilled as to the significance of a project codenamed 'Phoenix' (the portable Mulberry Harbours to be used in the Normandy invasion). The film is based on a true story: the real Louise survived the war, returning to France in 1949 where she received the Croix de Guerre and Légion d'Honneur for her valour. She died in 2004, aged 98. This style of behind-the-lines espionage film was parodied in the ill-conceived 'comedy' *All the Queen's Men* (2001), which featured male Allied agents (including Matt LeBlanc and Eddie Izzard) dressed in drag to infiltrate a factory.

Partisan activity elsewhere during the German occupation has resulted in some interesting, offbeat examples of world cinema. In Paul Verhoeven's thriller *Black Book* (2006), starring Sebastian Koch, Jewish singer Carice Van Houten joins the Dutch Resistance. Ole Christian Madsen's Danish-Czech-German co-production *Flammen & Citronen* (2008 – released internationally as *Flame & Citron*) depicted two heroes of the Danish Resistance: Bent Faurshou-Hviid, known as 'Flame' due to his distinctive red hair, and Jørgen Haagen Schmith, called 'Citron' because he worked in and sabotaged a Citroen car factory. They work as assassins for the Dutch Underground in occupied Copenhagen in 1944, fighting against the Germans and the Schalburg Corps, traitorous Danes in German uniforms. Bent and Jørgen are assassins who liquidate enemies of the Danish people, though they later discover they have been manipulated by their boss Askel Winther (Peter Mygind) into murdering innocent people. Thure Lindhardt played Bent and Mads Mikkelsen (Bond villain Le Chiffre in *Casino Royale* [2006]) was Citron. Both are excellent as the doomed, meditative heroes, who continue to carry out killings as their rewards rise and the German net closes.

Flame was shot on sets at Studio Babelsberg (also used for *Valkyrie* and *Inglourious Basterds*) and Christian Berkel played the heroes' nemesis, Karl Heinz Hoffmann, the head of the Gestapo: 'the biggest mass murderer Denmark has ever known'. In a bungled ambush meant for Hoffmann, the assassins accidentally kill a father and son, and realise they have been set up. Bent becomes romantically involved with courier Ketty Selmer (Stine Stengade), who is revealed to be a double agent working for Hoffmann, while Jørgen's wife Bodil (Mille Hoffmeyer Lehfeldt) leaves him for another man. Blessed with a thriller's pacing, realistic settings, artful grey cinematography by Jorgen Johansson and an ebbing, suspenseful score from Karsten Fundal, *Flame & Citron* is easily the best of recent 'resistance' movies. Flame and Citron were posthumously awarded the Medal of Freedom by the US government in 1951.

Jiri Menzel's *Closely Observed Trains* (1966 – *Closely Watched Trains* in the USA) was the quirky, bittersweet tale set towards the end of the war. Milos Hrma (Vaclav Neckar), a sexually frustrated apprentice signalman, works at the run-down, provincial Kostomlaty railway station in Czechoslovakia (filmed at Lodenice station, now in the Czech Republic). Milos comes from a long line of shirkers. His father is an ex-engine driver who took early retirement and his grandfather William was a hypnotist who did his bit to halt the German blitzkrieg towards Prague. He tried to stop the tanks with the power of thought, but 'The tank ran over him, cutting off his head'. When partisans blow up a bridge, a German military train carrying 28 carloads of ammunition is diverted to Milos' route and the partisan station staff (led by womanising Ladislav Hubicka [Josef Somr]) ambush it. The film won the Best Foreign Film Oscar in 1967 and is a perfectly crafted film that mixes pathos with comedy. Some moments of this grainy monochrome movie resemble Buster Keaton–style silent comedy, others neorealist drama, as in the scene when disconsolate Milos attempts to commit suicide by slitting his wrists in the bath. Like so many films made in the 1960s, it's really about sex. Trailers for the film were cut to resemble a bawdy sex comedy – which it isn't – but much of the story details Milos' attempts to woo pretty conductress Masa (Jitka Bendova) and the loss of his virginity to Viktoria Freie, a circus acrobat. It's an interesting, challenging take on the backwaters of the war.

Lewis Gilbert's underrated *Operation: Daybreak* (1975 – *Price of Freedom*) recreates events in Czechoslovakia that led to the assassination of Reinhard Heydrich in May 1942. Heydrich was deputy head of the Gestapo (after Heinrich Himmler) and Hitler's right-hand-man and governor of Prague (the Reichsprotector of Bohemia and Moravia). He was appointed to crush local resistance and to deport slave labourers to Germany – his zeal at both earned him the Czech nickname 'Heydrich the Hangman'. Three Czechs in exile in England – Jan Kubiŝ (Timothy Bottoms), Karel Ĉurda (Martin Shaw) and Joseph Gabĉík (Anthony Andrews) – parachute into Czechoslovakia. After careful planning with the local resistance in Prague, they attempt to shoot Heydrich (Anton Diffring) as he leaves for Berlin by train, but are foiled by a passing train, which obscures their view. They ambush his car en route to his office in Prague: Gabĉík's machine gun jams, but Kubiŝ mortally wounds him with a grenade. The assassins are sheltered in a church crypt by Father Petřek (Cyril Shaps), but are betrayed by Ĉurda, who fears for the safety of his wife and child.

Operation: Daybreak was based on Alan Burgess' 1960 novel *Seven Men at Daybreak*. It was artfully photographed on location in Czechoslovakia in Panavision by Henri Decaë and benefits from an unusual electronica score (performed on an A.R.P. Synthesiser) by David Hentschel. It was made with the collaboration of Československý Filmexport and at Barrandov Studios, Prague, and made excellent use of the authentic streets and architecture, which adds to the film's grandeur. The supporting cast included Joss Ackland as patriot leader Janák, Nicola Pagett as Anna (Kubiŝ' lover) and Diane Coupland as Aunt Marie, who houses the killers with her children, Ată (Kim Fortune) and little Jindríŝka (Pavla Matějuvská). Rene Kolldehoff played Gestapo officer Fleischer and Carl Duering was Heydrich's successor, Karl Frank. A reward is offered by the Nazi protectorate for the culprits and when that fails the SS razes the town of Lidice (called Liditz in German), 20 kilometres northwest of Prague. To wipe it from the map they destroy all the buildings, while the male population is executed, the women deported to labour camps and the children 're-educated'. Other films depicting the events surrounding Heydrich's killing include *Hangmen Also Die!* (1943 – *Lest We Forget*), *Hitler's Hangman* (1943 – *Hitler's Madman*) and *The Silent Village* (1943), which deployed the South Wales village of Cwmgiedd as Lidice.

For the razing of Lidice, *Operation: Daybreak* deploys some convincing Tiger tanks (built on T-34 chassis), as documentary filmmakers record the atrocity. Elsewhere German troops drive authentic Kübelwagons and half-tracks, and the film's historical accuracy is impressive. The story builds to an exciting, tragic climax, with the Czechs trapped in a church by the Germans. A gun battle fails to oust them and Fleischer calls for fire engines to flood the crypt. As the water rises, Kubiŝ and Gabĉík embrace each other and commit suicide. In the film's postscript, we learn that Ĉurda was executed for treason by the Czech authorities in 1947, that Father Petřek and Ată were executed by the Nazis in 1942, and that Anna and Jindřiŝka died in a concentration camp. Lidice wasn't wiped from maps, but was rebuilt after the war and many other towns are now named Lidice in its honour.

A Generation (1954 – *Pokolenie*), the first part of Andrzej Wajda's 'war trilogy', depicted partisan resistance in Poland and heralded the arrival of post-war Polish cinema internationally. Tedeusz Lomnicki starred as Stanislaw Mazuk (called 'Stach'), who also narrates the story. While working as an apprentice joiner Stach falls in love with political activist Dorato, whose real name is Ewa, an 'anti-fascist Polish patriot' (played by Urszula Modrzynska). As a member of the Organisation of Youth Fighters, Stach is given the cover name 'Bartek'. The workshop is used by the Polish Underground to store guns and Bartek steals a pistol. After an argument at a timber yard when Bartek is accused of stealing, he's beaten. In revenge, his friend Jacek (Ryszard Kotas) shoots the 'Werkschutz' (overseer) responsible in a bar. The Jewish ghetto revolts in April 1943 and the freedom fighters pitch in, but during an ambush of German soldiers, Jacek is cornered by troops and commits suicide by jumping from a staircase. The Gestapo close in and Dorato is taken away for questioning, while Bartek meets new resistance recruits and cries when one of them reminds him of Dorato.

Beginning in Warsaw in 1942 during the German Occupation, Wajda's film is filled with great moments, as he effortlessly mixes his love story with political allegory and social change. The inky cinematography and realistic locales add to the film's power and the style resembles Italian neorealism in its stark beauty and simple emotions. Working as a joiner's apprentice, Bartek learns the basics of capitalism when he is surprised to learn that his boss receives more zlotys for his carpentry than Bartek is paid for constructing it. Elsewhere Marxist theories are mentioned, including that workers are paid just enough to survive; most of the Warsaw businesses are run by the Germans. The love story between Lomnicki (who resembles a young Joe Pesci) and beautiful Modrzynska (who resembles Alida Valli) is touchingly handled by Wajda, as Bartek becomes aware of his non-political feelings for 'our political leader': 'I longed to stroke her hair', he notes. Smoke from the burning ghetto hangs over a German funfair, slave labourers are herded through the streets, ghetto fighters emerge from the sewers and executed partisans' corpses are hanged from telegraph poles. Jacek is told: 'Remember your job: you're a carpenter, not a hero', while a co-worker says of Bartek: 'They're starting politics early, this generation'. Wajda's depiction of ordinary people fighting for their freedom is also of note for the appearance by a young, skinny actor in the role of partisan Mundek: Roman Polanski. The film's credo – and also the credo for Wajda's trilogy – is uttered by Dorato in one of her speeches: 'The Germans have the slogan: "The wheels must roll for victory!" It's up to us to stop those wheels'.

Harry Keller's inept, US-made *In Enemy Country* (1968) was a lesser example of Polish partisan resistance. It begins in Paris in August 1939, with French agent Denise (Anjanette Comer) and German Baron (Paul Hubschmid) surmounting national boundaries – and their considerable height difference – to marry, enabling her to travel with him to Germany to become a French spy 'in enemy country'. Most of the plot details a fictitious mission to blow up a Polish torpedo factory. In early 1943, a new type of homing torpedo is causing havoc to Allied shipping. Tony Franciosa starred, unconvincingly, as Charles, a French secret agent of the Deuxieme Bureau, who impersonates, unconvincingly, a Polish electrician, to infiltrate the torpedo factory near Kiel. Tom Bell and Guy Stockwell played his accomplices: a British diver and a US explosives expert. They manage to call in an airstrike, which levels the works. When the remaining torpedoes are transported to a new factory, the commandos, with the help of the Polish underground, steal one from a moving train, carry it to an airfield and load it onto a B-25 Mitchell (the film's best aspect) to be flown back to England.

In Enemy Country was shot at Universal Studios. With its back-projected sets, matte shots, awful script and acting, and stock location establishing shots, it is so sloppily made as to resemble a send-up. The Polish factory work camp has a mitten-wearing warden, Ladislov (Michael Constantine), who pokes the labourers with an electric cattle prod and the German vehicles are American M3 half-tracks. Decked out in swanky costumes more appropriate for *Breakfast at Tiffany's* or *The Pink Panther*, beautiful Comer demonstrates why her star potential remained potential, while the male members of the cast coast through perfunctory performances and do little more than show off their Californian golf course suntans. No attempt is made by the leads to adopt the accents of their respective nationalities and Franciosa's drunken 'Zorba the Pole' dance on a beach has to be seen to be believed. This low-rent *Operation Crossbow* is more like 'Operation Slingshot'.

Germany too mounted special operations into enemy territory. Until the Allies gained a foothold in France in June 1944, the threat of a German invasion of Britain was never far away. It was expected that the Germans would land paratroopers ahead of any amphibious invasion, to secure vital objectives. This scenario is depicted in Alberto Cavalcanti's *Went the Day Well?* (1942 – also called *48 Hours*). On Saturday 23 May 1942, a 60-man squad of British sappers (engineers) arrive on exercises in the cosy fictional English country village of Bramley End. Despite the appearance of normality, all is not well. The engineers are actually German paratroopers, the vanguard of Hitler's invasion. They are to hold the village for 48 hours over Whitsun weekend and jam the region's radio signals in preparation for Hitler's invasion on Monday 25 May. By Sunday the paratroopers' cover is blown when a bar of German 'chokalade' from Wien (Vienna) is found in the commanding officer's kit and they resort to 'Plan B': the locals are imprisoned in the church and their children taken hostage. The paratroopers have an ally in Oliver Wilsford (Leslie Banks), a fifth columnist traitor, who helps them take over the village, but young George (Harry Fowler) manages to escape to nearby Upton Ferrars and raise the alarm.

Went the Day Well? was shot in Ealing Studios and on location in the village of Turville, Buckinghamshire in the Chilterns (also the setting for UK TV's *The Vicar of Dibley*). Landmarks include the church – where the villagers are imprisoned – and the hilltop Cobstone windmill, which the Germans commandeer as an observation post. The film is unequivocal in its anti-Nazi message – to ensure audience vigilance on the Home Front, the Germans are presented as monsters. The film often resembles a gothic horror movie, with its shadowy, evocative monochrome photography and some genuine shocks. Four cycling Home Guardsmen are callously mown down in a country lane ambush. When the vicar (C.V. France) attempts to ring the church bell to raise the alarm, the Germans kill him. The suspenseful drama also highlights heroism on the part of the village's women. Vicar's daughter Nora Ashton (Valerie Taylor) is suspicious of Oliver and when she discovers him dismantling their barricade in the manor house, she shoots him. Shopkeeper Mrs Collins (Muriel George) throws pepper in a German soldier's face and savagely kills him with a hatchet. When the soldier's cohort arrives, he bayonets her to death. Mrs Fraser (Marie Lohr), the manor's owner, selflessly saves some children, when she picks up a grenade and carries it into the corridor, where it detonates. Patricia Hayes and Thora Hird have early roles among the villagers. The struggle is initially poorly-armed villagers against professional soldiers, but with the arrival of regular troops and Home Guard from neighbouring Upton, the film ends with an incongruous gun battle in an idyllic setting. Following the Battle for Bramley End, a monument is erected in the churchyard to mark the burial place of the dead German paratroopers: 'The only bit of England they got', notes a local.

Went the Day Well? was sent-up in a 1975 episode of the UK TV series *Dad's Army*. In 'Ring Dem Bells', the 16-strong Home Guard platoon dress up as German soldiers for a training film. When they pop into the Six Bells pub for a drink, the landlord mistakes them for real German paratroopers. He raises the alarm and alerts the ARP warden, the vicar and the verger, who rush to the local church and ring the bells to warn the village. In a sequel to these events – the 1977 episode 'Wake-up Walmington' – Captain Mainwaring decides that by 1942 Walmington-on-Sea has become complacent and initiates 'Operation Wake-up' to give the locals a fright. The platoon disguises themselves as fifth columnists (enemy agents who have infiltrated Britain) and in a hilarious scene rendezvous in an old mill. Mainwaring wears a pirate's eye patch, as does Frazer, Pike arrives dressed as a Chicago gangster, Sergeant Wilson as a tramp and Corporal Jones a nun. Attempting to look shifty, furtive and suspicious as 'cutthroats and desperadoes' they eventually arouse suspicion in the Six Bells pub, whereupon the Home Guard from nearby Eastgate led by zealous Captain Square (Geoffrey Lumsden) is dispatched to apprehend them. As with many sitcoms of the 1960s and 1970s, there is a jarring difference between footage shot on film on location and scenes shot on studio interiors on videotape, but this is one of the better latter-day *Dad's Army* outings.

John Sturges' *The Eagle Has Landed* (1976) was based on Jack Higgins' 1975 novel of the same name. Oberst (Colonel) Kurt Steiner (Michael Caine) is an ace German paratroop commander, who is imprisoned on Alderney in the Channel Islands for opposing the extermination of Polish Jews. He is released to undertake a dangerous mission: in November 1943 he leads 16 German paratroopers disguised as Polish airborne troops (in Higgins' book British SAS) into the Norfolk village of Studley Constable to kidnap Churchill, who is staying in the village manor, Meltham House. The raiders are aided by local, Joanna Grey (Jean Marsh), a fifth columnist spy codenamed 'Starling'. She is a German-sympathising Boer whose mother and sister died in South Africa in British concentration camps. Romantic, motorcycle-riding IRA soldier Liam Devlin (Donald Sutherland) parachutes in and poses as the marsh warden, to make contact with Mrs Grey in preparation for the kidnapping. The 'Polish' troops pretend to be on manoeuvres, but are surprised to find a company of US Rangers stationed nearby. When one of the paratroops tries to save Susan, a little girl who almost drowns in the watermill stream, he is caught on the mill wheel: his disguise falls open, revealing an Iron Cross and German uniform. Steiner takes the villagers hostage in the church, but the US Rangers attack. Steiner manages to escape and under cover of darkness infiltrates Meltham House, where Churchill now resides. Realising that he can't kidnap Churchill, Steiner shoots him on the terrace, but it is not the great statesman who is dead but an impersonator: George Fowler, a variety artist. Churchill's in Persia, in conference with Roosevelt and Stalin in Tehran.

The Eagle Has Landed was the last film directed by Sturges. It was poorly received at the time, but has endured as a great World War II adventure. The twanging, atmospheric score by Lalo Schifrin helps and the opening title sequence, a flight over snow-capped mountains, is almost identical to *Where Eagles Dare. The Eagle Has Landed* was shot in Panavision on location, with interiors at Twickenham Studios, London. The snowbound railway depot where Steiner sees Jews being herded onto cattle trucks was in Rovaniemi, Finland. The German aircraft base at Landsvoort, Holland, was filmed at RAF St Mawgan, near Newquay, Cornwall. The harbour of Alderney, the Channel Island penal colony, was Charlestown in St Austell Bay, Cornwall; the pub, the 'Bell and Dragon' where Devlin is thrown through the window is now called the Pier House Hotel. The dunes and beach used for the coast near Studley Constable were Rock Beach, Cornwall. 'Studley Constable' and its environs was filmed on the country estate of the Berkshire village of Mapledurham, north of Reading. The watermill and St Margaret's Church feature prominently in the film and Mapledurham House (adjacent to the church) became Meltham House.

The book opens with author Higgins, a writer researching historical articles for an American magazine, discovering the concealed grave of the fallen German paratroops 'killed in action' in Studley Constable on 6 November 1943. In this way, Higgins establishes a grounding in reality for his fictitious story. This opening echoes *Went the Day Well?* In fact Sturges' film plays like a 1970s blockbuster version of Cavalcanti's film. Caine is good as Steiner and Sutherland is better as the IRA man who is able to calm savage guard dogs with his piercing high-pitched whistle. 'In the Middle Ages they'd have burned you for that', notes Steiner of Devlin's talent. Robert Duvall played the operation's planner, Colonel Radl. Wearing an eye patch and one leather glove he resembles a Bond villain. When the plan fails – Steiner and all the paratroops are killed, the E-boat that was supposed to pick them up is beached in an estuary on the receding tide and only Devlin survives – Radl is shot by a firing squad. Donald Pleasence portrayed Heinrich Himmler and Anthony Quayle played German Admiral Canaris. The character of Harvey Preston, a member of the Free British

Montage lobby still advertising John Sturges' *The Eagle Has Landed* (1976) featuring Michael Caine, Donald Sutherland, Jenny Agutter and Larry Hagman. Courtesy Kevin Wilkinson Collection.

Corps (an SS group of Nazi-sympathising Brits) was not included in the film version. Jenny Agutter was Molly Prior, Devlin's love interest in Studley Constable. Larry Hagman gave a barnstorming turn as glory-seeking American Colonel Clarence E. Pitts, whose blundering sortie into the village leads to a massacre. John Standing played village priest Father Philip Vereker and Judy Geeson was his sister, Pamela, whose lover Captain Harry Clark (Treat Williams) leads the US Rangers to save the day.

The action scenes in *The Eagle Has Landed* are staged with gusto, as when the Rangers shoot it out with the Germans in the church: stained-glass windows are smashed in and blown out, and tombstones are used for cover. The hardware on display includes bazookas, US M3 half-tracks and jeeps, and Steiner's men parachute from a DC-3 Dakota. With Sutherland as an Irishman, and Duvall and Pleasence as Germans, there's an interesting selection of accents to be heard, while Caine's variable cockney-German accent prompts you to expect him to order his paratroopers to 'Blow ze bloody doors off'. Three versions of the film exist: the US 123-minute print, a 145-minute 'Extended Edition' and the best version, the UK theatrical release, at 130 minutes.

Several World War II movies were set in the preparations for the amphibious D-Day landings during the spring of 1944, when Allied commando and French Resistance operations behind enemy lines were employed to disrupt German defences, disperse misinformation and cause confusion. In Alfonso Brescia's

Hell in Normandy (1968), US intelligence agent Strobel (Peter Lee Lawrence) impersonates a German officer and infiltrates the coastal bunker codenamed See Herr ('Sea Lord') on Omaha Beach. A squad of US paratroopers led by Captain Jack Murphy (Guy Madison) train for Operation Gambit. They will knock out the most sophisticated section of Hitler's Western Wall defences: this includes a minefield (the 'Devil's Garden') protecting the beaches, and gasoline which is pumped through pipes which turns the sea into an inferno when ignited (the 'Devil's Fountains'). Strobel makes contact with French Resistance agent Denise (Erika Blanc) and together with Murphy's squad they take over the bunker on the eve of D-Day. The slim budget stretched only to several motorcycles and Kübelwagons. French and English coastal scenes were filmed at Tor Caldara, on Anzio Cape in Italy, and the D-Day landings themselves are actual monochrome archive footage (though the rest of the movie is in colour). The film's wordy original title lost much in translation: *Testa di sbarco per otto implacabili* ('Head of the Landing for Eight Implacable Ones').

Robert Aldrich's *The Dirty Dozen* (1967), based on the 1965 novel of the same name by E.M. Nathanson, is one of the most notorious, debated World War II films. Major John Reisman (Lee Marvin) is assigned a top-secret mission, codenamed Rosedale. Reisman must train 12 convicted soldiers – some of whom have been condemned to hang – for an operation in Occupied France on the eve of D-Day. Theirs is a temporary amnesty, a stay of execution, nothing more, and an opportunity to die for their country. They will parachute into Brittany and attack a château near Rennes which is being used as a recreational rest centre and conference area for high-ranking German officers. Reisman bullies and cajoles his 12 charges into a crack fighting unit via his programme of Basic Training with-a-difference. If one of them steps out of line, they all go back to prison – a variation of 'one hang, we all hang' – which bonds the group.

Aldrich had tried to buy the rights to Nathanson's book before it was published, but the author sold them to producer Kenneth Hyman and MGM. Aldrich was then hired as director by Hyman. Five scripts later, Aldrich was almost satisfied with one by Nunnally Johnson. Lukas Keller worked on further script revisions, transforming it from what Aldrich called a '1945 war picture' into a '1967 war picture'. Both writers are credited with the screenplay, with two-thirds being Keller's modernist revisions and a third being Johnson's work, though the film is slightly overlong at 148 minutes and could have stood further editing. MGM originally hired John Wayne as Reisman, which displeased Aldrich: 'I'm a John Wayne fan. His politics don't bother me, that's his mother's problem. But you don't get John Wayne to play a Lee Marvin part'. War movie veteran Richard Jaeckel played MP Sergeant Bowren, who assists Reisman. In fact with Bowren and Reisman, 14 men actually land in France to undertake the mission.

Aldrich's big problem was making his indolent, anti-authoritarian mob of rapists, murderers, thieves and psychos endearing to audiences. He achieved this with shrewd casting decisions. Jim Brown, an American footballer with the Cleveland Browns, was breaking into acting and played Robert Jefferson (called Napoleon White in the novel). Singer Trini Lopez played Hispanic Pedro Jiminez and strummed the song 'The Bramble Bush' in the film. Telly Savalas was Archer

All guns blazing, GIs Wladislaw (Charles Bronson) and Franko (John Cassavetes), MP Bowren (Richard Jaeckel) and Major John Reisman (Lee Marvin) escape from the French château (a set at MGM British Studios, Borehamwood) in a German SdKfz 7 half-track, at the climax of Robert Aldrich's *The Dirty Dozen* (1967). Courtesy Kevin Wilkinson Collection.

Maggot, the worst of the bunch, a rapacious, Bible-quoting, redneck sadist zealot. John Cassavetes played Victor Franko, the twitchy wiseguy tough who becomes the dozen's spokesman. Clint Walker played Native American man mountain Samson Posey. Charles Bronson turned down the 'Ugly' role in *The Good, the Bad and the Ugly* (1966) to play stone-faced 'Polak' Joseph Wladislaw. Previously a member of the heroic groups in *The Magnificent Seven* and *The Great Escape*, Bronson's performance here is underplaying at its most effective. The scene when baseball-obsessed Wladislaw takes a psychological test with Captain Stuart Kinder (Ralph Meeker) is a great comedy moment. Donald Sutherland was memorable as dim-witted Vernon Pinkley, and Tom Busby (as Milo Vladek), Ben Carruthers (Glenn Gilpin), Stuart Cooper (Roscoe Lever), Colin Maitland (Seth Sawyer) and Al Mancini (Tassos Bravos) made up the numbers. The US top brass deployed Ernest Borgnine as General Worden and Robert Webber as General Denton. George Kennedy was Major Max Armbruster, Reisman's ally in HQ, and Robert Ryan was Reisman's arch-nemesis, Colonel Everett Dasher Breed, head of a parachute school which the dozen attend. The scene where Reisman passes unshaven Pinkley off as a general, to the humiliation of Breed's brass band reception and parade, is the film's funniest.

The Dirty Dozen was filmed from April to October 1966 on location in England with interiors at MGM British Studios, Borehamwood, on a $5.4 million budget. In the film's opening shot a hearse drives into bleak Marston-Tyne Military Prison, where an inmate is about to be hanged. It was filmed at Ashridge House, Little Gaddesden, Hertfordshire, which is now a management college. Colonel Breed's parachute school was at the aerodrome at Hendon, London. Reisman claims that his dozen are so well-trained that they can beat Breed's regulars in wargame army manoeuvres, during which they capture both his divisional HQ and the colonel himself. The 'Devonshire' village used for the wargame was picturesque Aldbury, Hertfordshire with its duck pond, stocks and manor house. When the dozen arrive in their Dodge truck, they pass the Greyhound pub twice. The French château and its grounds were constructed from scratch at Borehamwood: the gardens, including a brook and a stone bridge, involved the planting of six weeping willows, 5,400 square yards of heather, 400 ferns, 450 shrubs and 30 spruce trees. This spectacular set, first seen in a crane shot as the squad arrive, is an impressive setting for the night raid finale.

The squad earn their name the 'Dirty Dozen' from Sergeant Bowren, when 'courtesy of Mr Franko' they have their shaving and bathing rights suspended for insubordination. But it is a baker's Dirty Dozen of 13 men attacks the château in the film's finale – Pedro Jiminez dies off-screen when he breaks his neck in the parachute drop. Actor Lopez's agent had asked for more money and Aldrich altered the script to kill his character off without further ado. Reisman and Wladislaw infiltrate the château disguised as Nazi officers, with Pinkley as their staff car chauffeur, while the squad deploy around the building and its grounds. During these scenes, Richard Marner can be seen as a German sentry – he later played Colonel Kurt Von Strohm in sitcom *'Allo 'Allo!* Maggot betrays the group and runs amok in the château, calling for judgement day for his fellow sinners, and Jefferson is forced to kill him. An alarm sounds and the German officers and their female companions head underground to an air raid shelter, making the dozen's job easier. Reisman and Wladislaw lock the doors, trapping the officers below ground in arched cellar chambers which are also ammunition stores. Finding the shelter's chimney-like air vents, they pour in grenades and gasoline, then ignite the lethal cocktail with more grenades, frying the helpless Germans alive and blowing the château to smithereens. Meanwhile a column of German troops and light armour launch a surprise attack, decimating the squad. Franko, Bowren, Wladislaw and Reisman commandeer a half-track, but this is a Robert Aldrich film, so their escape vehicle isn't any old half-track, but the powerful German SdKfz 7. With its armour and roaring engine it ploughs over the wreck of a puny VW Kübelwagon. As they escape, Franko is shot dead and Reisman wounded. In the film's dénouement in a military hospital, Bowren, Wladislaw and Reisman are informed that Wladislaw will be reinstated in the army at his former rank and the dead men 'lost their lives in the line of duty'.

Aldrich's film is both anti-military and anti-Nazi. The dozen seem to exist in their own moral universe in which only they – criminals, looters and rapists – are right. The US top brass behind the operation are wargamers and their regulars are inferior to the dozen, who if nothing else are specialists in killing. Reisman

Turn Them Loose on the Nazis: US poster for the 70mm release, with full stereophonic sound, of Robert Aldrich's *The Dirty Dozen* (1967). Poster courtesy Kevin Wilkinson Collection.

notes that to impersonate a German, 'Just act mean and grunt' and refers to their mission as a 'turkey shoot'. The film's slam-bang finale was seen as patriotic stuff in 1967, but the intervening years have if anything intensified its sadism – in contrast to most war films made in this era. It was X-rated in the UK and is still rated 15 today. Posters stated: 'Train Them! Excite Them! Arm Them! … Then turn them loose on the Nazis!' Burning people alive – even if they are Nazis – is extreme, and the fact that the victims are trapped underground exaggerates the cruelty. The US army are absolved of moral blame, as General Worden has employed criminals to carry out the mission. On NBC's *Today* show, Judith Crist said the film, '(thumbed) its nose at authority and morality and at the compromise that is Hollywood's war cliché. It is cruel and unpleasant on an intellectual level, but that, of course, is war'. *Dirty Dozen* still has its detractors, but it was extremely popular on its original release, taking $19.5 million. It was the most successful film of 1967 and the fifteenth most successful of all time up to that point, no doubt helped by its release in the prestigious 'Roadshow' format, in impressive 70mm with six-track Stereophonic sound.

The Dirty Dozen was also highly influential, spawning many derivatives. There were three official TV movie sequels – *The Dirty Dozen: Next Mission* (1985 – with Marvin, Borgnine and Jaeckel), *Dirty Dozen: The Deadly Mission* (1987) and *Dirty Dozen: Fatal Mission* (1988 – both of which featured Ernest Borgnine, with Telly Savalas cast as Major Wright). On TV there were ten episodes of *Dirty Dozen: The Series* (1988) and the US series *Garrison's Gorillas* (1967–68) was inspired by Aldrich's film, with five convicts fighting as a crack team. Among many film title derivatives were *The Dirty Heroes* (1967), *The Dirty Two* (1969), *The Dirty Dam Busters* (1970 – *Churchill's Leopards*) and *The Inglorious Bastards* (1977). Gordon Hassler's *The Misfit Brigade* (1987 – *Wheels of Terror*), starring David Carradine, Oliver Reed and Bruce Davison, had convicts deployed in the German army. In the acrobatic *Five for Hell* (1969), gum-chewing Lieutenant Clem Hoffman (John Garko) led a group of specialists equipped with trampolines and exploding baseballs into Italian Villa Verdi to steal secret 'Plan K' from the SS, commanded by Colonel Hans Müller (Klaus Kinski). Umberto Lenzi's shot-in-Spain *The Battle of the Commandos* (1969 – *The Legion of the Damned*) starred Jack Palance as the commando leader with Wolfgang Preiss, Helmut Schneider and Curd Jürgens a formidable trio of German brass. Preiss or Jürgens must hold some kind of record for the most screen portrayals of German officers. *The Secret Invasion* and some of the derivatives mentioned above are leaner and briefer special mission movies. But there's no denying Aldrich's exhilarating, abhorrent action finale – magnificent and malfeasant – is one of the most powerful in combat cinema. It is a pure, visceral bullet-impact that anticipates Sam Peckinpah's and Quentin Tarantino's savage visions of war.

Chapter 13

SPECIAL OPS IN EUROPE II (1944–45)

Brian G. Hutton's *Where Eagles Dare* (1968) was set during the preamble to D-Day. Like *The Guns of Navarone*, it was based on a story by Alistair MacLean, who wrote the original screenplay and later adapted it into a novel. In the seven years since *Navarone*, cinema had changed considerably, with a noticeable escalation in screen violence. It was the era of *Bullit*'s high-octane car chases, the casual, explosive violence of *The Dirty Dozen* and *Bonnie and Clyde* (1967) and the gadget-laden espionage of James Bond, and the ante was upped as to what constituted 'high adventure'. Instead of a scene in *Navarone* when the commandos scale sheer cliffs in a raging storm, *Where Eagles Dare* served up cliff-hanging exploits on icy cable cars high above an alpine valley. In place of *Navarone*'s occasional action spots, when the heroes shoot it out with German patrols, Hutton's film had two Allied professionals – a double-agent and an OSS (Office of Strategic Services) assassin – shooting it out with the entire Wehrmacht.

Where Eagles Dare was influenced by *The Secret Invasion* – a mission to rescue a captured general from a Nazi fortress, with the heroes escaping disguised as Germans – but benefited from a $7.2 million budget. *Eagles* was based on MacLean's 'Adler Schloss' (Eagle Castle) which detailed a fictitious raid on a German mountaintop stronghold – Waffen SS fortress the Schloß Adler ('The Castle of the Eagles'), the HQ of the German Secret Service in southern Bavaria. British Intelligence (MI6) mount a special mission to free US General Carnaby (Robert Beatty) who has been captured when his Mosquito was shot down. He was flying to convene with the Russians on Crete, to discuss the establishment of a second front in Europe (Operation Overlord) and must be rescued before the Gestapo loosen his tongue. Major John Smith (Richard Burton) leads the crack rescue squad, which consists of US Ranger Lieutenant Morris Schaffer (Clint Eastwood), five British soldiers – James Christiansen (Donald Houston), Edward Berkeley (Peter Barkworth), Philip Thomas (William Squire), Harrod (Brook

US Ranger lieutenant – and OSS assassin – Morris Schaffer (Clint Eastwood) disposes of a German guard en route to the Schloß Adler in Brian G. Hutton's explosive *Where Eagles Dare* (1968). Courtesy Kevin Wilkinson Collection.

Williams) and Jock MacPhearson (Neil McCarthey) – and female agent Mary Ellison (Mary Ure). Mary poses as 'Maria Schenk' who visits her 'cousin' Heidi, an undercover agent working in the guest house Zum Wilden Hirsch (The Wild Stag). The squad parachute from a Junkers Ju-52, disguised as German mountain troops (Gebirgsjäger), but radio operator Harrod is killed on landing and MacPhearson is murdered shortly afterwards in the village of Werfen at the foot of the fortress. Realising that Christiansen, Berkeley and Thomas are traitors, Smith and Schaffer make preparations for their escape. They then infiltrate the eagle's nest, which can only be accessed by cable car, with help from Mary. Freeing Carnaby (actually an actor, Corporal Cartwright Jones, who is impersonating the general and whose 'crash' has been staged) they make good their escape with Mary and Heidi. They dash five-miles to Oberhausen military airfield (the HQ of the Bavarian Mountain Rescue) in a bus fitted with a snowplough, where they are picked up by the Junkers.

Elliott Kastner and Jerry Gershwin (fronting their London-based company Winkast) co-produced the film with MGM, with the formidable pairing of Burton and Eastwood in the leads. Michael Hordern played Admiral Rolland (codenamed Father Machree) at MI6 and Patrick Wymark was Colonel Wyatt Turner, who is revealed to be a Nazi double agent. Vincent Ball played the Junkers' pilot, Wing Commander Cecil Carpenter, and Derren Nesbitt was zealous Major Von Happen (called Captain Von Brauchitsch in the novelisation and Von Haggen on cast call sheets), the ever-suspicious, ever-delving Gestapo officer and ladies' man. Anton Diffring was the garrison commander Colonel Paul Kramer and Ferdy Mayne played his superior Reichsmarschall Julius Rosemeyer, who arrives in an anachronistic post-war helicopter to interrogate Carnaby – military adviser Major Grasteiger was present on set when this scene was shot, but he presumably ignored this oversight. Stuntman Bill Sawyer played Rosemeyer's helicopter pilot who is knifed by Schaffer to prevent Carnaby being whisked to safety by chopper. Richard Egan was an early choice for Schaffer and Leslie Caron was mooted as Mary. Future Hammer horror scream queen Ingrid Pitt was cast as Heidi, 'a pretty Alpine rose' and one of the top Allied agents in Bavaria since 1941. Though blonde Pitt is a busty Tyrolean serving wench, Mary Ure was not cast as mere set dressing and participates extensively as the action unfolds.

Shooting began on location in January 1968 and was completed at MGM's Borehamwood Studios in Hertfordshire by July. The 300-strong crew was based in Salzburg, Austria and travelled to the snowbound locales in 100 vehicles and three helicopters. The Schloß Adler was an actual eleventh century castle, the Burg Hohenwerfen, perched above the village of Werfen in the Salzach Valley. The castle exterior and courtyard were used, but all interiors were constructed at Borehamwood. The fortress interiors, with fireplaces, winding staircases and corridors, resemble Count Von Krolock's snow-shrouded, cobwebbed Transylvanian castle in *Dance of the Vampires* (1967), also shot at Borehamwood (Ferdy Mayne had played resident nosferatu Von Krolock in *Vampires*). Some of the cable car scenes were lensed in picturesque Ebensee, Austria, and a spectacular set incorporating cable cars, a craggy rock face, pine woods and the control room was constructed at Borehamwood. The bridge and tiered river weir scenes were shot in Ebensee, near Alpine Lake Traunsee, which was also the location of the railroad station and the German army barracks and training camp. The exterior of Zum Wilden Hirsch was in Lofer and the Oberhausen Airfield was filmed at Aigen Im Ennstal. Other scenes were shot near St Moritz, Switzerland, including the bus chase escape, the demolition of a bridge and the drop zone scenes, where the parachutists land in fir tree-fringed high alpine pastures. The Swiss Army provided the three-engined Ju-52 Junkers transport plane (a Lancaster in MacLean's book) and the Swiss European parachuting champions performed the drop.

Most of the action takes place at night, though some was filmed 'day-for-night': Arthur Ibbetson's picturesque Panavision snowscapes and the vast castle interiors are artfully lit and shot. *Where Eagles Dare* must be seen in widescreen: panned and scanned, or cropped TV prints fail to do Ibbetson's brittle, chilly exteriors justice. The second unit director was stunt ace Yakima Canutt, of *Stagecoach* and *Ben-Hur* fame. Stuntmen performed the eagles' daring exploits on location, with the stars' close-ups shot at Borehamwood. With the exception of a couple of process shots, the model work, effects and stunts are exemplary. Richard Burton's legendary offscreen drinking was apparent during the shoot. After the first screening of the finished film, Burton said to Hutton, 'I don't remember most of that, but I was pretty good in it, wasn't I?' The probable reason for this comment was that a large proportion of his performance was by his stunt double, Alf Joint. Even when Eastwood was on location he was often acting opposite

Joint. Eastwood suggested changing the title to *Where Doubles Dare.* For some stunts Eastwood was doubled by Eddie Powell and Gillian Aldam doubled Ure. Burton and Eastwood were required to scale the castle wall by rope. Eastwood climbed up himself, but Burton was suspended from a crane. According to Joint, 'He had more wires on him than Pinocchio'. Humorously, Smith comments to Mary, 'If I can climb up on my own, why can't he?' As Hutton remembered, 'We always said that it should have been called *Where Eagles Dare* starring Alf Joint with a few selected close-ups by Richard Burton'.

Hutton intended *Where Eagles Dare* to be a spoof of action movies. MacLean's convoluted, illogical plot has been unpicked and ridiculed by critics, but it didn't waste time on a lengthy preamble – ten minutes into the film we know the plan and its objective and are on the ground with the squad. The veiled purpose of Smith's mission is to expose German agents who have infiltrated MI6: Carnaby is a MacGuffin. The only people Smith can trust are Mary Ellison (his lover and partner in counter-espionage in Italy) and Ranger Schaffer. Smith's radio contact with MI6 opens with the now-classic call sign: 'Broadsword calling Danny Boy'. The three MI6 double-agents are tricked into revealing the names of their spy contacts and all three are killed: Thomas is shot as he abseils from the castle, while Smith kills Christiansen and Berkeley during a vicious fight on the roof of a cable car. The film ends with the revelation that Turner is the top German agent in Britain. He is allowed by Smith to cheat the hangman and jump from the rescue Junkers (in the book a Mosquito bomber) over the Alps without a parachute.

When the commandos first spy the inaccessible fortified castle, Schaffer notes, 'Somebody's got to be crazy'. Audiences would have to be crazy to take this fantasy escapism seriously and the preposterous action is what makes the film one of the most popular World War II films. As far as the stars were concerned, Burton handled the plot exposition and Eastwood did what he did best on screen in the 1960s: remain monosyllabic and shoot people. Their remarkable onscreen chemistry makes this one of WWII cinema's most memorable teamings – a loquacious, intelligent, manipulative double agent and a cold-hearted, fearless assassin. There's some underplayed humour in there too, notably when Smith impersonates the dreaded Heinrich Himmler's brother, to unnerve German officers in a tavern. Schaffer's mission is to liquidate the Schloß Adler's senior SS staff: Rosemeyer and Kramer. He also kills Von Happen and shoots a woman in the back, but it's morally justified, as she's Leutnant Anne-Marie Kernitser (Olga Lowe), a stern, uniformed Dr Death who administers Scopolamine truth serum with a hypodermic. In MacLean's book she's secretary Anne-Marie, a sexy-but-ruthless blonde 'pin-up girl for the Third Reich'. The heroes' escape from the castle includes the famous scene when Schaffer takes on the castle garrison during a shootout in a bullet-riddled corridor. During his rearguard action, Clint holds them off at the pass, selflessly picking up German stick hand-grenades (the Steilhandgranate, which the Allies called 'Potato Mashers') and throwing them back. He even fires two MP40 Schmeisser submachine guns simultaneously. Such improbable action drew derision from critics and historians.

As the action gains momentum, Smith and co flee the castle in a cable car and leap into a frozen river in the valley below. The commandos have set bundles of

Where Eagles Dare (1968): Top: Major Smith (Richard Burton) and Lieutenant Schaffer (Clint Eastwood) get their first sight of the Wehrmacht HQ. Middle: the inaccessible Schloß Adler ('The Castle of the Eagles'). Bottom: trapped inside the castle, Schaffer shoots his way out. Images courtesy Kevin Wilkinson Collection.

dynamite sticks detonated by tripwire or ticking timer, carefully orchestrated to affect their escape. Though the sticks were actually made from balsa wood, half-cut Burton informed Hutton: 'I don't handle explosives, Brian'. Smith, Schaffer, Mary, Heidi and Carnaby exit Werfen in a red bus. Smith uses the snowplough to detonate dynamite charges, felling fell trees and telegraph poles in their wake. This waylays the pursuing German convoy (an authentic selection of trucks, Kübelwagons and motorcycles and sidecars). The commandos blow up a bridge and speed on to Oberhausen Airfield's landing strip as the Junkers arrives. Smith swerves to swipe several German Focke-Wulf Fw190s fighter planes, blowing them up, and the incredible car stunts skid Kübelwagons across the icy tarmac, as the Junkers takes to the sky. One of the film's legacies is Ron Goodwin's enduring score. The grandiose, looming title theme – ascending, portentous chords and clattering machine-gun percussion – opens the film in style, as the Junkers soars above the majestic snowscape. The incidental, well-honed themes are suitably atmospheric, adding much to the action and tension. *Eagles* remains Goodwin's finest score.

Released in the UK in December 1968, *Where Eagles Dare* was exhibited in the US the following March. Posters publicised 'Alistair MacLean's epic adventure story of a wartime mission that cannot succeed – but dare not fail'. The trailer reminded audiences: 'From the company that brought you *The Dirty Dozen* and the author who gave you *The Guns of Navarone*'. *Variety* thought it was the best war movie since *The Great Escape*. *Eagles* was MGM's top earner of 1969, taking $21 million worldwide. The novelisation by MacLean was first published in 1967 and then reissued as a film tie-in in 1969. The novel's plot is similar to the film, though the dialogue differs significantly. An unpleasant scene in the novel – when Mary is forcibly and thoroughly searched by the Germans on her arrival at the schloß, to discover where her underwear was made (Piccadilly or Gorki Street) – didn't make it into the film. A proposed love affair between Heidi and Schaffer was removed from the screenplay (but is present in the novel) and Eastwood and Pitt featured prominently together in publicity stills, enjoying a stein of Holsten in Zum Wilden Hirsch with Ure and Burton. All references to Schaffer being a cowboy from Montana with a phobia of horses (present in MacLean's novelisation) were removed from the screenplay. In the finale of the book, the heroes jump from the cable car onto dry land (not into a river) and escape in a yellow post bus. They swipe some motorbikes with the plough, halt the pursuing convoy with crates of broken bottles, blow up a rickety wooden bridge and a Tiger tank shell passes through the entire length of the bus, but doesn't explode. Quoted on the cover of this paperback tie-in, Burton reckoned it was 'The best adventure story I have ever read', though if he didn't remember making the film perhaps his recommendation should be taken with a pinch of salt.

Though the Allies had a foothold in Europe after the invasion of France, there was still the need for behind the lines espionage and assassination – and not only by the Allies themselves. The pre-title sequence of Henry Hathaway's *The Desert Fox: The Story of Rommel* (1951) depicted a British commando assassination attempt on Rommel in North Africa. In November 1943, Rommel took over the Western Wall defences and the film also recreates Rommel's part in the most famous assassination attempt on Hitler, on 20 July 1944. Codenamed 'Valkyrie', part of the plan called for Colonel Claus Von Stauffenberg (Edward Franz, with one arm and an eye patch) to blow up 'The Bohemian Corporal's' Rastenburg headquarters in East Prussia, with an attaché case hidden under the table in a meeting room. *Desert Fox* boasts miles of archive footage and a good performance by James Mason as the anti-Hitler Rommel, a sympathetic Nazi who turns to treason. Leo G Carroll played Field Marshal Von Rundstedt and Jessica Tandy was Frau Rommel, Lucie. The film's main failings are its verbose script, lack of real drama and a ranting, Chaplinesque Hitler impersonation by Luther Adler, which anticipates *The Goons* and *Dr Strangelove*. Look out for the moment when Rommel's car is ambushed by an Allied fighter plane: the footage of the crash is lifted from a stock car rally, complete with a stand of spectators in the background. The July assassination attempt was covered by two West German films, G.W. Pabst's *Jackboot Mutiny* (1955 – *It Happened on the 20th July*) starring Bernhard Wicki, and *The Plot to Assassinate Hitler* (1955), with Wolfgang Preiss as Von Stauffenberg. A plan for US commandos to join up with Rommel and the conspirators was part of the mission in the Jack Palance action film *Battle Giants* (1969). The assassination plot also featured in Anatole Litvak's whodunit *The Night of the Generals* (1967), starring Peter O'Toole, Omar Sharif, Tom Courtenay, Donald Pleasence, Philippe Noiret and Charles Gray, with Christopher Plummer as Rommel.

Hitler's assassination attempt was also the focus of the US-German co-production *Valkyrie* (2008 – *Walküre*), with Tom Cruise as Von Stauffenberg. Filmed on location in Germany, the US and at Studio Babelsberg in Potsdam, Bryan Singer's film suspensefully depicts the planning and execution of 'Valkyrie'. While Hitler was to be assassinated in the Wolf's Lair HQ in East Prussia, other conspirators were to instigate a coup in Berlin, mobilising the Reserve Army to seize power from the SS and installing Dr Goerdeler (Kevin McNally) as Chancellor. The action opens in Tunisia in 1943, in the dying days of the Afrika Korps, when Stauffenberg is badly injured in an airstrike by US P-40s on the 10th Panzer Army. These desert scenes were lensed in Lucerne Valley, California. Stauffenberg loses his right hand, three fingers on his left hand and his left eye (he wore an eye patch or a false eye thereafter). In Berlin he becomes involved with the plan to oust the Führer and it is he who delivers the attaché case to the Wolf's Lair staff conference. Key members of the cell of disaffected German officers and politicians were played by familiar British actors, including Bill Nighy (General Friedrich Olbricht), Terence Stamp (Ludwig Beck), Kenneth Branagh (General Henning Von Tresckow), Tom Wilkinson (General Friedrich Fromm), Kenneth Cranham and Bernard Hill. Comedian and actor Eddie Izzard was good as General Erich Fellgiebel, the cell's contact within the Wolf's Lair. Carice Van Houten played Stauffenberg's wife, Nina, while both Thomas Kretschmann and Christian Berkel had appeared in another Hitler-themed film, *Downfall*. Harvey Friedman played Goebbels and several historical figures from Hitler's entourage are depicted, including Himmler and Göring. Hitler himself was an effective turn by David Bamber.

Valkyrie is based on a true story and although the filmmakers have 'Hollywooded up' history, it builds to a moving conclusion, as the conspirators are rumbled, captured and executed. Amid his mannered – mostly British – co-stars, Cruise could have stuck out like a sore thumb, but his immobility suits the rigid, militarist character and his star power doesn't overbalance or detract from the well-told, pacy story. The excellent sense of period detail also helps. So many 21st Century war films resemble either video games or awful TV drama-documentaries of historical events, a trap that *Valkyrie* admirably avoids.

There's a trend with Hollywood film stars such as Cruise to play Nazison screen, convincingly or otherwise. These include Roger Moore in *Escape to Athena*, Richard Burton in *Massacre in Rome*, Yul Brynner in *Triple Cross* and James Mason in *The Desert Fox* and *The Desert Rats*. Many other stars have donned Nazi uniforms as 'fashion accessory' disguises in war movies, including Lee Marvin and Charles Bronson (*The Dirty Dozen*), Gregory Peck and David Niven (*The Guns of Navarone*), Frank Sinatra and Trevor Howard (*Von Ryan's Express*) and Richard Burton and Clint Eastwood (*Where Eagles Dare*). As Howard says in *Von Ryan's Express*, 'That's what the bloody Bosch have: style'. The Ju-52 two-engined Junkers seen in *Valkyrie* as Hitler's personal aircraft is the same plane, now owned by JU-AIR in Switzerland, that carried Burton and Eastwood on their mission in *Where Eagles Dare*.

Terence Young's *Triple Cross* (1966) attempted a James Bond–style espionage film set during World War II. It tells the true story of Eddie Chapman (Christopher Plummer), a safe-cracker responsible for a series of robberies in London who is caught and imprisoned in St Helier on Jersey. When the Germans occupy the Channel Islands, Chapman is freed and becomes a German agent (winning the Iron Cross), though he also works as a double-agent for the British. Harry Meyen, Gert Fröbe, Romy Schneider and Howard Vernon played assorted German agents, officers and collaborators, with Trevor Howard and Anthony Dawson as British Intelligence. Claudine Auger appeared as Chapman's love interest, French Resistance agent, Claudette. The film features vignettes of the disastrous Dieppe Raid, the Normandy invasion and a sequence where Chapman redirects V-1 rockets bound for London, but is a spoofy, swinging sixties version of the war. Colonel Von Grunen (Yul Brynner), Chapman's superior at German Intelligence becomes disillusioned with the German cause and is involved in the plot to assassinate Hitler in July 1944, which costs Grunen his life.

Michael Anderson's all-star *Operation Crossbow* (1965) used as its basis the real life 'Operation Crossbow', a stratagem by the British government to counter the threat of Hitler's terrifying 'weapons of mass destruction', the V-1 flying bombs and V-2 rockets which were launched against England and the vital port at Antwerp in Belgium, in 1944. The V-1 (V for Vergeltungswaffe, or 'Vengeance Weapon') were unmanned flying bombs, resembling a small jet fighter. They were rocket powered and due to their distinctive throaty engines were christened 'Buzz Bombs'. When their fuel ran out, the 'buzz' ceased, to be followed by an ominous silence, as they glided to their targets, then exploded. They were very effective at random devastation and struck terror into the population of London when they were first used in June 1944. Britain's air defences soon learned to cope with this threat, as Spitfires and coastal batteries knocked them out, but 2,419 hit London, 30 dropped on Portsmouth and Southampton, and one on Manchester, killing a total of 6,000 people. The V-2 was a notable improvement on its predecessor – it looked like a missile and travelled at 2,500 miles an hour, making it impossible to waylay. Deployed in September 1944, its attacks were sudden and deadly, with no 'buzz' warning. 1,054 fell on England (half of these on London) and 900 on Antwerp. Like the V-1 it was a lottery as to where the V-2s landed and though they were effective, the cost of producing them drained Germany's resources.

Battle of the V-1 (1958 – *Missile from Hell* or *Unseen Heroes*), a low-budget UK production, told the story of a group of Polish Home Army resistance fighters who are drafted into the 'Volunteer Labour Service' to work on construction projects at Pennemünde on Germany's Baltic coast, where the V-1 missile is in development. The underground pass vital information to British Intelligence, who bomb the facilities at Pennemünde, delaying missile production and forcing the Germans to relocate out of bomber range to Western Poland. The resistance manage to steal a V-1 which has crashed on its test flight without exploding, and fly it back to England in a Dakota. Michael Rennie was Resistance fighter Novak, Patricia Medina, David Knight and Milly Vitale were his cohorts, and Christopher Lee had an early role as sadistic SS camp officer Brunner. Rocket sites in France were the target for Allied OSS agents in Henry Hathaway's *13 Rue Madeleine* (1947), starring James Cagney, Annabella, Frank Latimore and Richard Conte.

Operation Crossbow was produced by Carlo Ponti and released by MGM, with interiors shot at MGM's Borehamwood Studios. As Duncan Sandys (Richard Johnson) co-ordinates the British operation to halt rocket production, the film also depicts the Germans' technological development of the weapons. On the wide beaches of Pennemünde (filmed at Holkham Beach, Norfolk) the Germans test their new V-1 rockets, launched from ski runways. Barbara Rütting played pilot Hannah Reitsch, a historical figure who bravely test-piloted flying bombs to improve their design. A bombing raid by the RAF puts the rocket plant at Pennemünde out of action, but the Germans relocate deep into the heart of Germany, in an underground complex, to develop the V-2. The Germans are recruiting scientists and engineers from Occupied Countries to work on the project, so Sandys dispatches three Allied agents – Lieutenant John Curtis (George Peppard), Robert Henshaw (Tom Courtenay) and Phil Bradley (Jeremy Kemp) – to infiltrate the base disguised as Dutch engineers. They parachute into Holland, are recruited for the rocket project and taken to Germany. In the rush to activate the operation, the organisers haven't done their research on the identities stolen for the agents. Henshaw's appropriated 'persona' is actually that of a wanted murderer, while Curtis is confronted by his Italian ex-'wife' Nora, who shows up looking for her husband. During a night-time raid by Lancasters, Curtis manages to open the base's launching doors, guiding the bombers to their target: they obliterate the complex, at the cost of the agents' lives.

Operation Crossbow is largely fictionalised, using only the premise of the V-1 and V-2 campaigns as a framework for familiar spy hokum – the film was retitled *The Great Spy Mission* for some markets. It covers the period from early- to-late 1944. The underground rocket development plant (filmed in St Pancras Power Station, London) resembles a hewn-from-rock James Bond villain's subterranean lair, with gangways, blipping control rooms and a roof that opens to launch missiles. The long-range 'New York Rocket' which the

German's are developing towards the end of the film didn't exist – in reality their 'V-3' development was a super gun which would fire a powerful missile, but this was never perfected. The rocket and missile tests and the attacks on London are excitingly staged – with houses reduced to rubble and the emergency crews battling fires – and the destruction of the rocket plant is also above par, making this one of the most engrossing 'special mission' war movies of the 1960s.

The cast is a 'who's who' of British World War II movie cinema, with John Mills and Trevor Howard as the British planners of the operation, pipe-smoking General Boyd and sceptical Professor Lindemann. Intelligence officers Wing Commander Kendall (Richard Todd) and Constance 'Babs' Babbington Smith (Sylvia Syms) discover the rocket launching sites on aerial surveillance photographs, and a heavily disguised Patrick Wymark played Winston Churchill. Helmut Dantine, Ferdy Mayne, Paul Henreid and Anton Diffring played German officers of various echelons. Anthony Quayle was German double-agent Bamford who identifies Henshaw and has him interrogated, tortured and executed. With Ponti producing, it was natural for him to promote his wife Sophia Loren in the publicity, but she does little to warrant her top billing. She plays Nora, who almost exposes Curtis as an impostor to the German police. She blunders into the plot for a couple of emotionally overacted scenes and is shot by landlady Frieda (an Allied agent, played by Lilli Palmer) to safeguard the operation. Unusually for a English-language war film, over half the dialogue is rendered in German. As in *The Longest Day* and *Battle of Britain* the German characters speak German (with English subtitles) which adds an authenticity all-too-rare in such big-budget war cinema. In most UK and US WWII films, German officers speak to each other in English, but bafflingly issue orders to their men in German.

Bitto Albertini's *The War Devils* (1969) opened in Tunisia in 1943, for a US commando attack on a German gun emplacement, but provided audiences with two missions for the price of one. The second half of the film shifted the action to snowbound France in late 1944. The Germans are developing a 'super weapon' successor to their V-2 rockets and Captain George Vincent (Guy Madison) leads a group of US Rangers into France to rescue British Colonel Steele (Anthony Steel), a weapons expert, who has been captured when his RAF bomber is shot down. This brings Vincent into conflict with German Major Meinike (Venantino Venantini), his old adversary from Tunisia.

Alberto De Martino's *The Dirty Heroes* (1967) was originally entitled *Dalle Ardenne all'Inferno* ('From the Ardennes to Hell'). It was set in Holland near the end of the war, following the Germans' defeat in the Ardennes region of Belgium during the Battle of the Bulge. US escapees from German prison camp Lager 114 and Dutch partisans join forces to raid the canalside Wehrmacht headquarters of General Von Keist (Curd Jürgens) in Amsterdam. The squad are safecracker sergeant Joe 'Sesame' Mortimer (Frederick Stafford); US air force captain 'Lawyer' O'Connor (John Ireland); hardman POW Randall (Howard Ross); anti-Nazi German sergeant Rudolph Petrowsky (Michel Constantin); and partisans Luc Rollman, the 'Fox of Amsterdam' (Adolfo Celi) and Marta Van Staten (Faida Nichols). They plan to steal a cache of diamonds and secret information detailing V-1 and V-2 rocket production, ostensibly to aid the Dutch Underground.

Sesame, Lawyer, Randall and Petrowsky were Chicago gangsters before the war and have their eyes on the diamonds for themselves.

Martino mounts rousing action sequences, with German extras mown down by the dozen. The film also benefits from Gianni Bergamini's Techniscope cinematography and an emotive Ennio Morricone-Bruno Nicolai score. For their scheme to succeed, the Allies blackmail Kristina (Daniela Bianchi), Von Keist's wife. Kristina's a Jew, Hanna Goldschmidt, who has concealed her identity from her husband to avoid persecution. When Marta's partisan father and brother are captured by the SS, she betrays Sesame's men to the Nazis. For the heist on Von Keist, Sesame, Rollman and Randall drive a car into a canal, accessing the HQ via its cellar using scuba gear and flippers, while Captain O'Connor's plane keeps the German garrison occupied with a bombing raid. The gang escape in a tug, but are pursued in a heavily armed gunboat commanded by vicious SS General Hassler (Helmut Schneider – in his long leather coat, the villain of the piece). As the thieves make their getaway, the war torn wasteland – abandoned earthworks, gun emplacements and sandbagged bunkers littered with wrecked vehicles and aircraft – is enveloped in a pitched battle. Sesame's men hold off an attack by Hassler's Panzers (depicted by American M47s and M48s) until O'Connor and US paratroopers arrive. The scene of O'Connor convincing his colonel (Anthony Dawson) that now is the ideal time to attack the Germans – which is actually a ruse to save O'Connor's beleaguered, thieving cohorts – anticipates *Kelly's Heroes.* Sesame's 'vulgar hoodlums' plan to transport the diamonds to the US in a war hero's coffin, but the Dutch underground and the US military have other ideas, especially when the supposedly dead 'war hero' is spotted very much alive. A big-budget production financed by Edmondo Amati and shot on location in the Netherlands, *Dirty Heroes* is the most undeservedly forgotten World War II movie of the 1960s.

Chapter 14

OPERATION OVERLORD: THE D-DAY LANDINGS (1944)

In the spring of 1944 the Allies kept the Germans guessing as to where further landings in mainland Europe would occur. The Russians were eager for the Allies to open up a second front in France to divide Hitler's forces and resources. *I Was Monty's Double* (1958 – *Heaven, Hell and Hoboken*) told one of the most extraordinary war stories. To convince the Germans that the invasion would come from North Africa, General Montgomery made a tour of Gibraltar and North Africa in preparation for the attack. But the real Montgomery was planning Operation Overlord in England. The 'Monty' doing the rounds in Africa was in fact actor M. E. Clifton James, a lieutenant in the Pay Corps, whose remarkable resemblance to Montgomery earned him a unique place in history. James was appearing in theatre revue *Khaki Kapers* when he was convinced by British Intelligence to impersonate Montgomery. John Mills and Cecil Parker play the intelligence officers who engineer the ruse. German agents swallow the bait and begin to spread misinformation regarding Montgomery's whereabouts, which leads to assassination attempts and a kidnapping involving a U-boat. The film was based on James' 1954 book of the same name. For actor James it was the role of his life, in more ways than one. In the film James played himself and also portrayed Montgomery, in cleverly edited scenes which are spliced with archive footage of the real Monty. The film ends with James watching newsreels of the D-Day landings, having succeeded in diverting 60,000 German troops and a Panzer division into protecting a non-existent invasion attempt from North Africa.

Hitler also retained 12 Divisions in Norway as a result of the Allies creating a fictitious British Army who were stationed in Scotland and were preparing to invade. The Germans also suspected the invasion would land in the south of France, Yugoslavia or even Greece, but the real target was always to be France's

Atlantic coast. Preparations were afoot in England for Operation Overlord, the most important, complicated and decisive strategy of the war. The obvious invasion route from England was to the Pas-de-Calais. The shortest route was between Dover in Kent to Calais in Nord-Pas-de-Calais, France (the route the Channel Tunnel now uses). The Germans were kept guessing by subterfuge (as fake plans fell into the Germans' hands), while the French Resistance worked tirelessly to keep the occupying forces on their toes and Allied bombers destroyed vital bridges. Hitler's Atlantic Wall sea defences were at their strongest in the Pas-de-Calais area, with concrete and steel bunkers housing formidable guns, machine gun nests, webs of lethal barbed wire and minefields. There were also anti-tank and anti-landing craft defences: tetrahedral spikes that would disembowel landing craft and concrete 'Dragon's Teeth', making routes from the beach impassable. But large portions of this Atlantic Wall were poorly defended and some emplacements were dummies to confuse the Allies. The area of Normandy was equidistant from England's south coast ports – from Falmouth in the west to Newhaven in the east, which would be important in supplying Allied forces in the subsequent battle for France. Thus the coastline between Cherbourg (on the Cotentin Peninsula) and Le Havre became the most famous beaches in history.

Dwight D. Eisenhower of the Supreme Headquarters Allied Expeditionary Forces (SHAEF) oversaw the operation, with Montgomery in command of the ground troops. Operation Overlord was eventually set for midnight of the 5–6 June 1944, where a break in June storms would enable the 5,000-strong armada (including 600 warships) to travel safely across the Channel. The plan fell into two phases. The airborne assault was to secure important objectives inland. The amphibious assault would land ground troops and their equipment (including armour) on the coast. Infantry were ferried across the Channel on transporter ships and then loaded into landing craft as they neared the beaches. 176,000 troops travelled with the armada to land on five beaches – codenamed Sword, Juno, Gold, Omaha and Utah – in the Bay of Seine, roughly between the mouths of the Rivers Orne and Vire. On the left flank, British and French forces of the British 1st Corps landed at Sword, near Ouistreham. Canadian forces of the 1st Corps landed at Juno beach and the British 30th Corps landed at Gold. To the west, the US 5th Corps landed at Omaha and on the far right flank, the US 7th Corps landed at Utah, although due to navigational difficulties they landed in the wrong place. The invasion's exposed flanks were protected by airborne assaults. The British 6th Airborne Division secured vital bridges and disrupted communications on the left flank, while the US 82nd and 101st Airborne Divisions landed on the right. Arriving at night, in gliders and by parachute, they completely surprised the defenders, though the 82nd Airborne suffered heavy losses when some of them overshot the drop zone and landed on the fortified garrison town of Sainte-Mère-Église. Following a bombardment of the beaches – which commenced at 5.30 am – the invasion began landing troops onto the beaches at 6.30, with most assaults being highly successful. The naval barrages and concentrated air support weakened the German defences before the Allies landed. Only Omaha faltered, with sustained German fire pinning the US troops to the beach, though this was eventually overcome. By midnight of the 'longest day' five bridgeheads had been established.

Films which depict the D-Day landings are a mixed bag. TV movie *Ike: Countdown to D-Day* (2004) cast Tom Selleck as the Allies' supremo, deliberating over the most important decision of his life. In Charles Haas' *Screaming Eagles* (1956), the 101st Airborne Division set out to secure a strategically important bridge. Stuart Cooper's docu-drama *Overlord* (1975) mixed newsreel footage with a dramatised depiction of training for D-Day. It followed young British infantry conscript Tom Beddows (Brian Stirner) to the beaches of Normandy, where he's killed before he even leaves his landing craft. During his training he falls in love with a village girl (Julie Neesam) and the film's arty stretches are enlivened by a good score by Paul Glass. For Tom's twenty-first birthday, his parents send their son a fountain pen and the simple drama recalls A.E. Houseman's moving poem *A Shropshire Lad*. The film is particularly successful in its depiction of the inherent loneliness of military life, where for Tom everything outside the army and his comrades 'has faded away'. Defiantly '1970s' in its cynicism, *Overlord* is as good an advert for not joining the army as has ever been made.

Overlord uses of a wealth of very good D-Day archive footage, as one would expect from a production that trumpets 'The Imperial War Museum Presents'. This includes combat footage of the landings, but also interesting innovations during the lead-up to the operation, notably the two Mulberry harbours, which were towed across after D-Day – one in the US sector, one for the British. The Allies hadn't yet captured a port and these offshore breakwaters and sunken block ships created a safe haven which enabled vital supplies to be delivered and unloaded by sea. Other inventions for D-Day included minesweeping Crab tanks fitted with chain flails, Duplex Drive (DD) amphibious tanks, flamethrowing Crocodile tanks, Bobbin carpet laying anti-mine tanks and large, uncontrollable cartwheeling devices that fortunately never made it to the beaches of Normandy.

Twentieth Century-Fox's *D-Day the Sixth of June* (1956) has one of the most misleading titles of all time. The film begins promisingly on the dawn of D-Day, as 'Special Force Six', a commando unit made up of US, Canadian and British troops prepare to attack 'Angel Point', a clifftop fortified gun emplacement between the US and British–Canadian beaches (based on the German fortifications at Pointe du Hoc). Two of the mission's officers – American Captain Brad Parker (Robert Taylor) and British Captain John Wynter (Richard Todd) – are both in love with Valerie Russell (Dana Wynter), who works for the American Red Cross. Pre-battle nerves are settled with wistful soul-searching and most of the remainder of the film is an interminable flashback detailing their love affairs. In 1942 commando John was posted to Egypt and back home Valerie fell for Brad, who is himself married. The film, based on Lionel S.B. Shapiro's 1955 novel *The Sixth of June*, is a sappy romance, as Brad and Valerie enjoy romantic dinner dates and walks beside the seaside (the barbed wire defences notwithstanding). The Angel Point assault is well staged, as the troops arrive by landing craft, scale a cliff and knock out a huge artillery piece, though these scenes feel tacked-on. Brad is wounded in the engagement and is shipped back to England, while John wanders into a minefield on the beach and is killed. Edmond O'Brien played Brad's superior, Lieutenant-Colonel Timmer and John Williams played Valerie's brigadier father.

Interesting scenes delineate the friction between billeted Americans and local villagers, when GIs mock a group of drilling Home Guard. *D-Day* reinforces the stereotype of American soldiers running off with British women while their lovers and husbands were away fighting. Romantics may say that Valerie and Brad are thrust together in extraordinary circumstances, but the cynical message here is that in times of war, everyone's fair game.

Arthur Hiller's *The Americanization of Emily* (1964) written by Paddy Chayevsky used the landings as the backdrop to a cynical black comedy. Set in England during the preparations for D-Day, it followed the exploits of US Navy Lieutenant-Commander Charlie Madison (James Garner), a cowardly hustler. His commanding officer (Melvyn Douglas) decides to ensure that the navy aren't overshadowed by the army during the invasion, 'The first dead man on Omaha beach must be a sailor'. This martyr will then be buried with honours in the Tomb of the Unknown Sailor. Madison finds himself on Omaha beach during D-Day and is killed. He is feted as a hero, until it's discovered that he's very much alive. Julie Andrews played Madison's lover, motor pool driver Emily Barham, and the cast included James Coburn, Joyce Grenfell, Liz Fraser and Keenan Wynn. The convincing D-Day landings were filmed on Mandalay Beach in California.

When it comes to Operation Overlord in the cinema, there's only one contender: *The Longest Day* (1962). As a fitting tribute to the greatest operation of the war, Hollywood producer Darryl F. Zanuck's labour of love resulted in the finest World War II combat film. Cornelius Ryan's 1959 book *The Longest Day* was dedicated 'For all the men of D-Day' and told the epic story with alacrity and drama, which made it a page-turning bestseller. Ryan worked on the screenplay, with additional material by Romain Gary, James Jones, David Pursall and Jack Seddon. The book and film told the story from several protagonists' perspectives: French, German, British and American. To facilitate this narrative feat, with many speaking parts depicting real people, Zanuck assembled a stellar array of actors. He began casting in June 1961. This resulted in a once-in-a-lifetime 'spot the film star' cast, with some of the era's biggest names. The film is not only interesting as a historical document of the events of D-Day, but also a snapshot of the film stars of the day. There is no title sequence – simply the title *The Longest Day* – and the cast are listed alphabetically at the end, to prevent egotistic billing arguments.

The film begins in Occupied France at the moment of its deliverance. Radio messages convey coded instructions to the French Resistance. When a line from a Verlaine poem is broadcast ('The long sobs of the violins of autumn'), the Resistance know that when the next line is transmitted ('Wounds my heart with a monotonous languor') the invasion will begin within 24 hours. They disrupt the German lines of communication, destroying telephone cables and railway lines. In advance of the landings in Normandy, diversions convince the Germans that Cherbourg is under attack. 'Rupert' (a mechanical parachutist who explodes on impact with the ground) and many like him are dropped to confuse the enemy. In the dead of night, the Allies airborne assault begins – the pathfinders set up DZs and LZs (Drop Zones for paras and Landing Zones for gliders). British glider

British glider troops led by Major John Howard (Richard Todd) storm Pegasus Bridge on the Orne River in Darryl F. Zanuck's all-star production *The Longest Day* (1962). This lightning tactic demonstrated how effectively airborne troops could be used to secure and hold vital targets behind enemy lines. Courtesy Kevin Wilkinson Collection.

troops led by Major John Howard (Richard Todd) swoop on Pegasus Bridge on the Orne River, with instructions to 'Hold until relieved'. Their gliders land close to the bridge and the objective is swiftly secured. This surprise attack, deftly edited and staged for maximum impact, is a contender for the finest action scene in war cinema. When elements of the 82nd Airborne miss their DZs, most end up in a flooded swamp area, but many plunge into Sainte-Mère-Église, a Nazi garrison HQ. They drift helplessly into the town square, lit up by a building which has been ignited by a flare. Paratrooper John Steel (played by Red Buttons) is suspended from the church bell tower by his chute and watches the grim bloodbath unfold as few of his comrades hit the ground alive. Later their commander Colonel Ben Vandervoort (John Wayne) and the relief column discover the massacre, with paratroopers' corpses still limply hanging from telegraph poles and trees. Vandervoort's grittily snapped 'Get 'em down' is one of the Duke's finest screen moments.

The production boasted a long list of Military Consultants, many of whom are depicted in the film. Zanuck spent three months researching his subject. To ensure authenticity, he filmed his D-Day landings on the actual beaches and locations, with interiors directed by Zanuck himself at Studios De Boulogne. 31 separate exterior locations in Normandy were used. In the 1968 documentary *D-Day Revisited*, photographed by Henri Decaë and Walter Wottitz, and directed by Bernard Farrel, Zanuck returned to Normandy for the assault's twenty-fifth anniversary and discussed the locations he'd used in the film, including the concrete bunker gun emplacement atop a 100-foot cliff at Pointe Du Hoc, which still stands as a monument. Other locations used in the film include the town of Sainte-Mère-Église in Manche, the Orne crossing at Pegasus Bridge and the harbour fishing village of Ouistreham, Calvados, in Lower Normandy. The film was helmed by four directors (and uncredited Zanuck) but unlike *Tora! Tora! Tora!* you can't see the joins. Shooting simultaneously to save time, Ken Annakin filmed the British exterior episodes, Andrew Marton and Gerd Oswald shot the US episodes and Bernhard Wicki shot the German sequences. Co-producer Elmo Williams coordinated the battle episodes and the use of archive footage was kept to a minimum. Principal photography began in August 1961 and by autumn they were shooting the beach landings. By then the assigned budget of $8 million from Twentieth Century-Fox had been eaten up and Zanuck was financing the project himself.

The film's monochrome cinematography reinforces the film's realism, while the widescreen 2.35:1 CinemaScope ratio adds to its epic scope. Jean Bourgoin and Walter Wottitz won Oscars for their cinematography. Best Special Effects Oscars also went to Robert MacDonald (visual) and Jacques Maumont (audible). Maurice Jarre composed the memorable score, which deploys rolling, relentless marching drums to create tension. The opening scene – a fade from inky blackness to a shot of a wave-lapped beach, with an upturned GI's helmet lying in the sand (an image used for the film's poster) – is accompanied by ominous timpani. The distinctive 'dun-dun-dun-daarr!' opening notes of Beethoven's Fifth Symphony are heard. This is the 'V' for victory sign in Morse Code (dot, dot, dot, dash). Only at the film's conclusion, with victory won, do we hear Jarre's famous theme song. Composed by singer Paul Anka and arranged by Mitch Miller, this lively march tells of the longest day's heroism ('Many men will count the hours, as they live the longest day'). In the film it is sung rousingly by a chorus, though Anka also recorded a version of the song as a tie-in with the film.

The Longest Day boasts the most impressive cast list of all time. Advertising trumpeted '42 International Stars' on display (later posters noted '43', having added Sean Connery, post-James Bond, to the list). Even with the film's 168-minute running time, few had time to shine for long and some appearances are literally to deliver one or two lines, or as a face in the crowd. John Wayne was top of the pile as Colonel Ben Vandervoort, who breaks his ankle on landing and is towed through the action on a wheeled ammo limber. Wayne received $250,000 for the role, while his co-stars received $25,000 each. Robert Mitchum was similarly prominent as Brigadier General Norman Cota of the US 29th Division on Omaha beach and Henry Fonda played arthritic General Theodore Roosevelt, the president's son, who was the oldest member of the assault team. Zanuck took out what he termed 'a little insurance' in the casting of several young actors – many of whom were also singers – as US Rangers, infantrymen and paratroopers, to hook the teenage audience. The youngsters briefly on display during *The Longest Day* include Fabian, Paul Anka, Tommy Sands and Sal Mineo, but their names appeared prominently on posters and ensured the film drew a wide audience. There were many established American names in supporting roles. Robert

Ryan played Brigadier General James Gavin, Rod Steiger was a destroyer commander off Normandy, Eddie Albert was Colonel Thompson on Omaha beach, Stuart Whitman played paratrooper Lieutenant Sheen, Edmund O'Brien was General Raymond 'Tubby' Barton, Mel Ferrer played Major General Robert Haines and Steve Forest was the 82nd Airborne's Captain Harding. Other US soldiers were played by Mark Damon, Ray Danton and Roddy McDowell, while Richard Beymer (Tony in *West Side Story*) had a key role as paratrooper 'Dutch' Schultz, who manages not to fire his gun throughout the entire day and ponders at the film's close: 'I wonder who won?'

Richard Todd, Kenneth More, John Gregson and Richard Burton were familiar to audiences from 1950s British war films. Bearded More played Captain Colin Maude, the Royal Navy Beach Master, who orchestrates the landing on Sword with his bulldog Winston. John Gregson played the 6th Airborne's padre, who is seen diving in a river for his lost Communion set. Burton played RAF pilot Flight Officer David Campbell, who is found slumped, badly wounded, in a farmyard – his leg is held together with safety pins. No one can deliver lines like 'Ack-ack over Calais' or 'Split right open from the crotch to the knee', like Burton, with his distinctive clipped Welsh tone. Peter Lawford played commando Lord Lovat of the Green Beret British Special Service Brigade, whose troops go ashore on Sword to the accompaniment of Scots piper Bill Millin. Richard Wattis played a paratrooper, Leo Genn was Brigadier General Edwin P. Parker, Michael Medwin played a Bren Gun driver stalled on the beach and Donald Houston played an RAF pilot. Canadian Alexander Knox was Major General Walter Bedell Smith. As bickering comic relief, Norman Rossington played cockney Private Clough and soon-to-be 'Agent 007' Sean Connery played Irishman Private Flanagan on Sword. Leslie Phillips can be seen briefly as Mac, an RAF officer who is being sheltered by the Resistance – his character is a precursor of the British airman in the TV sitcom *'Allo 'Allo!*

As the film employed 'Top talent of four countries', the French and German contingent was considerable. Among the famed French players was Arletty as Mother Superior to a group of nuns (trained nurses who tend the French wounded); Jean-Louis Barrault was Father Louis Roulland; Jean Servais was naval Amiral (Admiral) Jaujard of the Forces Françaises Libres; and Bourvil was the excitable Mayor of Colleville. Christian Marquand played Commandant Philippe Kieffer of the Commando Français, with Georges Rivière his aide, Sergeant Guy De Montlaur. Irina Demick played Resistance fighter Janine Boitard and Italian Maurice Poli was her fiancé Gille. The German top brass included Major General Günther Blumentritt (Curd Jürgens), Colonel General Alfred Jodl (Wolfgang Lukschy), Major General Dr Hans Speidel (Wolfgang Büttner), Field General Gerd Von Rundstedt (Paul Hartmann), General Wolfgang Hager (Karl John) and General Erich Marcks (Richard Münch). Wolfgang Preiss played Major General Max Pemsel and Heinz Reincke played Luftwaffe colonel Josef 'Pips' Priller, whose depleted squadron consists of two planes. Future 'Goldfinger' Gert Fröbe played slobbish Sgt Kaffekanne, who delivers coffee to the coastal gunners on a horse that looks as lethargic as he is. Some world famous historical figures were also depicted: Admiral Sir Bertram Ramsay (played by John Robinson),

Montgomery (Trevor Reid), Rommel (Werber Hinz) and Lieutenant General Omar N. Bradley (Nicholas Stuart), who surveys the invasion from his flagship, *Augusta.* Henry Grace played Dwight D. Eisenhower. Ike was going to play himself, but makeup artists couldn't achieve the transformation convincingly.

Once the longest day is underway, the film is a succession of memorable action vignettes. The first sight of the armada through the slit of a German coastal bunker as it materialises from the morning mist is accompanied by Beethoven's Fifth shuddering on the soundtrack. From his bunker, Major Werner Pluskat (Hans Christian Blech) feels the full force of the Allied naval salvo and yells down the phone to Lt-Col Ocker (Peter Van Eyck): 'Those five thousand ships you say the Allies haven't got – well, they've got them!' For the action sequences, the French Army loaned the production 3,000 men as extras and impressive ordnance gathered from around the world poured onto the beaches, including Sherman tanks, trucks, Bren Gun carriers, jeeps, M3 half-tracks and amphibious DUKWs. These were the so-called Army 'Ducks', which were GMC 6x6 trucks with boat-shaped hulls, making them resemble wheeled pontoon barges. For one scene, a real train was blown up to depict the Resistance's activities. The action scenes are intercut with the German commanders' attempts to counter the invasion and their incredulity at their own ineptitude: the invasion inconveniently coincides with the absence of many top officers on training exercises. When they request reinforcements, senior German field commanders are informed that the Führer has taken a sleeping pill and can't be woken. Thus vital Panzer divisions remain in reserve, when their deployment may have turned the tide.

The film's beach scenes resemble newsreels, as the camera dollies alongside the charging US troops on Omaha beach. A swooping attack by two Luftwaffe planes, which strafe Gold and Juno beaches, is filmed from the perspective of the pilots as they wreak havoc. An impressive helicopter shot (filmed by Ken Annakin on the eighth take, when all other directors had failed) captured the French Commandos from Sword rushing the waterfront of Ouistreham to take a heavily fortified hotel and casino – a brilliantly orchestrated scene which is a swirl of smoke, noise and movement. As they make their way at night through the silent countryside, US paratroopers use click-click 'crickets' as signalling devices. Sal Mineo is unfortunate when the two 'clicks' which answer his signal are a German soldier levering his bolt-action Mauser rifle. At Pointe Du Hoc, 225 specially trained US Rangers led by Robert Wagner (and including Fabian and George Segal) scale the cliffs under heavy enemy fire with grappling hooks and ladders to take the gun emplacement with 75 per cent losses: in vain as it turns out the guns have never been installed. It is during this scene that a US Ranger mows down German soldiers and then wonders what 'Bitte, bitte!' means (it means 'please', as in 'Please don't shoot us, we're surrendering'). Jeffrey Hunter had a pivotal role at the film's climax as engineer Sergeant John H. Fuller, who bravely sets tubular Bangalore torpedoes and explosives to blow a breach in the German defences so the 'Fighting 29th' can scramble off Omaha beach. The film ends as troops pour inland into the bridgehead, with Robert Mitchum as Cota enjoying a celebratory cigar and hitching a ride on a jeep ('OK, run me up the hill son'), as the whistled 'Longest Day' march swells.

The Longest Day (1962): Images from Darryl F. Zanuck's World War II blockbuster re-enactment of the Allied assault on the Normandy coast on 6 June 1944. Top (left and right): Allied troops assail the beaches in landing craft and amphibious DUKWs (Army 'Ducks'). Bottom left: General Theodore Roosevelt (Henry Fonda, right) takes cover behind a jagged German beach defence. Bottom right: US Rangers scale the cliffs to the gun emplacement at Pointe du Hoc. Images courtesy Kevin Wilkinson Collection.

The Longest Day premiered in Paris (as *Le Jour De Plus Long*) on 25 September 1962, to great success. Edith Piaf sang from the Eiffel Tower for the premiere. The New York premiere followed a month later and the film was a hit with both critics and public. In Italy, *The Longest Day* won a David Di Donatello Award in 1963 for Best Foreign Film. There was also an all-star Italian spoof called *The Shortest Day* (1963), directed by Sergio Corbucci and headlining the comedy team Franchi and Ingrassia. Mark Damon wrote in his autobiography that he was the only actor to appear in both films. *The Longest Day* trailer contains alternative takes of some scenes (for example, the dialogue between Beymer and Burton in the farmyard) and scenes cut from the final version (Mel Ferrer making an announcement to a press conference). In the most widely seen English version, the actors of various nationalities speak their own languages, with English subtitles. There is also a version with everyone dubbed into English and another version is colourised. *The Longest Day* grossed $18 million in the US and in its first year took $25 million – according to Zanuck it was seen by more people than any other black-and-white film. It stands as a testament to the producer's vision and determination in bringing this great story of the 'Longest Day' in history to the screen.

Chapter 15

THE BATTLE FOR FRANCE (1944)

Having breached the Atlantic Wall defences and attained a foothold in Normandy, the Allies' priority was to push inland. The German armour mounted a defence that slowed the Allies' advance to a crawl during the so-called Battle of the Hedgerows through the Normandy 'bocage'. The bocage country consisted of tightly packed fields and hedgerows that made the Allies' progress inland painstakingly tedious, as armour was useless and ambushes were easily mounted in this dense landscape patchwork of fields and lanes. The US troops in the west pushed into the Cotentin Peninsula and the US 7th Corps took Cherbourg on 29 June 1944. Other elements of Bradley's US 1st Army pushed south and reached St Lô on 18 July. The British and Canadians broke out from Gold, Juno and Sword and battled for control of Caan, which finally fell 33 days after it should have been taken – it was originally one of the objectives for D-Day itself. By the time they were captured, both Caan and St Lô were bombed-out ruins. As a GI observed in St Lô, 'Gee, we sure liberated the hell outa this place!' It wasn't until Operation Epsom (26–29 June) and Operation Goodwood (18–21 July) that the British started to make inroads against the SS Panzer troops. Goodwood was particularly costly. It was conceived as an attack on a 4,000-yard front by Montgomery's armour, following carpet bombing by the RAF. The 5,000 tonnes of bombs did little damage and on the plains of Caan, Rommel ambushed and halted Montgomery's advance. But during Hitler's purges following the assassination attempt on his life on 20 July, Rommel was replaced by Field Marshal Von Kluge.

The initial inland push from the Normandy beachhead in the first week of the invasion is the setting for Steven Spielberg's multi-award winning *Saving Private Ryan* (1998). Following the landings on Omaha beach in Normandy, Captain John H. Miller (Tom Hanks) of the 2nd Rangers is assigned to lead a 'rescue mission' ordered by General Marshall (Harve Presnell). Miller and his seven-man squad must locate Private James Francis Ryan, whose three older brothers have been killed in action – on Omaha and Utah beaches and in New Guinea. Their mother in Iowa receives all three telegrams informing her of their deaths on the same day. James is being withdrawn from the front and given a ticket home. He has landed behind enemy lines with the 101st Airborne as part of the invasion. On D-Day +3 (three days after the landing) Miller and his men move inland to the ruined town of Neuville-au-plain, held by airborne troops under Captain Hamill (Ted Danson). They find a Private Ryan, but he is from Minnesota. Miller's men arrive at the 101st glider troops' rally point, where they find that their Ryan is in the town of Ramelle on the Merderet River. US airborne troops are holding a bridge which Rommel plans to use to move armour into combat. Miller's men ambush an SS recon half-track and encounter Ryan. When he's told of his brothers' deaths, Ryan refuses to leave his post and promises to remain at the undermanned Ramelle bridge defences – his comrades are his only brothers now. As a result of Ryan's noble act, Miller discovers that he must sacrifice the lives of his own men to save Ryan during the ensuing German armoured counterattack on 13 June.

Working with a $70 million budget, Spielberg filmed on location in Ireland, England and France, including an actual US war cemetery near Omaha beach. The beach at Curracloe, Ballinesker in County Wexford, Ireland was used for the D-Day landing re-enactment. Twenty-five hundred Irish soldiers appeared as extras. Thame Park in Oxfordshire stood in for the fields and hedgerows of the wartorn Normandy bocage, littered with corpses ripening in the summer heat. The rubble-strewn French towns of Neuville and Ramelle were the same set, which was built on a disused airfield at Hatfield Aerodrome in Hertfordshire. Much of the battle footage was staged with the help of an army of skilled stuntmen. This was augmented with special effects provided by George Lucas' Industrial Light & Magic, which used computer-generated imagery (CGI) and other digital effects. Among the roster of German vehicles on display are SdKfz 250 half-tracks, self-propelled guns and some authentic-looking Tiger tanks, which are converted Russian T-34s: the distinctive wheels are the giveaway. One of the most unusual vehicles of the war makes an appearance: the German SdKfz 2, a speedy motorbike/half-track hybrid, which was originally designed to pull light artillery.

Miller's squad consists of tough Sergeant Mike Horvath (Tom Sizemore), cynical East coaster Private Reiben (Edward Burns), ace marksman Private Jackson (Barry Pepper), Private Mellish (Adam Goldberg), Private Caparzo (Vin Diesel), T/4 Medic Wade (Giovanni Ribisi) and timid cartographer Corporal Upham (Jeremy Davies), a translator attached to the group. Edward Burns had been offered the small-but-crucial role of Private Ryan, but turned it down to play Reiben, enabling Matt Damon to be cast. Miller's men are war movie clichés – a tough-as-nails sergeant, a cowardly pen-pusher – but their unchivalrous treatment of German prisoners is unusual for an American war film. When German soldiers emerge on fire, having been flushed from their bunker with flamethrowers, GIs reason: 'Don't shoot, let 'em burn'. Prisoners are shot and there is more than a hint of Vietnam's confused ethics in the unit's exploits in the field. Joerg Stadler played a German soldier billed as 'Steamboat Willie' in cast lists, who is captured by Miller's men when they overrun a bunker and radar station. Willie saves his life by trying to appear sympathetic to America. He reels off several US cultural icons (Betty Grable, Betty Boop, Mickey Mouse) before resorting to the rather more blunt 'Fuck Hitler'.

Saving Private Ryan offers an interesting twist on a World War II mission movie. As the tagline stated, 'The mission is a man'. It was written by Robert Rodat and is loosely based on the true story of the Niland brothers, three of whom were thought to have been killed in action. The Niland brother lost in Burma was later found alive and the fourth brother (who was in the 101st Airborne) couldn't be contacted but he also managed to survive. In reality there was no battle for Ramelle Bridge, though the River Merderet was one of the US Airborne's objectives and Neuville-en-plain was north of Sainte-Mère-Église. In the film, Miller voices the simple rationale that the lives of the men he has lost during the fighting are outweighed by the number of men he has saved. That is

Captain John H. Miller (Tom Hanks) rallies his men in the deadly crossfire on Omaha Beach in Steven Spielberg's Oscar-winning *Saving Private Ryan* (1998). Courtesy Kevin Wilkinson Collection.

the crux of Spielberg's film. Having exhibited a tremor since the landing, Miller holds his nerve during the mission but is mortally wounded during the defence of the bridge, at the very moment P-51 Mustang 'tank busters' fly overhead and rout the attacking Germans. With his dying breath, Miller tells Ryan to 'Earn it' – that is, to earn the right to live when all bar Reiben and Upham have been killed protecting Ryan and the bridge. The film has a modern-day prologue and epilogue, two nostalgic Spielberg scenes, when elderly Ryan (Harrison Young) visits the Normandy American Cemetery and Memorial at Colleville-sur-Mer, a sea of thousands of white crosses. Ryan stands beside Miller's grave with his wife, children and grandchildren, to prove to his fallen comrade that he is indeed a good man who has lived a good life. Ryan has made their sacrifice worthwhile and he salutes Miller's cross.

Spielberg's film opens and closes with a shot of the 'Stars and Stripes' back-lit by sunshine – it's as patriotic as a wartime flag waver – and is bookended by two grandiose battle scenes, on Omaha beach and the Battle of Ramelle Bridge. These two scenes account for almost a third of the film's 162-minute running time. The opening re-enactment of the disastrous US landing from rough seas onto Omaha Beach under heavy fire is one of the most kinetic sequences in action cinema. With its blood-splatters, slow-motion photography, oozing guts, lost limbs, whizzing bullets, vomit and perforated heads, this is 'D-Day, the Sam Peckinpah Years'. Pinned at the water's edge amid corpses and dead fish, the Americans gradually crawl up the beach, as the sea runs red and German defences crumble. This action scene is praised for its realism, but its heightened presentation, shock editing and heavy debt to computer-generated graphics make parts of it resemble a video game. As the GIs move through the CGI, there's a sense of wallowing in gore for gore's sake, which undermines the film's effectiveness – this is particularly noticeable in a scene where the squad tend wounded medic Wade. The hand-to-hand street fighting in ruined Ramelle is convincing: death lurks around every corner, in every window and in every room, as the German armour and their infantry support overrun the town. Under-equipped and low on ammunition, Miller and his men attempt to halt the German column with 'sticky bombs', a TNT and axel grease combo wrapped in a sock, which when exploded derails the attacking Tigers' tracks.

The camerawork by Janusz Kaminski is often jerkily handheld, which lends the film a distinctive look. The Technicolor stock was desaturated in post-production, leaving only 40 percent of the colour, to fade out the images for added realism. John Williams provided the lush, emotive score. The horn solos were played by Gus Sebring and trumpet solos by Tim Morrison and Thomas Rolfs. The cues are a mixture of the sentimental – as in the end title music, with the Boston Symphony Orchestra and the Tanglewood Festival Chorus – and the elegiac, as in the trumpet 'last post' for a picturesquely composed graveside sunset for medic Wade.

In its depiction of men under extreme pressure, *Saving Private Ryan* has an authentically pithy script with some profanity, which marks it as a modern war film for a modern audience: it was rated R in the USA and 15 in the UK. It also includes the oft-repeated wartime acronym 'FUBAR' (fucked-up beyond all

Saving Private Ryan (1998): Top: Sergeant Mike Horvath (Tom Sizemore, middle left) and Captain Miller (Tom Hanks, middle right) apprehensively approach Omaha Beach in a landing craft. Middle: Miller, Ryan (Matt Damon) and Reiben (Edward Burns) man the Ramelle Bridge defences. Bottom: Miller's squad in battle torn Ramelle. Images courtesy Kevin Wilkinson Collection.

recognition). It was released by Paramount and the poster featured a solitary soldier on a sun-burnished horizon, with portraits of Sizemore, Hanks, Damon and Burns in the sky as heroic gods watching over Ryan. The film won five Academy Awards: Spielberg was Best Director, Kaminski Best Cinematographer, plus Best Effects (Sound Effects Editing), Best Film Editing and Best Sound. Best Picture went to period costume romance *Shakespeare in Love.* This seems to sum up *Ryan*: its success in the technical categories is well deserved, as it is a good war film with great battle scenes, but it is somewhat hamstrung by its plodding midsection. *Ryan* struck a chord with audiences and was the most successful film of its year, taking over $200 million in the US alone.

Saving Private Ryan was a tremendously influential film, which rejuvenated interest in World War II cinema and history, and created a boom in the production of war subjects for the cinema, TV and video gaming audience. The UK videotape had the tagline: 'The Film that Inspired the World to Remember'. Among the spin-offs was the 1999 Playstation game *Medal of Honor*, which was created by Spielberg for DreamWorks Interactive and spawned several sequel games set in various theatres of war. Spielberg and Hanks also produced a ten-part TV series for HBO based on Stephen E. Ambrose's 1992 novel *Band of Brothers* (2001), which followed American paratroopers of Easy Company of the 101st Parachute Infantry, through Normandy, Holland and Belgium to their capture of Hitler's 'Eagle's Nest' at Berchtesgarden. War expert Ambrose had worked as 'historical consultant' on *Saving Private Ryan.*

By 24 July 1944 the Allies were in a position to mount a breakout. The US troops on the Cotentin Peninsula pushed south down France's western coast and took Avranches on 30 July. This enabled them to drive south for Nantes and to attack the Brittany ports in Operation Cobra (25 July), though Lorient, St Nazaire and Brest held out (Brest fell on 18 September). To the east, the Allies' gains enabled them to encircle and squeeze a large German force on 20 August in the Falaise Gap (sometimes called the Falaise Pocket) where 20,000 Germans died and 50,000 were captured. Once German resistance in France was broken, progress was swift. Patton's 3rd Army swept south to Nantes, then east to Chartres and on to Fontainebleau. On 20 August, the US 15th Corps established the first bridgehead across the River Seine. Paris itself was liberated on 25 August, after which the Allies advanced on a wide front north of the Seine, through France and into Belgium – Montgomery in the east and Bradley in the west – from 26 August 1944. By 17 September the Allied front line had reached Holland.

Twentieth Century-Fox's *Up from the Beach* (1965), starring Cliff Robertson, continued the story of the D-Day landings, with US troops liberating French locals. It was based on George Barr's 1959 book *Epitaph for an Enemy* and was released in France as *The Day After*. David Aboucaya's *The Cross Roads* (2009), which saw a platoon lost behind enemy lines in France, 1944, was from the 'combat scenes as video game' school of filmmaking. *The True Glory* (1945) was an Oscar-winning documentary which depicted the D-Day operation. Other war movies set in D-Day and its aftermath include *Breakthrough* (1950) starring David Brian and John Agar, and Edmondo Amati's *From Hell to Victory* (1979). Budd Boetticher's *Red Ball Express* (1952) starred Jeff Chandler, Alex Nicol, Hugh

O'Brian, Sidney Poitier, Jack Worden and Jack Kelly and depicted a US Army supply truck convoy racing to keep Patton supplied from Normandy on his advance through France during August 1944. There have been few German depictions of the battle for France ('Saving Private Von Ryan'?), which is surprising, as there have been several German films about the Eastern Front, which was just as disastrous for the Wehrmacht.

Terence Young's *They Were Not Divided* (1950) followed tank crew members of the Welsh Guards – part of the Guards Armoured Division – from training in England in 1941 to their first action in France in June 1944, as part of the Normandy Breakout: in Operation Goodwood and fighting around Falaise. Edward Underdown played English officer Philip Rodney Hamilton, Ralph Clanton was New Yorker David Morgan and Michael Brennan played Irishman 'Smoke' O'Connor. The supporting cast included Christopher Lee and Anthony Dawson as tank commanders, Desmond Llewelyn (later Q in Young's James Bond films) as Welshman Jones, and Michael Trubshawe as their bewhiskered commander, Major Bushey Noble, who is killed, not in combat, but in a car accident. The Welsh Guards' tanks are inscribed with the names of Welsh towns – Llangollen, Llanelly and Llandudno – and 'Men of Harlech' and John Hughes' 'Cwm Rhondda' feature on the soundtrack. Filmed in grainy monochrome by Harry Waxman, the film is notable for its realistic scenes of combat and real Sherman and Tiger tanks: the film was made with the collaboration of the War Office, the British Army of the Rhine and the Brigade of Guards. The recreation of Operation Goodwood, with the Guards' Shermans charging forward under smokescreen cover, is particularly memorable. The battlefields are littered with burning, burned-out tank wrecks, which the troops describe as having been 'brewed up'. Later the Guards liberate Brussels and are involved in operations in Holland, until Philip and David are killed together in a German ambush while on a reconnaissance mission in the snowbound Ardennes forest during the Battle of the Bulge in the winter of 1944–45.

The US 1st Infantry Division took part in the D-Day landings and their involvement on Omaha Beach is depicted in Samuel Fuller's *The Big Red One* (1980). Rifleman Griff (Mark Hamill) detonates a Bangalore torpedo to blow a hole in a barbed wire barricade which blocks their exit from the bullet-peppered beach (actually the coast of Israel). The rifle squad fight through France and pass a cenotaph to the dead of the 1st US Division. The soldiers note that it hasn't taken them long to erect a memorial to the war. 'That's a World War I memorial', comments their sergeant (Lee Marvin), a seasoned veteran of the Great War. 'But the names are the same'; 'They always are', the sergeant replies. They are passing over the same land where the sergeant fought years before. At a distinctive carved crucifixion monument they are ambushed by Germans and the sergeant spills enemy blood on this land once more. By September, the squad have reached Belgium and the River Meuse. They help resistance fighter Walloon (Stephane Audran) destroy a German stronghold based in an insane asylum, where the GIs wonder who are the mad ones – the inmates or themselves?

Marcel Ophuls' four-and-a-half-hour documentary *The Sorrow and the Pity* (1970) depicted life in occupied France, while René Clément's *Is Paris Burning?*

(1966) was a French–US co-production recreating the liberation of the city. General Dietrich Von Choltitz (Gert Fröbe) is instructed by Hitler (Billy Frick) 'If you can't hold Paris, burn it'. Choltitz makes plans with demolition expert Captain Von Ebernach (Wolfgang Preiss) to destroy the city if the Allies capture it. Free French fighters learn that the Allies plan to encircle Paris. This will allow the Germans to level the city, resulting in 'One thousand years of history turned to dust'. Resistance fighter Jacques Chaban-Delmas (Alain Delon) watches German newsreels of the destruction of Warsaw following the Polish uprising and worries that the same fate will befall Paris. Resistance fighter Major Gallois (Pierre Vaneck) infiltrates the German lines and convinces the Allies to come to Paris' aid. As resistance factions of all stripes, including communists and anti-communists, rise up and fight their oppressors in the streets, the US and French armies rush to take the city.

This vast sprawling epic is French cinema's answer to *The Longest Day*, with an all-star cast enacting historical events. It was based on Larry Collins and Dominique Lapierre's 1965 novel of the same name and was adapted for the screen by Gore Vidal and Francis Ford Coppola. Additional dialogue for the French sequences was written by Marcel Moussy and for the German sections by Beate Von Molo. Maurice Jarre composed the score, which ranged from cymbal-clashing dramatics to the film's famous lilting accordion theme. It was shot on location in Paris, at Notre Dame, Île de la Cité, the Seine bridges, L'Arc de Triomphe and the Eiffel Tower. It was an amazing logistical feat, staging machine-gun skirmishes and ambushes in iconic broad, tree-lined avenues, and a small-scale tank battle in Place de la Concorde. These re-enactments were intercut with archive footage of the battle for Paris. Marcel Grignon's Panavision monochrome switched to colour for aerial shots of modern day Paris during the end titles. His artful cinematography, which sometimes resembles French 'New Wave' vérité style, was nominated for an Academy Award.

The cast is impressive, though many only appear for single scenes. The French Resistance and the army feature Charles Boyer, Claude Dauphin, Michel Piccoli, Marie Versini and Jean-Paul Belmondo. Yves Montand played a French tank commander, Claude Rich was General Leclerc, Jean-Pierre Cassel played Lieutenant Henri Karcher, Bruno Cremer was the Resistance's Colonel Rol Tanguy and Simone Signoret popped up for two seconds as a café owner. Hannes Messemer (the camp Kommandant from *The Great Escape*) played General Jodl and Konrad George played Field Marshal Model, while Helmut Schneider can be seen as a German officer berating a slovenly enlisted man (Otto Stern) on the Paris Metro. Peter Neusser and war-movie perennial Karl Otto Alberty played two SS men who attempt to liberate the Bayeux Tapestry for Hitler. Kirk Douglas played General Patton, Robert Stack was General Sibert and Glenn Ford was General Omar Bradley (who gives the go-ahead for the Allies to enter Paris). Anthony Perkins and George Chakiris appeared as GIs. Jean-Louis Trintignant (in shades and Borsalino) had a cameo as Parisian double agent Captain Serge, who pretends to help naïve young freedom fighters, then turns them over to the Gestapo. Those betrayed are then shot as they are thrown from the back of a truck. In the film's most effective scenes, Françoise Labe (Leslie Caron) commandeers the neutral Consul General for Sweden, Nordling (Orson Welles) to save her husband, Bernard Labe (Tony Taffin), from deportation. Bernard is a respected leader who can unite the factious Resistance. Françoise and Nordling arrive at the railroad yard, crammed with civilians being loaded into cattle trucks bound for Buchenwald camp, in scenes that anticipate *Schindler's List* (1993). Françoise desperately searches the carriages, while Nordling argues with a sadistic SS officer (Guenter Meiser). In the confusion, Bernard is machine-gunned. Vignette follows vignette and the film is partially ruined by its awful English language dubbing, but the human interest and shear power of the piece are still impressive. As the Allies arrive, Choltitz disobeys Hitler and surrenders the city. 'Is Paris burning?' shouts the Führer down the telephone, to no avail, as the great bell of Notre Dame swings to life, tolling the chimes of freedom. Often slated by critics for its overblown nature, *Is Paris Burning?* is an understated war film that is of more interest to military historians than cinephiles.

John Frankenheimer's *The Train* (1964) was based on a true incident as the Allies were about to liberate Paris. On 2 August 1944 art-loving Colonel Von Waldheim (Paul Scofield) loots the Musée du Jeu de Paume Impressionist collection in Paris of its priceless archive of paintings, packs them safely in crates and commissions a train to transport them back to Berlin. The French Resistance, informed of the plan by the museum curator Mlle. Villard (Suzanne Flon), divert the train. Chief among the Resistance is Paul Labiche (Burt Lancaster), an area inspector on the railways, who is chosen by Von Waldheim to drive the engine. He takes the train on a detour and with the aid of Resistance operatives throughout France they reroute the engine, taking it back to the station where its journey began.

The Train was based on *Le Front de L'Art: Défense des Collections Françaises, 1939–1945* ('The Art Front: Defence of the French Collections') a 1961 book by Rose Valland, who was the basis for Mlle. Villard in the film. The film was shot on a $6.7 million budget provided by French, Italian and US finance: Les Films Ariane, Dear Film Produzione and Les Productions Artistes (the European wing of United Artists). This international concoction, a good example of a successful co-production, is the finest action movie to depict the exploits of the French Resistance. The production was based in Vaires-sur-Marne near Paris and was able to deploy an abandoned railway marshalling yard and 40 disused railcars in Acquigny near Rouen. This was destroyed in the first of two impressive set pieces, when a British air raid bombs the German railway yard, obliterating a heavily armoured troop train, as the art train snakes to safety, miraculously undamaged. In the second set piece, the Resistance halt the art train and orchestrate a three-engine pile-up, an impressive collision that was staged for real.

The Train was the last of the large-scale 1960s action war movies to be filmed in then-unfashionable monochrome. Frankenheimer uses long tracking shots and cranes to survey his rolling stock and the cinematography by Jean Tournier and Walter Wottitz adds documentary realism to the action, despite Lancaster's larger-than-life heroics. Lancaster's not particularly plausible as the French train inspector and when the action commences, Labiche transforms into the Crimson Pirate. His distinctive darting run – that head-down sprint of Lancaster's

French Resistance fighter Paul Labiche (Burt Lancaster) halts art-loving Colonel Von Waldheim (Paul Scofield) and his precious loot at the climax of John Frankenheimer's *The Train* (1964). Courtesy Kevin Wilkinson Collection.

many acrobatic leading roles – make it difficult to wholly suspend belief, though he performed all his own stunts. Labiche's relationship with widowed Christine (Jeanne Moreau), a hotelier who shelters him from the Nazis, is more convincing. Donal O'Brien, Howard Vernon and Richard Münch cropped up as German officers. Wolfgang Preiss was Major Herren, who cares little for art and tries to reason with Von Waldheim's increasingly excessive demands. French character actor Michel Simon played grumpy train driver Papa Boule, who is summarily shot by the Germans for placing Francs in the locomotive's oil pipe, which blocks the flow and delays the train. Charles Millot and Albert Remy were Labiche's accomplices, Pesquet and Didont, and Jacques Marin was stationmaster Jacques – all are killed in their attempt to protect the paintings. Resistance workers across France change the names of the stations. The German escort have no idea they're not heading towards Zweibrüken in Germany, until they arrive in Vitry, France. In reality, the art train didn't get far from Paris, paralysed by the molasses of French bureaucracy.

According to Lancaster, when the art-loving German officer returned to Germany, he was so depressed 'he drank poisoned champagne'. In *The Train* Von Waldheim also perishes. As the Allies approach, the Resistance paint the boxcar roofs white, as a signal to the RAF not to bomb it. Labiche manages to derail the train and Von Waldheim executes the French hostages who have been tied to the front of the loco (to prevent Labiche blowing it up). The German escort join a retreating convoy, leaving Von Waldheim alone with his treasures. Labiche confronts him, amid the half-unloaded crates. Von Waldheim taunts Labiche: 'Some of the greatest paintings in the world. Does it please you Labiche? Give you a sense of excitement in just being near them? A painting means as much to you as a string of pearls to an ape'. Without a word, Labiche machine-guns the colonel, who dies having snobbishly reasoned that, 'Beauty belongs to the man who can appreciate it'. Frankenheimer intercuts shots of the crates with the dead French hostages. The art is worth millions and in wartime, money is a weapon. But is the preservation of great art ever worth human lives? US audiences didn't care for such cerebral war fare. On its release it took only $3.5 million in the US, but a further $6 million worldwide. *The Train* is an intellectual war film which has since gained a reputation as one of the key World War II films of the 1960s.

In Carl Foreman's *The Victors* (1963), following the day the 'Great secret is divulged' (D-Day), GIs find themselves fighting through a muddy and rain-sodden France and Belgium towards Germany. Like *The Longest Day*, it deploys the dramatic opening bars of Beethoven's Fifth Symphony, but Foreman's film is the anti-*Longest Day* and strives to subvert GI heroism. GIs trap a group of Germans inside a concrete bunker in a valley, until French regulars arrive and take over the operation. The Germans emerge under a white flag to surrender, but the French shoot at them and force the Germans to retaliate. The French soldiers then rig the bunker with explosives and obliterate it. A French lieutenant (Maurice Ronet) reminds the disgusted Americans that it was his country that has been living under German occupation. Jeanne Moreau had a cameo as a French woman who is found by Sergeant Craig (Eli Wallach) living in the cellar of a house which she refuses to evacuate. Michael Callan played a GI who transforms French cabaret violinist Regine (Romy Schneider) into a moneymaking prostitute and George Peppard's soldier has a transient relationship with bar owner Magda (Melina Mercuri). Peppard travels to a rehabilitation hospital in Britain to visit injured Sergeant Craig and is shocked to discover the sergeant is hideously disfigured, having had his face blown off. In a Golden Globe–nominated performance, Peter Fonda plays a young soldier who adopts a puppy, but the other GIs won't let him keep the animal. When the troops pull out, the puppy runs after their truck and the soldiers take bets on who can shoot it. One succeeds, in the film's most unheroic moment.

A unique take on the Allies' dash through France was provided by Brian G. Hutton's caper comedy *Kelly's Heroes* (1970). Having landed on Omaha Beach, a motorised US reconnaissance platoon commanded by Sergeant Big Joe (Telly Savalas) is about to take the town of Nancy, but is replaced by clean-looking reserve troops for the liberation. GI Kelly (Clint Eastwood) learns from captured German Colonel Dankhopf (David Hurst) the details of Operation Tannenbaum ('Fir Tree'), a $16 million gold bullion shipment sitting in a bank in Claremont, 30 miles behind German lines. Kelly and his cohorts – including Big Joe, hustler Supplies Sergeant Crapgame (Don Rickles) and three Sherman tanks led by loose screw Oddball (Donald Sutherland) – set out to perpetrate the 'perfect crime'. Oddball notes, for millions of dollars 'we could become heroes for three days', while the film's posters proclaimed: 'They set out to rob a bank … and damn near won a war instead!'

Originally titled *The Warriors* and *Kelly's Warriors*, *Kelly's Heroes* was a US-Yugoslavian co-production filmed in Yugoslavia in 1969 for $4 million. The story takes place around the town of Nancy, Lorraine (west of Paris and en route to Germany). The crew were based at the Petrovaradin Fortress in Novi Sad (now in Serbia) and in Umag, a port on the Adriatic. Claremont itself was Vizinada, with Marshall Tito Square the setting for the final confrontation outside the bank. The Yugoslavian army played GIs and Nazi stormtroopers, and locals portrayed the French townspeople. In 1969 there was still plenty of army surplus hardware in Yugoslavia, including machine guns, jeeps, half-tracks and authentic Sherman tanks, though the Tiger tanks (Panzer VIs) guarding Claremont were replicas built over Russian T-34s. Big Joe's platoon travel in two Willys 4x4 jeeps and a pair of M3 half-tracks. Oddball's Shermans have 1960s-style modifications – they fire shells filled with paint to freak-out their opponents, have speedily souped-up engines and emerge from a railway tunnel to attack a marshalling yard with 'All for the Love of Sunshine' and 'I've Been Working on the Railroad' blasting from loudspeakers. 'A Sherman can give you a very nice edge' notes Oddball. In reality, Shermans were outclassed by German Panthers and Tigers. The Germans called Shermans 'Tommycookers' and US troops nicknamed them 'Ronsons', after the famous lighter. When hit, the Shermans lit first time.

Stoic Eastwood was surrounded by an overacting crew of GI reprobates. Savalas and Rickles bicker throughout in broad New York accents, while the dozen-strong platoon's yammering voices resemble the cast of TV cartoon *Top Cat* (you expect to hear 'Gee TC' at any moment). Sutherland's shaggy Oddball is the story's most interesting and bogus aspect, dating the film in the wider context of the hippy era. Oddball's dopey crew, including mechanic Moriarty (Gavin MacLeod) and Turk (Shephard Sanders), cloud his day with 'negative waves'. Even the film's title song, the funky sing-along 'Burning Bridges' performed by the Mike Curb Congregation, is clearly 1960s in origin.

Gabriel Figueroa's Panavision cinematography during the expensive set pieces – a battle for a bridge, rocket plane attacks, minefields, ambushes, burning towns, troop columns and tank battles – looks tremendous, but makes a mockery of war. The platoon's commander, Captain Maitland (Hal Buckley), is only concerned with shipping out his looted yacht. Kelly's crew discover all bridge crossings have been destroyed by the Allies, so Oddball simply enlists the 42nd Engineers to throw a pontoon across a river, for 'a piece of the action'. Alf Joint was the stunt coordinator and Andrew Marton directed the busy second unit. The heroes' enthusiasm and greed, as they punch a hole in the German frontline, is misconstrued by klaxon-voiced General Colt (Carroll O'Connor) at US HQ as bravery and he mobilises his forces to follow in their wake.

As to be expected post–*Dirty Dozen*, the ending is cynical. The treasure hunters arrive in Claremont and following a protracted shootout strike a deal with the German Tiger tank commander (Karl Otto Alberty) to divide the gold. In homage to Eastwood's cowboy heroes, Kelly, Big Joe and Oddball stride down the street accompanied by spaghetti western music from Lalo Schifrin. By the time Colt arrives, greeted as a liberator, Kelly's heroes are nowhere to be seen. *Argosy* called the film, 'a superbly acted, exquisitely photographed, howling

The roguish mercenaries of Brian G. Hutton's *Kelly's Heroes* (1970), including Kelly (Clint Eastwood, background left) and tank commander Oddball (Donald Sutherland, foreground left), hitch a ride on a Sherman en route to a fortune in Nazi gold bullion. Courtesy Kevin Wilkinson Collection.

spoof of wartime heroics' and christened it, 'The Sons of Patton's Dirty Dozen Go Where Eagles Dare'. Both US and UK posters featured Eastwood and crew, but in the UK copy Rickles wears a helmet, in the USA a Vietnam War *Deer Hunter* – style red headband. *Kelly's Heroes* was almost the last of the 'War is Swell' jokey World War II movies, as by the early 1970s Vietnam deterred audiences from war films. If they wanted to see American soldiers shot and blown up, they only had to switch on the news.

In the South of France, the US 7th Army and the French 2nd Corps landed west of Cannes in the Anvil landings, also called Operation Dragoon, on 15 August 1944. Audie Murphy's biopic *To Hell and Back* (1955) depicts the landings – Dragoon was the 'anvil' to D-day's 'hammer'. It was a great success, with the Allies taking Toulon, Marseilles and Avignon before heading north, through Lyon and Grenoble and towards Dijon, southeast of Paris.

Operation Dragoon and the fight for the South of France was depicted in Rachid Bouchareb's French-Moroccan-Belgian-Algerian co-production *Indigènes* (2006 – literally 'Natives'), which was retitled *Days of Glory* for international release. Following the liberation of North Africa in 1943, Algerians and Moroccans are recruited to fight in the French army. They are trained at Sétif in Algeria, before being pressed into service in the Italian campaign in 1944. The North African light infantry are assigned to take a German hilltop position, but their suicidal attack is simply to enable their French commanders to pinpoint the German machine gun and mortar emplacements, so French artillery can pick them off. The North Africans fight selflessly for their 'Motherland' (France) and soon fight on their 'home soil'. They take part in Operation Dragoon in August 1944 and campaign through Provence into the Rhone Valley (October 1944), the forested Vosges mountains (November 1944) and into Alsace. These auxiliary troops are sent on a rescue mission (with pack mules loaded with ammunition) to beleaguered US soldiers, but they are ambushed and decimated. Five survivors liberate a small village, but during a battle on 15 January 1945, they face a German patrol which is armed with machine-guns and a Panzerschreck (German antitank bazooka).

Days of Glory's battle scenes are impressively stage – particularly the Italian assault and the village battle – and the film benefits from an emotive North African-flavoured score by Armand Amar and Khaled. Illiterate Algerian soldier Saïd observes: 'I free a country, it's my country. Even if I never saw it before', but the 'natives' soon discover that they have little in common with their French allies, nor with the country they are liberating. The French reward themselves: while valorous African soldiers are passed over for promotions, are issued with inferior rations and are entertained with the French's idea of culture (a ballet) which leads to mutinous thoughts. The Germans exploit this dissention in the ranks by dropping propaganda leaflets telling the Africans that their leaders send them to die as cannon fodder. Bernard Blancan played the troops' commander, Sergeant Martinez, a French North African, and Jamel Debbouze played Saïd Otmani, his batman, who discovers that Martinez is also an Arab. Samy Nacery and Assaad Bouab played Moroccan brothers Yassir and Larbi. Roschdy Zem was marksman Messaoud Souni, who meets and falls in love with French woman Irène (Aurélie Eltvedt) in Marseilles. Their story is perhaps the film's saddest, as their letters are intercepted by the French censure and Messaoud dies thinking his lover has forgotten him. Sami Bouajila portrayed Corporal Abdelkader, the unit's sole survivor of the final battle, who watches as a cameraman films a newsreel of the French Forces – the white French Forces that arrive as reinforcements – liberating Alsace. His colonel (Antoine Chappey) had promised Abdelkader a promotion but reneges on his word. Abdelkader, seen 60 years later visiting his comrades' graves in a vast Alsace war cemetery, wonders what exactly they were fighting for. This rewarding war film, made with intelligence and heart, was a deserved Best Foreign Film Oscar nominee.

The Battle Giants (1969 – *Fall of the Giants*) was set on the Freiburg Front, on the Alsace-Swiss-German border, in the autumn of 1944. A crack squad of five US officers led by Major John Heston (Jack Palance) are dropped beyond the Rhine disguised as German paratroopers. They are to contact Rommel (who is under house arrest in his villa) and his conspirators, following their failed assassination attempt on Hitler. But the mission's real objective is to take a fortified bridge and concrete gun emplacement at Kesselberg Pass. This diversionary attack will attract all the German forces in the area and allow for a push through the now-undefended Zella Pass. The movie is undermined by its Madrid locations, with searing Spanish sunshine, picturesque pine forests (in the Guardarrama Mountains) and dusty roads depicting a German 'autumn'. Director Leon Klimovsky (as 'Henry Manckiewicz') includes some cockeyed historical references, with Rommel committing suicide rather than face a trial for treason. Rommel didn't shoot himself, but took poison on 14 October 1944. The action scenes – an attack on an armoured train, the final confrontation between Heston's commandos and the German forces – are above par for an Italianate *Dirty Dozen* derivative. The Battle of Kesselberg Pass deploys plenty of tanks (US M47s), trucks, half-tracks (US M3s) and assault troop infantry, as its II Panzer Division. Only Heston and a Nazi double-agent (Alberto De Mendoza) survive the onslaught. Heston wins the DSO and his men receive the award posthumously. Palance is his usual larger-than-life self as Heston – one moment quiet and reflective, the next a rabid lunatic. Listen too for the mission's ridiculous call sign: 'Kangaroo calling Swordfish'.

The Battle of the Last Panzer (1968) was set in France during 1944 and follows Tiger tank 'Panzer 71', the lone survivor of a US army ambush, as it attempts to make its way through no man's land to the German lines. Stan Cooper played Lieutenant Hunter, the Panzer's fanatical commander, and his crew are predictably named Fritz, Hans and Schultz. Guy Madison was the US officer in charge of the tank hunt and Riccardo Palacios (in beret and eye patch) played Rene, a French partisan. Shot near Madrid, the film features a wholly unconvincing, arid Spanish landscape as France and the French town of 'Villebois' is depicted by a wild west cowboy set. There is also much post-war army kit on display – the Panzer 'Tiger' tanks are US M48s – and US GIs wear German helmets painted green.

Enzo G. Castellari's cult war movie *The Inglorious Bastards* (1977 – *Counterfeit Commandos, Hell's Heroes* or *Deadly Mission*) is set in France, after D-Day but before Patton had crossed the Rhine. It was advertised as 'Whatever the *Dirty Dozen* do, they do it dirtier!' A quintet of US military prisoners escape while they're being transferred to a stockade and head for the Swiss border. They accidentally wipe out a group of US paratroopers who are disguised as German soldiers and take on the dead soldiers' identities and carry out their special mission – to steal a gyroscopic guidance system for V-2 rockets, which is being transported by an armoured train – the Italian title, *Quel maledetto treno blindato*, translates as 'That Cursed Armoured Train'. The misfit convicts are redneck Tony (Peter Hooten), Fred Canfield (Fred 'The Hammer' Williamson), hippy Nick (Michael Perglani), Berle (Jackie Constantin) and their leader, pilot Lieutenant Yeager (Bo Svenson). They capture a German soldier, Adolf Sachs (Raimund Harmstorf), who acts as their guide and Ian Bannen had a cameo as Colonel Buckner, the mastermind behind the mission. The convicts team up with a group of Free French fighters for the train attack. The partisans are led by Veronique (Michel Constantin) and include nurse Nicole (Debra Berger), Tony's love interest. Regular Castellari collaborator John Loffredo played a sadistic MP and Donal O'Brien played the SS officer at a command post (actually Odelscalchi Castle, near Bracciano Lake, Lazio) where the convicts steal explosives.

Inglorious Bastards is a 'spaghetti western' war movie, with big close-ups, a blaring score, migraine-inducing machine-gun action and slow-motion blood spurts. As a spoof it's even more implausible than *Kelly's Heroes*. The film was made on locations in Lazio, Italy, in the verdant countryside of Manziana and at the Monte Gelato waterfall in the Treja Valley. The train sequences were filmed on the railway between Capranica and Viterbo. The comic-strip title sequence is cut to Francesco De Masi's bombastic cue, featuring blaring trumpets and clashing cymbals. A.T.A. supplied the military vehicles, including US M3 half-tracks, trucks, Kübelwagons and an SdKfz 2 tracked motorbike. Fred Williamson, who refers to his Tommy gun as 'Baby' and the Germans as 'Fuzz with guns', appears to have walked off the set of a blaxploitation movie. Hippy Nick drives a stunt motorbike like Steve McQueen in *The Great Escape* and stone-faced Svenson wears the expression of a man who has stepped on a rake. Director Castellari appears as a German officer in command of a mortar detachment and is everywhere among the German stunt extras – he can be seen to die innumerable times. The incredible stunts are the film's greatest accomplishment. Castellari also uses trick shots and miniatures to good effect to depict a busy US Army depot or a shelled, ruined town. In the finale, a model train with the armed V-2 rocket warhead on board crashes headlong into a German ambush at Pont Mosson station.

Quentin Tarantino, an aficionado of cult action movies, borrowed a misspelling of Castellari's movie for his gloriously over-the-top, intricately constructed *Inglourious Basterds* (2009). Lieutenant Aldo Raine (Brad Pitt) leads a squad of eight Nazi-hating Jewish-American commandos, 'The Basterds', behind enemy lines in France. They strike terror into their German adversaries with their savage methods, which include scalping their victims and branding survivors by carving swastikas into their foreheads with hunting knives. In June 1944, in collaboration with British film critic-turned-commando Lieutenant Archie Hicox (Michael Fassbender), they carry out Operation Kino. Instigated by the British OSS, the plan is to blow up *Le Gamaar* cinema in Paris, where the Führer (Martin Wuttke) is due to attend the prestigious premiere of *Nation's Pride*, the latest propaganda effort by Joseph Goebbels (Sylvester Groth). The owner of the cinema, Emmanuelle Mimieux (Mélanie Laurent), plans to kill the high-ranking Germans present at the gala, by torching reels of celluloid film stock during the screening. Emmanuelle is actually Shosanna Dreyfus, a Jew who has survived the massacre of her family by SS 'Jew Hunter' Colonel Hans Landa (Christoph Waltz). Landa has been put in charge of security for the event.

The film was shot in widescreen by Robert Richardson, on location in Paris and Germany (interiors at Studio Babelsberg, Potsdam) and much of the dialogue is in German, French and Italian. The colourful visuals, vivid costumes and stunning art direction are a feast for the eyes in this, Tarantino's first 'period film'. Tarantino planned the project as a spaghetti western in World War II garb and the film begins: 'Once upon a time ... in Nazi-occupied France'. This is 147 minutes of comic strip history, where historical figures (Hitler, Goebbels and Churchill) meet larger-than-life action heroes, such as 'The Bear Jew', Sergeant Donny Donowitz (Eli Roth), a member of the Basterds, who beats up Nazis' with his baseball bat. Tarantino rewrites history, as the German high command is incinerated in Operation Kino, while they watch *Nation's Pride*, propaganda which depicts the exploits of celebrity war hero Private Fredrick Zoller (Daniel

International poster for Quentin Tarantino's anarchic World War II movie, *Inglourious Basterds* (2009), starring (clockwise from top) Christoph Waltz, Diane Kruger, Til Schwieger, Brad Pitt, Eli Roth and Mélanie Laurent.

Brühl). He's an ace German sniper, who held innumerable American troops at bay from a bell tower during the battle for Italy. Zoller hopes to become 'the German Van Johnson' and *Nation's Pride* itself is included as an extra on DVD releases. Hitler was a cinema enthusiast and when he took breaks in the Berghof, his residence in the Bavarian Alps, he would watch two movies, mostly 'escapist fare', each night.

Tarantino's biggest financial success to date, *Inglourious Basterds* remoulds established formulas and motifs, and is a must-see for film and war buffs alike. There are references to German cinema (G.W. Pabst, Emil Jannings and the 'mountain films' genre) and German literature (the *Winnetou* western novels and Edgar Wallace thrillers). At one point Shosanna tells Zoller: 'I'm French, we respect directors in our country', a line every cineaste will applaud. The scalp-hunting Basterds resemble *The Dirty Dozen*'s cutthroats and the climax, with the German top brass locked inside the burning, exploding cinema, recalls the sadistic, inferno finale of Aldrich's film, as Donny machine-guns Hitler's face. Shosanna has spliced her own home movie, a vengeful address to the assembled Nazis, at the end of *Nation's Pride* and as flames engulf the screen, Shosanna's projected monochrome image oversees her revenge.

The director's references are always interesting and often unexpected. He alludes to several Clint Eastwood movies: a massacre at a French dairy farm – when Landa visits homesteader Perrier LaPadite (Denis Menochat) who is sheltering Shosanna's family – is straight out of *The Good, the Bad and the Ugly*. A tavern scene in the village of Nadine resembles 'Zum Wilden Hirsch' in *Where Eagles Dare* and Lalo Schifrin's 'Tiger Tank' cue from *Kelly's Heroes* is reused. Tarantino deploys a range of cult film music as his soundtrack. The film opens with Dimitri Tiomkin's 'The Green Leaves of Summer' from *The Alamo* (1960) and Jacques Loussier's cue from the Congo-set war movie *The Mercenaries* (1968 – *Dark of the Sun*) also features. Its star, Rod Taylor, appears here as Winston Churchill. Ennio Morricone cuts from *The Big Gundown*, *Death Rides a Horse* and *A Professional Gun* invoke spaghetti western atmosphere. Gianni Ferrio's lilting harmonica from *One Silver Dollar* wafts through a French café. Morricone's agitated *Battle of Algiers* cue scores a prison break, when the Basterds release champion Nazi killer, Sergeant Hugo Stiglitz (Til Schwieger). From *The Return of Ringo*, Morricone's dramatic 'The Meeting with the Daughter' (a reorchestration of Mussorgsky's 'Night on the Bare Mountain') scores the murder of Shosanna's family, who are hiding under the farmhouse's wooden floorboards. The score's only false note is the deployment of David Bowie's 'Cat People (Putting Out the Fire)' for Shosanna's entrance (wearing a bright red dress) to the gala, when The Passions' 1981 hit 'I'm in Love with a German Film Star' would have been perfect. Tarantino's use of the instrumental 'Un Amico', one of Morricone's most underrated compositions (from the 1973 thriller *Revolver*) for the final confrontation between Shosanna and Zoller, is masterful.

As moustachioed, neck-scarred Tennessee country boy 'Aldo the Apache' – a part-Native American descendant of mountainman Jim Bridger – Pitt channels Burt Reynolds' 'good ol' boy' screen persona. Charles Bernstein's music from Reynolds' moonshine classic *White Lighting* (1973) appears on the soundtrack. At the gala, Aldo (in a white Armani tux) impersonates Italian stuntman 'Enzo Gorlomi', with Donny posing as cameraman 'Antonio Margheriti'. Jacky Ido was Marcel, *La Gamaar*'s projectionist, and Christian Berkel, who usually plays German officers, was cleverly cast against type as tavern keeper, Eric. A heavily disguised Mike Meyers played Operation Kino's coordinator, General Ed Fenech (a reference to Italian starlet Edwige Fenech) and Diane Kruger played German film star (and Allied double agent) Bridget Von Hammersmark, who attends the premiere but is unmasked by Landa when her shoe is found at the scene of a tavern massacre. Landa himself is the film's most memorable creation – an infamous, feared hunter of Jews. Christoph Waltz is terrific and terrifying in the role of the delving, overly polite psychopath. He won Best Supporting Actor awards at both the BAFTAs and the Oscars. Packed with in-jokes and bursting with flair and imagination, this is the best war movie in years. As Aldo the Apache says at the film's close, having given Landa a forehead scar to remember him by: 'I think this might just be my masterpiece'.

Patton (1970) featured the Allies' breakout from Normandy, a deadlock that was broken by master tactician General George Patton (George C. Scott). Throughout the planning and execution of D-Day, disgraced Patton has been used as a decoy by Eisenhower in Corsica, Malta and North Africa, to convince the Germans that the invasion of France will begin from the Mediterranean. The Germans think Patton's Sicilian 'slapping incident' is a propaganda ruse by the Allies and can't believe they are not deploying their most effective commander in Europe. To keep the Germans guessing, Patton is moved to London, then to the Cheshire town of Knutsford. Eisenhower created a 'dummy army', complete with fake logistics and communiqués: the fictitious 1st US Army Group (FUSAG). This convinced Hitler that the Allies would strike in Calais. In *Patton*, the general doesn't want to sit out the war as a decoy and Eisenhower appoints him to collaborate with General Omar Bradley (Karl Malden) on Operation Cobra. Patton's thrust towards the Seine is so successfully that he drives clear off the HQ strategists' map. In *Patton* the US war machine on the march is vividly depicted, as the mechanised US columns roll on. At the moment when it looks as though Patton is about to single-handedly win the war, he is stalled. His supply lines are severed and redirected to Montgomery's forces driving through Belgium into Holland. Patton's offensive literally ran out of gas. In *Patton* this is illustrated by Patton's tanks grinding to a halt and fighting a night-time pitched battle from which they cannot escape. Meanwhile their fuel has been diverted to Montgomery to enable him to mount perhaps the most daring manoeuvre of the war, the ill-fated Operation Market Garden.

Chapter 16

OPERATION MARKET GARDEN (1944)

As Patton's army drove through France, pulverising everything is its path, it was stopped short. Montgomery had convinced Eisenhower to divert vital supplies from Patton to concentrate on an offensive into Holland. Brussels had fallen on 3 September 1944, followed by the port of Antwerp the following day, but the Allies couldn't sustain their attacks on all fronts. On 10 September, Eisenhower and Montgomery met in Brussels and Montgomery pitched his plan, codenamed Operation Market Garden. Ignoring Eisenhower's preference for an advance on a wide front, Montgomery proposed an audacious combined operation between ground and airborne forces, which would conquer Holland and open up a route into Germany's Ruhr, thereby ending the war by Christmas.

Montgomery planned to deploy the Allies' airborne troops the way Hitler had during the Blitzkrieg. They would secure vital objectives – in this case a series of seven canal and river bridges – ahead of a land offensive, which would link up with the airborne troops. 'Market' was the airborne elements, while 'Garden' was the ground troops. The plan was for three airborne contingents to drop into Holland. The Germans were launching rocket attacks against Britain from sites in Holland. The US 101st Airborne Division (the 'Screaming Eagles') would land near Eindhoven and Son and the US 82nd Airborne Division would land in the vicinity of Nijmegan and Grave to take bridges spanning the Wilhelmina and Willems Canals, and the rivers Maas and Waal respectively. The furthest and most risky target was the bridge at Arnhem, which would take the Allies across the Neder Rhine (Lower Rhine) and into Germany. This was the objective of the British 1st Airborne Division, which included the 1st Polish Parachute Brigade. British XXX Corps commanded by Lieutenant General Brian Horrocks would advance from the Belgian border and drive north into Holland to relieve the airborne troops.

There were two main problems with the plan. Firstly, the front's offensive was narrow, essentially a single road, which if blocked would stall the entire attack by XXX Corps. Secondly, the airborne objectives were some distance from the Allies' front lines and depended on light resistance from the Germans to be able to retain possession of their targets until the relief column arrived. The Arnhem bridge was the mission's raison d'être and the airborne commanders were assured by Montgomery that XXX Corps would relieve them in two days. 'We can hold them for four', commented Lieutenant General Frederick 'Boy' Browning, the British 1st Airborne's commander, to Montgomery, 'But sir, I think we might be going a bridge too far'.

The operation was blighted by a catalogue of disasters. On the fine morning of Sunday 17 September 1944, Market Garden went into action. The airborne forces consisted of paratroopers and glider-borne troops. The gliders also conveyed the troops' heavier equipment and supplies. The landing zones (LZs) and drop zones (DZs) for Major General Robert Urquhart's British 1st Airborne, their commander in the field, were eight miles from the Arnhem Bridge, to the west of the town of Oosterbeek. The plan was for Freddy Gough's light reconnaissance troops to rush to the bridge in jeeps, but most of their equipment was damaged and they were ambushed en route. The British paras had to walk to the bridge and only the 2nd Parachute Battalion (2 Para) commanded by Lieutenant Colonel John Frost reached their objective, securing the north end of the crossing. Resistance was far heavier in the area than reported. Expecting Hitler Youth and old men on bicycles, the British troops faced the II SS Panzer Corps: the 9th 'Hohenstaufen' Division under Lieutenant Colonel Harzer and the 10th 'Frundsberg' Division under Brigadier General Harmel, which were in the area for a refit. Reconnaissance and intelligence photographs, and reports from the Dutch Underground, had revealed German armour in the area, but the omens had been ignored.

As XXX Corps set off they too met heavy resistance and their route up the single road was often obstructed by their own wrecked vehicles. The US paratroops landed and moved to take their objectives, but the canal bridge at Son was demolished by the Germans and the Nijmegan Bridge was heavily defended, causing further delays. Due to a lack of aircraft the airborne forces – some 35,000 men – couldn't be dropped in one lift, so they arrived in three waves over three days. For the men at Arnhem this proved disastrous, as the Germans overran the drop zones, capturing their supplies. In the case of the Polish Brigade under Major General Stanislaw Sosabowski, their drops were delayed until 22 September by bad weather. When they landed on the south side of the river at Driel, they were decimated as they hit the ground. Early in the battle a full set of Market Garden's 'Top Secret' plans fell into German hands. They were found in a wrecked glider and detailed the entire operation, but Field Marshal Model, the German commander, dismissed them as fake. On the 18 September XXX Corps reached the 101st in Eindhoven and by the 19 September linked up with the 82nd in Nijmegan. On 20 September paratroopers commanded by Major Julian Cook mounted a daring amphibious crossing of the Waal in canvas boats and secured the north side of the Nijmegan Bridge and the Germans' demolition charges on the structure failed to detonate.

But in Arnhem time was running out. Frost's battle for the bridge too far was defined by fearsome house-to-house fighting, an often point-blank bloody melee, as the paras fought tooth and nail to cling on against crack SS troops. The ferocious battle took its toll and on 21 September Frost was forced to surrender. The rest of the British airborne division never reached the bridge and were pinned down in a dwindling perimeter in Oosterbeek with their backs to the Rhine. During a vital period of the battle Urquhart was separated from his command and spent 39 hours trapped in an attic behind German lines, while few of the paras' radios worked so the British Airborne HQ had no way of coordinating troop movements. On the 23 and 24 September, the Poles failed to cross the Rhine to reinforce Urquhart's men and on the 25 September, nine days after the mission began, the remains of the 1st Airborne were evacuated in an amphibious operation to the south bank of the Rhine. Of the 10,000 men who had attempted to secure the Arnhem bridge, only 2,163 crossed back. Montgomery famously asserted that the operation had been '90 percent successful', while Urquhart's official report in January 1945 concluded: 'The operation … did not end quite as we intended. The losses were heavy but all ranks appreciate that the risks involved were reasonable. There is no doubt that all would willingly undertake another operation under similar conditions in the future. We have no regrets'.

Market Garden and the Battle of Arnhem are remembered today for their extraordinary heroism and extreme ill fortune. There are many US films depicting their military disasters – witness the dozens of dramatisations of General Custer and the Battle of the Little Bighorn, or Vietnam – but few British equivalents. Rare examples include *Dunkirk*, *The Charge of the Light Brigade* (1968) and *Zulu Dawn* (1979 – the Battle of Isandlwana). The first film of the Battle of Arnhem was *Theirs Is the Glory* (1946 – *Men of Arnhem*), co-directed by Brian Desmond Hurst and Terence Young. It was unique among war films in that it was filmed on location in Arnhem using men who had actually fought in the battle, as a documentary-style re-enactment. In fact it is often passed off unknowingly in TV documentaries as actual World War II footage, due to the presence of real German armour, including Tiger tanks. Young also included scenes of Operation Market Garden in *They Were Not Divided* (1950), with the Welsh Guards at the vanguard of XXX Corps, uniting with US paratroopers at Grave and taking the bridge at Nijmegan. Their push ends with their Shermans bogged down in mud and rain on 25 September, as they fail to reach Arnhem.

Colin Teague's *The Last Drop* (2005), which is set against the backdrop of the Battle of Arnhem, could have been titled 'A Vault too Far'. This wartime heist movie has four groups of soldiers converging on the riverside farm. A fortune in Nazi loot – priceless antiques, rare coins and paintings – has been stashed in an underground vault and is about to be airlifted out to Berlin before Holland falls. Renegade German Leutnant Jürgen Voller (Alexander Skarsgard) plans to steal the loot to seek revenge on his sworn enemy, scar-faced SS Major Kessler (Laurence Fox, actor James' son). As Voller observes, 'The fog of war – what better time for a robbery?' Meanwhile as part of Operation Market Garden, a band of British paratroopers are dispatched by Warren (UK comedian Jack Dee) on Operation Matchbox, to save the haul from the Nazis. Along the way a band of US Screaming Eagles led by Colonel J.T. Colt (Michael Madsen), who have secured a nearby bridge, learn of the cache and join the treasure hunt.

Taken for what it is – a historically inaccurate, implausible, never-dull action movie – *Last Drop* is entertaining. It is a UK-Romanian co-production, shot on location in Romania and at Media Pro Studios, Bucharest. The cast included Billy Zane as gung-ho Canadian glider pilot Bobby Oates, Karel Roden as Voller's ursine sidekick Hans Beck and Steve Spiers as snivelling Nazi Gustav Hansfeldt, who knows the cache's location. Among the British paratroopers was Neil Newborn as SOE agent Powell, Tommy Flanagan as morphine addict Baker, Sean Pertwee as Sergeant McMillan, Rafe Spall as medic Wellings and Nick Moran as spiv Bren-gunner Ives, who declares at one point 'We're here on the rob'. Coral Beed and Lucy Gaskell played Saskia and Benitta, two Dutch women at the lakeside farm: this picturesque location includes a windmill and jetty, where in the all-action finale a German seaplane arrives to take the treasures to Berlin. Best of all is the appearance of French ex-footballer David Ginola as Corporal Dieter Max, Voller's marksman henchman. Ignore the hilarious videogame CGI effects of towed gliders, the inaccurate British paratrooper helmets, the horrible tacked-on ending (a museum heist of the treasures) and Michael Madsen's completely over-the-top cameo as gravel-voiced Patton imitator Colt (named after Carroll O'Connor's character in *Kelly's Heroes*). Jack Dee appears in the film's trailer for longer than he does in the actual film. *Last Drop* features Imperial War Museum archive footage and is welcome relief from most modern po-faced treatments of the war. 'Look for it on DVD' said the trailer, helpfully, as it didn't make it to cinemas.

By far the best-known film version of Market Garden is Richard Attenborough's massive *A Bridge Too Far* (1977), based on Cornelius Ryan's account of the same name which was first published in 1974 shortly before Ryan's death in November of that year. Since *The Longest Day* in 1959, Ryan had written *The Last Battle* in 1966, which recounted the final battle for Berlin and is yet to be filmed. As in *Longest Day*, Ryan brought history vividly to life in *A Bridge Too Far*, with hours of interviews and detailed eyewitness accounts creating a superb sense of narrative storytelling. The film version is crammed with famous faces, both to facilitate the story's telling and to attract audiences to cinemas.

Ryan's book was adapted for the screen by William Goldman, the Academy Award winning writer of *Butch Cassidy and the Sundance Kid* and *All the President's Men.* He also wrote the book *William Goldman's Story of A Bridge Too Far* in 1977 to tie-in with the film's release, which recounted how producer Joseph E. Levine financed the film himself and pre-sold it worldwide on the roster of 14 star names he had attracted. Levine, who came out of retirement to produce it, noted, 'In the past I've often claimed I would never risk my own money in the hazardous film world. But I feel differently about this one. It's the best damn story I've ever read'. Levine paid $800,000 for the screen rights. Goldman's wonderful, literate script made the story accessible to those unfamiliar with the battle. *A Bridge Too Far* begins with a 'story so far' of archive footage, narrated by Liv Ullman, recounting the state of play on the Western Front since D-Day. It then depicted in meticulous detail the operation's planning and execution – the mistakes made, the opportunities lost, the valour – with many historical vignettes effortlessly woven into the film's fabric. The story only occasionally blurs out of focus, and when it does Goldman's chronology and Attenborough's powerful imagery steer it back on course.

The well-chosen cast were billed alphabetically, to preclude billing arguments. The key players were Dirk Bogarde as 'Boy' Browning, Gene Hackman as Sosabowski, Sean Connery played Urquhart and Robert Redford as Major Cook. Attenborough and Levine had wanted to cast Steve McQueen, but his role was taken by Redford. Roger Moore was an early choice to play Horrocks, but Edward Fox was finally cast. Fox did an excellent job, in a memorable scene telling the assembled officers of XXX Corps in their HQ in Leopoldsburg on the Belgian-Dutch border: 'This is a story you will tell your grandchildren – and mightily bored they'll be!' Ryan O'Neal played Brigadier General James M. Gavin, the commander of the 82nd Airborne, and Paul Maxwell was Major General Maxwell Taylor of the 101st. Anthony Hopkins was a highlight as Frost, who rallies his men on the drop zone with a blast of his hunting horn. Michael Caine portrayed Lieutenant Colonel 'J.O.E' Vandeleur of the Irish Guards, who led the vanguard of XXX Corps. The producer and director ran into Caine in a restaurant, who demanded: 'Every other bloody actor in town's in your movie, why not me?' and a part was found for him. Paul Copley played Private Wicks, Frost's batman, Jeremy Kemp was an RAF briefing officer and Denholm Elliott was an RAF meteorologist. Elliott Gould played one of the few fictitious characters – Colonel Bobby Stout of the 101st – who witnesses the destruction of the Son canal bridge. Stout was based on Colonel Robert Sink. James Caan played Staff Sergeant Eddie Dohun (real name Charles Dohun), who guarantees his captain's life before the battle. When his captain is thought to have been killed, Dohun recovers his body and drives it by jeep through German lines to a US medical station and forces a surgeon at gunpoint to check his captain – it turns out that the captain is still alive and Dohun avoids a court martial, in one of the most effective episodes of the film. Stars received between a quarter and half a million dollars a week, which for the time was staggering. Their agents, unconvinced of the film's success, asked for payment in advance, which cost Levine $10 million before the film even began shooting.

On the German side Maximilian Schell portrayed SS Lieutenant General Wilhelm Bittrich, Walter Kohut played Field Marshal Model, Hans Von Borsody played General Blumentritt and war movie stalwart Wolfgang Preiss was Field Marshal Von Rundstedt. Hardy Krüger was convincing as SS Major General Ludwig, a composite of the SS Panzer commanders Harzer and Harmel. As the Dutch contingent, Laurence Olivier played fictitious Dr. Spaander in Arnhem, who negotiates a ceasefire with the Germans on behalf of the British, so that the wounded paratroopers can be taken into care by the Germans. This truce was actually negotiated by Dr Graeme Warrack, the 1st Airborne's chief medical officer. Liv Ullman played Kate Ter Horst, whose house became a military field hospital for wounded paras (Audrey Hepburn had been considered for the role). Siem Vroom played a Dutch Underground leader, who with his son (Eric Van't Wout) feeds information to British intelligence. When Vroom's wife and son are killed, their bodies become part of a human barricade of corpses to block the streets of Arnhem, delaying the German armour – a true occurrence during the battle. Spaander travels through the ruined Arnhem streets, littered with civilian dead and scavenging dogs and the film's final shot is of Spaander, Ter Horst and her children leaving devastated Arnhem pulling a handcart, amid a lyrical sunset. In this way the huge civilian cost of the battle is depicted too, reinforcing Attenborough's assertion that *Bridge Too Far* was 'a major antiwar movie'.

Levine wanted the film in cinemas by June 1977, so Goldman worked on the screenplay while preparations were made for shooting in Holland. The eventual budget was almost $26 million, making it the most expensive British film made up to 1977. By pre-selling the film to distributors on the basis of screened snippets of the work in progress and the star names, Levine was $4 million in the black before the film was released. Levine's investment is evident onscreen during the 169-minute duration. It was photographed spectacularly in Panavision and Technicolor by Geoffrey Unsworth on location in Holland over a dry summer, beginning on 26 April 1976, for six months. Initially there was a possibility that they wouldn't be allowed to film on the distinctive circular span style bridges in Holland. This would have meant filming in Yugoslavia, which according to Goldman 'has lots of tanks but no bridges'. Levine would have had to build them. The area around the actual Arnhem Bridge was now surrounded by modern buildings, a result of its regeneration after the war, so the bridge at Deventer, north of Arnhem, was used instead. The real Nijmegan Bridge across the Waal was used, with other scenes shot in and around Bemmel, Bronkhorst, Grave and Lent. Some exteriors were filmed at Moor Park Golf Club in Hertfordshire and interiors were shot in Twickenham Studios, London.

Battle of Arnhem: The 9th SS Panzer Reconnaissance Battalion under Captain Gräbner is ambushed on Arnhem Bridge by Lieutenant Colonel John Frost's 2 Para, in Richard Attenborough's epic re-enactment *A Bridge Too Far* (1977). Courtesy Kevin Wilkinson Collection.

A Bridge Too Far is notable both for its large-scale battle scenes and for its historical accuracy. The stunt coordinators were Alf Joint and Vic Armstrong, and the military consultants were Horrocks, Gavin, Vandeleur, Frost and Urquhart. Associate producer John Palmer scoured Europe, the Middle East and North Africa for authentic World War II vehicles. The production deployed 11 real DC-3 Dakota aircraft (four owned by the company, the rest from the Finnish and Danish air forces) for the recreation of the parachute drop (which was filmed with 19 cameras). The large-scale parachute drop is the best such scene in World War II cinema. The Horsa gliders used by the airborne troops had to be constructed from scratch, as none had survived the war. The production had 11 authentic Sherman tanks, with more created by casting moulds over VW Beetles. Further ordnance onscreen included four Harvard fighters, an Auster reconnaissance plane, seven Bren gun carriers, 13 half-tracks and 93 jeeps, plus a selection of artillery (25-pounders, 17-pounders and anti-tank guns). The scenes of XXX Corps' advance are impressive, deploying M3 half-tracks, jeeps, armoured cars and tanks. The German armour too is authentic, with Panzers, armoured cars and VW Kübelwagons. There are several large-scale battle scenes recreated throughout. Notable among these is the initial breakout by XXX Corps up 'Hell's Highway', with Vandeleur's armour advancing and the German artillery ambushing them from cover in woodland. In another scene, US paratroopers cross the surging Waal in canvas boats to attack the north side of Nijmegan Bridge.

The film's finest scenes are the three-day Battle for Arnhem Bridge. An initial assault on the bridge is led by Major Carlyle (Christopher Good), carrying his distinctive umbrella into battle, but the Germans hold the south side. During a follow-up attack at night, Corporal Davies (Alun Armstrong) accidentally detonates an ammo dump on Arnhem Bridge when he tries to destroy a pillbox defending the bridge approaches. The paras billet in houses overlooking the bridge's iconic elliptical steel arc; this vantage point gives them a clear view of the crossing's raised concrete highway ramp. In the film's best sequence, the 9th SS Panzer Reconnaissance Battalion under Captain Paul Gräbner (Paul Williams) attack across the bridge in armoured cars, half-tracks and light vehicles, and are successfully ambushed by Frost's 2 Para, who open up with machine guns, grenades and Piats. Fired from the shoulder like a rifle, the Piat fired a bulbous anti-tank missile. This action scene was rehearsed in a local car park, with the Kübelwagon skids achieved using a carpet of plastic ball bearings. Later, Bittrich orders 'Flatten Arnhem' and the Panzer troops go to work. Tanks and troops move from house to house, as Frost's defenders are stalked by the German Panzergrenadiers through the smoking ruins. The fate of the rest of the 1st Airborne is also depicted, with foxholes around the Hartenstein Hotel, their HQ in Oosterbeek (the hub of the paras' dwindling perimeter). One desperate soldier runs the gauntlet of German fire to retrieve a parachute supply canister, but he's shot – the canister falls open to reveal that it contains not food, ammunition or medical supplies, but dozens of red berets. As the Germans arrive at the Hartenstein at the battle's close, wounded paratroop survivors gently hum the hymn 'Abide With Me'.

A Bridge Too Far was released in June 1977 by United Artists in the US and UK to mixed reviews. The *Monthly Film Bulletin* called it 'wearily, expensively predictable', while the *Sunday Times* noted that, 'When celluloid death is so random and so spectacular, so mechanised and so grotesque ... then it is impossible not to fill the screen, intermittently, with pictures which stun the mind and bruise the conscience'. In the US it was panned by critics, who refused to take the film's unbelievable action as historical fact, claiming they had 'Hollywooded' the story up for cinema audiences. This particularly riled Goldman, who maintained: 'We killed ourselves to be accurate, sure it rankles – still does'. According to Attenborough the film's unsympathetic portrayal of Browning didn't go down very well in some circles – in the film, blame for ignoring the Dutch intelligence reports is placed firmly at Browning's door, making him the villain of the piece. *A Bridge Too Far* was not the financial bomb many contemporary reviewers have branded it – it took over $50 million in the US alone. It was ignored by the Oscars, but in the UK it was nominated for eight BAFTAs and won four, including Fox as Best Supporting Actor and John Addison's score. His music is a major plus to the film. The opening title music – stirringly heroic and yet bittersweet in its minor key melody – has become a classic war movie theme, which is now a popular standard of military brass bands' repertoires.

Urquhart's 1958 memoir *Arnhem* was reissued in 1977 on the back of the film's success. That same year Sir Brian Horrocks published his memoir *Corps Commander* and in 1980 Frost published *A Drop Too Many*, his own recollections of the Bruneval Raid, Sicily and Arnhem. *The Tenth Virgin Film Guide*'s opinion ('A movie too long') is typical of the film's standing today with film fans, while its reputation is considerably higher with historians and war buffs. Like *The Longest Day* and *Tora! Tora! Tora!*, it brings history to life in an entertaining, informative way. *A Bridge Too Far* is the last great war film – that is the last great 'old style' war movie, with a stellar cast, a great score, and widescreen action recreated at great expense. Unlike Urquhart, Browning and Horrocks, Attenborough, Goldman and Levine achieved their goal.

Many US histories of World War II barely mention Market Garden, or if they do it is as a footnote to history – sometimes as though it never happened and sometimes as a calamitous demonstration of Montgomery's folly. There are still yearly ceremonies in Holland to commemorate Market Garden and one para's gravestone bears the inscription: 'When you go home, tell them of us and say "For your tomorrow, we give our today"'. The operation was a costly gamble, but had it succeeded it would have saved many lives. Instead it cost many, many more.

Chapter 17

THE PACIFIC WAR II (1942–45)

After the US victory at Midway in June 1942, American forces continued to exact revenge for Pearl Harbor. The American national outcry following the Pearl attack resulted in a hatred of the Japanese which was evident in the savage warfare in the Pacific. The US tactics involved 'island-hopping' – that is moving their forces from island to island, clearing it of Japanese occupying forces and then moving on to the next one – until they were close enough to invade Japan itself.

The US forces in the Pacific divided into three commands: the South-west Pacific Area under General Douglas MacArthur, the South Pacific Area under Admiral Halsey and the Central Pacific Area under Admiral Nimitz (replacing Kimmel as CINCPAC, or Commander-in-Chief Pacific Fleet). The tactics employed to take each island rarely differed. The US Marines transferred from their transporters, climbing down cargo nets into landing craft. Naval and aerial bombardments would 'soften up' the Japanese defences on the islands, but the effects of these sustained barrages were often negligible. The Japanese defenders were organised and well-established. They dug tunnels, built concrete defensive pillboxes, set lethal, crippling booby traps and fought to the last man. They even became human bombs, carrying mines and being run over by tanks. The best way for the US troops to clear the concrete bunkers and pillboxes was with flamethrowers – weapons that fired a jet of ignited gasoline and nitrogen (replaced in 1943 by napalm). They were carried by infantryman (with the lethal liquid fuel tanks strapped to their backs) or larger versions were mounted on adapted Sherman tanks. If the defenders weren't fried alive by the jets of flame, then the burning liquid sucked the oxygen out of the air and they were asphyxiated. During this campaign, photographs of Marines trudging through smouldering jungles past dead Japanese soldiers bore hauntingly prophetic echoes of Vietnam.

Japanese Pacific expansion reached its zenith in August 1942. At the beginning of August, US forces landed on Guadalcanal, one of the Solomon Islands.

They captured the half-completed jungle airbase and completed its construction, naming it Henderson Field. After sustained, bloody fighting, during which the US troops and their reinforcements repulsed several Japanese offensives, they secured the island on 9 February 1943. This was the first significant land battle of the Pacific conflict. It is during the Battle of the Teneru River in November 1942 on Guadalcanal that Al Schmid (John Garfield) was blinded by a grenade in Delmer Daves' *Pride of the Marines* (1945), a moving true story of rehabilitation. Schmid returns home to his wife Ruth (Eleanor Parker) and the film made the *New York Times*' yearly 'ten best' list.

There have been more films made about the Pacific War than any other World War II theatre. US war films set in this theatre usually depict the US Army's westward assaults on island strongholds – the island-hopping campaign. Gaining these footholds, many of which were flyspecks on Pacific maps, would enable the US forces to capture enemy airfields, essential for their assault on Japan itself. These Pacific films follow a strict formula of training, romance and domesticity combined with re-enactments of the beach assaults. In most Hollywood depictions of Pacific island warfare, rookies are bloodied in battle, becoming battle-hardened veterans, who are subsequently contrasted with their 'green' replacements.

Guadalcanal Diary (1943) is the archetypal example of such fare, which was released in the US in October 1943, only eight months after the battle itself. It is based on Richard Tregaskis' 1943 book of the same name. The film depicts in some detail the 1st US Marines' assault on Guadalcanal. The film begins on 26 July 1942, aboard a transport ship packed with Marines. They land on Guadalcanal unopposed and secure the airfield, but soon the Japanese counterattack begins and the Marines defend their perimeter. The protagonists include Corporal Taxi Potts (William Bendix), padre Father Donnelly (Preston Foster), Mexican soldier Jesus Alvarez (Anthony Quinn), Sergeant Malone (Lloyd Nolan) and Captain Davis (Richard Conte). Lionel Stander cropped up in an early role as rasping voiced Marine, Butch. Particularly memorable was Richard Jaeckel as 'Chicken' Anderson, a rookie with much to learn, who claims to have a girl back home, but is in fact dutifully writing to his mother.

Interestingly these are cine-literate soldiers: troops sing a hymnal rendition of the cowboy favourite 'Home on the Range' around the camp fire, one soldier mentions Gary Cooper starring as *Sergeant York* and another only knows the Civil War as 'the war in *Gone With the Wind*'. The action is well staged, with much of it recreated on Santa Catalina Island, near California, including the amphibious landing sequences, a battle for some caves and the final confrontation on the island which drives the Japanese into the sea. The Marines' appalling conditions during the defence of the airfield perimeter are illustrated in the film, as they endure intense Japanese air and naval bombardment. Their boredom too is well delineated, as the troops listen to the World Series on the wireless, write letters home and chat (termed 'shooting the breeze'). As propaganda *Guadalcanal Diary* is more realistic in its depiction of the soldiers' lot than most, with the Japanese defenders depicted as fanatics. When Alvarez – the lone survivor of a patrol – makes his escape by swimming out to sea, he looks back to see Japanese soldiers bayoneting his fallen comrades. The film ends optimistically with the Marines marching past a sign reading 'Tokyo 3,380½ miles', as the Marines' anthem 'The Halls of Montezuma' ('From the Halls of Montezuma to the shores of Tripoli!') swells rousingly on the soundtrack.

James Jones' Guadalcanal-set novel *The Thin Red Line*, published in 1962, was filmed under that title by Andrew Marton in 1964 and more famously by Terrence Malick in 1998. In Marton's adaptation, written by Bernard Gordon, C ('Charlie') Company of US infantry land on Guadalcanal and are ordered to secure the Japanese held village of Boola Boola in 'a classical infantry operation'. To do this they must battle through a swamp, cross a river and scale a steep, heavily mined and barb wire strewn ravine (the 'Bowling Alley'), all of which are riddled with enemy troops, booby traps, machine gun nests and pillboxes. They succeed and eventually overrun a fortified Japanese cliff emplacement of caves christened the 'Dancing Elephant'. The film was shot in monochromed CinemaScope on location near Madrid, Spain: the Boola Boola village set was at Embalse De Santillana (Santillana Reservoir) at Manzanares El Real. Kier Dullea played Private Doll, who married Judy (Merlyn Yordan) only eight days before he departed for action. Doll is mercilessly bullied by First Sergeant Welsh (Jack Worden) throughout the operation. Ray Daley was their caring commander, Captain Stone (Stein in the novel), who is replaced by Captain Gaff (Jim Gillen) when he wilfully disobeys orders from their glory-seeking superior, Colonel Tall (James Philbrook). Marton's handling of the action scenes, visceral human drama and wasteful tragedy – as many of the company, including Welsh, are killed in action – make this Allied Artists production one of the most realistic, thoughtful combat movies of the 1960s. As Stone notes, 'There's only a thin red line between the sane and the mad'.

Malick's arty, reflective *The Thin Red Line* also follows Charlie Company of US infantrymen as they assault Guadalcanal. The Marines have done their job and cleared the beaches: now the battle for the island begins. Charlie Company is instructed to take 'Hill 210', a Japanese machine gun and mortar bunker which controls the surrounding valley. The infantry's assault is repelled, despite being supported by an artillery barrage. Lieutenant Colonel Tall orders Captain Jim Staros to lead Charlie Company in a frontal attack, rather than a flanking manoeuvre, but Staros refuses to sacrifice his men in such a suicidal endeavour. Nevertheless, through the extreme valour of a party led by Captain Gaff, the bunker is taken.

The Thin Red Line was shot on location in Guadalcanal (the Solomon Islands), in San Pedro (California) and in Queensland (Australia). The *SS Lane Victory* appeared as a troop transporter for the invasion scenes (as it would in *Flags of Our Fathers*). Jim Caviezel's philosophical, unruly Private Witt is the standout portrayal, but the film is filled with excellent actors, many of whom appear in brief cameos. Sean Penn was Witt's tormentor, First Sergeant Welsh, the company's 'rock' who cries beside Witt's graveside at the film's close. Adrien Brody was Corporal Fife and Woody Harrelson played Sergeant Keck, who accidentally pulls the pin on a grenade which is still attached to his belt and blows his 'butt off'. Nick Nolte played bulging-veined, gravelly-voiced Tall, a bitter, passed-over-for-promotion officer who cares for results, not lives. Elias Koteas resembles Robert De Niro in his intense portrayal of Captain Staros, who pays for caring too much about his men ('you are my sons') by being relieved of his command by Tall. John Cusack played Staros' replacement, Captain Gaff. John Travolta was Brigadier General Quintard and George Clooney appeared as Captain Bosche, Charlie Company's new commander.

The film is eloquently narrated in voiceover by several characters, from C Company's officers to its enlisted men. Private Jack Bell (Ben Chaplin) reminisces happily about his wife Marty (Miranda Otto) back home. He has been true to his wife since he was shipped out, but his loyalty counts for nought when he receives a letter which reveals she has 'just got too lonely'. Having met an airforce captain she wants a divorce from Jack, her 'friend of all these shining years', a revelation which destroys him.

Malick's *The Thin Red Line* is the antithesis of *Saving Private Ryan*, though the timing of its release the same year inevitably invited comparison with Spielberg's film. *Red Line* won nothing at the Oscars, even though it was nominated in many categories, including Best Picture, Best Director, Best Adapted Screenplay and Best Score. Malick's film is more thoughtful, ethereal and dreamlike, and more imaginative in its presentation of valour. *Ryan* is a straightforward narrative which goes hell for leather, while the often hallucinatory imagery and pacing of Malick's film is strictly arthouse. *Red Line* begins quietly, lyrically – with deserter Witt hiding out in a tropical paradise, where he and a colleague have 'gone native' – and builds in intensity with the attack on the island, before calming for the finale, as the troops (now augmented by replacements) embark on landing craft for their next mission. When the troops land on Guadalcanal, Malick's technique allows the horror of war to gradually permeate the film. As Charlie Company approach the front line, they pass gruesome dead and dying soldiers, while stretcher bearers wash bloody stretchers in a river. When they enter the killing ground of tall grassland which surrounds Hill 210, their enemy are seldom glimpsed and the unsettling atmosphere of the assault's build-up creates a crackling tension.

The Oscar-nominated Panavision cinematography by John Toll makes *Red Line* one of the most picturesque war films. This terrible battle rages in an ancient, primeval paradise, through the sun-dappled umbrella of tropical jungle or the rolling, beautiful hill country. Moments resemble a wildlife documentary, almost to the point of distraction, as Malick picks out colourful birds, owls, struggling fledglings, bats, crocodiles, snakes and other vivid flora and fauna. The film's artistry is enhanced by the eerie, mythical score, with original compositions by Hans Zimmer and additional cues, including 'Requiem in Paradisum' and Francesco Lupica's echoing 'Cosmic Beam Experience'. *The Thin Red Line* has been branded as simply a displaced Vietnam War film – the jungle atmosphere, the burning villages and the film's questioning tone are reminiscent of such works as *Apocalypse Now* and *Platoon*. But it is successful on its own terms, as a marvellous war film, filled with nuance, emotion, beauty and fleeting moments of genius.

Otto Preminger's *In Harm's War* (1965) was a sprawling Hollywood melodrama, in monochrome and Panavision, which was based on James Bassett's 1962 novel, *Harm's Way*. It begins on the eve of Pearl Harbor and depicts an implausible love pentagon. US naval commander Rockwell 'The Rock' Torrey (John Wayne) falls for nurse Maggie Haynes (Patricia Neal), who rooms with feisty young nurse Annalee Dohrn (Jill Haworth), who romances Commander Paul Eddington (Kirk Douglas), Torrey's friend and lieutenant, whilst being engaged to young naval Ensign Jeremiah, called 'Jere' (Brandon De Wilde), Torrey's estranged son. Most of the film is concerned with the resolution of this emotional spider's web on Hawaii. Eddington has lost his drunken, wayward wife Liz (Barbara Bouchet) when she's killed in a car accident during the attack on Pearl, following an adulterous skinny-dipping tryst with flyer Hugh O'Brian. Embittered Eddington later assaults Annalee when he discovers that she's engaged and she OD's on sleeping pills. During 'Operation Skyhook' (commanded by Rock), Eddington embarks on an aerial suicide mission to discover the Japanese strength during the US island-hopping campaign in August and September 1942 in the Solomon Islands.

Though the island's names have been changed for *In Harm's Way* (to Gavabutu and Levu-Vana, amongst others), this is the Guadalcanal campaign. Jere is posted to a PT boat – the US Navy's fast-moving torpedo launches – and is killed in the heroic action during the naval battle around the islands with the Japanese Task Force and the super-battleship *Yamato*. This confrontation is loosely based on the fighting around Savo Island, Santa Isabel, Cape Esperence and in Ironbottom Sound (so-called for the number of wrecks on the seabed). There's a scene featuring a broadcast by 'Tokyo Rose', the name given to the Japanese propaganda radio transmissions aimed at undermining US morale, which are depicted in many Pacific War films (for example, *MacArthur, Up Periscope* and *Flags of Our Fathers*). The supporting cast of star names included Dana Andrews as Admiral Broderick, George Kennedy as Paramarine commander Colonel Gregory, Franchot Tone as Admiral Kimmel and Henry Fonda as Admiral Nimitz (a role he would reprise in *Midway*). Others in the lengthy cast list include Bruce Cabot, Christopher George, Larry Hagman, Burgess Meredith, James Mitchum, Carroll O'Connor and Slim Pickens. Tom Tryon played brave naval captain Mac and Paula Prentiss was his worrisome wife, aircraft spotter Bev. Stanley Holloway had an unlikely cameo as Australian 'coast watch' and guide Clayton Canfil, and Patrick O'Neal was memorable as slimy press officer Owynn. The film's minimal use of stock footage and impressive production design worked in its favour. The naval engagement was staged with large-scale models and the film ends with Rock's ship going down as part of this heroic US victory. Rock has his leg amputated and Nimitz visits him on a hospital ship, before Rock begins his new life with Maggie. The film's soap opera elements anticipate the TV miniseries *The Winds of War*, as does Preminger's irritating technique of constantly fading to black, as though he's expecting TV adverts. At almost three hours this 'From Here to Eternity' does actually seem to last an eternity.

Robert Aldrich's *Too Late the Hero* (1970) relocated the cynicism of Aldrich's *The Dirty Dozen* to the Pacific War. In the spring of 1942, US naval code expert

Lieutenant Sam Lawson (Cliff Robertson) is seconded by his superior officer, Captain Nolan (Henry Fonda), to a British combat unit on the New Hebrides, south of the Solomon Islands. Able to speak Japanese, he joins a British commando raid on a ship-watch radio station. Lawson will send a fake radio report from the transmitter, allowing a US sea convoy to pass through the island's northern straits unscathed. The squad – led by Captain Hornsby (Denholm Elliott) and including tough cockney medical orderly Tosh Hearne (Michael Caine) – battle through the jungle and are whittled down in a series of encounters with Japanese patrols. When they reach the radio station the operation descends into a fiasco, Hornsby is killed and the radio transmitter destroyed. As they flee, the remains of the squad discover a Japanese airfield in the area and realise that they must make it back to base to inform the US convoy of the danger.

Too Late the Hero was co-written by Aldrich and Lukas Keller (from *Dirty Dozen*) and shot on location in the Philippines in 92 days, from January to June 1969, near Subic Bay naval base, at Los Banos (a resort south of Manila), in a rainforest nearby and in a mocked-up jungle on Stage 2 of Aldrich's own studio in Hollywood. At $6.25 million it was the biggest film ever shot in the Philippines and the Japanese airstrip featured eight authentic Zeroes. The bickering, volatile unit of jungle fighters resembles its equivalent in *The Long and the Short and the Tall* and the robust supporting cast included Ian Bannen, Harry Andrews, Lance Percival, Percy Herbert and Ronald Fraser. Though set in the New Hebrides, with all the Scottish accents on display it might as well be the Outer Hebrides. Caine is excellent in one of his most overlooked performances and the tension-filled film builds to a fine climax. With most of the squad killed or captured, Lawson and Tosh are pursued by the Japanese, whose commander, Major Yamaguchi (Ken Takakura), attempts to convince them to surrender, via mind game tannoy announcements which echo through the jungle. Arriving back at the jungle perimeter near their base, Lawson and Tosh find it patrolled by the Japanese. The exhausted duo manage to kill Yamaguchi and in the confusion they run the gauntlet, making a frantic, zigzagging dash across open country under heavy enemy fire to safety – a sprint which only one of them will survive. The film's alternative TV title was *Suicide Run* and it was a considerable, undeserving box office flop on its original release.

Fritz Lang's *American Guerrilla in the Philippines* (1950) cast Tyrone Power as Ensign Chuck Palmer, whose PT boat is sunk in the spring of 1942, so he takes refuge in the jungles of Leyte. There he makes contact with the local Filipino guerrillas and finds himself shanghaied into organising a resistance army against the occupying Japanese, eventually establishing the Provincial Government of Free Leyte. They are resupplied by US submarines and print their own money and newspaper, run cars on palm juice gasoline, make their own rifles and cannon, string barbed wire from trees to become telegraph wires and create radio observation posts, all the while avoiding Japanese patrols, naval activity and radio interceptions. Tom Ewell appeared as Palmer's PT shipmate Jim Mitchell and Jack Elam had a trademark cameo as an unscrupulous mercenary, who takes collections from the locals to buy arms he has no intention of purchasing. Palmer becomes involved with French plantation owner's widow Jeanne

Martinez (Micheline Prelle), who hides out with the Filipino patriots and wears full makeup throughout, even when she's washing her clothes on a rock in the river. Based on Ira Wolfert's 1945 book of the same name, the film is a tribute to the Filipino freedom fighters and benefited from beautiful location filming in the Philippines in saturated Technicolor. The film features several shots of Douglas MacArthur's promise 'I Shall Return' which was printed on cigarette packets (and was also the UK release title for the film). In the finale, MacArthur liberates Leyte, which was secured by Christmas Day, 1944.

Events in the Philippines were also depicted in *MacArthur* (1977), a biopic of the war hero, as played by Gregory Peck. It begins with General MacArthur's reluctant escape by PT boat from Corregidor in the Philippines to Australia in March 1942, at the express wishes of US president Roosevelt. There he organises his raw recruits and vows 'I shall return'. He masterminds the invasion of New Guinea, cutting off Japanese supply lines by bypassing and starving out strongholds, and by using air power to deploy his men. Radio broadcasts by Tokyo Rose warn the US troops: 'The jungle where we live is where you die'. US forces then land on Leyte Gulf on Luzon on 20 October 1944, to take back the Philippines. This is depicted with a combination of colour archive footage and recreations of the amphibious landings. Supreme Allied Commander MacArthur strides down the ramp of a landing craft, accompanied by the island's president and watched by journalists and cameramen, and gives a patriotic, rousing speech. He stands fearlessly in the battle's front line and is present at the liberation of Japanese internment camps, including those holding survivors from the Bataan Death March. The film's soft-focus cinematography makes the film resemble a flattering TV movie. Peck, wearing MacArthur's trademark sunglasses and conveying the general's resolute dignity, gives a fine portrayal of the publicity-loving commander, who harbours political ambitions. His courage under fire inspired his men and his tactical mastery won him many victories. MacArthur won the Congressional Medal of Honor, as his father had at Missionary Ridge during the American Civil War.

Guadalcanal is also the setting for Nicholas Ray's *Flying Leathernecks* (1951), which depicted the Marine Corps Wildcat fighter-bombers flying sorties from an under-fire island airfield during the campaign. Much of the story concerns a clash of the titans between Major Dan Kirby (John Wayne) and his subordinate Captain 'Griff' Griffin (Robert Ryan). Jay C. Flippen played roughish Sergeant Clancy on the ground. Having secured Guadalcanal by using the Wildcats as 'close air support' to Marine ground forces, the action shifts to the Battle for Okinawa in 1945. The film's impressive combat scenes, on land and in the air, are colour Korean War footage spliced with re-enactments.

As *Guadalcanal Diary* described it, island-hopping enabled the US Army to 'strike closer and closer to the heart of the Japanese octopus'. After Guadalcanal and nearby Tulagi, US forces continued with their stepping stone strategy, as island after island was wrestled from Japanese control over a protracted three-year period. The Aleutian Islands off Alaska fell on 16 August 1943, followed by amongst others: Tarawa Atoll in the Gilbert Islands (captured on 23 November 1943), the Marshall Islands (which fell in February 1944), Bougainville (captured in March 1944), Saipan (captured July 1944) and the Marianas, Tinian (August 1944) and Guam (August 1944, though the last Japanese surrendered there in 1960). During the US assault on Saipan, the Japanese defenders abandoned their usual tactic of defending the beaches and dug in with a defensive network of bunkers and tunnels inland – a tactic they later deployed in the defence of other islands. The Battle of the Philippine Sea defeated the Japanese naval air force in the Pacific in June 1944 and the Battle of Leyte Gulf in October 1944 finished off the navy. To clear the Philippines, US forces took Luzon and Corregidor (with the latter secured on 28 February 1945) then moved on to Mindanao. The last two island assaults were Iwo Jima (February-March 1945) and Okinawa (April-June 1945). Only 1,000 Japanese soldiers of 23,000 survived the Battle of Iwo Jima and an estimated 110,000 perished on Okinawa.

As the Japanese began to lose their grip on the Pacific, their master tactician Yamamoto was assassinated while on a tour of inspection. He was ambushed in Operation Vengeance on his way from Rabaul, whilst travelling in a lightly escorted bomber, by US planes on 18 April 1943 off Bougainville. As the campaign wore on, the Japanese commanders became increasingly desperate. Kamikaze fighter pilots (named after the 'divine wind', a storm which generations before had wrecked the Mongol invasion fleet) were the most deadly of the Japanese suicide squads. They flew their planes, which were loaded with explosive, headlong into US ships. Little could be done against such desperate measures. Kosako Yamashita's *Father of the Kamikaze* (1974) depicted the creation of the 'suicide airforce', by Naval Vice-Admiral Onishi (Koji Tsuruta). Under their Bushido credo of 'victory or death', foot soldiers mounted suicidal Banzai charges and fought to the death. For example, on Tarawa only 100 of the 4,700 Japanese defenders were taken prisoner. The Imperial Army told the civilian populations of islands such as Okinawa and Saipan that the US forces would rape and murder them, resulting in mass suicides. Chilling footage exists of these horrific suicides, as women throw their children from cliffs and then leap to their deaths. By the end of the campaign, the US forces were close enough to launch attacks on Japan itself.

One of the first Hollywood films to depict US Marine action in the Pacific was Roy Enright's *Gung Ho! The Story of Carlson's Makin Island Raid* (1943). The United States Marine Corps (USMC) were elite shock troops, the toughest of the tough who always got the dirtiest jobs – they were the navy's front-line assault troops, specialists in survival and killing. Randolph Scott starred as Colonel Thorwald, who trains and leads the newly formed Second Marine Raider Battalion in an attack on the Japanese stronghold on Makin Island in the Gilbert Islands, in August 1942. Thorwald was based on the leader of the raid, Lieutenant Colonel Evans F. Carlson, who served as one of the film's three technical advisors. Eight days out of Pearl Harbor in two submarines, the Marines invade Makin in rubber dinghies and set about ridding the island of Japanese troops and destroying their installations: oil tanks, supply depots, radio masts and aircraft. The film's title is inspired by the Raiders motto, 'Gung' (to work) and 'Ho' (in harmony), which Thorwald learned from his time fighting alongside the Chinese Army against the Japanese. On the way from their Californian training base, the Marines survey the wreckage of Pearl Harbor, motivation enough for these men who want to fight Fascism, who have lost brothers in the attack on Pearl or who 'just don't like Japs'. Among the Marines were Sam Levene and Rod Cameron. David Bruce and Noah Beery Jr quarrel over Grace McDonald in fortunately brief romantic subplot padding. Robert Mitchum scored in an early role as ex-boxer 'Pig-iron' Matthews and Harold Landon, as Brooklynite Frankie Montana, memorably sprinted through the jungle to knock out a machine gun nest with grenades.

For the first 50 minutes of the 87-minute film, *Gung Ho!* details the Marines' training and their journey to Makin, while the remainder of the story is non-stop action as the Marines take the island, then return to their submarines, their job done. The combat sees the Marines outnumbered 6–1, but they have been taught in their training 'always do the unexpected': for example, a traction engine steamroller is driven into a radio installation, destroying it, and the Marines paint a large 'Stars and Stripes' banner on a corrugated roof, resulting in Japanese aircraft bombing and machine-gunning their own men. The hand-to-hand action, fought with guns, bayonets and knives, is surprisingly graphic and bloody for a 1940s war film, though Scott delivers a predictable, rousing patriotic speech straight to camera at 'The End'.

Lewis Milestone's *Halls of Montezuma* (1950) follows B Company, the First Marine Battalion, which has fought on Guadalcanal and Tarawa. Six months after Tarawa, they embark on another assault and the film depicts in detail their operations taking an island from Japanese occupation. Richard Widmark starred as Lieutenant Carl Anderson and Richard Boone portrayed commander Lieutenant-Colonel Gilfillan, overseeing the operation. The film's supporting cast is a strong one, filled with familiar and soon-to-be familiar faces: Jack Palance (as soft-spoken ex-boxer Pidgeon Lane), Karl Malden (as pipe-smoking Corpsman 'Doc'), Jack Webb (as war correspondent Dickerman), Reginald Gardiner (as British intelligence officer, Sergeant Johnson), Robert Wagner, Skip Homier, Richard Hylton, Martin Milner, Bert Freed and Neville Brand. After they land, the marines are pinned down by sustained Japanese resistance and rocket fire. Anderson's mission is a race against time to locate the rocket launch sites before the US counterattack at H-hour. *Halls of Montezuma* was made with US Marine Corps cooperation and partially shot at Camp Pendleton Marine Base, California. The large-scale battle and amphibious landing scenes deploy authentic LVT2 and LVT4 (Landing Vehicle Tracked) amphibious landing craft, plus Sherman tanks as the marines' armoured support. The staged sequences were intercut with actual colour archive footage of beach landings and Shermans fitted with flamethrowers clearing Japanese defences. There's also a hymnal score by Sol Kaplan and vivid Technicolor cinematography by Winton C. Hoch and Harry Jackson. Widmark is excellent as traumatised ex-science teacher Anderson, who suffers 'psychological migraines' in combat. With no romantic subplots, this was a male-only drama that established Widmark as a war movie screen hero rival to John Wayne.

The American attack on Iwo Jima island is one of the most celebrated engagements in USMC history – and its most costly. Iwo Jima had three airfields (two completed and one under construction) and was vital to the US campaign. The island, five-and-a-half miles long and two-and-a-half miles wide, was dominated at the southern tip by a dead volcano, Mount Suribachi, which was defended by heavy artillery. On 19 February 1945, the US 5th Amphibious Corps landed on the beach at the southern sector of the island, below Mount Suribachi. 23,000 Japanese soldiers were entrenched on the highly fortified island, in a sophisticated system of concrete pillboxes, foxholes and earthworks, while the island was riddled with an underground network of tunnels. To the Japanese it was sacred ground, their home soil, and they would defend it to the last man. The first US amphibious wave was able to land, but was then caught in a firestorm crossfire, as the Japanese opened up. By the end of the first day 30,000 US troops had landed and the engagement became a merciless pitched battle, as the Marines prised the Japanese from their positions. The battle raged until 26 March as the Marines pushed northward across the island. The last Japanese resistance capitulated near Kitano Point in the north and the US lost almost 7,000 men.

On 23 February at 10.20, am, five days into the operation, the Marines captured Mount Suribachi. Men of the 2nd Battalion, 28th Regiment of the 5th Marine Division raised the US flag, 'Old Glory', atop the mountain and the moment was captured by photographer Joe Rosenthal. This image, of six men struggling to erect the flagpole, became to Americans an iconic portrait of fortitude, patriotism and victory.

Sands of Iwo Jima (1949) was Allan Dwan's famed saga of and tribute to the USMC. John Wayne was cast as Marine Sergeant John M. Stryker. Beginning shortly after Guadalcanal, Stryker whips his squad into shape with an unforgiving training regime: 'I'm gonna ride you 'til you can't stand up, but when you do stand up, you're gonna be Marines'. His squad includes Pete Conway (John Agar), Al Thomas (Forrest Tucker), Benny Regazzi (Wally Cassell), Charlie Bass (James Brown), Soames (James Holden), Shipley (Richard Webb) and Corporal Robert Dunne (Arthur Franz), who also acts as the story's narrator. Richard Jaeckel and William Murphy played the quarrelsome, brawling Flynn brothers. Following their training in New Zealand (via a montage of Marines exercising and Stryker barking orders), they are shipped out to fight, firstly on Tarawa and then on Iwo Jima.

Sands of Iwo Jima was released by Republic Pictures, where Wayne made many films, and was shot mainly in California. Wayne's tough-as-boot-leather sergeant is an archetypal performance from the actor. As in Wayne's westerns he plays a drinker and a brawler and there are few problems Stryker can't solve with his fists. When Thomas, a boxer who has faced Stryker in the ring, causes the death of two Marines in combat through negligence, Stryker risks a court martial when he beats Thomas up. Stryker's courage under fire is immense, an example to his squad – Wayne didn't serve in the armed forces during the war, unlike many of his contemporaries, and was at pains to reinforce his heroism onscreen. Stryker tells his men to 'saddle up!' (move out) and also uses the phrase 'lock and load' at several points in the film. *Sands* depicts both the Marines in action and their romances and personal quarrels whilst on leave. The troops let off steam in Honolulu and Stryker romances Mary (Julie Bishop), a woman who has become a prostitute to support her infant son. Such scenes show a softer side to Wayne's screen persona, as he kind-heartedly gives Mary some money. By contrast, during the assault of Tarawa, Stryker ignores a dying comrade's cries, rather than give the Marine's defensive position away to the enemy.

Sands of Iwo Jima closely resembles Wayne's cavalry and Indians westerns with John Ford – such as *Fort Apache* (1948) and *She Wore a Yellow Ribbon* (1949) – both of which also starred Agar as the young romantic lead. These films depicted army life as one of contrasts, between calm, often boring, domesticity and the heat of battle. In *Sands*, Pete Conway falls in love at first sight with Allison Bromley (Adele Mara) and marries her. Their sappy romance is the film's major failing, as Mara is no Shirley Temple or Joanne Dru (Agar's love interest in the westerns). When they first meet, Pete and Allison dance cheek to cheek and exchange facile dialogue: 'Pete's my name, Pete Conway'; 'Allison', she replies; 'Hello Allison', 'Hello Pete'. When Pete tells Allison that they're going to make the most of their brief time together ('We'll make it seem a long time'), they certainly succeed.

Fortunately *Sands of Iwo Jima* also has plenty of combat. Dwan deploys extensive archive footage, but rarely has such footage been so seamlessly woven into a film, making *Sands* one of the finest depictions of Pacific War combat. The US force's tactics – naval barrage and bombing by the 'fly fly boys', followed by amphibious landings – is recreated. For the landing at Tarawa, the Marines arrive on shore in landing craft and in LVT 2 landing vehicles, which were tracked, hulled armoured personnel carriers. The combat, amid the battered vegetation of ravaged palm trees, their leaves hanging limp like flags on a windless day, is convincingly savage. A Japanese bunker which pins Stryker's squad to the Tarawa beach is dealt with by a flamethrower and Stryker's heroics with a satchel charge.

US Marines Pete Conway (John Agar) and Sergeant John Stryker (John Wayne) dig in amid the *Sands of Iwo Jima* (1949). Courtesy Kevin Wilkinson Collection.

After their part in the taking of Tarawa, the squad return to Hawaii to recuperate, retrain and have their depleted numbers swelled with raw recruits. Now it is Stryker's men who are the hardened vets, teaching the rookies the ropes. In most of these Hollywood Pacific War films, the Japanese soldiers are referred to as 'Japs', 'Nips' and at one point in *Sands* Stryker calls them: 'Those little lemon-coloured characters'. Soldiers may have used such insults and jingoistic, xenophobic language was commonplace in war films of the time, but today it's offensively racist. The US troops' hatred of their enemy was fuelled by Japan's terrible treatment of captured Allied soldiers, a result of it not being a signatory of the Geneva Convention.

The melodrama, romance and chit-chat are really only a lead-in to the main event – the Marines' attack on heavily fortified Iwo Jima. The assault is a combination of archive and staged footage, with the Marines storming up the beach and Sherman flamethrower tanks spitting plumes of fire. The real explosions, drifting smoke and scores of extras make this superior to later, computer generated depictions of the battle. In the shock ending, as the summit of Mount Suribachi is secured, Stryker is killed by a sniper, moments after noting, 'I never felt so good in my life'. In his long career, Wayne died only five times onscreen – in three westerns (*The Alamo*, *The Cowboys* and *The Shootist*), *The Fighting Seabees* and here. *Sands of Iwo Jima*'s poster announced: 'A great human story makes a mighty motion picture' and it was a mighty success at the box office, with Wayne voted the most popular actor of the year in screen polls. Also available in a computer colourised version, *Sands* has been shown by the USMC to new recruits and with *The Quiet Man* remains Wayne's most popular non-western film. It was for his performance as Stryker that he received the first of two Best Actor Oscar Nominations.

At the climax of *Sands of Iwo Jima*, three of the famous flag-bearers appeared in cameos – they are among the squad Stryker hands the standard to before the raising scene, which was recreated in the film. They were Rene A. Gagnon, Ira Hamilton Hayes and John H. 'Doc' Bradley. The title sequence of *Sands* includes the historic note: 'The first American flag was raised on Mt Suribachi by the late Sgt Ernest I. Thomas Jr USMC on the morning of Feb 23, 1945'. Why would the film need to clarify this? The answer can be found in director Clint Eastwood's *Flags of Our Fathers* (2006), which was based on a book of the same name by James Bradley and Ron Powers, published in 2000. Bradley was the son of 'Doc' Bradley and the film exposes the bizarre story behind Rosenthal's famous photograph.

Flags of Our Fathers follows the three survivors – navy corpsman (medic) 'Doc' Bradley (Ryan Phillippe), Rene Gagnon (Jesse Bradford) and Ira Haynes (Adam Beach) – from their ordeal fighting on the sands of Iwo Jima, to their exploitation as war heroes back in the US by Bud Gerber (John Slattery), who recruits them for a publicity tour advertising War Bonds. It later transpires that Gagnon has misidentified one of the dead flag-raisers in Rosenthal's photograph and that the picture is actually of a second, staged flag-raising. Though Gagnon and Bradley think their efforts will help their comrades at war, Native American Haynes is deeply troubled by their exploitation. His story is the saddest, as

The historical flag-raising by US troops on Mount Suribachi, Iwo Jima, on the morning of Feb 23, 1945, as recreated in Allan Dwan's *Sands of Iwo Jima* (1949). Courtesy Kevin Wilkinson Collection.

haunted by guilt he died an alcoholic. *The Outsider* (1961) is a biopic of Hayes, with Tony Curtis as the Pima Indian.

As Iwo Jima is a vast war grave and access is limited, Eastwood shot little footage there. He filmed the publicity tour in Illinois, Los Angeles, Chicago and Texas, and the battle scenes on the coast of Iceland, as the black Icelandic sand was a good match for Iwo Jima's ashen beaches. *SS Lane Victory* appeared as a cargo troop ship deployed in the invasion. Barry Pepper (from *Saving Private Ryan*) played platoon sergeant Strank and Jaime Bell (from *Billy Elliot*) was 'Iggy' Ignatowski, one of Strank's men, who is pulled beneath the sand by the Japanese into the bowels of the island and tortured. For the present day scenes of the Iwo Jima veterans, elderly John Bradley was played by George Grizzard. Much of the battle footage was created using special effects, which creates epic-scale depictions of the engagement. As in *Sands of Iwo Jima*, you'll be rooting for the Marines as they slowly oust their enemies with grenades and flamethrowers. The initial ambush on Iwo Jima beach is the film's best sequence: the Marines disembark from landing craft and proceed unopposed up the beach, until the Japanese spring their trap and the Marines are pinned down, dismembered and filleted in the ebbing tide. The film was rated 'R' in the US for 'graphic war violence and carnage'. Posters depicting the flag-raising ran with the tagline: 'A single shot can end the war'.

War Bonds were a vital part of the American war effort and earned $49 billion (a sixth of the war's cost to the US). Many wartime Hollywood films included an end title card prompting: 'For Victory – US War Bonds and Stamps – Buy Yours in This Theatre'. Movie stars made guest appearances on hullabaloo tours – Dorothy Lamour was reckoned to have been responsible for selling $350 million worth of bonds, while Clark Gable's wife Carole Lombard was killed in a plane crash in January 1942, on her way back to California following a Midwestern bond tour. The fundraising in *Flags* demonstrates how the 'Heroes of Iwo Jima' were used for political ends back in the US, and how it affected the heroes' lives. Rosenthal's photograph catches the public's imagination, the celebrities are mobbed wherever they go and the publicity tour sees them paraded before the populace as heroic examples to all. Unscrupulous Gerber has them mouth platitudes: 'The real heroes are dead on that island and we'd appreciate it if you bought bonds in honour of them'. At Chicago's Soldier Field stadium, Gerber stages a re-enactment of the triumphant climb, with the three heroes scaling a papier-mâché replica of Suribachi. The film ends with a reflection on heroism: 'Maybe there's no such thing as heroes', says the voiceover, 'They may have fought for their country, but they died for their friends'. The real heroes are the men who died on Iwo Jima, to whom the monument seen at the end of the film is dedicated.

In an interesting venture, Eastwood also made *Letters from Iwo Jima* (2006), which told the battle from the Japanese perspective. It was based on *Picture Letters from Commander in Chief* by Tadamichi Kuribayashi, the general in command of Japanese forces on the island, which was adapted into a screenplay with the working title 'Red Sun, Black Sand'. Most of the navy's Combined Fleet has been destroyed in battle off the Marianas, while the air force has been recalled to protect the Japanese mainland. When he realises there will be no reinforcements, Imperial commander General Kuribayashi (Ken Watanabe) fortifies Mount Suribachi: 'If our children can live safely for one more day, it would be worth one more day that we defend this island'. Within five days of the USMC assault, Suribachi is lost. Young soldier Saigo (Kazunari Ninomiya) and his squad are ordered to commit suicide, but Saigo doesn't. He scrambles across the island to Kuribayashi's HQ, witnessing many horrors en route. The Imperial forces have run out of food, water and ammunition, and live on earthworms. Kuribayashi instructs Saigo to burn all documentation in the HQ, but Saigo buries many of the records instead, including letters from Kuribayashi to his wife in Japan. Years later, these letters from Iwo Jima are discovered by archaeologists and reveal the true story of the battle.

Letters from Iwo Jima was mainly filmed in California, with some brief shots actually on Iwo Jima. Battle and invasion fleet footage from *Flags* reappears in *Letters* – now presented from the Japanese perspective. *Letters* was filmed completely in Japanese, with Japanese actors in all the principal roles. Its washed-out photography provides an authentic, almost newsreel look, recalling the Japanese war trilogy *The Human Condition* (1959–61). Consisting of *The Human Condition I: No Greater Love, The Human Condition II: Road to Eternity* (both 1959) and *The Human Condition III: A Soldier's Prayer* (1961), it starred Tatsuya Nakadai as Kaji the Idealist, a soldier and conscientious objector, who witnesses dreadful horrors as he struggles through wartime.

Letters demonstrated the Japanese Army's suicidal defence of their homeland, where surrender is not an option. Japanese commanders lead suicidal 'Banzai' charges or order their men to kill themselves (by grenade, sword or bullet) to find their 'place at the Yasukuni Shrine'. 'I'll see you there', says one officer, before blowing his brains out. In *Letters* we see Japanese soldiers bayoneting a helpless US Marine and a Marine shoots dead two Japanese soldiers who've surrendered, because he can't be bothered capturing them. When a Japanese patrol discovers the bodies, one still clutching a white flag, it reinforces their preconceptions of the US troops. Japanese soldiers are instructed to identify and kill US troops wearing red crosses, the insignia of medics. Japanese soldiers are burned alive in the rabbit warren of tunnels as the Marines' flamethrowers dispense liquid fire. In a shocking scene, Japanese soldiers kill themselves on Suribachi with grenades, as human beings are reduced to bloody carcasses before our eyes. Kuribayashi's tank commander is Baron Nishi (Tsuyoshi Ihara), a lieutenant colonel and former equestrian gold medallist at the 1931 Los Angeles Olympics, whose prized stallion Jupiter is killed in an American air raid. Nishi is later blinded by a US shell blast and dies alone in the caves, killing himself by pulling the trigger of his rifle with his toe. In this way the Japanese perspective of the battle is depicted, as *Flag of Our Fathers*' flipside. *Flags* is the most accessible film of the two for general audiences and was the most successful at the box office, while *Letters* is the better film.

Tim Burstall's Australian-Taiwanese co-production *Attack Force Z* (1980) depicted commandos on a rescue mission in January 1945 to save Imoguchi (Wang Yu), a defecting Japanese war minister, whose plane has crashed on the Japanese-occupied Chinese island of Sembalong. A five-man team of 'Z Men', from the Australian army's Z Special Force, is dispatched to rescue him. The squad included John Phillip Law, Sam Neill and Mel Gibson, who team up with the Chinese resistance, led by Lin Chan-Lang (Koo Chuna Hsiung). This action-packed film is small-scale, but effective and very violent, with few protagonists surviving the final shootout. It has added cult value today for the appearances of pre-stardom Neill and Gibson.

Other Pacific War movies include Phil Carlson's *Hell to Eternity* (1960), Monte Hellman's *Back Door to Hell* (1964 – starring a young Jack Nicholson) and director-star Cornel Wilde's *Beach Red* (1967). Steven Spielberg and Tom Hanks produced a follow-up to *Band of Brothers*, the ten-part HBO miniseries *The Pacific* (2010), which was shot on location in Australia. It followed various US soldiers from enlistment to combat, as they fight for 'tiny specks of turf that we have never heard of' dotted across the Pacific Ocean. The action proper begins in August 1942, with the assault on Guadalcanal, as the USMC land and meet no opposition, only to run headlong into savage Japanese assaults in the jungle. The well-told human story of the conflict is enacted by a capable cast including Joseph Mazzello, James Badge Dale and Jon Seda as the principle characters. It features several battles from the campaign, such as Peleliu, Iwo Jima and Okinawa, and is beautifully written and paced. The firefights, ambushes and amphibious landings are probably the most realistic Pacific War combat scenes ever recreated, highlighted by the never-gratuitous deployment of blood and gore, and a great stereo sound mix of gunfire and explosions.

Raoul Walsh's *Battle Cry* (1955), based on Leon M Uris' 1953 novel of the same name, starred Van Heflin as US Marine Corps battalion commander Major Sam Huxley, whose men are involved in the battles for Guadalcanal, Tarawa and finally the assault on Saipan, in June 1944. It was a familiar tale of training, romance and combat, filmed in colour and CinemaScope with the cooperation of the USMC, which provided hundreds of troops and many vehicles, so the battle scenes look tremendous. The amphibious assault and attack footage were staged on Veiques, an island near Puerto Rico. Other sequences were shot at Camp Pendleton Marine Base, California and in San Diego. The amphibious assault deploys many tracked LVT 2s and DD (Duplex Drive) amphibious Shermans, while the Japanese tanks are disguised US Shermans. Gregory Walcott played the boot camp's drill sergeant and the squad included sergeant James Whitmore, argumentative Perry Lopez, bookworm John Lupton, lumberjack Aldo Ray, guitar-strumming Texan Fess Parker and street hoodlum William Campbell. Tab Hunter played a naive soldier who is torn between his girl back home (Mona Freeman) and adulterous Mrs Yarborough (Dorothy Malone). The film's fashions are more 1950s than 1940s, and the battle footage closely resembles the Korean War. L.Q. Jones appeared in his film debut under his real name Justus E. McQueen. He played a character – the company's joker – called 'L.Q Jones', which he then took as his stage name.

PT 109 (1963), starring Ty Hardin and Robert Culp, told the story of the title torpedo boat, which boasted future US president John F Kennedy (Cliff Robertson) as its commander. John Ford directed *Mister Roberts* (1955) an adaptation of the hit play, with Henry Fonda recreating his stage role as Lieutenant Doug Roberts. Jack Lemmon played Ensign Frank Thurlowe Pulver (and won a Best Supporting Actor Oscar) and James Cagney was the tyrannical captain of the *USS Reluctant*. Ford and Fonda fell out over Ford's liberal interpretation of the material. Their disagreements ended when they came to blows on location on Midway. Thereafter Ford began to drink and was eventually rushed to hospital to have his gallbladder removed. The film was finished by Mervyn LeRoy and Joshua Logan (the director of the stage version) and its success spawned a sequel *Ensign Pulver* (1964), also directed by Logan. Following *Mister Roberts* Fonda and Ford, once a powerhouse creative partnership, never again worked together.

With its wacky title, big band jazz theme tune and a cast featuring comedian Jack Lemmon and pop singer Ricky Nelson, *The Wackiest Ship in the Army* (1960) would appear to be a slapstick farce. That's certainly how it begins, as in February 1943 Lieutenant Rip Crandall (Lemmon) at Allied HQ, Brisbane, is assigned his first command, a run-down, decrepit scow sailing ship, the *USS Echo*, that's to be taken to New Guinea. Crandall whips the clueless crew into shape to complete a top secret mission. They pass the scow off as a native fishing vessel and drop Australian lookout Patterson (Chips Rafferty) on a Japanese-held island. In the process they spot an enemy convoy, are captured by the Japanese and Crandall is wounded, but they manage to escape, getting a message through to HQ. The convoy is destroyed by US aerial attack, which is based on the Battle of the Bismarck Sea in March 1943. Nelson played Crandall's second in command, Ensign Tommy Hanson and crooned a pop song, 'Do you Know what it Means to miss New Orleans?' *The Wackiest Ship in the Army* was also the model for a short-lived TV series in 1965.

Lloyd Bacon's exciting *The Frog Men* (1951) offered an interesting viewpoint of the Pacific War. Richard Widmark starred as John Lawrence, who is put in command of Underwater Demolition Team (UDT) #4. The fearless frogmen of the UDT carried out sabotage and diversionary actions against the enemy. The film is set post–Iwo Jima – the UDT team's previous commander has been killed during that battle. In preparation for an amphibious assault on an island, the UDT team swim in close to the shore under cover of smoke and artillery fire, to reconnoitre and destroy 'hedgehogs' (jagged metal girders set in concrete designed to rip the bottom out of landing craft). Later they are posted to a submarine and sent on a dangerous mission to blow up a Japanese submarine pen in an island harbour. Eventually, Lawrence earns the respect of his men, who throughout the film have been unwilling to adopt his strictly by-the-book methods. Lawrence's chief adversary is Jake Flanagan (Dana Andrews) with others members of the UDT played by Jeffrey Hunter and Harvey Lembeck. The frogmen, in flippers and goggles, leap from the back of their launch into a dingy in tow at high speed and flop into the sea to swim inshore. Having laid explosives and carried out their sabotage missions, they are then picked up in similar fashion by the launch. Widmark is good as always – he must rank as one of the most consistent actors of all time – and the underwater and action scenes are excellently staged, the fast pace leaving little time for chat. In perhaps the film's greatest scene, a dud Japanese torpedo hits the UDT's transport ship and lodges in the hull. As the sickbay floods, calm Lawrence disarms the warhead with a screwdriver.

Frank Sinatra directed and starred in *None But the Brave* (1965), a Pacific-set war movie shot on Kauai, Hawaii. His only crack at directing, Sinatra also produced it for Sinatra Enterprises, in a co-production deal with Tokyo Eiga Co Ltd and Toho Film, Japan. On an unnamed island in the Pacific Ocean, a Japanese garrison are cut off from the world, forgotten by the war. The outpost's idyll is interrupted by the arrival of a crashed US transporter plane carrying US Marine replacements. The two enemies initially quarrel, but negotiate an uneasy truce, which is soon broken when the Americans manage to repair their radio and are able to contact the US navy. As a relief ship approaches, the two factions fight it out – the Americans emerge, decimated but victorious, while the Japanese are wiped out and the film ends with the reminder: 'Nobody Ever Wins'. *None But the Brave* boasts a fine Anglo-Japanese cast: Sinatra played US corpsman Francis, towering Clint Walker was pilot Captain Dennis Bourke, who assumes command of the US contingent, Marine lieutenant Blair was played by Sinatra's then-son-in-law, singer Tommy Sands, and Brad Dexter was Marine sergeant Bleeker. Dexter saved Sinatra from drowning off Kauai in May 1964, during the making of this film, when Sinatra was pulled out to sea by a riptide. Tatsuya Mihashi (who later appeared in *Tora! Tora! Tora!* and Woody Allen's Japanese spy spoof *What's Up, Tiger Lily?* [1966]) played the Japanese garrison commander Lieutenant Kuroki. Takeshi Kato was antagonistic Sergeant Tamura and Homare Suguro played suicidal Lance Corporal Hirano. The film looks tremendous in Technicolor and Panavision, the special effects (particularly an aerial dogfight and a tidal wave) are convincing, and John Williams supplied the fine score, but the odd mixture of acting styles, and the tragicomic tone don't quite gel.

The most unusual of the Pacific War films sounded like a piece of 'gung ho!' action, but was a different kind of war drama which owed something to *None But the Brave.* In John Boorman's allegorical *Hell in the Pacific* (1968) a US flier (Lee Marvin) is marooned on an idyllic Pacific island, which is also the refuge of a Japanese soldier (Toshirô Mifune). With no guns, the adversaries prowl around one another, bringing their primitive enactment of the war to this tropical paradise. Both actors – the only performers in the entire film – are powerful screen personalities and great physical actors, perfect for a story told with little dialogue that required moments of mime, broad comedy, pathos and action. They quarrel pettily over Mifune's scant water supply, until it rains and they find something else to fight about. Mifune captures and imprisons Marvin, then the roles are reversed, but Marvin can't cook and has to release Mifune to survive. Eventually they call a truce and agree to build a raft. After an arduous voyage they hit land, where they find the ruins of war, but no people. Images of dead Japanese soldiers in an abandoned copy of *Life* magazine remind Mifune that they are only temporary allies: the two quarrel once more and go their separate ways. This is the ending shown in widescreen on UK BBC2 in the 1980s. The more widely released alternative ending – where the ruined house the two men are sheltering is flattened by a stray artillery shell, killing both protagonists – is truly awful. Lalo Schifrin's ultra-weird atonal score is an ideal musical commentary to this unique cinema experience, which was artfully shot in Panavision and Technicolor on location in the Palau Islands by Conrad Hall. In the film's most memorable scene, Marvin attempts to convince his yoked captive Mifune to fetch a stick like a dog, but ends up repeatedly retrieving it himself.

On April Fool's Day 1945, US forces invaded Okinawa. In contrast to Iwo Jima, this time they were allowed to land unopposed and were drawn into a protracted land battle. The US forces first cleared the north of the island, then the south, as the Japanese manned the Shuri Line defences. Lieutenant General Buckner, the US invasion commander, was killed by shrapnel during the muddy, vicious encounter. Kamikaze plane attacks took a terrible toll on the US navy, while the *Yamato* was sacrificed in a last-ditch action: it was sunk by US aircraft having steamed into action with only enough fuel for a one-way trip. The island was finally taken on 22 June 1945, with the US having lost 12,000 men in the assault. The Kamikaze attacks featured in *Okinawa* (1952), which depicted destroyer *USS Blake*, commanded by Pat O'Brien. The battle for the island was also depicted in Kihachi Okamoto's Japanese epic *Battle of Okinawa* (1971), starring Tatsuya Nakadai and Tetsuro Tamba. The securing of Okinawa was the last US operation in the Pacific. Their next target was Japan itself, with the invasion planned for November 1945, but one final twist to this campaign loomed in the rising sun.

Chapter 18

THE ARDENNES OFFENSIVE (1944–45)

Despite their Market Garden setback in Europe, the Allies were approaching the German border by the autumn of 1944. When Antwerp fell on 4 September, they finally had a port large enough to resupply their ground forces. But the Germans still occupied the approaches to the port on both sides of the Scheldt estuary and it took a hard-fought campaign by Montgomery's British-Canadian forces (the British 21st Army Group) and commandos to secure it. The Canadians bottled up German forces on the mainland in the Breskens Pocket, which was taken on 2 November. Having fought through the South and North Beveland Peninsulas, Walcheren Island in the middle of the estuary fell on 8 November, but the estuary waters were not operational until 26 November, when all mines were cleared by minesweepers.

Omar Bradley's US 12th Army Group meanwhile was pushing through France and Belgium towards the German border. Germany's frontier was marked by the formidable Siegfried Line, Hitler's 'West Wall'. The US 1st Army under Lieutenant-General Hodges was making for the Ruhr, Germany's industrial heartland, while Lieutenant-General Patton's 3rd Army attacked the fortress at Metz, which lay in the path of an advance into the Saar, Germany's second biggest industrial centre. Patton met stiff opposition, but eventually took Metz on 22 November and prepared to make a push for the Saar and its chief city, Saarbrücken. On 21 October Hodges captured the city of Aachen, over the German border. Now the German army was defending its own soil, the Fatherland. The Battle of the Hürtgen Forest beyond Aachen in December was costly for the Allies. Samuel Fuller's *The Big Red One* (1980) featured a sequence depicting the battle for Hürtgen (filmed in Ireland), which cost the US 1st Army 34,000 casualties.

Don Siegel's gritty, black-and-white *Hell Is for Heroes* (1962) featured US soldiers fighting on the French-German border in late 1944. GIs led by Sergeant Pike (Fess Parker, TV's Davy Crockett) are ordered to defend a stretch of the

Siegfried Line, here represented by rows of distinctive 'Dragon's Teeth' anti-tank defences (filmed in soaring temperatures in Cottonwood, Northern California). Their section is undermanned and under attack, so the squad attempt to appear more numerous to their German attackers. Mechanic Henshaw (James Coburn) rigs a jeep to sound like a tank, by causing it to backfire and by wrapping chains around the wheels. When they discover their defences are bugged, the GIs send bogus telephone messages to HQ, enabling guest star comic relief Bob Newhart (as supplies officer Private Driscoll) to perform a humorous but out-of-place spoof telephone routine. The interesting cast included singer Bobby Darin, L.Q. Jones, Siegel favourite Harry Guardino and a sullen, indolent Steve McQueen as embittered Reese: his heroic act at the film's close, during an assault on a German pillbox, sees him blow up the fortification (and himself) with a satchel charge. Much of the film resembles a made-for-TV movie – the story was written by Robert Pirosh, who soon afterwards created the war TV series *Combat!* (1962–67), which starred Rick Jason and Vic Morrow as GIs fighting through post-D-Day France.

Following the Battle of Hürtgen Forest, many US troops were sent to the 'Ghost Front' – so-called because nothing happened there – in the Ardennes region. It was here that the Germans had launched their initial Blitzkrieg in 1940. In the fall of 1944, Hitler planned one last attack, which he hoped would punch a hole in the thinly spread advancing Allied lines and drive through Luxembourg and Belgium to the port of Antwerp. This would split the US forces. Hitler mustered his forces in secret in the Eifel Mountains. The attack, originally codenamed 'Wacht am Rhein' (Watch on the Rhine) but renamed 'Herbstnebel' (Autumn Mist), came through the forested, snowy Ardennes region and struck an overstretched point in the Allies' line – the 'Ghost Front' of the US 8th Corps. The assault began at dawn on 16 December, when bad weather and cloud cover meant that the Allies couldn't make their air superiority count. Eight German Panzer divisions of Army Group B, including Waffen SS troops, burst across the German border into Luxembourg in the south and Belgium to the north, along an 85-mile front.

The concentrated attack took the Americans by surprise and they were soon driven back. This offensive formed a 'bulge' in the US lines, hence the engagement's name: the Battle of the Bulge. The Americans managed to slow the German advance and the main US command centres and road junctions in the towns of St-Vith and Bastogne held out, though the defenders of St-Vith were forced to withdraw on 22 December. The defenders of Bastogne, the 101st Airborne Division, endured a terrible siege but when offered the chance to surrender, their commander General McAuliffe famously replied 'Nuts!' Bastogne was named by its defenders 'Bastion of the Battered Bastards of the 101st'. All delays to the German attack were vital, as they only had finite resources. The Germans' top priority was capturing fuel dumps to refill their tanks – this Blitzkrieg was Antwerp or bust. In the north, the US 1st Army and in the south the US 3rd contained the German advance. When the weather broke, the Allies were able to deploy air cover and Patton's men relieved Bastogne on 26 December. The Germans mounted a final spearhead towards Dinant on the River Meuse but the II Panzer Division were halted four miles short of the river in a tank battle near Celles by the US 2nd Armoured Division on 25–26 December 1944. A US counterattack was launched and by 4 January 1945 the Germans were repulsed. US forces from the north and south met at Houffalize, north of Bastogne on 16 January, and by 18 January the front line was east of Bastogne. By the end of the month the battle was over and the Allies had smoothed the bulge. The Germans were forced back across their own border, first to the Siegfried Line and then to the natural defence of the River Rhine.

The Battle of the Ardennes was a potential fiasco that became a resounding triumph for the US, as they snatched victory from the jaws of defeat. It was the US troops on this 'Ghost Front', many of whom were green recruits or battle-weary veterans in need of recuperation, who fought so valiantly. As such it has been popular with Hollywood filmmakers, as it was primarily a US-versus-German operation. Interestingly, producer-director Robert Aldrich chose this moment in US history as the backdrop to one of the most cynically anti-militarist films ever made. *Attack* (1956 – sometimes billed as *Attack!*) begins during the Battle of Aachen, with Lieutenant Joe Costa (Jack Palance) leading US Fox Company to attack a German pillbox. His commanding officer, Captain Erskine Cooney (Eddie Albert) fails to give his attack proper support, causing the deaths of 19 of Costa's platoon including Sergeant Ingersol (Strother Martin). After the battle, while holed up in a town in Belgium to recuperate, Costa and Lieutenant Harry Woodruff (William Smithers) try to have Cooney removed from command, but Colonel Clyde Bartlett (Lee Marvin) refuses. Bartlett harbours political ambitions and Cooney's father, a judge, can help him. Bartlett knows Cooney is a liability, but Cooney craves a medal to finally prove his worth to his father. Costa hates 'gutless wonder' Cooney and is a proper soldier, one who cares for his men and despises freeloaders and cowards. Bartlett assures Fox Company that they'll never see combat again as the war is almost won, but the Germans' Ardennes offensive thrusts Fox Company back into the frontline. They are ordered to take and hold the nearby village of Lanelle. The badly planned attack is aborted when the town is found to be crawling with SS and tanks. Costa and four men make it to a ruined house on the outskirts of town. The Germans counterattack, Cooney panics and doesn't send support to relieve them and Costa vows to avenge his decimated company, assuring Cooney by radio: 'I'm comin' back ...'

Attack is one of the realistic portrayals of World War II combat and also one of the most controversial. It is based on the play *Fragile Fox* by Norman Brooks; working titles for the project included *The Fragile Fox* and *Command Attack*. The US Defence Department refused to co-operate with Aldrich, as the film presents certain (fictitious) members of the US Army in a wholly inglorious light. Despite a budget of only $810,000 and no help from the US Army, *Attack* proved popular, taking $2 million when it was released by United Artists. The army's lack of cooperation can be seen in the German Panzers on display, which are a figment of the production designer's imagination. Action was lensed on the Albertson Ranch in California and on the European Village set at Universal City, with the streets littered with fallen masonry and army ordnance. Regular Aldrich collaborators Joseph Biroc provided the grainy, stylised monochrome cinematography and Frank DeVol the hymnal score. As with all Aldrich's films, the supporting cast is strong and well chosen. Peter Van Eyck played an SS captain captured by Costa in a cellar near Lanelle (Costa pushes him outside and the captain is shot by his own men) and Steven Geray was the captain's subordinate Otto (who is taken back to HQ for questioning by G2 intelligence). Among Costa's squad were Buddy Ebsen (later Jed Clampett in TV's *The Beverly Hillbillies*) as marksman Sergeant Tolliver, Robert Strauss (from *Stalag 17*) as wisecracking comic relief Private Bernstein, Jimmy Goodwin as Private Ricks and Richard Jaeckel as Private Snowdon.

Road signs at a crossroads intersection for Spa, Verviers, Limbourg and Malmédy indicate that *Attack* is set in the northern sector of the Battle of the Bulge. Having overrun Lanelle, the Germans attack the US HQ nearby. The town is an important crossroads and Cooney is ordered by Bartlett to hold it at all costs until the 10th Army Task Force arrives. Drunk and hysterical, Cooney isn't fit for duty and Woodruff assumes command. The GIs hold the town, but Costa and Cooney are both killed. Albert and Palance make feral adversaries. Albert's spoiled brat, a snivelling, psychotic, drunken little coward, lives long in the memory, while Palance is perfectly cast as the cynical realist who is transformed into a primal avenger. The scene when limping Costa takes on two Panzers with a bazooka amid a ruined town ends with the second tank running over Costa's left arm and pinning him to the ground. Demonic Costa, his arm smashed, confronts Cooney but dies before he can exact revenge. Woodruff shoots Cooney and other members of Fox Company also pump bullets into his corpse, so that blame can't be apportioned for his death: they know a court martial would favour Cooney and 'railroad' Woodruff. Bartlett promotes Woodruff to captain and reports will indicate Cooney died a hero's death – this 'hero' will get his Distinguished Service Cross. But Woodruff refuses to become another of Bartlett's pawns and the final scene sees him making a call to General Parsons at Divisional HQ, to tell the real story of the battle.

Ken Annakin's *Battle of the Bulge* – released by Warner Bros in 1965 but one of the commercial hits of 1966 – gave the engagement the big-budget treatment. It threw everything at its audience: an all-star cast, the biggest screen process available at the time and action on a grand scale. It was based on a screenplay by Philip Yordan, Milton Sperling and John Melson. Ace German Panzer commander, Colonel Martin Hessler (Robert Shaw), recently of the Russian Front, is appointed by General Kohler (Werner Peters) to lead the attack, which deploys the Germans' brand new tank, the King Tiger (the Panzer VI Tiger II, produced by Henschel). The armoured attack is supported by mechanised Panzergrenadiers commanded by Major Von Diepel (Karl Otto Alberty). The offensive kicks off on 16 December 1944, with enough resources to last 50 hours. Lieutenant Colonel Kiley (Henry Fonda) from US intelligence tries to convince General Gray (Robert Ryan) in the Divisional HQ in Amblève that the Germans are about to attack through the Ardennes region but Gray's staff, particularly Colonel Pritchard (Dana Andrews), doubt his evidence. When the German surprise attack begins, they roll over the American defences and besiege Amblève and Bastogne.

It seemed as though every 'epic' film of the 1960s was shot on location in either Italy, Yugoslavia or Spain. *Battle of the Bulge* was filmed near Madrid in Spain, which worked both for and against the production. It enabled the film-makers to stage impressive battle scenes, with hundreds of extras and ranks of armour. The pine forests of the Sierra De Guardarrama mountain range resemble the Ardennes region, especially when wreathed in fog and blanketed in snow. Elsewhere, the mud-strewn roads and desolate, miserable landscape convincingly passes for war-torn Belgium. But a scene when a US Army munitions train is seen hurtling through a sunny, arid landscape is risible. The final tank battle, on dusty desert plains and rolling hill country near Madrid, more closely resembles El Alamein and there are many Spanish-looking 'German soldiers' in the battle scenes.

The landscape cinematography was by Jack Hildyard (an Academy Award winner for *The Bridge on the River Kwai*) in the vast 'Cinerama' format in Ultra Panavision 70 (a 70mm process). Cinerama, which had been used to great success on *How the West Was Won* (1962), was a three-screen process, which joined together to form a single widescreen image and was shown on a curved screen. By the time *Battle of the Bulge* was filmed, the process had been improved and was a single image, projected onto a curved screen, which dispensed with the vertical 'joins' in the earlier format. *Battle of the Bulge* makes certain concessions to the format – there are two 'roller coaster' rides in the film, which place the audience in the thick of the action: Hessler's car careers down a mountain road and a US train speeds through mountain tunnels. The effective score was composed by Benjamin Frankel and performed by the New Philharmonia Orchestra. He also deployed the German military's Panzer song, the 'Panzerlied' (with lyrics by Kurt Wiehle), which is sung rousingly by Hessler's tank officers prior to the offensive.

Fonda's Kiley, an ex-police inspector, is the principal US protagonist who does most to stifle the German advance. He joins up with US troops led by Major Wolenski (Charles Bronson) in captured concrete bunkers on the Siegfried Line and witnesses the German attack. This scene, with the German tanks rumbling out of the mist-shrouded woods, is the film's most memorable. Hastily dug-in, the GIs offer little resistance to the armour and mechanised infantry. Their bazooka missiles and tank shells bounce off the heavily armoured Tigers and the US troops are routed. The plot soon resembles an immense detective story, with Kiley piecing together the evidence and solving the case. He sees empty German fuel barrels floating in the River Ourthe and captured German soldiers are found to be carrying lengths of rubber hose used for siphoning. From this Kiley deduces that the Germans are low on fuel.

The cast is peppered with famous and not-so-famous names. Telly Savalas played tank sergeant Guffy, a black-marketeer whose Sherman (the 'Bargain Basement') is festooned with crates of booze, nylons, cigarettes and perfume. Pier Angeli played Louise, Guffy's fellow smuggler. She is killed when the Germans level Amblève, which transforms Guffy from a selfish profiteer into a machine-gun wielding avenger. Barbara Werle played Elena, a courtesan sent by Kohler to 'entertain' Hessler. Robert Woods was spotter pilot Joe, who ferries Kiley on daredevil reconnaissance missions over the Eifel Mountains. Hans Christian Blech (from *The Longest Day*) played Hessler's caring batman Corporal Conrad, an archetypal Hollywood 'good German'. James MacArthur played inexperienced US Lieutenant Weaver and George Montgomery was his battle-hardened sergeant, Duquesne. Both are captured by the Germans and are present at the Malmédy Massacre, a real-life atrocity perpetrated by the Waffen SS near Malmédy in Belgium at noon on 17 December 1944. It was attributed to Taskforce Peiper, under Lieutenant Colonel Joachim Peiper, in the northern sector of the German advance. Records vary of the number of victims, from 86 to 120 US POWs. As a result of the massacre, some US troops were instructed to execute German prisoners, especially SS men. This atrocity was a rare example of an event on the Western Front that was commonplace in the Eastern sector.

Battle of the Bulge concentrates both on the steamrollering German advance and events in the US Divisional headquarters in Amblève, to the north west of St-Vith. The vast set and model work used to create the bombarded streets of Amblève were based on archive photos of Bastogne during the siege. The film includes several historical events – the Malmédy Massacre, McAuliffe's 'Nuts!' at Bastogne – as sideshows to the main action. An interesting subplot depicted a group of English-speaking German commandos disguised as US Army MPs, who parachute behind enemy lines to disrupt communications, causing chaos with false directions and switched roads signs. Otto Skorzeny (the crack paratrooper who had rescued Mussolini in 1943) and his men dressed in captured uniforms and drove purloined jeeps to infiltrate the US lines. In the film Ty Hardin played their commander, Lieutenant Schumacher. The 'MPs' misdirect traffic, take the Ourthe bridge and pretend they are about the blow it up, when in fact they allow Hessler's tank column to cross it. Later they seize a vital fuel dump, but Kiley, Guffey, Weaver and others outwit the bogus MPs and retake the depot. Weaver asks Schumacher – whom he recognises from earlier in the battle – 'Does the road to Amblève still lead to Malmédy?' In the final tank battle, Hessler breaks away from the fighting with 15 tanks and trucks in an effort to take this vital fuel dump. Kiley and the defenders roll gasoline barrels down the road and ignite the fuel, halting Hessler's tanks in their tracks. Hessler is burned alive in his command vehicle as the 'Panzerlied' strikes up on the soundtrack.

Though it recreates several historical events, *Battle of the Bulge* is not known for its factual accuracy. Shortly after its release, Eisenhower denounced the film as fiction, though in its defence it ends with a dedication to the one million men who fought in the battle and points out that places, names and characters have been 'generalized' and action 'synthesized': 'in order to convey the spirit and the essence of the battle'. This explains the 50-hour, one cycle countdown clock in Kohler's operations room, which suggests the entire offensive lasted just over two days, when in fact the film ends with the massed tank battle near the Meuse on 25 December, nine days after the initial spearhead. There's a great scene when Hessler confronts Kohler with a captured American chocolate cake. Kohler fails to see its significance, but Hessler points out that if the Americans have enough fuel to fly chocolate cake from Boston across the Atlantic, they are going to have more than enough fuel for their armour. The

'Does the road to Amblève still lead to Malmédy?' Top: US troops, including James MacArthur and George Montgomery (both foreground in jeep), are diverted by road signs switched by German saboteurs. Bottom: the Malmédy Massacre of captured US soldiers recreated in Ken Annakin's *Battle of the Bulge* (1965). Images courtesy Kevin Wilkinson Collection.

massed tanks on display throughout the film look impressive, but are wholly inaccurate. Hessler is told by Kohler that the new King Tigers are one of Germany's new secret innovations in armaments: the delay caused by the German attack will enable Hitler to produce jet planes to defeat the Allied airforce and Kohler alludes to the development of atomic weapons. These 'King Tigers' are indeed innovative, for they are all Korean War US M47 Pattons with German livery. The Americans' 'M4 Shermans' are actually Light Tank M24 Chaffees and the German Panzergrenadiers travel in US M3 half-tracks.

Battle of the Giants: The Panzers roll in this Italian poster for Warner Bros all-star Cinerama presentation *Battle of the Bulge* (1965), headlining Henry Fonda, Robert Shaw and Robert Ryan. Poster courtesy Kevin Wilkinson Collection.

Battle of the Bulge's original theatrical release included a musical introduction ('Overture'), an 'Intermission' (just after Hessler is allowed to launch an all-out night attack on Amblève to 'reduce it to ashes') and extended 'Exit Music'. TV versions are the uncut print of the film, running at 163 minutes. Some UK home video versions are cropped to fit the TV screen (ruining the Cinerama experience) but retain the Overture, Intermission and Exit Music. Even including this extra music, this version runs 149 minutes. Various battles are trimmed and five whole scenes are missing: Hassler and Kohler meet Schumacher's commandos in Kohler's HQ; Hassler inspects rows of new King Tigers; Wolenski tells Kiley how Germany should be treated after the war (he suggests wiping it off the map); a Belgian boy attempts to assassinate Hassler (the boy is set free, but his father is executed); and Wolenski accuses Hassler of the Malmédy Massacre. In the cut version, we are first aware of the bogus MPs when General Grey receives a tip-off that English-speaking Germans have been recruited for a special mission – this creates more tension, as we don't know what the German commandos look like. Despite its jumble of anachronistic hardware, *Battle of the Bulge* remains one of the great 1960s war epics. Not a meticulous re-enactment of the engagement in the manner of *The Longest Day*, it still mixes history and drama to entertaining effect. But like the GIs duped by the phoney 'MPs', don't take everything at face value.

William A. Wellman's *Battleground* (1949 – *Bastogne*) told the story of the defence of Bastogne, where the 101st 'Screaming Eagles' paratroopers held out against huge odds whilst starving and frozen in the besieged town. The film begins in France in December 1944. The 101st, still recovering from their ill-fated involvement in Market Garden, are expecting leave in Paris, but instead are deployed as stopgap infantry when the Germans break through. The muddy landscape is soon frozen, snowy and fogbound. The film depicts in some detail the paratroopers' exploits, firstly dug in foxholes defending the wooded Bastogne perimeter and later – when they are forced back by German armour – the siege of Bastogne itself. The fog ensures that the US can't deploy their airpower and the ground troops are at the mercy of the German assault troops, armour and artillery, which pound them mercilessly: this bombardment is dubbed 'incoming mail'. As their supplies and ammo dwindle, the walking wounded are armed but when the Germans close in for the kill, the skies clear, the US Air Force break up the ground attack and the town is relieved.

Battleground was written by Robert Pirosh, who had fought in the Ardennes. It is a deftly written, balanced, well-constructed screenplay which deservedly won Pirosh a Best Story and Screenplay Oscar. Pirosh noted that he consciously avoided three key clichés of combat movies: 'There is no character from Brooklyn … nobody gets a letter from his wife saying she has found a new love and nobody sweats out the news of the arrival of a newborn baby back home'. The battle is seen though the eyes of the men of 'I Company', Third Platoon. These include journalist Jarvess (John Hodiak), Bettis (Richard Jaeckel), false-teeth clicking 'Kipp' Kipperton (Douglas Fowley), Standiferd (Don Taylor), Wolowicz (Bruce Cowling), Abner Spudler (Jerome Courtland), wisecracking Holley (Van Johnson) and rookie Jim Layton (Marshall Thompson). James Whitmore (himself a Marine veteran of the Pacific War) played baccy-spitting Sergeant Kinnie. Throughout the film the squad is decimated – Standiferd catches pneumonia, Wolowicz is wounded, Abner killed – and the film is notable for its downbeat, bleak atmosphere and realistic combat. The one concession to Hollywood is the character of Bastogne local Denise (sexy French actress Denise Darcel), but her role is brief. The soldiers look malnourished, unshaven and scruffy in their battered greatcoats – their hands gloved, their feet bandaged against the harsh winter cold. When the soldiers talk of visiting Paris, it is to the Pigalle Red Light district, rather than sightseeing. The only moment of jingoism is when the army's Lutheran chaplain (Leon Ames) says that never again must an evil force such as Nazism be allowed to rise and encourages the beleaguered defenders to pray in their own way 'to their own God'.

Battleground's grainy monochrome photography by Paul Vogel resembles newsreels and won the Best Cinematography in Black and White Oscar (the film is also available in a colourised version). 20 'Screaming Eagle' veterans of the actual battle appeared in the film as extras. Most of the action was shot at MGM Studios. Two soundstages were knocked into one to create the snowy 'exteriors' of the Ardennes forest. Unlike many studio-bound war movies, this soundstage is completely convincing, as the 'forest' consisted of 520 trees brought in from Northern California. Sets were also recreated of the ruined streets and houses of Bastogne. The film delivers some fine moments of action – foggy firefights and snowstorm shootouts – but also displays the confusion of war. The squad seldom understand the big picture and learn more about the battle from issues of the *Star and Stripes* newspaper, where they discover they have been mounting a 'heroic stand'. There is much black humour – Holley carries precious eggs through combat (hoping one day to make an omelette in his helmet) and Pop Stazak (George Murphy) is due to return home to help his ailing wife look after their two children, but by the time he receives the letter granting him leave, the encirclement of Bastogne is complete and he can't go. Other memorable moments include Hispanic soldier Roderigues (Ricardo Montalban) whooping like a kid when he sees snow for the first time (he later dies of exposure). There are incongruous snowball fights, McAuliffe's famous 'Nuts!' and German spies disguised as GIs. *Battleground* is the finest of the immediate post-war Hollywood war films and the best film depicting action in the snowbound Ardennes.

Of the other Ardennes-set films, Keith Gordon's *A Midnight Clear* (1992) had a group of GIs (led by Ethan Hawke) temporarily becoming friends with their German enemy. Sydney Pollack's allegorical *Castle Keep* (1969) had GIs Burt Lancaster (wearing a Crimson Pirate eye patch), Peter Falk, Patrick O'Neal and Bruce Dern defending a Belgian châteaux loaded with art treasures from the Germans. Like many 1960s Hollywood war films, it was shot in Yugoslavia. Roger Corman's *Ski Troop Attack* (1960) followed a five-man US recon ski patrol in the snowbound Hürtgen Forest during Christmas 1944. Cut off by the Bulge offensive, the patrol decides to halt the Germans' advance by blowing up a railroad trestle, as a train crosses it, with mortar charges and a mine set on the rail. But once they shoot a local German woman in her cabin, a German ski patrol dogs their tracks. The film is low-key but fast moving, with several actionful skirmishes (including bayonet-versus-ski pole jousting). When the US ski troops spot the German offensive, Corman deploys archive footage of advancing German Panzer columns and infantry. Michael Forest starred as Lieutenant Factor and Frank Wolff played sadistic Sergeant Potter. *Ski Troop Attack* looks good in grainy monochrome. It was shot in Deadwood, South Dakota, with members of local ski teams cast as the combatants. In typical Corman style, the director ended up playing the pursuing German ski patrol commander, when the German-born ski instructor hired from Sun Valley for the role broke his leg two days before filming began.

Producer-director Ryan Little's atmospheric *Saints and Soldiers* (2003) was set in the immediate aftermath of the Malmédy Massacre, with four US survivors – Corporal Greer (Corbin Allred), Medic Steve Gould (Alexander Niver), Private Shirl Kendrick (Lawrence Bagby) and Sergeant Gordon Gunderson (Peter Holden) – trapped behind enemy lines. In the eerie, snowbound landscape (filmed in Utah), they encounter downed RAF reconnaissance pilot Flight Sergeant Oberon Winley (Kirby Heyborne), who has crucial intelligence information on the German offensive which could save hundreds of US soldiers' lives. As they struggle to get back to their own lines before the German Panzers reach the Meuse River, deeply religious Greer, known as 'The Deacon', suffers hallucinations of a group of women and children he accidentally killed in a grenade blast, while the group attempt to avoid the roving German patrols. Eventually Kendrick and Gunderson are killed in a firefight in a ruined town and the three survivors make a risky break for it towards the US lines, disguised as German soldiers in a purloined jeep.

Amid the grittily photographed snowscape, *Saints and Soldiers* strives for religious significance – Medic Gould is eventually converted to Greer's faith and inherits his Bible. The Malmédy massacre opens the film eerily. Ethan Vincent played Rudolf 'Rudi' Getz, a German soldier who is captured by the company. Ace shot Greer never misses his mark, but he misses Rudi and takes this as an omen, especially when he discovers that he knows Rudi from Greer's time working as a missionary in Germany. The overall ramshackle Ardennes milieu is convincing, the ordnance on display mostly accurate and when the US soldiers find a German half-track, it has an authentically empty tank. The US soldiers shelter at the farmhouse of Catherine (Melinda Renee) and her daughter Sophie (Ruby Chase O'Neil), and when Greer allows Rudi to escape (in return for geographical details and information on German troop movements), the German leaves a model of an angel made from tinfoil for Sophie. The snowbound combat scenes were populated by many World War II re-enactors, rather than CGI'd GIs. The special effects are kept to a minimum, with the accent on human drama, which results in an interesting, low-key surprise of a war film.

The German commandos subplot from *Battle of the Bulge* was the focus of *The Last Blitzkrieg* (1958), starring Van Johnson, Kerwin Matthews and Dick York. Carl Foreman's episodic *The Victors* (1963) was based on Alexander Baron's 1953 novel *The Human Kind*. During the Ardennes campaign, the GI squad which is the film's focus led by Sergeant Craig (Eli Wallach) are transported by truck through the snow (with the carol 'Jingle Bells' in the background). The squad are enlisted to act as witnesses to the execution of a US army deserter. In a vast snowy waste, the GIs watch as the deserter is led out and prepared for his execution, as Frank Sinatra sings 'Have Yourself a Merry Little Christmas' on the soundtrack. When the hooded prisoner has been shot, 'Hark the Herald Angels Sing' is heard. This powerful juxtaposition of music and image is the film's finest moment.

Twentieth Century-Fox's *Patton* (1970) also featured the Battle of the Bulge, in particular the siege of Bastogne. During a strategy meeting, the Allies discuss how to save Bastogne. General Patton (George C. Scott) pipes up that he can mobilise three divisions in 48 hours and rush to their aid. When a British officer mentions that Patton should be falling back, consolidating his position, the general answers, 'I don't like to pay for the same real estate twice'. The film depicts Patton's relief column on the march through deep snow, deploying M48s as the US tanks and authentic M7 Priest self-propelled, tracked artillery: they were called 'Priests' by British troops due to their pulpit-like turret which mounted a 12.7mm machine-gun (their main weapon was a 105mm Howitzer). *Patton* was made with the collaboration of the Spanish Army and much of the footage was filmed in Spain. The snowbound Belgian scenes were filmed in the Sierra De Urbasa, Navarra, north of Madrid. Patton drives though the German lines but on the eve of reaching Bastogne the weather forecasts predict snow, which will mean Patton will have to attack without air cover. A deeply religious man, Patton asks his chaplain for a prayer to guarantee good weather. Patton reads the prayer (intercut with scenes of combat as US troops smash into Bastogne) and God delivers, with perfect weather for the offensive.

Over New Year 1944–45, Hitler launched a diversionary attack codenamed 'Nordwind' (North Wind) in the Alsace region of France, to the south of the Ardennes through the Vosges Mountains, to little avail. It was intended to draw US resources away from the Bulge. This little-known campaign is the setting for Byron Haskins' *Armored Command* (1961), a budget retelling of Nordwind, shot in monochrome in Germany over the winter of 1960–61. A recon squad of GIs led by Sergeant Mike Gillespie (Earl Holliman) find wounded Alsatian woman Alexandra Bastegar (Tina Louise) in the snowbound Vosges Mountains. They billet in a nearby village, 18 miles from the Siegfried Line, and take care of Alexandra, but her seductive manner causes rivalry between Mike and one of his men, cocky 'Polak' Skee (Burt Reynolds). As the Germans launch an offensive on New Year's Eve, Alexandra is revealed to be a German spy. In only his second film role, Reynolds gives the best performance in a mediocre film; he was constantly mistaken for Marlon Brando on location in Germany. Howard Keel played the US commander Colonel Mark Devlin, who guesses that the Germans plan a surprise attack – on New Year's Eve cognac is given to the GI defenders in an attempt to inebriate them.

An interesting scene depicts US soldiers on Christmas Eve listening to German propaganda broadcasts intended to cause resentment and spread misinformation and fear, but lumbered with a moronic script, *Armored Command* is mostly a disappointment. Alexandra is referred to throughout as a 'girl' not a 'woman', in that quaintly hip 1960s way that all 'women' are 'girls' – the legacy of too many Elvis and Beach Party movies. *Armored Command*'s awfulness is dispelled in its final 13 minutes, as a well-staged operation Nordwind gets underway. German armour and infantry attack a US-occupied village, in muddy, smoky action which sees Skee die a hero's death, firing a M3 half-track heavy machine-gun at the onrushing German assault troops, until he's picked off by sniper Alexandra. No matter that both the US and German tanks are US M47s,

General George Patton prays for clear skies and good weather during the siege of Bastogne. George C. Scott on location in the Sierra De Urbasa, Navarra, north of Madrid for Franklin J. Schaffner's *Patton* (1970). Courtesy Kevin Wilkinson Collection.

the film aptly captures the excitement and confusion of battle in this snowbound theatre of war.

With the Bulge contained, the Allies planned their final offensive into Germany. Eisenhower favoured an advance on a broad front, rather than a single hammer blow to the heart. In theory this would enable the British and Americans to advance at the same rate through the Rhineland, though the reality was quite different. In the northern sector Montgomery's forces attacked towards the Ruhr in a series of operations (codenamed Veritable, Blockbuster and Grenade) from 8 February to 13 March, while in the south Patch's 7th Army drove through the Saar. In the Allies' centre, Bradley's 12th Army Group attacked from 23 February to 10 March in Operation Lumberjack. As part of this offensive, Hodges' 1st Army headed for Cologne and Bonn, and was the first to secure an intact Rhine crossing, the Ludendorff railway bridge at Remagen, on 7 March 1945. Montgomery was supposed to cross the Rhine first, in a complicated assault on a 20-mile front, south east of Arnhem in Operation Plunder, but when the Americans took the bridge at Remagen, they beat Monty to the western bank. Montgomery crossed on 23–24 March, while Patton had already landed on the eastern bank under cover of night at Nierstein, southeast of Remagen, on 22 March.

Jose Merino's *Hell Commandos* (1969) opens with newsreel footage of the atomic bomb blasts in Japan and victory celebrations at the end of the war, but is actually set in France and Germany before the Third Reich's defeat, in the final phase of the European war. As a last throw of the dice, Hitler has ordered Dutch Professor Van Kolstrom (Alfredo Mayo) to develop germ warfare which causes blindness. Major Carter (Guy Madison) and his crack US Marines parachute in disguised as SS troops, but are accidentally massacred by Sergeant Nolan (Stan Cooper) and his US Marines. Carter survives and convinces the bunglers to take on the secret mission. They must trek into Germany to attack the fortified villa at Truniger, to free – or kill – the professor, before he invents an antidote to the germ warfare. With help from the professor's daughter, Sara (Raffaella Carra), they infiltrate the villa. The villa is manned by the SS commanded by Gestapo Colonel Krautzfeld (Piero Lulli), who is blown to bits in the finale when his faithful Alsatians retrieve a lit stick of dynamite. Carter's squad manage to kill the SS garrison by slipping the professor's deadly germ into the villa's water supply.

The German defence of their homeland was depicted in Bernhard Wicki's West German production *The Bridge* (1959), a Best Foreign Film Oscar nominee. It told the true story of a group of drafted teenage boys who are ordered to stall the Allied armoured advance by holding a vital bridge. It was remade under the same title as a German TV movie by Wolfgang Panzer in 2008. The battle towards the German border also featured in Audie Murphy's biopic, *To Hell and Back* (1955), which depicts an amphibious river crossing. The story of the first Rhine bridgehead is retold in John Guillermin's *The Bridge at Remagen* (1969). At German HQ in early March 1945, General Von Brock (Peter Van Eyck) decides to blow up the Remagen railway bridge, the last remaining Rhine crossing, even though it will mean trapping 75,000 men of the German XV Army. Major Paul Krueger (Robert Vaughn) is assigned the task of overseeing its destruction. Krueger disobeys orders and stalls, trying to allow as many refugees and retreating German soldiers to cross the bridge as possible. In the vanguard of the advancing US 9th Armored Division, a recon unit led by Captain Colt (Paul Prokop) is instructed to take the town of Stadt Meckenhiem to the west of Remagen. Colt is blown up in his jeep and Lieutenant Phil Hartman (George Segal) assumes command. Meckenhiem falls more easily than expected and the recon unit push on to Remagen, where after fierce fighting they secure the town. When the main US force commanded by Brigadier General Shinner (E.G. Marshall) arrives, they launch an attack with Hartman's men as the spearhead. They manage to take the bridge, despite huge losses, and remove most of the explosives before Krueger detonates the bridge, which suffers only minor damage. For his failure to level the crossing, Krueger is executed: in reality Hitler had the German officers who failed to blow the Ludendorff Bridge shot.

Another example of a big-budget American production filmed in Europe (here Czechoslovakia and Italy), *Bridge at Remagen* fused the historical aspect of *The Longest Day* to the cynicism of *The Dirty Dozen*. The film is virtually non-stop action and even though you know the outcome there's still tension.

The US mechanised units use 4x4 Jeeps, M3 half-tracks and M24 Chaffee tanks. The Germans even have authentic SdKfz 251/1 half-tracks. The action scenes are among the finest in 1960s combat cinema, with the speeding Allied push towards the Rhine aptly conveyed. The opening scene depicts US armour dashing for the Obercassel Bridge, which is obliterated by the Germans moments after a German hospital train has safely crossed it. Elmer Bernstein's punchy score and Stanley Cortez's picturesque Panavision DeLuxe cinematography contributed to the film's pace. Remagen, its railroad line and bridge were filmed on location in the picturesque Czech village of Davle, south of Prague, with the River Vltava standing in for the Rhine. Actual buildings were dynamited for the impressive street fighting scenes in Remagen, which were filmed in Most, Czechoslovakia. Shooting was interrupted in August 1968 when the liberal reforms of the 'Czech Spring' were overturned by the Soviet invasion, so the movie was completed in Italy.

Segal is good as the war-weary GI at odds with his rigid commander, Major Barnes (Bradford Dillman). Vaughn is suitably aloof as Krueger, wearing shades and a long leather coat. Ben Gazzara was cynical Sergeant Angelo, who spends most of his time looting German prisoners, and Matt Clark and Bo Hopkins played members of Hartman's squad. At Remagen, Hans Christian Blech played Captain Carl Schmitt, commander of the ragtag German forces ('old men, riffraff, the sweepings from the road'). On paper he has 1,600 men at his disposal (with two Panzer divisions due to arrive), but in reality only 200. Joachim Hansen was Captain Otto Baumann (the engineer who rigs the bridge) and Heinz Reincke played innkeeper Councillor Holzgang, who is also the head of local militia and whose son has been killed at Stalingrad. The German civilian population are mobilised to man the barricades of Remagen and this is one of few films to depict this 'Volkssturm' – Hitler's People's Army (a Home Guard) which consisted of all German males able to fight between the ages of 16 and 60. In another scene, a cowardly German officer is executed as an example to others.

The battle for the bridge is impressively staged, as US tanks fire from a ridge overlooking the river at the German 88mm artillery on the opposite bluffs; 88s were anti-aircraft flak guns that the Germans also used with deadly accuracy against Allied tanks. In other scenes a US B-25 Mitchell bomber unloads on the retreating Germans crossing the bridge and a German munitions train is destroyed by advancing US tanks. When Kruger attempts to blow up the bridge, the explosives detonate but when the smoke clears the structure, despite minor damage, still stands. The actual Remagen Bridge collapsed into the Rhine on 17 March 1945 and was never rebuilt. By then however it had been used by the Americans to form a bridgehead for their final attack into Germany.

Epilogue

THE END OF DAYS

The final defeat of Germany and Japan has proved to be a difficult subject for filmmakers. For the majority of the participants, the end of the war was welcomed, but the final blows in the conflict – and the subsequent revelations and recriminations, even among the Allies – are still controversially debated today.

In perhaps the British and American Allies' costliest decision of the war, they stopped short west of Berlin, at the River Elbe, and allowed the Russians to take the city. On 16 April 1945, the Red Army under Marshal Zhukov and Marshal Konev massed on the east bank of the River Oder and attacked Berlin. On 20 April (Hitler's 56th birthday), the Russian artillery bombardment of the city began, reducing it to rubble. American and Russian troops met at Torgau to the south-west of Berlin on the River Elbe on 25 April. Meanwhile Berlin's defenders fought tenaciously but eventually they disintegrated and capitulated – many were old men and young boys, Hitler's makeshift Volkssturm. By 27 April, the defenders were compressed into a pocket ten miles long and three miles wide – Fortress Berlin's last stand. On 30 April, Russians stormed the Reichstag and raised the Red Flag over the city. The same day, the Führer shot himself and his body and that of his wife Eva were burned by his aides before the Red Army arrived. On 2 May, German troops in Italy surrendered and two days later German forces in Denmark, Holland and Northern Germany surrendered to Montgomery. Hitler's successor was Admiral Karl Dönitz and on 7 May, German General Alfred Jodl surrendered to the Americans, British, French and Russians at Reims at 2.41 pm, ending World War II in Europe. The actual ceasefire began at 00.01 on 8 May, which was designated V-E (Victory in Europe) Day triggering widespread street parties and celebrations across the world.

Hitler's demise was depicted from the German point of view in G.W. Pabst's *Ten Days to Die* (1954 – *The Last Act*) and also in Ennio De Concini's Italian-UK co-production *Hitler: The Last Ten Days* (1973), with Alec Guinness in the title role and a supporting cast that included Simon Ward, Philip Stone, Mark Kingston, Adolfo Celi, Diane Cilento and Gabriele Ferzetti. John Bennett played propagandist Goebbels, Barbara Jeffords was his wife, Magda, and German actress Doris Kunstmann (in her English-speaking debut) portrayed Eva Braun. Guinness noted: 'I'm glad the picture is over. I can't wait to get out of the skin of Hitler. It hasn't been a very comfortable one'. On TV, Frank Finlay played Hitler in *The Death of Hitler* (1973) and Anthony Hopkins portrayed him in *The Bunker* (1981).

By far the finest recreation of Hitler's last days is Oliver Hirschbiegel's *Der Untergang* (2004), which was released internationally as *Downfall*. It was based on several sources, including Joachim Fest's book *Inside Hitler's Bunker* and a first-hand account of life inside Hitler's bunker by Traudl Junge, who was played in the film by Alexandra Maria Lara. Junge can also be seen as an interviewee in the 1970s TV documentary series *The World at War*. Renowned Swiss-born actor Bruno Ganz gave a chilling, almost sympathetic portrayal of Adolf Hitler, who loses all sanity amid the confines of the concrete foxhole which becomes his tomb.

Downfall begins in November 1942 at the Führer's HQ in East Prussia, when Traudl Junge is recruited as Hitler's personal secretary. The action then shifts to 20 April 1945 (Hitler's 56th birthday) in his bunker below the Chancellery. From here the deluded leader plans strategies for his decimated, imaginary armies, plots to recapture oil fields for 'long range operations' and appoints new commanders for his fictitious airforce. The Russian artillery rains down a constant barrage on the city and the Volkssturm (with little training and equipment) are mobilised as the city's cannon fodder. Hitler implements Operation Clausewitz, turning Berlin into 'a frontline city', a battleground, with no regard for the three million civilian population of women, children, wounded and the elderly. Old men are shot as deserters by the military police when they refuse to fight. A subplot details the short Volkssturm career of Peter Kranz (Donevan Gunia), a boy soldier who is decorated by Hitler for successfully knocking out Russian tanks with a Panzerfaust (a bulbous anti-tank weapon). When Peter returns home after his unit is decimated, he finds his mother dead and his father, one-armed war veteran Wilhelm (Karl Kranzkowski), hanged. Many German civilians committed suicide, as the 'barbaric' Russians sacked the city.

Scared of confronting their fanatical leader, Hitler's commanders make the most of what little resources they have, but results are not forthcoming. In a famous scene, Hitler learns during a staff meeting that Steiner, one of his commanders, couldn't muster enough men to mount an assault. He explodes, unleashing a torrent of bile as he raves at his officers for their incompetence, betrayal and cowardice. Eva Braun, Hitler's lover, throws a party, a last bash for the Third Reich, which is abruptly curtailed by a direct hit from a Russian shell. Later she becomes Frau Hitler in a brief wedding ceremony, before they commit suicide together on 30 April. To prevent the Russians putting the corpses on display, their cadavers are immediately burned on a petrol-fuelled funeral pyre. As the Russians close in, many of the staff flee the Chancellery, including Traudl, who disguises herself as a German soldier. When the troops she is travelling with through the ruined city are surrounded and surrender, she and young Peter make it through Russian lines – hand-in-hand – and escape.

Presented by Constantin Film, Munich, the film was lensed by Rainer Klausmann on location in St Petersburg (Russia), in Munich, Berlin and at Bavaria Filmstudios. By night, the ruptured city is lit by bonfires – either from damaged buildings or from the Nazis incinerating incriminating documents. There's no gas, electricity, clean water, transport or coal. For its realism and meticulous attention to detail, *Downfall* is heavy going at times, particularly towards the end of its 160 minutes, when many of the main characters commit suicide. The film depicts the last ten days of bunker life and doesn't hold back the horror, as in the scenes depicting the Goebbels family's demise: mother Magda (Corinna Harfouch) administers sleeping drug 'medicine' to her six children (Helga, Heide, Helmut, Hedda, Holde and Hilde) and then slips them a fatal pill in their slumber. She is then shot by her husband, Joseph (Hitler's propaganda minister and briefly the German Chancellor following Hitler's death), who then shoots himself. There are little details from Hirschbiegel too – such as Hitler testing a suicide capsule out on his beloved Alsatian, Blondi – and some truly odd moments, as when the Goebbels' children sing for the Führer, which resembles a demented outtake from *The Sound of Music.* Most surprising is the touching relationship between Hitler and Traudl, which presents a seldom seen facet of Hitler's persona. Ganz is excellent as the Führer, his hand constantly quivering, his moods erratic. The tremor in Hitler's left hand was actually an early sign of the onset of Parkinson's disease. Lara is also outstanding as Traudl, whose panicky demeanour and emotional reaction to events are the audience's eyes. Her tentative walk with Peter, through throngs of Russian soldiers, is as terrifying as their final scene – pedalling away to freedom on a purloined bike – is joyous. Documentary footage of the real Traudl bookends the film, where she ponders if she was too young and naive to fully understand what it meant to be a Nazi and that she cannot forgive herself for being part of such important world events. Traudl lived in Munich until her death in 2002.

Other key female roles in *Downfall* were taken by Birgit Minichmayr, as secretary Gerda Christian who also escaped the bunker (she died in 1997), and Juliane Kohler, as Hitler's cold, delusional Eva. She is honoured to be allowed to remain with her lover and gives away a fur coat to Traudl, an empty, pointless gesture amid the madness in the bunker. Thomas Kretschmann played SS-Gruppenführer Herman Fegelein, Eva's brother, who absconds from the bunker. Captured in a stupor in a decadent, hedonistic brothel, he is summarily executed. Heinrich Himmler (Ulrich Noethen) attempts to broker peace with the Allies in Lübeck. Professor Dr Ernst-Günter Schenck (Christian Berkel) discovers the hospitals have been emptied of supplies and the patients left to fend for themselves. Michael Mendl played General Helmut Weilding, who is handed the poisoned chalice of commanding the defence of Berlin and Heino Ferch played Hitler's architect Albert Speer. When asked by the Führer if he should escape Berlin, Speer tells his leader: 'You must be on stage when the curtain falls'.

The Germans hoped the Allies would arrive from the west before the Red Army swept in from the east, but in the event it is the Russians who bring the curtain down. In *Downfall* they are depicted as Cossack-dancing, singing soldiers. Their horrendous sacking of the city and mistreatment and abuse of the German civilian population, as recounted in Cornelius Ryan's book *The Last Battle*, is not recreated onscreen and would surely have made the film even more difficult viewing. Max Färberböck's *A Woman in Berlin* (2008 – *The Downfall of Berlin*) is a more realistic depiction of the Russians' arrival and their appalling treatment of the Germans. *Downfall* was nominated for the Best Foreign Language Film Oscar in 2005, but lost out to *The Sea Inside. Downfall* is a product of the public's continued interest – via TV documentaries and shelves full of books – in the allure and enigma of Hitler and the Third Reich. But this masterful film is definitive and is perhaps the last word on its subject.

Giuliano Montaldo's bleak Italian-Yugoslavian *The Fifth Day of Peace* (1969 – *Crime of Defeat* and *Got Mit Uns*), was set in the last days of the war in a stockade for German soldiers at Emmen prisoner of war camp in Holland. It is a grimy, wintry film, photographed by Silvano Ippoliti in grainy Eastmancolor. The film centres on the battle of wills between the camp's commander, Canadian Captain John Miller (Richard Johnson), and Colonel Von Bleicher (Helmut Schneider), the leader of the 2,000 German inmates. Bleicher sentences to death two deserters, Corporal Reiner Schultz (Larry Aubrey) and Ensign Bruno Grauber (Franco Nero). To keep the peace, Miller allows the execution to take place. The unusual cast included Relja Basic as Miller's assistant Lieutenant Romney, Renato Romano was Miller's batman, Sergeant O'Mally, and Bud Spencer was supplies officer Corporal Jelenek. Michael Goodliffe, a veteran of many British war movies, played Miller's superior General Snow, who tells Miller: 'They've lost the war – don't let 'em forget it'. Ennio Morricone provided the haunting theme music.

The first day of the ceasefire is the setting for Andrzej Wajda's *Ashes and Diamonds* (1958), which offered an interesting snapshot of the uncertainty and political rivalry which resulted when peace broke out in Poland. On 8 May 1945, three Polish anti-communist resistance fighters ambush a car that is supposed to be carrying Szczuka (Waclaw Zastrzezynski), the communist District Party Secretary, but they kill two innocent cement workers instead. Hiding out in a hotel in a nearby town, the would-be assassins discover that Szczuka is staying in the same hotel to attend a celebratory banquet thrown by Mayor Swiencki, who is to be appointed a communist minister. Two of the assassins, Maciek (Zbigniew Cybulski) and Andrzej (Adam Pawlikowski), decide to carry out the assassination, while the third, Drewnowski (Bogumil Kobiela), is the mayor's secretary and is hoping for a promotion under the new communist regime. Maciek takes a room next to Szczuka's and spends his time chatting up the barmaid, Krystyna (Ewa Krzyzanowska). Drewnowski gets drunk and embarrasses himself at the banquet, letting off a fire extinguisher and climbing on a table. Maciek and Krystyna make love, dance and walk through town in the rain. In a ruined chapel they discover the two corpses of the cement workers, laid out for burial. Maciek tells Andrzej that he doesn't want to kill Szczuka, but is eventually convinced otherwise. As Szczuka leaves in the dead of night, Maciek shoots him in the street. The next morning, Maciek bids Krystyna farewell and leaves to catch the morning train, but he's accosted by Polish troops and shot dead.

Based on the novel by Jerzy Andrzejewski, *Ashes* is the most accessible of Wajda's war trilogy. Zbigniew Cybulski, a bit part player in *A Generation*, was a handsome actor who with his quiff and indolent rebellious manner was tagged the 'Polish James Dean', though he more closely resembles Alain Delon. He died in 1967 aged 39, when he was run over by a train. Maciek's wears shades throughout the film, which is conveniently explained – he is a survivor of the Warsaw Uprising and his eyes are sensitive to light, having spent time in the sewers.

Ashes and Diamonds is an idealist's film, its downbeat ending notwithstanding. Communist Szczuka is a veteran of the Spanish Civil War and is trying to locate his estranged 17-year-old son. Szczuka later learns that his son is an anti-communist resistance fighter who has been captured by the Russians. The Russian presence in the town is strong – T-34s and troops move through the streets past posters of Stalin – as it was for many years in Poland after the war. Maciek's blossoming love for Krystyna gives him a reason to live. In the ruined chapel she begins to read an inscription by Norwid, which Maciek completes: 'Beneath the ash a diamond will sparkle like the dawn star of victory'. But the new dawn of 9 May 1945 is a false dawn for Maciek. The sunlight that floods the hotel the following morning merely reveals the previous night's stumbling, woozy revellers. It doesn't bring new life and a new start to Maciek, and Krystyna is left alone. Drewnowski is disowned both by his communist employer and his partisan friends and only Andrzej achieves his aim – the death of Szczuka. As in the earlier films of Wajda's trilogy, little details – such as the woebegone hotel clerk (Jan Ciecierscki) who longs for the old Warsaw before the war – add much to the film. Maciek lighting glasses of liquor, like candles, on the hotel bar (in memory of his dead comrades) or the fireworks that erupt behind Maciek as he assassinates Szczuka, mark this as art cinema, rather than simply a political or genre piece.

Patton (1970) contains a scene where the US general attends a celebration thrown by the Russians and refuses to share a toast with the Russian commander. Patton (George C. Scott) was well known for his anti-Russian stance and in the film insults the Russian allies in a speech to a ladies' group at the 'Doughnut Dugout' in Knutsford, for which he's reprimanded. Patton also thinks that the Allies should turn their attention to tackling the Russians as they gain a foothold in Berlin, but his premonition of the Cold War is ignored. Patton is criticised for not adopting Eisenhower's 'De-Nazification' policy and continues to employ Nazi notaries to help govern. After the war Patton bids farewell to his staff and like so many biopics depicting national heroes, the film allows its hero to survive the end credits, achieving immortality. We don't see Patton's ignoble death in a road accident on 21 December 1945. The film closes with Patton bemoaning the fact that in ancient times, the Romans savoured their moments of triumph with victory parades and celebrations, exulting the victor and humiliating the vanquished.

As the Allied forces fought through Germany, the full scale of Hitler's methodical campaign of genocide was revealed. In Germany the victors discovered the concentration camps – political prisons at Dachau, Sachsenhausen and Buchenwald – where 'resettled' opponents of the Nazi party were tortured and starved. Above their entrance gates was forged the motto: 'Arbeit macht Frei' – work sets you free. Dachau in Bavaria, southwest Germany, was the first of these camps, opened in March 1933, when the Nazi's came to power. But it was the discovery of the 'killing factories' to the east of Germany that was most troubling. These macabre inventions carried out murder on a vast scale and in great secrecy, Hitler's attempt to wipe out the Jewish race, his 'Final Solution'. Among the six death camps overseen by the SS were Dachau, Treblinka and Belsen, but the most notorious and efficient was Auschwitz in Poland. Between June 1940 and January 1945, an estimated 4 million people were executed there. Killing on such scale required planning. The death trains carrying detainees to their doom had priority over all else on the railroads. The camps themselves were well organised in their slaughter. Hundreds and thousands of victims were killed in huge gas chambers, by monoxide gas, or zyklon-B (crystallised prussic acid), and their bodies were incinerated in vast ovens. This massacre of European Jews and others deemed racially inferior to Hitler's vision of a pure Europe, became known as the Holocaust. Of the 3 million Polish Jews, only 100,000 survived the Holocaust.

Alain Resnais' harrowing 30-minute documentary *Nuit et Brouillard* (1955 – *Night and Fog*) depicted the concentration camps. In *Europa, Europa* (1990) Marco Hofschneider played Solomon Perel, a young German Jew, whose evasive action to avoid deportation goes so far as to join the German army. George Stevens directed *The Diary of Anne Frank* (1959). Anne kept a record while she and other Jewish refugees were in hiding in Nazi-occupied Amsterdam from 1942 until their betrayal in 1944. Her diary was published posthumously by her father in 1947 (she died in Bergen-Belsen concentration camp in 1945). Millie Perkins portrayed Anne in the film. John Erman's TV movie *The Attic: The Hiding of Anne Frank* (1988) also recounted this story, from the perspective of Miep Gies (Mary Steenburgen), the Dutch woman who sheltered the Franks. Concentration camps have even been used as the setting for comedies – notably the Oscar-winning *Life Is Beautiful* (1997), directed by and starring Italian comedian Roberto Benigni.

The finest film depicting the Holocaust is Steven Spielberg's *Schindler's List* (1993), a worthy Best Picture and Best Director winner at the Oscars. Based on Thomas Keneally's novel of the same name, it told the true story of Austrian businessman Oskar Schindler (Liam Neeson), who saved the lives of 1,100 Polish Jews by claiming they were needed to operate his factory, despite the attentions of Nazi commander Amon Goeth (Ralph Fiennes). In Hungary, Swede Raoul Wallenberg saved an estimated 100,000 Jews through paperwork subterfuge, even though Hungary was a member of the Axis. Stanley Kramer's *Judgement at Nuremberg* (1961) dramatised the trials held in their city from November 1945 to October 1946, when 22 prominent Nazis were tried before a military tribunal, with 12 of them being sentenced to hang. Many German officers distanced themselves from Nazism, maintaining that they were simply 'following orders'. War trials eventually established who gave those orders. The 190-minute running time and heavyweight cast – Burt Lancaster, Spencer Tracy, Richard Widmark, Marlene Dietrich, Judy Garland, Maximilian Schell and Montgomery

Clift – reflected the film's important subject matter. Based on Ira Levin's novel of the same name, Franklin J. Schaffner's *The Boys from Brazil* (1978) depicted famed Nazi hunter Ezra Lieberman (Laurence Olivier) on the trail of 'Angel of Death' Dr Josef Mengele (Gregory Peck). Mengele, who hides out in South America with a cadre of neo-Nazis and wanted war criminals, has cloned the Führer. This was a typically overblown, globetrotting Sir Lew Grade production, shot in Portugal, the US, England and Austria. The all-star cast included James Mason, Lilli Palmer, Uta Hagen, John Dehner, Denholm Elliott, Walter Gotell, Wolfgang Preiss, Michael Gough, Steve Guttenberg, John Rubinstein, Richard Marner, Prunella Scales and Bruno Ganz. The sinister little 'Hitlers' – genetic experiments who are the 'boys' from Brazil – were all played by Jeremy Black. Mengele was also portrayed by Howard Vernon in Andrea Bianchi's Uraguayan-shot, Franco-Spanish *Angel of Death* (1986 – *Commando Mengele*).

Samuel Fuller's *The Big Red One* (1980) was one of the few World War II combat films to look beyond the battlefield. The film is semi-autobiographical – Fuller had fought in the US 1st Infantry Division in North Africa, Sicily, France, Belgium and Germany – and the story follows the unit through various theatres of war. In reality, it was nearly impossible for a US soldier fighting in Europe to make it from D-Day to the war's end without suffering injury. During the Pacific War, Marines' chances of even making it through a single operation without a scratch were slim.

The Big Red One was originally to have been made in 1945 with John Wayne in the lead. Producer Gene Corman wanted Steve McQueen as the sergeant, but Fuller always envisioned Lee Marvin in the role: he had the right rugged, monolithic presence for the World War I veteran. As Fuller noted, 'I've rarely been locked in on the same wavelength with an actor'. In 1978 Fuller finally realised his dream project, but at a price. The budget was whittled down by financiers Lorimar from $12 million to less than $4 million and Fuller's four-and-a-half-hour cut was abridged to 109 minutes for theatrical release, against his wishes. In 2004 a 162-minute 'Director's Cut' was assembled after Fuller's death, which is billed on DVD as 'The Reconstruction'.

The Big Red One goes where other war films feared to tread and ends in Czechoslovakia in May 1945. Having repulsed the Germans at the Battle of the Bulge, the rifle squad are sent to liberate Falkenau, a concentration camp, which due to production costs was filmed in Israel. It was an abandoned armoury in the middle of Jerusalem called Camp Schneller. The GIs shoot it out with the SS guards and witness the terrible killing factory: the hollow-eyed inmates, the ovens, the bones and the chimneys. An SS soldier hiding in an oven is executed by manic Griff (Mark Hamill), who is unable to comprehend the horror, whilst a young boy survivor befriends the tough sergeant and dies as he's carried aloft on his saviour's shoulders. Later the sergeant stabs a surrendering German and then learns that the war has been over for four hours. This mirrors the film's opening scenes, set in France in November 1918, when the young sergeant stabs an enemy after the November Armistice has been signed. *Big Red One* is choppy, episodic and erratic. There are moments of brilliance, brutality and banality – but that's Fuller and that's war.

The dénouement of Edward Dmytryk's sprawling, CinemaScoped *The Young Lions* (1958) takes place after the discovery of the concentration camps by advancing US troops. The story's antagonists come face to face and GI Whiteacre (Dean Martin) kills German Diestl (Marlon Brando) – during training Whiteacre's friend, young Jewish-American GI Noah Ackerman (Montgomery Clift), has had to endure anti-Semitic torment and beatings from sadist Sergeant Ricketts (Lee Van Cleef) and his cronies.

When Germany surrendered, Berlin was divided into four military zones: British, American, French and Russian. When East Germany was formed in 1949, the Russian sector became East Berlin, the remainder West Berlin. The war had begun when Poland was invaded by Germany, but Poland was now occupied by Russia. In 1961, a wall was built across Berlin to stop anyone escaping from east to west. It remained the capital of East Germany, while Bonn became the capital of West Germany. The Berlin Wall was finally dismantled in 1989, after the fall of Communism.

Robert Aldrich's *Ten Seconds to Hell* (1959) depicted bomb disposal squads working in Berlin, diffusing unexploded 1,000-pound Allied bombs. Steven Soderbergh's *The Good German* (2006) was a monochrome mystery set in post-war Berlin, starring George Clooney, Cate Blanchett and Tobey Maguire. *Germany Year Zero* (1948) was also set during this period when the population of Berlin began to dig themselves out of the rubble. It is the last of Roberto Rossellini's three dramas depicting the war and its aftermath, and was filmed on studio interiors and on location in Berlin. The film follows the Köhlers, a German family. The father (Ernst Pittschau), a widower, is infirm: the victim of a weak heart and poor diet. His daughter Eva (Ingetraud Hinze) works at night as a prostitute and his eldest son Karl-Heinz, an ex-soldier who fought at Tobruk and in Russia, is a sponger-in-hiding, who fears being carted off to a prison camp. The Russians marched many of their German prisoners off to Siberia. Youngest son Edmund (Edmund Meschke) falls in with gangs of petty thieves and street kid urchins, and hawks wares on the street for his old schoolteacher, Mr Henning (Erich Gühne). Their elderly father is admitted to hospital and with care and nourishment makes a full recovery, but when he returns to their crowded apartment, he bemoans that he has become a burden to his family. Edmund, misunderstanding his father's ramblings ('I wish I were dead'), kills him with poison stolen from the hospital. Distraught at his actions, Edmund dazedly wanders the streets and throws himself from a ruin, killing himself.

Rossellini's documentary neorealism and good performances ensure the degradation of post-war life in war torn Berlin is palpable. The director's brother Renzo provided the score and piles of real Berlin masonry, as photographed by Robert Juillard, are the haunting backdrop to the story. *Year Zero* is a routinely shocking film. Edmund is introduced working with other Berliners as a gravedigger and a dead horse's corpse is carved up by a crowd in the street. Surreally, the trams still run, while basic supplies of electricity, hot water and gas are erratic; the apartment's electricity is cut off due to meter tampering. Edmund plays one of Hitler's speeches on a gramophone amid the ruins of the Chancellery, which once again rings to the master's voice: 'Victory will be ours!' is the Führer's empty rallying cry. Edmund and his cohorts steal everything, from coal to potatoes, and a girder which has crashed through an apartment floor becomes his slide: to Edmund, the ruined city is his playground.

The US implemented the Marshall Plan, a programme of regenerative economic aid to European countries. From 1948–51, $12 billion was given to 16 countries. Even as the victors, Britain endured post-war 'austerity'. The rationing measures of essential foodstuffs began in January 1940 and continued until 1954. In the immediate post-war period there was a noticeable dearth of British war films in cinemas, as audiences sought entertainment and escapism – not reminders of their lost love ones. On 26 July 1945, Churchill, the leader of the coalition government, who had inspired Britain to great resilience during the war, lost the General Election to his deputy prime minister in the War Cabinet, Labour's Clement Attlee.

Carl Foreman's *The Victors* (1963) is a rare example of a World War II film depicting the fractious post-war period, with Berlin shown to be riven with animosity between the Russians, Germans and Americans. US GI George Hamilton dates German woman Helga (Elke Sommer) in the barren Soviet Zone of 1946. She and her parents hate the Russians, while Helga's sister Trudi (glamorous Senta Berger) dates a Russian officer and wears furs and expensive jewellery. As Hamilton makes his way though Berlin's deserted, shattered streets, he encounters a drunken Russian soldier (a bizarre cameo by Albert Finney). The two victors squabble over the right of way across a plank 'bridge' which spans a puddle. They draw knives and both are killed. The camera pulls back from the two one-time allies, now enemies, who are lost in a vast ruined city. At the beginning of the Cold War, as the 'Iron Curtain' (as Churchill christened it) descends across Europe, who, asks Foreman, are the victors?

With the war in Europe over, the US planned to invade Japan on 1 November 1945 (Operation Olympic) and on 1 March 1946 (Operation Coronet). The Japanese readied the entire civilian population to defend their homeland, so a US invasion was ruled out. The saturation bombing of European cities by Bomber Command and the USAAF, and the firestorm of Dresden were overshadowed by the distinctive mushroom clouds that rose over two Japanese cities. By 1945, US physicists working on the Manhattan Project had created two atom bombs: one uranium, one plutonium. On 6 August 1945, the Japanese city of Hiroshima in the south of Honshu Island was hit by a uranium-based atomic bomb named 'Little Boy', which was dropped by US B-29 bomber 'Enola Gay' (named after pilot Colonel Paul Tibbetts' mother). On 9 August, the plutonium bomb called 'Fat Man' landed on Nagasaki on the southern island Kyushu. Both blasts caused widespread destruction, both to the civilian population and the landscape, with thousands of people killed and many more scarred and injured. The effects of radiation from the blasts caused illness, deformities and death for years after the attacks. Shocked and awed, Japan surrendered on 15 April 1945, although it was 14 August that was designated V-J (Victory in Japan) Day in America, due to the time difference between the US and Japan.

Dramas based around these events included several Japanese movies – *Children of Hiroshima* (1953 – *Children of the Atom Bomb*), *Shadow of Hiroshima*

(1956), *Hiroshima Heartache* (1962 – *A Night to Remember*) and *Heart of Hiroshima* (1966). Other films that addressed the blasts include *Hiroshima – Remembering and Repressing* (1986) and *Hiroshima – Out of the Ashes* (1990). The 24 hours of 15 August – as those in power in Japan engage in political wrangling, revolt and indecision – are depicted in *Japan's Longest Day* (1967 – *The Emperor and the General*) directed by Kihachi Okamoto. It featured an all-star Japanese cast including Takashi Shimura, Sô Yamamura and Toshirô Mifune, with narration by Tatsuya Nakadai. David Lowell Rich's *Enola Gay* (1980), starring Patrick Duffy, Gregory Harrison and Kim Darby, was a rare example of a US film depicting the planning and dropping of the bombs.

Throughout the 1950s, global science fiction cinema became obsessed with nuclear power and radioactivity was blamed for many of the world's ills. One of the most lasting effects of the mushroom clouds in Japan was its popular cinema's preoccupation with monsters mutated by nuclear tests and by the effects of radioactivity. This resulted in the 'Godzilla' monster movies (called 'Kaiju Eiga') and allegories such as *Matango, Attack of the Mushroom People* (1963 – *Fungus of Terror*) where shipwrecked tourists mutate into giant fungi, their facial disfigurements post-nuclear in their appearance. The best of this genre, including the trendsetting *Godzilla* (1956 – *Godzilla, King of the Monsters*), *Godzilla versus Mothra* (1964) and *Destroy All Monsters* (1968), were powered by a Honda – director Ishirô Honda that is.

Another example of the generational repercussions of events in August 1945 was Alain Resnais' Franco-Japanese co-production *Hiroshima Mon Amour* (1959). Resnais had planned to shoot a documentary in modern day Hiroshima in the style of *Night and Fog*, but eventually adapted this scenario into a love story between two nameless protagonists. A French actress (Emmanuelle Riva) arrives in Hiroshima to appear as a nurse in an international anti-war film, but meets and falls in love with a Japanese architect (Eiji Okada). Both are married with children and she is due to leave Hiroshima for Paris the following day. Their all-too-brief affair is filmed amid the backdrop of rejuvenated Hiroshima – their night of passion takes place in the 'Hotel New Hiroshima' and travelogue shots of the city include tours of the neon-lit streets by night and the 'Hiroshima Gift Shop'. There are scenes in a hospital (where the actress prepares for her film role) and a museum commemorating the city's destruction, where Resnais camera dwells on photographs, newsreel footage and dramatic re-enactments of the carnage and its aftermath: levelled wreckage, horrific radiation burns, loss of hair, burned stones, refugees, a three-legged dog, fish poisoned by acid rain and artefacts such as 'bouquets' of fused bottle tops. This much remains of Resnais' original documentary idea. The actress recounts the grim facts: '200,000 dead, 80,000 wounded. In 9 seconds'.

The two protagonists have different perspectives on the bomb blast. In France the actress recalls that it meant the end of the war, mixed with 'Amazement that they dared. Amazement that they brought it off'. The architect, who was away fighting in the Japanese army but whose parents were present in the city, notes bitterly, 'The whole world rejoiced'. As with Resnais later *Last Year in Marienbad* (1961), the storytelling relies heavily on voiceover monologues, abstract juxtapositions of imagery, and is interspersed with fragments of flashbacks, creating vivid evocations of displaced time, place and memory. The actress remembers her younger life in Nevers, France, during the German occupation, when she had a relationship with a German soldier and was ostracised by the locals. The film's dreamlike eeriness is underpinned by a delicate avant-garde score from Georges Delerue and Giovanni Fusco. *Hiroshima Mon Amour* is an extraordinarily brave, moving anti-war and anti-nuclear film masquerading as a love story. It was at the forefront of the French 'New Wave' school of filmmaking.

The inglorious end to the Pacific War, indeed to World War II, is seldom depicted on film – the horrific archive images of the widespread destruction are reminder enough. In Hollywood cinema, the defeat of Japan is almost always seen through the heroic battles for the string of islands across the Pacific during the US force's island-hopping strategy. Biopic *MacArthur* (1977) depicted the uncertain period in the Far East at the end of the war. MacArthur (Gregory Peck) is ready to invade Japan, but following the death of Roosevelt, newly incumbent president Harry S. Truman scraps the plan and drops the atomic bombs. MacArthur is a key figure in America's occupation policy regarding the rebuilding of a New Japan, transforming it from a feudal past to an 'Americanised' future. There are considerable land, industrial and political reforms (including granting women the vote) and an effort to dispel militarist power in the country. The film biography continues beyond the conflict's end and follows MacArthur into the Korean War (1950–53), a war which he terms: 'One last gift to an old warrior'. As the relatives and loved ones of the 50 million who lost their lives in World War II would no doubt attest, war is one 'gift' the world can do without.

BIBLIOGRAPHY AND SOURCES

Books, Magazines & Articles

Ambrose, Stephen E. *Band of Brothers* (Simon & Schuster, 1992)

Atkinson, John, *The Oscars* (Pocket Essentials, 2001)

Bailey, Ronald H., *Prisoners of War* (Time-Life Books, 1978)

Barry, Lieutenant Colonel Simon, *D-Day to VE Day: The Liberation of Europe* (Castle Books, 1995)

Bergen, Ronald, *The United Artists Story* (Octopus, 1986)

Bishop, David, *Starring Michael Caine* (Reynolds & Hearn, 2003)

Boulle, Pierre, *The Bridge on the River Kwai* (Secker & Warburg, 1954)

Brickhill, Paul, *The Great Escape* (Faber & Faber, 1951)

Buford, Kate, *Burt Lancaster – An American Life* (Aurum, 2001)

Burt, Robert, *Rockerama – 25 Years of Teen Screen Idols* (Blandford, 1983)

Carden, Jeremy (trans.), *A New Illustrated History of World War II: Rare and Unseen Photographs 1939–1945* (David & Charles, 2005)

Chant, Christopher, Brigadier Shelford Bidwell, Anthony Preston and Jenny Shaw, *World War II: Land Sea & Air Battles 1939–1945* (Sundial Books, 1977)

Davenport, Robert, *The Encyclopedia of War Movies* (Checkmark Books, 2004)

De Agostini, *The Clint Eastwood Collection: Volume 7 (Kelly's Heroes); Volume 20 (Where Eagles Dare)* (De Agostini, 2004)

Dewey, Donald, *James Stewart: A Biography* (Warner Books, 1998)

Eames, John Douglas, *The MGM Story: The Complete History of over Fifty Roaring Years* (Octopus, 1977)

—— *The Paramount Story* (Octopus, 1985)

Evans, Alun, *Brassey's Guide to War Films* (Brassey's, 2000)

Eyman, Scott and Paul Duncan (ed.), *John Ford: The Complete Films* (Taschen, 2004)

Ferguson, Ken (ed.), *Photoplay Film Annual 1974* (Argus Press, 1974)

—— *Photoplay Film Year Book 1978* (The Illustrated Publications Company, 1978)

Fiegel, Eddi, *John Barry: A Sixties Theme* (Boxtree, 2001)

Flaherty, Thomas H., *The Wolf Packs* (Time-Life Books, 1989)

Fox, Keith & Maitland McDonagh (eds), *The Tenth Virgin Film Guide* (Virgin, 2001)

Frank, Alan, *The Films of Roger Corman 'Shooting My Way out of Trouble'* (Batsford, 1998)

Frayling, Christopher, *Sergio Leone – Something to Do With Death* (Faber and Faber, 2000)

Frost, Major-General John, *A Drop too Many* (Cassell & Co, 1980)

Fuller, Samuel, *A Third Face: My Tale of Writing, Fighting and Filmmaking* (Applause, 2002)
Goldman, William, *William Goldman's Story of a Bridge Too Far* (Coronet, 1977)
Goodenough, Simon, *War Maps: Great Land, Sea and Air Battles of World War II* (Macdonald & Co, 1982)
Guérif, François, *Clint Eastwood: From Rawhide to Pale Rider* (Roger Houghton Ltd, 1986)
Guttmacher, Peter, *Legendary War Movies,* (Metrobooks, 1996)
Higgins, Jack, *The Eagle Has Landed* (William Collins Sons, 1975)
Hirschhorn, Clive, *The Warner Bros. Story* (Octopus, 1983)
Horrocks, Sir Brian, *Corps Commander* (Sidgewick & Jackson Ltd, 1977)
Hyams, Jay, *War Movies* (Gallery Books, 1984)
Jewell, Richard B. & Vernon Harbin, *The RKO Story* (Octopus, 1982)
Kaminsky, Stuart M., *Don Siegel: Director* (Curtis, 1974)
Katz, Ephraim, *The Macmillan International Film Encyclopedia* (HarperCollins, 1998)
Kay, George, *The Beaver Book of War Stories* (Beaver Books, 1981)
Lloyd, Ann (ed.), *Good Guys and Bad Guys* (Orbis, 1982)
——*Movies of the Sixties* (Orbis, 1983)
Luck, Steve (ed.), *Philip's Compact Encyclopedia* (Chancellor Press, 1999)
MacLean, Alistair, *The Guns of Navarone* (Collins, 1957)
——*Force 10 from Navarone* (Collins, 1958)
——*Where Eagles Dare* (Collins, 1967)
Malloy, Mike, *Lee Van Cleef* (McFarland & Company, 1998)
Maltin, Leonard, *2001 Movie and Video Guide*
Marshall Cavendish, *Great Battles of World War II: A Visual History of Victory, Defeat and Glory* (Imperial War Museum, 1995)
Masheter, Philip, *Broadsword Calling Danny Boy – Where Doubles Dare: The Making of Where Eagles Dare* (Movie Collector) (Volume Two, Issue Two, 14 March 1995)
Maule, Henry, *The Great Battles of World War II* (Hamlyn, 1972)
McBride, Joseph, *Searching for John Ford* (Faber and Faber, 2003)
McGilligan, Patrick, *Clint Eastwood – The Life and Legend* (HarperCollins, 1999)
Mosley, Leonard, *Battle of Britain* (Pan Books, 1969)
Nathanson, E.M., *The Dirty Dozen* (Arthur Barker, 1966)
Niven, David, *The Moon's a Balloon* (Hamish Hamilton Ltd, 1971)
Nourmand, Tony & Graham Marsh, (editors) *Film Posters of the 60s: The Essential Movies of the Decade* (Aurum, 1997)
O'Brien, Daniel, *Clint Eastwood – Film-Maker* (Batsford, 1996)
O'Neill, William L. *The Oxford Essential Guide to World War II* (Berkley Books, 2002)
Pfeiffer, Lee and Dave Worrall, *Cinema Retro 'Movies Classics' Special Edition: Where Eagles Dare* (Cinema Retro, 2009)
Ryan, Cornelius, *A Bridge Too Far* (Hamish Hamilton Ltd, 1974)
——*The Last Battle* (William Collins Sons & Co, 1966)
——*The Longest Day* (Victor Gollancz Ltd, 1960)
Scheuer, Steven H. (ed.), *Movies on TV* (Bantam Books, 1977)
Schickel, Richard, *Clint Eastwood* (Arrow, 1997)
Shepherd, Donald and Robert Slatzer with Dave Grayson, *Duke: The Life and Times of John Wayne* (Time Warner, 2003)
Slide, Anthony (ed.), *De Toth on De Toth* (Faber and Faber, 1996)
Smith, Frederick E., *633 Squadron* (Hutchinson & Co, 1956)
Tonks, Paul, *Film Music* (Pocket Essentials, 2003)

Trevor-Roper, H.R., *Hitler's War Directives 1939–45* (Pan Books, 1966)
Trewhitt, Philip, *Armoured Fighting Vehicles: 300 of the World's Greatest Military Vehicles* (Grange Books, 1999)
Urquhart, Major-General R.E., *Arnhem* (Cassell & Co, 1958)
Weddle, David, *Sam Peckinpah: 'If They Move ... Kill 'Em'* (Faber and Faber, 1996)
Weldon, Michael J., *The Psychotronic Video Guide* (St Martin's Griffin, 1996)
Whiting, Charles, *'44: In Combat on the Western Front from Normandy to the Ardennes* (Century Publishing, 1984)
Whitney, Steven, *Charles Bronson – Superstar* (Dell, 1975)
Williams, Eric, *The Wooden Horse* (Collins, 1949)
Zinnemann, Fred, *An Autobiography: A Life in the Movies* (Scribners, 1992)

Further sources

Documentaries

Jeremy Isaac's landmark 26-part *The World at War* (1973–74) is an exhaustive Thames Television World War II documentary series narrated by Laurence Olivier. *The Nazis: A Warning from History* is easily the finest documentary depicting Hitler's rise to power and the Final Solution, which was shown in 6 parts on BBC TV in 1997. The BBC's 3-part *D-Day to Berlin* (2005) narrated by Sean Bean is essential viewing too. Also worthy of note, if only for its bizarreness, is Susan Winslow's documentary *All This and World War II* (1976), which features archive combat, newsreels and war movie clips set to The Beatles' back catalogue as performed by the likes of Elton John, The Bee Gees, Leo Sayer, David Essex, Bryan Ferry, Rod Stewart and Status Quo.

Internet Sources

The Internet Movie Database (www.imdb.com), the official British Board of Film Classification site (www.bbfc.co.uk), You Tube (www youtube.com), Amazon UK (www.amazon.co.uk) and the Motion Picture Association of America (www.mpaa.org)

INDEX OF NAMES

This index includes film personnel, such as actors, directors, composers, cinematographers and producers, as well as servicemen and women, politicians and other historical figures. Page entries in bold denote an illustration.

INDEX OF FILMS

Films are listed by their best-known English language title. Alternative titles are listed in parenthesis. TV = TV series, miniseries or TV movie, doc = documentary.